Camping Oregon

A Comprehensive Guide to Public Tent and RV Campgrounds

Third Edition

Rhonda and George Ostertag

FALCONGUIDES

GUILFORD, CONNECTICUT
HELENA, MONTANA
AN IMPRINT OF **ROWMAN & LITTLEFIELD**

Copyright © 2013 by Rowman & Littlefield

Previous editions of this book were published by Falcon Publishing, Inc., in 1999 and 2005.

ALL RIGHTS RESERVED. No part of this book may be reproduced or transmitted in any form by any means, electronic or mechanical, including photocopying and recording, or by any information storage and retrieval system, except as may be expressly permitted in writing from the publisher.

Falcon, FalconGuides, and Outfit Your Mind are registered trademarks of Rowman & Littlefield
All photos by George Ostertag

Maps by Daniel Lloyd © Rowman & Littlefield

Distributed by NATIONAL BOOK NETWORK

Library of Congress Cataloging-in-Publication Data is available on file.

978-0-7627-8158-4

Printed in the United States of America

Contents

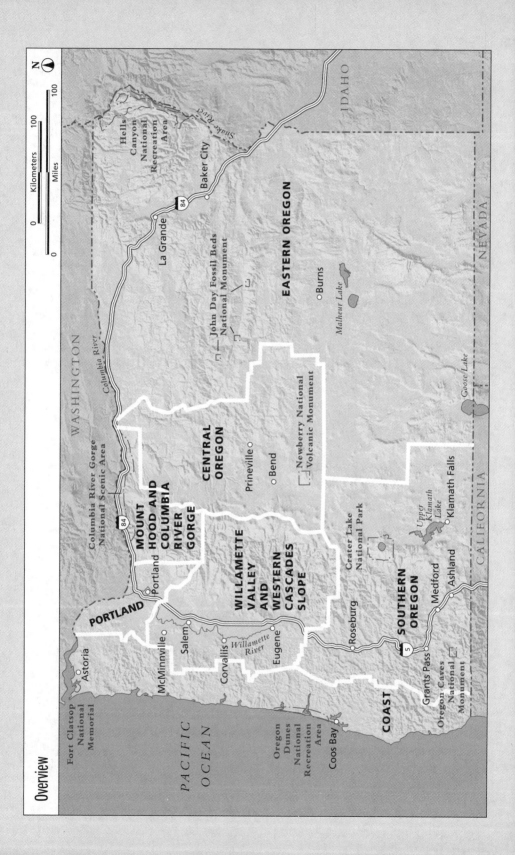

Overview

N

Kilometers 0 100

Miles 0 100

PACIFIC OCEAN

WASHINGTON

IDAHO

NEVADA

CALIFORNIA

Fort Clatsop National Memorial

Astoria

Columbia River

Columbia River Gorge National Scenic Area

84

Portland

PORTLAND

MOUNT HOOD AND COLUMBIA RIVER GORGE

La Grande

84

Baker City

Snake River

Hells Canyon National Recreation Area

John Day Fossil Beds National Monument

EASTERN OREGON

Burns

Malheur Lake

McMinnville

Salem

Corvallis

Willamette River

Eugene

WILLAMETTE VALLEY AND WESTERN CASCADES SLOPE

CENTRAL OREGON

Prineville

Bend

Newberry National Volcanic Monument

Oregon Dunes National Recreation Area

Coos Bay

COAST

Roseburg

Crater Lake National Park

5

SOUTHERN OREGON

Grants Pass

Oregon Caves National Monument

Medford

Ashland

Upper Klamath Lake

Klamath Falls

Goose Lake

Acknowledgments

We would like to thank the staffs of the local chambers of commerce, the visitor centers, the city and county parks departments, the state parks and forest departments, the state and federal fish and wildlife offices, Crater Lake National Park, and the district offices of the USDA Forest Service and Bureau of Land Management for the help they provided us in compiling this book. We also would like to thank the people we met along the way who shared their enthusiasm for camping in Oregon.

About This Edition

Well, a few years have passed, and we decided it was high time we took a look at our camping resources. Once again we hit the roads and hit the phones. We went back to where it all began.

The news on the whole ranges from fair to good. Although some smaller, more remote campgrounds have closed or are trending toward management as dispersed-use sites, the state has gained others, and many of the campgrounds have undergone facelifts. The campsites that remain have become more serviceable, attractive, and accessible for all.

However, it is still advisable to phone ahead to check on seasons, services, and campground status, especially if your destination is a small or remote camp. Also, for the smaller no-fee sites, it's a good idea to come prepared with water, toilet paper, and trash bags to haul back your garbage for disposal.

For some good news: In the years since the previous edition, Oregon campgrounds escaped harm from natural disasters. Although we did find water systems in some back reaches abandoned, toilets at many camps have been upgraded. Site turnouts at several campgrounds have been leveled and surfaced, and other camps have new tables. While our recreation providers can always use more funds for maintenance and upgrades, conditions are holding stable for the core campground resource.

Equestrians have seen an increase in their campground inventory, and state and county parks have expanded.

There have been some changes in roads, road and camp names, and signing. We've updated this information and have added the Global Positioning System (GPS) coordinates for each campground. This should help guide you now and in the future. Much of the contact information has changed since the second edition, with reorganizations and with new web addresses and phone numbers. As this is a perpetual condition, you'll probably need to pencil in changes now and again.

We've done our best to keep up with all that's occurred. You will see a host of changes throughout this new edition. I guess what it all adds up to is a healthy resource that hasn't been forgotten.

Now, with all this new information, let's go camping Oregon!

Introduction

Oregon is one of the most naturally diverse states in the Union, with elevations ranging from sea level to 11,000 feet. Along the Pacific Coast, you may encounter quiet coves, uninterrupted sandy strands, and the exciting collision of wave and headland. As you move east toward the Cascades, you pass through temperate rain forests, chiseled coastal mountains, and the fertile Willamette Valley—destination of settlers following the Oregon Trail. The Cascade Range will captivate you with its chain of conical volcanic peaks, extensive fir forests, and high-mountain lakes, including its crown jewel, Crater Lake.

In the shadow of the Cascades, shaping the central part of Oregon, are plateaus, lava fields, desert plains, and, to the south, a sweeping expanse of playas, lakes, and wildlife lands. Farther to the east, the signature peaks and meadows of the Blue Mountains set the stage. The state's northeastern corner features a stirring juxtaposition: the glacial high country of the Wallowa Mountains and the arid steppes of Hells Canyon National Recreation Area. Secreted in the southeastern corner are colorful canyons, rocky rims, and lonesome sagebrush flats.

This amazingly varied terrain combines with distinctive climatic differences to produce habitats for a menagerie of wildlife. A number of public and private wildlife lands harbor native and migrant species. Antelope congregate in Hart Mountain National Antelope Refuge, Kiger wild horses gallop at Steens Mountain, great gray owls nest in the Blue Mountains, elk gather at the winter feeding stations in Union and Baker Counties, and gray whales migrate along the Oregon coast each spring and fall. Each of these events suggests a potential vacation theme.

Other seasonal changes and natural events may serve as impetus for a camping trip: the blaze of fall foliage, the bloom of rhododendrons, the harvest season, the ripening of the huckleberries, or the Perseid meteor showers, to name a few. At the annual Mosquito Festival in Paisley ("if you can't beat 'em, celebrate 'em") there is even a tongue-in-cheek crowning of Oregon's very own "Miss-Quito." (By the way, the birding in the area is fabulous.)

Oregon's many spectacular rivers, which served as highways for the Native Americans, early explorers, and arriving settlers, now guide contemporary explorers through the best the state has to offer. Among the contiguous United States, Oregon leads the way in protecting its waterways. As a result, the recreational opportunities are superb. You can indulge in summer swimming; salmon, steelhead, sturgeon, and trout fishing; whitewater rafting, canoeing, and kayaking; drift boating; mailboat rides; and stern-wheeler tours. There is also an impressive collection of waterfalls and hot springs. You will be surprised by what Oregon can do with a raindrop!

While Oregon's natural bounty is unparalleled, the state also caters to more-refined tastes, with fine museums, concerts, wineries, art galleries, aquariums, a zoo, and shops. The Ashland Shakespeare Festival has an excellent national reputation, and

Falls Creek National Recreation Trail, Umpqua National Forest

seasonal festivals, Saturday markets, community theaters, and art fairs add to the allure of town-and-country outings. If you are ready to "let 'er rip," the Pendleton Rodeo is an ideal venue, or you may choose to try your luck at one of the tribal casinos.

Best of all, Oregon has fine public campgrounds from which to explore its exciting attractions.

How to Use This Guide

This book focuses on public campgrounds and parks that are readily accessible by car, motor home, and recreational vehicle. While the list is not exhaustive, it is comprehensive. Some public campgrounds were excluded because they were unreasonably isolated, were in disrepair, or had rough access roads, too few sites, or no facilities. Group campgrounds and strictly walk-in facilities were also omitted.

Choosing a Campground

To help you locate and select a campground, we have basically organized the book using the seven travel regions established by Oregon's Department of Tourism: Coast, the Portland area, the Willamette Valley (and Western Cascades Slope), Mount Hood and the Columbia River Gorge, Southern Oregon, Central Oregon, and Eastern Oregon. Within these regions we have assembled the campgrounds based on their proximity to key towns or landmarks. In each subsection, campgrounds are listed alphabetically.

Each campground description includes key information on location, season, the number of sites, maximum RV length, availability of facilities and services, fee per night, the management agency, contact information, how to get there, and what you can expect to see and do once you are at the campground. The numbers assigned to the campgrounds coincide with those on the regional maps. By consulting the appropriate regional map and scanning the descriptions, you should be able to select a campground that both appeals to your interests and is most convenient for your travel plans.

Helpful Information

The specific categories in the campground sections are Location, Season, Sites, Maximum length, Facilities, Fee per night, Management, Contact, and Finding the campground. The following explains some of the information within these categories, along with a few tips.

Season: Many campgrounds remain open during fair weather, closing when frost, ice, and snow threaten plumbing and safety or when rain makes the ground and roads unsuitable for camping. We have listed the typical operating seasons, but check with the managing agency if your trip occurs at the edge of the operating season.

For some of the USDA Forest Service and Bureau of Land Management (BLM) campgrounds, the more remote and primitive offerings can remain open year-round but go without service after the summer visitor season (June through August). Snow, though, still can prevent access. When frequenting these camps after the peak camping season, bring your own toilet tissue, water, and other comforts, and pack out all garbage—never leave unburned garbage in a fire ring or grill.

In some parks winter camping may be restricted to self-contained RVs or have limited sites, reduced services, or dry camping only. For general information on the state parks, including their operating seasons, call the Oregon Department of Parks and Recreation (800-551-6949).

Keep in mind that listed operating times are subject to change. Weather, budget cuts, ongoing events, a changeover in the concessionaire, and vandalism can all influence opening and closing policies. The price of a phone call is small relative to the cost of a misspent trip.

Within camp descriptions, the nearby attractions mentioned may also have seasonal schedules. If the success of your trip depends on visiting a particular museum or attraction, you may wish to call ahead.

Sites: The sites are labeled as hookup, basic, RV, tent, or walk-in tent. Throughout this book, "RV" refers to the broad class of recreational vehicles on the road: trailers, campers, motor homes, tent trailers, and vans. Basic sites are those suitable for either tent or RV camping but without hookups.

Under this heading we have also indicated if cabins, tepees, or yurts are available for rent. Yurts are domed canvas structures with wooden floors, heating, electricity, lock-secured doors, and bunks. Yurt users bring their own bedding or sleeping bags and have access to the camp restroom/shower facilities.

Fee per night: The price codes used throughout the book are based on the prices in 2012. A range is used because prices can fluctuate year to year. The symbols will assist in cost comparisons and provide a relative idea of out-of-pocket cost.

$ = $0–$10
$$ = $10–$19
$$$ = $20 or more

The price refers to single campsites only. Expect cabins, yurts, tepees, and double sites to cost more. Many camps have add-on fees for additional vehicles, pets, or large parties, which could increase your costs.

In some cases a Northwest Forest Pass may be required in lieu of the campground fee. These passes are required for many of the state's trailheads. Northwest Forest Passes can be purchased from the forest service.

Reservations: Making reservations is a good idea, especially during peak summer travel months, holidays, fish runs, or when your travel plans hinge on getting a campsite and there are no alternative camping options in the area. The state park system has a contract with a fee reservation service to handle the booking of state park campsites (800-452-5687).

Although most forest service campgrounds are offered on a first-come, first-served basis, the agency does have a reservation line for a few of its larger, more popular campgrounds; this too is a fee service. Contact the National Recreation Reservation Service at (877) 444-6777, or visit www.recreation.gov. Many forest service campgrounds in Oregon are run by concessionaires, which set their own pricing and rules for reservations.

Water: We have tried to list each of the campgrounds that have developed drinking water systems. Because these systems can pass water quality tests one week and fail the next, you should always carry an emergency supply of safe drinking water and be prepared to treat campground water by boiling. This becomes especially true the farther you travel from safe urban water sources.

Pets: Unless it is specified otherwise in the campground descriptions, leashed pets are generally allowed.

The quick reference charts with each area give information about the campground services available. Following is a key to abbreviations used in these charts:

Hookups: W = Water, E = Electric, S = Sewer, C = Cable, P = Phone, I = Internet

Total Sites: T = Tents only

Max. RV length: Given in feet

Toilets: F = Flush, NF = No flush

Recreation: H = Hiking, S = Swimming, F = Fishing, B = Boating, L = Boat launch, O = Off-highway driving, R = Horseback riding, C = Cycling

Getting to the Campground

The best way to reach your intended campsite is to use the campground directions in conjunction with a detailed state map or the appropriate forest service or BLM map. Maps in this guide are meant to be used only as general locator tools.

Outdoor and Camping Refresher Course

Responsible use of the outdoors and the campground and trail facilities is the best way to protect and preserve the privilege of a quality outdoor experience. It is also the best way to control campground costs.

Preparation

The drive: Traveling to campgrounds and parks along major highways poses little problem. The roads are well maintained, a town or passing vehicle is never far off, and the reception of your cellular phone seems just fine.

But backcountry roads are a different story. For this type of travel, it is mandatory that you keep your tires and engine in good repair. Top the gas tank at the last point of civilization, and carry emergency vehicle gear: jack, spare tire and belts, tire pump, jumper cables, and, if the weather is foul, tire chains.

Basic survival gear: This includes water, food, blankets, matches, a first-aid kit, and a flashlight. You may also want to add a shovel and bucket to the list. A downed tree, road washout, or rockslide need not spoil a trip if you carry supplies for an unintended stop and maps for plotting an alternative destination or route. Before any long

Trip planning at camp

journey from home, it is advisable to phone the appropriate agency about facility openings and road conditions.

Notification safeguard: Because being stranded or injured in the wild poses a greater problem than similar situations at home or in town, it is critical before heading out on any outdoor adventure to notify a responsible party of your intended destination and time of return. Contacting that individual when you get back completes the safety procedure. This also works in reverse: If an emergency occurs on the home front, someone will be able to alert you or help authorities locate you.

Camping

Zero-impact camping should be the goal of everyone, even at developed camp-grounds. Do not rearrange the site, pound nails, remove ground cover, or dig drainage channels. If you build a campfire, keep it small and inside the provided container. If grills or fire rings are not provided, do not build a campfire. Heed all regulations on campfires, smoking, and wood gathering.

Setting up: Exercise courtesy with your site selection, and keep it neat. Avoid blocking roads and spilling out of your assigned space into your neighbor's site.

Storing food: Food should be stored in closed containers when not in use. At night, be sure all foods and coolers are stowed away in the vehicle. In some areas you will also want to cover the coolers—bears have learned that coolers hold food and have ripped open car doors just to reach them.

Garbage: Dispose of litter properly and often. If no facility is provided, pack your garbage out. Use sturdy garbage bags to collect the garbage at your site, storing the bags where they are handy for use but not an eyesore to fellow campers. At night you should stash the garbage bags in a vehicle to avoid raids by raccoons or bears. Never put garbage down toilets, leave it in the outhouse, or abandon it in the fire pit. If you did not burn your flammable garbage during your stay, pack it out.

Sanitation: Dispose of wastewater in the sites provided at campgrounds. Bathing or washing dishes should be done well away from natural waters such as lakes or streams and away from the campground supplies of drinking water.

Smoking: Where fires present extreme danger or where habitats are particularly sensitive, smoking may be prohibited; heed regulations. Where and when smoking is allowed, stop to have your smoke; never smoke while hiking. Use an ashtray at camp. In the wild you'd clear an area to the mineral soil, smoke the cigarette, and then crush it out in the dirt. Pack out cigarette butts.

Pets: In campgrounds that allow pets, keep your animal(s) at your site, restrained, and quiet. If your pet is not comfortable around strangers, it does not belong in a public campground. Pets must be leashed at all times on trails to protect habitat and wildlife. Always clean up after your pet.

Courtesy: Keep your noise down and your site neat, ration your use of showers, and clean up after yourself and your youngsters in the restrooms. There is no maid service here!

Stay limits: Public campgrounds typically have stay limits ranging from a few days up to two weeks, although a few facilities accommodate campers on a monthly basis.

Gearing Up for the Outdoors

Clothing: Layering is the way to go. Wool is the fabric for cold, wet, or changeable weather conditions. It retains heat even when wet. Cotton is the fabric of warm summer days. In Oregon a good suit of rain gear—jacket and pants—is a clothing necessity.

Footgear: Sneakers are appropriate for town walks or nature trails, but for longer hikes boots provide both comfort and protection.

Equipment: The quantity and variety of equipment you carry will depend on where you are going and how long you will be away from the vehicle or campsite. Daypacks with padded straps or fanny packs offer convenient storage and portability while keeping hands free. Water, snacks, a sweater, money, keys, tissues, sunglasses, a camera, and binoculars are fine for short hops. The greater the adventure, the greater the quantity of gear, including safety and first-aid materials, will be required.

Atlases, maps, and brochures: Maps are important tools. They provide an orientation to the area, suggest alternative routes, present new areas to explore, and aid in planning and preparation. Be sure to have the correct maps for your trip. The farther your travels take you from the beaten path, the more important specific area maps become. County, forest service, BLM, and topographic maps can all show greater detail than the standard state road map.

Fees and permits: Trail park passes, wilderness permits, and day-use permits may be required to travel the trails in the area where you are camped. While some permits may be picked up or purchased at the site, others must be secured in advance at the ranger station.

Activities
Beachcombing: Learn the rules for tide pooling and collecting, and check on any wildlife closures; these are generally posted at each beach. Before taking a long stroll on the beach, find out the times and heights of high and low tides to avoid becoming

Fishing on the upper McKenzie Wild and Scenic River, Willamette National Forest

stranded. Make sure there will be adequate time to complete your hike or reach safety before the incoming tide. Irregular "sneaker" waves occur along the Oregon coast and can arrive suddenly, sweeping you off your feet. Drift logs do not provide a safe haven from incoming waves because the logs can shift in the surf, unseating and striking would-be riders.

Fishing: A current fishing license from the state of Oregon is a must, and for a few places along the Deschutes River, you will also need to purchase an Indian fishing license from the Confederated Tribes of Warm Springs. It is essential that you possess and study a copy of the current year's *Oregon Sport Fishing Regulations.* The booklet specifically outlines what state waters are open to angling, the season, what types of bait are allowed, catch limits, and size restrictions. Copies may be picked up where fishing licenses are sold and at bait and tackle, sporting goods, and outdoor stores. A state map will help you sort out your options and ensure compliance with the rules, which can vary depending on your location along a river or stream.

Since the initiation of the Salmon Recovery Program in 1997, and with the evolving federal and state listings of threatened and endangered fish species, regulations are changing continuously. Do not trust memory or hearsay. What was acceptable in the past may no longer be permissible. Use only barbless hooks in catch-and-release waters, and always wet your hands before handling fish. Minimize your contact with fish being returned to the wild.

Swimming: Swimming areas mentioned in this book are typically unguarded, so swim at your own risk. Visitors should never swim alone. Also, always supervise children; survey the area for hazards beforehand; and use common sense with regard to water levels, flow, and water temperature. Chilly temperatures and undercurrents can disable even the strongest swimmer. Horseplay, drinking, and diving are inappropriate and dangerous.

Hiking with children: When hiking with young children, choose simple destinations and do not insist on reaching any particular destination. Allow for their differences in attention span, interests, and energy level. Encourage children's natural curiosity, but come prepared for sun, mosquitoes, wasps, and poison oak. Do not become so focused on what you want to share with your children that you dismiss their discoveries. Get down on your hands and knees, peer into that puddle, admire that ugly rock. For safety's sake, discuss what to do should you become separated (hug a tree); even small ones should carry some essential items: a sweater, water bottle, and food.

Hiking shared-use trails: Unless otherwise posted, mountain bikers are expected to yield the right of way to hikers and horseback riders; hikers, in turn, should yield to equestrians. Because horses can spook and put riders at risk, yielding means stopping, with all party members stepping to the same side of the trail. Avoid any sudden movements, but feel free to speak in normal tones. Voices reassure the horse that you are indeed human and not some alien creature; backpacks, tripods, and walking sticks can confuse or alarm horses.

Hiking with pets: Owners should strictly adhere to posted rules for pets. Controlling your animal on a leash is not just a courtesy reserved for times when other campers and hikers are present; it is an ongoing responsibility to protect wildlife and ground cover. Know that dogs represent a threat to horses and may create problems with bears. Clean up after your pet, keeping trails free of debris.

Safety

While this guide attempts to alert users to safe methods and warn of potential dangers, it can only accomplish so much. Nature is unpredictable, and humans are fallible. Good judgment and common sense remain your best allies. When you travel the backcountry, you assume the risks, but you also reap the rewards.

Water: To avoid dehydration, carry ample drinking water with you. When taking water from an outdoor source, be sure to treat the water by using an approved filter or by boiling it for 10 minutes. Even if you plan to use trailside sources, you should carry an emergency supply in case those sources have dried up or become fouled. Even on short nature walks and city outings, water is a good companion. If you are thirsty, you cannot enjoy what the trail or area has to offer.

Getting lost: Before venturing on any hike, leave word with someone about your planned destination and time of return. Then keep to your plan and notify the informed party upon your return. Do not go alone. If you become lost, sit down and try to think calmly. You are in no immediate danger as long as you have packed properly and followed the notification procedure. When hiking with a group, you should stay together and not wander off on your own. If you do become separated, try signaling to the others by shouting or whistling in sets of three, universally recognized as a distress call. If it is getting late, use the remaining light to prepare for night and conserve your energy.

Hypothermia: Hypothermia is a dramatic cooling of the body. Cold, wet, and windy weather conditions demand respect. Eating properly, avoiding fatigue, and being alert to the symptoms (sluggishness, clumsiness, and incoherence) remain the best protection. Should someone display symptoms, stop and get that person dry and warm. Hot fluids can help restore body heat.

Heat exhaustion: Overwhelming your body's own cooling system during warm weather is also a danger. Wear a hat, drink plenty of water, eat properly, and take rests as needed.

Poison oak and ivy: To avoid the irritating oils of these plants, learn what the plants look like and in what environments they grow. There are creams and lotions that can be applied both before and after contact with the plant to reduce the risk of rash. Avoidance, though, is the best tactic.

Stings and bites: The best protection against stings and bites is knowledge. It is important to become aware of any personal allergies or sensitivities that you may have and to learn about the habits and habitats of snakes, bees, ticks, and other potential threats. If you are experiencing any unexplained symptoms or poor health, seek medical advice and volunteer the information that you have been hiking or camping, which can help with the diagnosis. In the case of a tick bite, after removal of the tick, watch for signs of redness and swelling, which could be an early indication of Lyme disease. Consult a physician when bites or wounds show any sign of infection.

Bears: Bears have a supersensitive sense of smell and tend to be curious, so avoid any strong smells that could intrigue them. In particular, be careful of how and where you store food, and never store food in your tent. If you are tent camping, avoid sleeping in clothes that may have picked up cooking odors. Also be wary of sweet-smelling creams, cosmetics, or lotions that may be enticing to a bear. While hiking, make ample noise, and never intentionally come between a sow and her cubs. If you should see a bear, do not try to get closer for a better look.

Outdoor Awareness

There is risk associated with any trip into the backcountry. Changes occur all the time, in nature and in the maintenance of roads, campgrounds, and trails. Just because a campground or trip is represented within these pages does not mean it will be safe when you get there. Common sense and good judgment, paired with careful preparation and a realistic assessment of your skills and abilities, are the best means for ensuring a safe, fun, fulfilling outing.

Map Legend

Transportation

Interstate Highway   =⟨5⟩=

US Highway   ={26}=

State Road   =⟨18⟩=

Hydrology

Body of Water

River/Creek

Intermittent River

Symbols

Campground   ❶

Capital   ✪

City   ○

Land Use

National Park/
Forest/Preserve

State Park/
Forest

Help Us Keep This Guide Up to Date

Every effort has been made by the author and editors to make this guide as accurate and useful as possible. However, many things can change after a guide is published—campgrounds open and close, grow and contract; regulations change; facilities come under new management, and so forth.

We appreciate hearing from you concerning your experiences with this guide and how you feel it could be improved and kept up to date. While we may not be able to respond to all comments and suggestions, we'll take them to heart, and we'll also make certain to share them with the author. Please send your comments and suggestions to the following address:

Globe Pequot Press
Reader Response/Editorial Department
P.O. Box 480
Guilford, CT 06437

Or you may e-mail us at:

editorial@GlobePequot.com

Thanks for your input, and happy camping!

Coast

Next to thick carpets of trees and, of course, rain, Oregon is probably best known for its coastline. In the shadow of the Coast Range and Siskiyou Mountains, rumpled dunes, sandy strands, natural spits, rugged headlands, sea lion rookeries, sea stacks, and verdant coastal valleys combine to create one incredible welcome mat. The explorers who first visited the coast—James Cook, Robert Gray, Lewis and Clark, and Don Bruno de Heceta—live on in the place names. Gold rushes and Indian encounters pepper the coastal tale, while lighthouses and shipwrecks supply the romance. To preserve this 350-mile-long treasure, the state has elected to keep its beaches public; nearly one hundred state parks and waysides help to do just that, providing residents and visitors with unmatched coastal access.

The coastal mountains and the rivers that drain them extend the bounty, with elk herds, waterfalls, hidden lakes, record-size trees, pockets of old-growth, natural meadows, and Oregon's lone redwood forest. Historically the rivers hosted sizable salmon and steelhead runs, but modern-day pressures leave the fishing in question. Today's anglers must keep current with sportfishing regulations and restrictions.

Nonetheless, outdoor activities abound. Hiking, kite flying, beachcombing and tide pooling, whale watching, birding, surf and freshwater fishing, crabbing and clamming, dune play, off-highway-vehicle driving, and horseback riding will get you started. Shopping, museums, and aquariums allow you to dodge the raindrops when necessary. Festivals crowd the beach calendar, with kites, sandcastles, storms, azaleas, rhododendrons, and cranberries all providing reasons to celebrate.

Coastal recreation is year-round. In winter, storm fronts laden with rain pass over the coast interspersed with bold breaks of sunshine. In summer, soaring temperatures in the Willamette Valley create an inversion that sucks in coastal fog and summons sea-cooled afternoon winds. (Keep those jackets at the top of your suitcase.) Spring and fall promise clear skies, mild temperatures, and less wind. In the coastal mountains you will find a vibrant temperate rain forest in winter and sun-drenched peaks and shady canyons in summer.

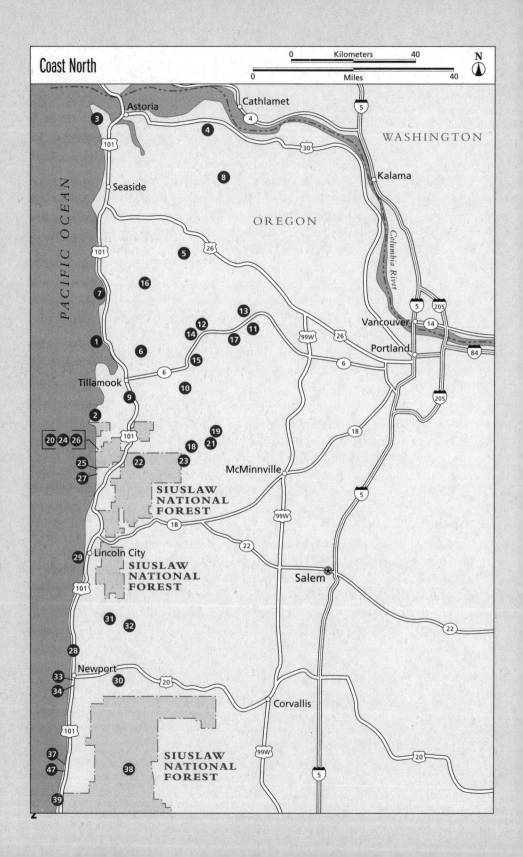

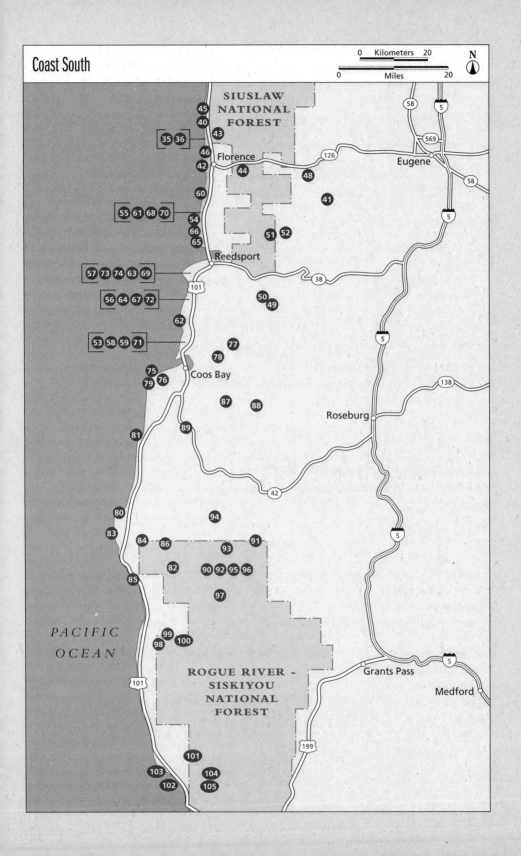

Astoria-Tillamook Area

	Hookup Sites	Total Sites	Max. RV Length	Hookups	Toilets	Showers	Drinking Water	Dump Station	Recreation	Fee	Can Reserve
1 Barview Jetty County Park	73	315	40	WES	F	X	X	X	HSF	$$-$$$	X
2 Cape Lookout State Park	39	212	60	WES	F	X	X	X	HSF	$$-$$$	X
3 Fort Stevens State Park	476	482	50	WES	F	X	X	X	HSFBRC	$$-$$$	X
4 Gnat Creek		6	Small		NF				HF	$	
5 Henry Rierson Spruce Run		37	30		F, NF		X		HFB	$-$$	
6 Kilchis River County Park		63	40		F	X	X	X	SFBL	$$	X
7 Nehalem Bay State Park	265	282	60	WE	F	X	X	X	HSFRC	$$	X
8 Northrup Creek Horse Camp		11	40		NF		X		HR	$$	
9 Port of Tillamook Bay RV Park		52	50		F		X			$$	
10 Trask County Park		63	40		NF		X		HSFBL	$$	X

1 Barview Jetty County Park

Location: In Barview, about 12 miles north of Tillamook
Season: Year-round
Sites: 73 hookup sites, 242 basic sites; water, electric, and sewer hookups
Maximum length: 40 feet
Facilities: Tables, flush toilets, drinking water, showers, dump station, wireless (fee)
Fee per night: $$-$$$
Management: Tillamook County
Contact: (503) 322-3522, reservations accepted; www.co.tillamook.or.us/gov/parks/Campgrounds.htm
Finding the campground: From US 101 in Barview, 1.5 miles north of Garibaldi, turn west onto Cedar Street and follow it 0.2 mile to its end at the campground and beach.
GPS coordinates: N45 34.361' / W123 57.184'
About the campground: Occupying a large coastal flat, this campground is framed by a tall dune bank to the east and a wild beach strewn with drift logs to the west. Sites are roomy and private in a natural setting of low, twisted shore pine and salal. Fishing from North Jetty is popular. Youngsters will like romping, sliding, and exploring the dune.

Walking the beach, Cape Lookout State Park

2 Cape Lookout State Park

Location: About 12 miles southwest of Tillamook
Season: Year-round
Sites: 39 hookup sites, 173 basic sites, 13 yurts, 6 cabins; water, electric, and sewer hookups
Maximum length: 60 feet
Facilities: Tables, grills, flush toilets, drinking water, showers, dump station
Fee per night: $$-$$$
Management: Oregon State Parks and Recreation Department
Contact: (503) 842-4981; (800) 452-5687 for reservations; www.oregon.gov/OPRD/PARKS/camping.shtml
Finding the campground: From US 101 in Tillamook, head west and southwest on Netarts Highway-Three Capes Scenic Route for 12 miles. The park entrance is west off the scenic loop.
GPS coordinates: N45 21.889' / W123 58.077'
About the campground: This large coastal campground, with closely spaced beachside or forest sites, provides campers with convenient access to a dramatic ocean headland and an ocean spit with 5 miles of uninterrupted beach, dunes, and bay shoreline. Harbor seals haul out on the spit's tip. Three Capes Scenic Route provides easy outward exploration to Cape Meares State Park to the north, with its lighthouse and octopus spruce, and Cape Kiwanda State Park to the south, with its hang gliders and dory fleet. Scenic offshore rocks along this coast delight photographers and provide seabird nesting.

3 Fort Stevens State Park

Location: About 5 miles west of Astoria, near Hammond
Season: Year-round
Sites: 476 full and partial hookup sites, 6 basic sites, 15 yurts, 11 cabins; water, electric, and sewer hookups
Maximum length: 50 feet
Facilities: Tables, grills, flush toilets, drinking water, showers, dump station, playground, nearby boat docks and launch
Fee per night: $$-$$$
Management: Oregon State Parks and Recreation Department
Contact: (503) 861-1671; (800) 452-5687 for reservations; www.oregon.gov/OPRD/PARKS/camping.shtml
Finding the campground: From the junction of US 30 and US 101 in Astoria, go 2.7 miles south on US 101. Turn right onto East Harbor Drive and travel 4.4 miles to Hammond. Turn south onto Lake Drive, and continue 1 mile to the campground.
GPS coordinates: N46 10.860' / W123 57.757'
About the campground: This large campground could be considered a miniature town. Sites are closely spaced, but you are not likely to spend much time in camp when you can bicycle, explore the historic military bunkers, fish Coffenbury Lake, hike the trails, or walk the beach either along the ocean or at the mouth of the Columbia River—all without ever leaving the state park. From mid-December to mid-May, you will want to take along your binoculars; bald eagles congregate near the river mouth to feed on migrating shorebirds weakened from their journey south. Astoria-area attractions include the Column, the Columbia River Maritime Museum, and Fort Clatsop National Memorial, where Lewis and Clark wintered on the Oregon coast before their return east.

4 Gnat Creek

Location: About 17 miles east of Astoria
Season: Year-round
Sites: 6 tent sites; no hookups
Maximum length: Small units only
Facilities: Tables, fire pits, nonflush toilet; no drinking water
Fee per night: $
Management: Clatsop State Forest
Contact: (503) 325-5451; www.oregon.gov/ODF
Finding the campground: The campground is north off US 30 at milepost 78, about 17 miles east of Astoria and 1 mile west of the Gnat Creek Fish Hatchery.
GPS coordinates: N46 10.623' / W123 30.139'
About the campground: Along Gnat Creek near Gnat Creek Fish Hatchery, this rustic forest campground appeals to anglers and hikers. A foot trail links the camp to the hatchery, where additional trails enter the Nicolai Watershed and lead to a waterfall. Area anglers find 2.5 miles of fishing access; consult current fishing regulations before casting your line. The hatchery rears both

summer and winter steelhead. Hatchery visitors will find a show pond with large rainbow trout and sturgeon, as well as picnicking spots.

5 Henry Rierson Spruce Run

Location: About 32 miles southeast of Seaside
Season: Year-round
Sites: 32 basic sites, 5 walk-in tent sites; no hookups
Maximum length: 30 feet
Facilities: Tables, fire rings, flush and nonflush toilets, drinking water (flush toilets and drinking water maintained in summer only)
Fee per night: $-$$
Management: Clatsop State Forest
Contact: (503) 325-5451; www.oregon.gov/ODF
Finding the campground: From US 26, east of Elsie and west of Jewell Junction, turn south at a sign onto Lower Nehalem River Road; proceed 7 miles to camp.
GPS coordinates: N45 48.687' / W123 36.751'
About the campground: In the Nehalem River valley, this 128-acre camp claims a tree-shaded and grassy flat parted by Spruce Run Creek. A 2.4-mile trail runs between the campground and Spruce Run Lake. The lower Nehalem River is open to canoeing for a short season, and river sightseeing is always inviting. Visitors may wish to make an excursion to Jewell Meadows Wildlife Area for elk viewing. Wild turkeys too can sometimes be seen at the wildlife area.

6 Kilchis River County Park

Location: About 7 miles northeast of Tillamook
Season: May–Sept
Sites: 59 basic sites, 4 walk-in sites; no hookups
Maximum length: 40 feet
Facilities: Tables, fire rings, flush toilets, drinking water, showers, dump station, playground, horseshoe pits, primitive boat launch
Fee per night: $$
Management: Tillamook County
Contact: (503) 842-6694, reservations accepted; www.co.tillamook.or.us/gov/parks/Campgrounds.htm
Finding the campground: From US 101, 1.5 miles north of Tillamook, turn east onto Alderbrook Road. At the fork in 1 mile, bear right onto Kilchis River Road; proceed 4 miles to the park.
GPS coordinates: N45 32.320' / W123 47.115'
About the campground: This family campground sits along the Kilchis River. The lower paved loop through camp rings a playing field; sites are grassy with framing alders and statuesque Sitka spruce. An upper tier of sites occupies a grassy clearing with a few big trees, all at the edge of the forest. The Kilchis is a beautiful coastal canyon river. Drift boating, fishing, relaxing, and birding help guests while away the day.

7 Nehalem Bay State Park

Location: Near Manzanita, about 24 miles north of Tillamook
Season: Year-round
Sites: 265 hookup sites, 17 horse campsites, 18 yurts; water and electric hookups
Maximum length: 60 feet
Facilities: Tables, grills, flush toilets, drinking water, showers, dump station, corrals at horse sites
Fee per night: $$
Management: Oregon State Parks and Recreation Department
Contact: (503) 368-5154; (800) 452-5687 for reservations; www.oregon.gov/OPRD/PARKS/camping.shtml
Finding the campground: The campground is located 1.5 miles west off US 101, 21 miles south of the US 101–US 26 junction and 3 miles south of Manzanita.
GPS coordinates: N45 42.071' / W123 56.213'
About the campground: Sheltered by a coastal dune, this bayside campground offers convenient access to the old-growth Sitka spruce forests at Oswald West State Park and Cape Falcon and to summit views from Neahkahnie Mountain, all to the north. Within Nehalem Bay State Park, visitors can stroll a 2-mile-long spit and 6 miles of coastal beach. Binoculars bring birds, whales, and harbor seals into focus. Boating and fishing similarly top lists of things to do. Tent campers, however, may prefer the walk-in sites in the deep old-growth woods of Oswald West State Park.

8 Northrup Creek Horse Camp

Location: About 40 miles east of Astoria
Season: Mid-May–Nov
Sites: 8 horse campsites, 3 basic sites; no hookups
Maximum length: 40 feet
Facilities: Tables, grills, nonflush toilets, drinking water, site horse corrals, manure bin
Fee per night: $$
Management: Clatsop State Forest
Contact: (503) 325-5451; www.oregon.gov/ODF/FIELD/ASTORIA/State_Forest_Management/recreation_main.shtml
Finding the campground: From US 26 at Jewell Junction, take the Jewell exit and head north on OR 103, crossing under US 26. Go 9.5 miles and turn right (east) onto Oregon 202. Drive 6.1 miles and turn left (north) onto Northrup Creek Road, which begins paved but changes over to gravel. Continue on this main road at junctions, remaining in the drainage bottom to reach the campground in 4.7 miles. The car camp is on the left, the horse camp on the right.
GPS coordinates: N46 01.158' / W123 27.182'
About the campground: This attractive camp with separate areas for equestrian and traditional family camping offers ample, leveled sites in a second-growth Douglas fir forest with classic Coast Range understory. Trails link the campground and a day-use trailhead located 0.4 mile beyond the camp turnouts. The 8.5-mile multiuse loop of Northrup Creek Trail draws explorers from camp, as does the Big Tree Nature Trail, for foot-use only, which starts from the car camp. The latter travels

along beaver-enhanced Northrup Creek and has some surprising big neighbors. An old-growth fir, cedar, and bigleaf maple shoot skyward.

9 Port of Tillamook Bay RV Park

Location: South end of Tillamook
Season: May–Oct
Sites: 40 basic sites, 12 tent sites; no hookups
Maximum length: 50 feet
Facilities: Tables, barbecue pits, flush toilets, drinking water
Fee per night: $$
Management: Port of Tillamook Bay
Contact: (503) 842-7152; www.potb.org/airport/rvpark.html
Finding the campground: From the junction of US 101 and OR 6 in Tillamook, go 2.8 miles south on US 101. Turn east onto Matlock Way and drive 0.2 mile to the campground.
GPS coordinates: N45 25.112' / W123 49.217'
About the campground: Located near Tillamook County Airport and the Air Museum, this large campground sits on an open grassy plain with views of the coastal foothills. Sites have gravel parking pads and ample room for setting out chairs or raising tents. Shade sources can make a stay more pleasant. The attractions of Tillamook and the Tillamook–Three Capes coast await.

10 Trask County Park

Location: About 14 miles east of Tillamook
Season: Year-round
Sites: 63 basic sites; no hookups
Maximum length: 40 feet
Facilities: Tables, grills, nonflush toilets, drinking water, horseshoe pits; boat launch 4 miles downstream at Peninsula Day Use
Fee per night: $$
Management: Tillamook County
Contact: (503) 842-4559, reservations accepted; www.co.tillamook.or.us/gov/parks/Campgrounds.htm
Finding the campground: From US 101 in Tillamook, go east on OR 6 for 2.5 miles. Turn right (south) onto Trask River Road and drive 1.8 miles. Bear left to remain on Trask River Road; proceed another 10 miles to the park.
GPS coordinates: N45 26.496' / W123 36.615'
About the campground: Along the Trask River and its North Fork, this rustic campground is woodsy, with earthen roads and parking; some sites are more level than others. The park day-use area claims the grassy flat above the river. When adequately high, the Trask River is popular with rafters. Its fast channels are interspersed with quiet flows. A foot trail allows exploration along the river at the Peninsula boat launch.

Tillamook State Forest

	Hookup Sites	Total Sites	Max. RV Length	Hookups	Toilets	Showers	Drinking Water	Dump Station	Recreation	Fee	Can Reserve
11 Browns Off-Highway-Vehicle Campground		30	40		NF		X		HO	$$	
12 Diamond Mill		20	40		NF		X		O	$	
13 Gales Creek		23	25		NF		X		HFR	$-$$	
14 Jones Creek		43	40		NF		X		HSF	$$	
15 Jordan Creek Off-Highway-Vehicle (OHV) Staging Area		6	40		NF				O	$$	
16 Nehalem Falls		20	30		NF		X		SFB	$-$$	
17 Stagecoach Horse Camp		10	25		NF				HR	$$	

11 Browns Off-Highway-Vehicle Campground

Location: About 21 miles northwest of Forest Grove
Season: Apr–Oct
Sites: 30 basic sites; no hookups
Maximum length: 40 feet
Facilities: Tables, grills, nonflush toilets, drinking water, off-highway-vehicle (OHV) loading ramps and staging area
Fee per night: $$
Management: Tillamook State Forest
Contact: (503) 357-2191; www.oregon.gov/ODF/tillamookstateforest/Recreation.shtml
Finding the campground: At the highway summit on OR 6, 19 miles west of Forest Grove and 31.3 miles east of Tillamook, turn south at the sign for Browns Camp. Quickly bear right, following a single-lane dirt road riddled with potholes. Go 0.8 mile and again bear right, proceeding 0.4 mile. There bear left, coming to a T-junction in another 0.2 mile. Head left for 0.3 mile and then bear right, continuing 0.4 mile to the campground on Scoggins Creek Road.
GPS coordinates: N45 36.654' / W123 20.931'
About the campground: Edged by alders and conifers, this campground for the OHV enthusiast lays out like a three-leaf clover, with each camping loop nudging the central revegetated area. Boulders shape the graveled sites and avenues, while Scoggins Creek threads past camp. Trails and roads open to OHVs are the primary draw, so you can expect a noisy neighborhood. Elsewhere in historic Tillamook State Forest, visitors can enjoy the quieter pursuits of horseback riding, hiking, fishing, and sightseeing.

12 Diamond Mill

Location: About 24 miles east of Tillamook
Season: Year-round
Sites: 20 basic sites; no hookups
Maximum length: 40 feet
Facilities: Tables, nonflush toilets, drinking water
Fee per night: $
Management: Tillamook State Forest
Contact: (503) 842-2545; www.oregon.gov/ODF/tillamookstateforest/Recreation.shtml
Finding the campground: From OR 6, 23 miles east of Tillamook and 29 miles west of Forest Grove, head north on gravel North Fork Road for 0.3 mile. Bear right and proceed 1.3 miles to the campground.
GPS coordinates: N45 36.267' / W123 32.877'
About the campground: Tables mark off the campsites that border a central, gravel off-highway-vehicle (OHV) staging area. A fir-and-alder forest shapes the perimeter. Although noisy, the camp attracts a like-minded group interested in OHV riding.

13 Gales Creek

Location: About 17 miles northwest of Forest Grove
Season: Mid-May–Sept
Sites: 19 basic sites, 4 walk-in tent sites; no hookups
Maximum length: 25 feet
Facilities: Tables, grills, nonflush toilets, drinking water
Fee per night: $-$$
Management: Tillamook State Forest
Contact: (503) 357-2191; www.oregon.gov/ODF/tillamookstateforest/Recreation.shtml
Finding the campground: The campground sits 0.7 mile north of OR 6, 17 miles west of Forest Grove and 33.6 miles east of Tillamook.
GPS coordinates: N45 38.581' / W123 21.546'
About the campground: In historic Tillamook State Forest, this campground offers family campsites in a second-growth forest of alders and firs along Gales Creek. The series of fires that burned the forest in the 1930s are considered one of the worst disasters to strike the Pacific Northwest; the reforestation is one of the region's great success stories. From camp, hikers may access the historic Gales Creek Trail, which in turn leads to University Falls Loop. Additional trails in the state forest serve hikers, equestrians, and off-highway-vehicle users. Fishing, sightseeing, and relaxing also engage campers. Tent campers might prefer Elk Creek Campground, 7 miles farther west on OR 6. It has fifteen forested walk-in sites with similar services. Elk Mountain Trail leaves from that camp, and the Wilson River Trail connects the Elk Mountain and Kings Mountain Trails.

14 Jones Creek

Location: About 22 miles east of Tillamook
Season: Mid-May–Sept
Sites: 29 basic sites, 14 walk-in tent sites; no hookups
Maximum length: 40 feet
Facilities: Tables, grills, nonflush toilets, drinking water, horseshoe pit
Fee per night: $$
Management: Tillamook State Forest
Contact: (503) 842-2545; www.oregon.gov/ODF/tillamookstateforest/Recreation.shtml
Finding the campground: From US 101 at Tillamook, go east on OR 6 for 21.5 miles. Turn left, crossing the river bridge, to reach the campground in 0.3 mile.
GPS coordinates: N45 35.349' / W123 33.455'
About the campground: In historic Tillamook State Forest, this campground offers beautiful sites in a mature, even-aged Douglas fir forest riddled with alders. The campsites are aesthetically pleasing and spacious, with long, gravel parking pads. A few sites sit close to the Wilson River. The park offers convenient access to the varied recreation of the forest: off-highway-vehicle driving, horseback riding, hiking, fishing, and sightseeing, with swimming and kayaking also possible. River Trail offers a short walk to a picturesque rock ledge.

15 Jordan Creek Off-Highway-Vehicle Staging Area

Location: About 20 miles east of Tillamook
Season: Mid-May–Sept
Sites: 6 basic sites; no hookups
Maximum length: 40 feet
Facilities: Tables, fire rings, nonflush toilets; no drinking water
Fee per night: $$
Management: Tillamook State Forest
Contact: (503) 842-2545; www.oregon.gov/ODF/tillamookstateforest/Recreation.shtml
Finding the campground: From the junction of US 101 and OR 6 in Tillamook, go east on OR 6 for 17.4 miles. Turn right onto gravel Jordan Creek Road at the sign for the off-highway-vehicle (OHV) staging area. Continue 2.2 mile to the staging area and take a right. The campground is 0.1 mile ahead.
GPS coordinates: N45 32.214' / W123 34.142'
About the campground: This campground serving OHV enthusiasts sits beside Jordan Creek and consists of a large central gravel parking area with the site tables and grills dispersed in the perimeter forest. Alders overhang the picturesque creek. State forest roads and designated trails provide OHV users ample opportunities.

16 Nehalem Falls

Location: About 11 miles northeast of Nehalem
Season: Mid-May–Sept
Sites: 14 basic sites, 6 walk-in tent sites; no hookups
Maximum length: 30 feet
Facilities: Tables, grills, nonflush toilets, drinking water
Fee per night: $–$$
Management: Tillamook State Forest
Contact: (503) 842-2545; www.oregon.gov/ODF/tillamookstateforest/Recreation.shtml
Finding the campground: From US 101, 8.5 miles north of Rockaway Beach and 1.5 miles south of Nehalem, turn east onto OR 53 toward Mohler and Portland. Go 1.4 miles and turn right, following signs toward Nehalem River and Foley Creek. In another 0.9 mile turn left onto Foss Road; follow it 7 miles to the campground entrance on the left.
GPS coordinates: N45 43.728' / W123 46.325'
About the campground: Within earshot of the Nehalem River, this pleasant family campground sits among alders, bigleaf maples, and mixed conifers. The walk-in sites are tucked away in an old-growth stand. A few old stumps pierce the undergrowth of thimbleberry and fern. The river shows dark, deep pools alternating with riffles. A path leads to the river falls contained in an outcrop gorge. A fish ladder bypasses the falls.

17 Stagecoach Horse Camp

Location: About 24 miles west of Forest Grove
Season: Year-round; camp reserved for horse-users only Apr 1–Oct 31
Sites: 10 basic sites; no hookups
Maximum length: 25 feet
Facilities: Tables, grills, nonflush toilets, shelter, corrals, stock water; no drinking water
Fee per night: $$
Management: Tillamook State Forest
Contact: (503) 357-2191; www.oregon.gov/ODF/tillamookstateforest/Recreation.shtml
Finding the campground: At the highway summit on OR 6, 19 miles west of Forest Grove and 31.3 miles east of Tillamook, turn south at the sign for Browns Camp. Quickly bear right, following a single-lane gravel road riddled with potholes. Continue to bear right at the junctions at 0.8 mile, 1.2 miles, 2.7 miles, and 4.4 miles, staying on the primary gravel road. At 4.7 miles turn left onto Rutherford Road for a steep 0.3-mile descent into camp. A state forest map will help you find your way.
GPS coordinates: N45 35.801' / W123 24.852'
About the campground: Equestrians will appreciate this relaxing camp snuggled in a second-growth fir forest with a lush understory. An information board in camp shows the location of trailheads. Tillamook State Forest's historic trails (all signed) are open to hikers and equestrians only. For the most part these trails keep your horses safely away from off-highway vehicles. Still, when riding the trails, remain attentive at intersections.

Pacific City-Nestucca River Area

	Hookup Sites	Total Sites	Max. RV Length	Hookups	Toilets	Showers	Drinking Water	Dump Station	Recreation	Fee	Can Reserve
18 Alder Glen Recreation Site		11	40		NF		X		F	$$	
19 Dovre Recreation Site		10	30		NF		X		F	$$	
20 East Dunes and West Winds		140	40		F, NF		X		HSFO	$$	
21 Fan Creek Recreation Site		11	24		NF		X		F	$$	
22 Hebo Lake		12	18		NF		X		HFB	$$	
23 Rocky Bend		6	30		NF				F	None	
24 Sandbeach		96	30		F		X		HFO	$$$	X
25 Webb County Park	7	38	30	WE	F		X	X	HSF	$$	
26 Whalen Island County Park		33	25		F		X		HFBL	$$-$$$	
27 Woods County Park	5	12	40	WES	F		X		FBL	$$-$$$	

18 Alder Glen Recreation Site

Location: About 16 miles northeast of Beaver and 28 miles northeast of Pacific City
Season: May–Sept; limited off-season service for hunters until the first snowfall
Sites: 11 basic sites; no hookups
Maximum length: 40 feet
Facilities: Tables, grills, nonflush toilets, drinking water (usually through mid-Sept), fishing dock
Fee per night: $$
Management: Bureau of Land Management—Salem District, Tillamook Resource Area
Contact: (503) 815-1100; www.blm.gov/or/
Finding the campground: From US 101 at Beaver, turn east onto Nestucca River Road, a BLM Backcountry Byway, and go 16.4 miles to the campground.
GPS coordinates: N45 15.965' / W123 34.851'
About the campground: In a moss-draped alder and maple setting, this welcoming Nestucca River campground sits across the river from a lacy, pyramid-shaped waterfall. Sites have paved parking spaces, and a paved path leads to a small fishing dock. The relaxing sound of the water erases campers' cares.

19 Dovre Recreation Site

Location: About 25 miles northeast of Beaver, 37 miles northeast of Pacific City
Season: May–Sept
Sites: 10 basic sites; no hookups
Maximum length: 30 feet
Facilities: Tables, grills, nonflush toilets, drinking water (usually through mid-Sept), covered picnic shelter
Fee per night: $$
Management: Bureau of Land Management—Salem District, Tillamook Resource Area
Contact: (503) 815-1100; www.blm.gov/or/
Finding the campground: From US 101 at Beaver, turn east onto Nestucca River Road; continue 25 miles to the campground.
GPS coordinates: N45 18.953' / W123 28.697'
About the campground: At this Nestucca River campground, the sites terrace the riverside slope of tall hemlocks and Douglas firs. Mossy rocks and cascading ferns dress the opposite shore, and a large side creek adds to the river's song. If quiet is your goal, you will find it at this campground. Most sites have paved parking pads, but a few have graveled road-shoulder parking. The lower reaches of camp provide direct access to the river, which alternately shows riffles and glassy pools.

20 East Dunes and West Winds

Location: About 12 miles north of Pacific City
Season: Year-round
Sites: 100 basic sites at East Dunes, 40 basic sites at West Winds; no hookups
Maximum length: 40 feet
Facilities: Flush and nonflush toilets, drinking water, playground
Fee per night: $$
Management: Siuslaw National Forest
Contact: (503) 392-5100; www.fs.usda.gov/recmain/siuslaw/recreation
Finding the campground: From the junction of US 101 and OR 6 in Tillamook, go south on US 101 for 10.7 miles. Turn west onto Sand Lake Road and proceed 4.3 miles. Turn left to remain on Sand Lake Road; continue another 0.9 mile. Turn right onto Galloway, go 2.3 miles, and keep right at the junction. The campgrounds are just ahead, with West Winds at road's end.
GPS coordinates: N45 17.218' / W123 57.470'
About the campgrounds: This pair of campgrounds caters to off-highway-vehicle (OHV) enthusiasts. Large, open, paved parking areas serve the RVers and truck campers pulling OHV trailers. Sites sit side by side. At the edge of the parking lot, a few determined individuals manage to pitch tents where the pavement meets the dunes. The roar of engines can be heard 24 hours a day, so be prepared.

21 Fan Creek Recreation Site

Location: About 22 miles northeast of Beaver, 34 miles northeast of Pacific City
Season: May–Sept
Sites: 11 basic sites; no hookups
Maximum length: 24 feet
Facilities: Tables, grills, nonflush toilets, drinking water (usually through mid-Sept)
Fee per night: $$
Management: Bureau of Land Management–Salem District, Tillamook Resource Area
Contact: (503) 815-1100; www.blm.gov/or/st/en.html
Finding the campground: From US 101 at Beaver, turn east onto Nestucca River Road and go 22.4 miles to the campground. From McMinnville the campground is 30 miles northwest of town via Meadow Lake and Nestucca access roads.
GPS coordinates: N45 17.458' / W123 29.603'
About the campground: In a mixed forest of hemlocks, firs, and alders, this campground occupies the shores of Nestucca River and Fan Creek. Thorny salmonberry abounds in the understory, helping assure site privacy. All sites have paved parking, with some more level than others. Tent campers may opt instead for the five walk-in sites under a canopy of bigleaf maples at Elk Bend, 3.5 miles west, which has river access and similar amenities.

22 Hebo Lake

Location: About 5 miles east of Hebo, 15 miles northeast of Pacific City
Season: Mid-Apr–mid-Nov
Sites: 12 basic sites; no hookups
Maximum length: 18 feet
Facilities: Tables, grills, nonflush toilets, drinking water, rustic picnic shelter, barrier-free fishing docks
Fee per night: $$
Management: Siuslaw National Forest
Contact: (503) 392-5100; www.fs.usda.gov/recmain/siuslaw/recreation
Finding the campground: From OR 22 at Hebo, turn east onto FR 14 just north of the Hebo Ranger District office. Proceed 4.5 miles to the campground on the right.
GPS coordinates: N45 13.874' / W123 47.813'
About the campground: Centerpiece to the camp is Hebo Lake, a coastal mountain lake stocked with pan-size trout and said to have some big catfish. Rafts or small rowboats may ply the water, but three is definitely a crowd. Rich coastal woods enfold the lake and camp, and a barrier-free trail travels two-thirds of the way around Hebo Lake. Lily pads, alder reflections, and newts add to the lake's charm. From camp, the 7-mile Pioneer-Indian Trail leads hikers over Mount Hebo and past vegetated North Lake, ending at the larger, more isolated South Lake, which also offers fishing.

23 Rocky Bend

Location: About 14 miles northeast of Beaver, 26 miles northeast of Pacific City
Season: Year-round
Sites: 6 basic sites; no hookups
Maximum length: 30 feet
Facilities: Tables, grills, nonflush toilets; no drinking water
Fee per night: None
Management: Siuslaw National Forest—Hebo Ranger District
Contact: (503) 392-5100; www.fs.usda.gov/recmain/siuslaw/recreation
Finding the campground: From US 101 at Beaver, turn east onto Nestucca River Road and go 13.8 miles to the campground.
GPS coordinates: N45 14.376' / W123 36.339'
About the campground: In Hebo Ranger District, this tiny, primitive camp occupies an alder-clad shore along the Nestucca River. Sites have gravel parking.

24 Sandbeach

Location: About 12 miles north of Pacific City
Season: Year-round
Sites: 96 basic sites; no hookups
Maximum length: 30 feet
Facilities: Tables, grills, flush toilets, drinking water
Fee per night: $$$
Management: Siuslaw National Forest—Hebo Ranger District
Contact: (503) 392-5100; (877) 444-6777 for reservations; www.fs.usda.gov/recmain/siuslaw/recreation
Finding the campground: From the junction of US 101 and OR 6 in Tillamook, go south on US 101 for 10.7 miles. Turn west onto Sand Lake Road and proceed 4.3 miles. Turn left to remain on Sand Lake Road, continuing another 0.9 mile. Turn right onto Galloway and continue 2.3 miles. Turn left at the junction for Sandbeach Campground.
GPS coordinates: N45 17.092' / W123 57.407'
About the campground: Although off-highway vehicles (OHVs) are prohibited from driving through camp, engine roars carry over the dunes 24 hours a day. A designated bypass links the camp to the riding dunes. For quieter pursuits, the beach, closed to OHVs between the campground and Fisherman's Parking, is just 0.1 mile away via Sand Lake Estuary. Sand Lake is a big, shallow tidal lake that reduces to a sand flat at low tide. The lake holds flounder and perch, which attract feeding eagles and other birds at low tide. Because the campground sits in a weather gap between coastal capes, it often basks in sun when the rest of the coast is cloaked in fog. Sites have fairly good privacy in the dune–shore pine setting.

25 Webb County Park

Location: In Pacific City
Season: Year-round
Sites: 7 hookup sites, 31 basic sites; water and electric hookups
Maximum length: 30 feet
Facilities: Tables, grills, flush toilets, drinking water, dump station
Fee per night: $$
Management: Tillamook County
Contact: (503) 965-5001; www.co.tillamook.or.us/gov/parks/Campgrounds.htm
Finding the campground: From Cape Kiwanda Drive, 1.1 miles northwest of Pacific City center, turn right onto Webb Park Road (opposite the parking for Cape Kiwanda State Natural Area); follow it into the park.
GPS coordinates: N45 12.972' / W123 58.015'
About the campground: Inland from Haystack Rock, this pleasant campground claims a private, out-of-the-way, shore pine–shaded spot. The campground sits within easy walking distance of a state beach where dories (flat-bottomed fishing boats) are launched into the surf and where hang gliders soar from the Cape Kiwanda headland. Other area activities include driving Three Capes Scenic Route, hiking the spit at Robert W. (Bob) Straub State Park, and fishing the Nestucca River or tiny Hebo Lake.

26 Whalen Island County Park

Location: About 7 miles north of Pacific City
Season: Year-round
Sites: 31 basic sites, 2 hike/bike tent sites; no hookups
Maximum length: 25 feet
Facilities: Tables, fire rings, flush toilets, drinking water, boat launch
Fee per night: $$–$$$
Management: Tillamook County
Contact: (503) 965-6085; www.co.tillamook.or.us/gov/parks/Campgrounds.htm
Finding the campground: From the junction of US 101 and OR 6 in Tillamook, go south on US 101 for 10.7 miles. Turn west onto Sand Lake Road and proceed another 4.3 miles. Turn left to remain on Sand Lake Road and continue 3.3 miles. Turn right and cross a Sand Lake levee road to enter the camp in 0.2 mile.
GPS coordinates: N45 16.352' / W123 56.998'
About the campground: Most of the campsites here stretch across a treeless, grassy flat overlooking the Sand Lake estuary; a few occupy a rise at wood's edge. Bald eagles, shorebirds, and frogs contribute amusement to your stay. Fishing, crabbing, and exploring the Three Capes Scenic Route or area dunes engage campers. This camp offers a quiet alternative to the area's popular off-highway-vehicle campgrounds.

27 Woods County Park

Location: Less than 1 mile east of Pacific City
Season: Year-round
Sites: 5 hookup sites, 7 tent sites; water, electric, and sewer hookups
Maximum length: 40 feet
Facilities: Tables at tent sites, shelter with tables and fireplace, flush toilets, drinking water; public boat launch and fishing access 0.4 mile west of camp
Fee per night: $$–$$$
Management: Tillamook County
Contact: (503) 965-5001; www.co.tillamook.or.us/gov/parks/Campgrounds.htm
Finding the campground: From the center of Pacific City, go 0.8 mile east on Brooten Road. The campground is on the corner at Woods Bridge.
GPS coordinates: N45 12.685' / W123 57.218'
About the campground: In a rural-residential setting, this small campground occupies a corner green at Woods Bridge above the Nestucca River. The camp's small, sandy river access often holds the tracks of the previous night's wildlife, and the river shows a tidal influence. Meadowlarks serenade campers from the open field across from the park. Sites occupy an open lawn, but trees grow toward shore. RVers should avoid camping here when conditions are wet; the soft grassy sites can turn to mud under the weight of the vehicle.

Lincoln City–Newport Area

	Hookup Sites	Total Sites	Max. RV Length	Hookups	Toilets	Showers	Drinking Water	Dump Station	Recreation	Fee	Can Reserve
28 Beverly Beach State Park	128	256	65	WESC	F	X	X	X	HSF	$$$	X
29 Devils Lake State Recreation Area	33	87	45	WESC	F	X	X		SFBL	$$-$$$	X
30 Elk City Park		12	40		F		X		FBL	$$	
31 Jack Morgan County Park		14	40		F		X		FBL	$$	
32 Moonshine County Park		38	40		F	X	X		FBL	$$	
33 Newport Marina RV Park	143	143	60	WESC	F	X	X	X	FBL	$$$	X
34 South Beach State Park	228	287	60	WE	F	X	X	X	HSF	$$$	X

28 Beverly Beach State Park

Location: About 7 miles north of Newport
Season: Year-round
Sites: 128 full or partial hookup sites, 128 basic sites, 21 yurts; water and electric hookups; sewer and cable hookups available at some sites
Maximum length: 65 feet
Facilities: Tables, grills, flush toilets, drinking water, showers, dump station, playground, visitor center
Fee per night: $$$
Management: Oregon State Parks and Recreation Department
Contact: (541) 265-9278; (800) 452-5687 for reservations; www.oregon.gov/OPRD/PARKS/camping.shtml
Finding the campground: From Newport go about 7 miles north on US 101. The campground is on the east side of the highway.
GPS coordinates: N44 42.698' / W124 03.243'
About the campground: Threaded by Spencer Creek, this campground occupies a coastal forest setting of Sitka spruce, wax myrtle, and rhododendron. It features beach access and a short nature trail and lies within easy reach of Yaquina Head Outstanding Natural Area, with its visitor center, historic lighthouse, and wildlife watching. Visitors to the natural area can spy nesting seabirds on Colony Rock, migrating gray whales, and harbor seals. Newport adds its city, port, and beach enticements.

Yaquina Head Lighthouse, Yaquina Head Outstanding Natural Area

29 Devils Lake State Recreation Area

Location: In Lincoln City
Season: Year-round
Sites: 33 full or partial hookup sites, 54 basic sites, 10 yurts; water and electric hookups; sewer and cable hookups available at some sites
Maximum length: 45 feet
Facilities: Tables, grills, flush toilets, drinking water, showers, boat launch, dock, moorage slips
Fee per night: $$–$$$
Management: Oregon State Parks and Recreation Department
Contact: (541) 994-2002; (800) 452-5687 for reservations; www.oregon.gov/OPRD/PARKS/camping.shtml
Finding the campground: From US 101 in Lincoln City, head east on Sixth Street for 0.1 mile to enter the campground.
GPS coordinates: N44 58.244' / W124 00.669'
About the campground: Attractive shore pines shade and seclude these campsites, which are not far from the shore of Devils Lake. The individual sites are level, with paved parking pads. Lake access is available at the dock here and at the park's day-use area off First Street. The park also offers guided kayak tours in summer for a fee. Besides fishing and boating at the lake, you can spend your time prowling the coastal beaches, visiting the shops and eateries of Lincoln City, joining in the spring or fall kite festival, or taking a chance at Chinook Winds Indian Casino.

30 Elk City Park

Location: About 10 miles southeast of Toledo, 20 miles southeast of Newport
Season: Apr–Oct
Sites: 12 basic sites; no hookups
Maximum length: 40 feet
Facilities: Tables, grills, flush toilets, drinking water, horseshoe pits, concrete boat ramp and dock
Fee per night: $$
Management: Lincoln County
Contact: (541) 265-5747; www.co.lincoln.or.us/lcparks
Finding the campground: From the junction of Main Street and Butler Bridge Road in Toledo, follow Butler Bridge Road for 0.8 mile as it rounds south past the Georgia-Pacific Paper Mill and crosses the Yaquina River. Bear left at the fork onto Elk City Road. Continue 8.7 miles upstream to this park at the intersection of Elk City and Harlan Roads.
GPS coordinates: N44 37.242' / W123 52.518'
About the campground: At the confluence of Big Elk Creek and the Yaquina River, this campground occupies a large flat meadow with a handful of shade trees. It mainly attracts anglers and boaters, with ample boater parking in addition to the campsites. Vultures commonly soar overhead. In 1866 the first stage line between the Willamette Valley and the coast stopped here; coast-bound travelers then had to continue by boat on the Yaquina River.

31 Jack Morgan County Park

Location: About 20 miles southeast of Lincoln City
Season: Apr–Nov
Sites: 14 basic sites; no hookups
Maximum length: 40 feet
Facilities: Tables, grills, flush toilets, drinking water, drift/car-top boat launch (across road from camp)
Fee per night: $$
Management: Lincoln County
Contact: (541) 265-5747; www.co.lincoln.or.us/lcparks
Finding the campground: From US 101 south of Lincoln City, turn east onto OR 229 to reach the campground in 17 miles. The campground is 6 miles northwest of Siletz.
GPS coordinates: N44 48.018' / W123 54.327'
About the campground: Across the highway from the Siletz River, this campground occupies a grassy spot beneath towering western hemlocks and spruces. Some of the well-spaced sites are more open than others. The camp has paved roads and parking. The coastal river draws campers away for fishing or drift boating.

32 Moonshine County Park

Location: About 12 miles northeast of Siletz
Season: Apr–Oct; in winter, dry camping only
Sites: 24 RV sites, 14 tent sites; no hookups
Maximum length: 40 feet
Facilities: Tables, grills, flush toilets, drinking water, coin-operated showers, drift/car-top boat launch, horseshoe pits
Fee per night: $$
Management: Lincoln County
Contact: (541) 265-5747; www.co.lincoln.or.us/lcparks
Finding the campground: From OR 229 at Siletz, 23 miles southeast of Lincoln City and 7 miles north of Toledo, go east on East Logsden Road, which becomes Upper Siletz Road. Drive 7.5 miles to Logsden. Turn left (north) at a sign for the park and continue another 4 miles to the camp.
GPS coordinates: N44 46.602' / W123 50.107'
About the campground: This park serves up Siletz River hospitality in an attractive river valley location. Campsites occupy a large, open lawn above the river, with dispersed pine, spruce, and cedar trees distributing bits of shade. Paved pads are available at the RV sites, while tent sites dot the lawn. Across from camp, a tributary waterfall spills into the coastal river that supports salmon and steelhead.

33 Newport Marina RV Park

Location: In Newport
Season: Year-round

Sites: 143 hookup sites; water, electric, sewer, and cable hookups
Maximum length: 40 feet at marina sites, 60 feet at the south RV area
Facilities: Flush toilets, drinking water, showers, laundry, dump station, wireless (available), camp store, cafe, pier, charters, dock, boat rental, fish-cleaning station
Fee per night: $$$
Management: Port of Newport
Contact: (541) 867-3321, reservations accepted
Finding the campground: From the south end of Yaquina Bay Bridge in Newport, take Southeast Pacific Way. Follow the signs for the Oregon Coast Aquarium to reach the marina in 0.6 mile. The park sits east of the bridge.
GPS coordinates: N44 37.355' / W124 02.964'
About the campground: RVers may choose between the two camp areas: the paved lot of the marina for waterfront camping or the inland coastal flat of the south RV area, which has grass and a few shore pines. The marina offers everything that nautical and fishing enthusiasts might want, and its sites are within a hat's throw of a microbrewery, the Oregon Coast Aquarium, and the Mark O. Hatfield Marine Science Center. Seasonal attractions include jigging for herring, crabbing on the pier, clamming in the bay, and watching larcenous sea lions or diving loons. Newport and the coastal beaches may lure you away from camp.

34 South Beach State Park

Location: About 1.5 miles south of Newport
Season: Year-round
Sites: 228 hookup sites, 59 basic sites, 27 yurts; water and electric hookups
Maximum length: 60 feet (40 feet for basic sites)
Facilities: Tables, grills, flush toilets, drinking water, showers, dump station, playground, volleyball and basketball courts
Fee per night: $$$
Management: Oregon State Parks and Recreation Department
Contact: (541) 867-4715; (800) 452-5687 for reservations; www.oregon.gov/OPRD/PARKS/camping.shtml
Finding the campground: From the Yaquina Bay Bridge in Newport, drive 1.5 miles south on US 101; turn west to enter the park.
GPS coordinates: N44 36.329' / W124 03.673'
About the campground: This jumbo campground occupies a broad coastal plain behind the swale and low dunes of a prized beach. Shore pines isolate and lend shade to the campsites, which are nicely spaced for privacy and comfort. The paths to the beach range between 0.25 and 0.5 mile in length. Hiking north along the beach, you reach a jetty where you can fish or watch the sea lions and harbor seals in the bay. The park also offers guided kayak tours in summer for a fee. The state park is within easy drive of the tourist shops and Old Town attractions of Newport, coastal offerings, Oregon Coast Aquarium, and Mark O. Hatfield Marine Science Center.

	Hookup Sites	Total Sites	Max. RV Length	Hookups	Toilets	Showers	Drinking Water	Dump Station	Recreation	Fee	Can Reserve
35 Alder Dune		39	45		NF		X		HSF	$$$	X
36 Baker Beach Recreation Site		4	25		NF				HSFR	$$	
37 Beachside State Recreation Area	32	74	30	WE	F	X	X		HSF	$$-$$$	X
38 Blackberry		32	40		NF		X		FBL	$$	X
39 Cape Perpetua		38	32		F		X	X	HF	$$$	X
40 Carl G. Washburne Memorial State Park	58	65	45	WES	F	X	X	X	HSF	$$-$$$	
41 Clay Creek Recreation Site		21	32		NF		X		HSFBL	$$	
42 Harbor Vista	38	38	40	WE	F, NF	X	X	X		$$$	X
43 Horse Creek Trailhead		10	60		NF				HR	Donation	
44 Port of Siuslaw RV Park and Marina	91	104	40	WESC	F	X	X	X	FBL	$$$	X
45 Rock Creek		15	22		NF		X		HF	$$$	
46 Sutton Creek Recreation Area	22	77	40	E	F		X		HFBL	$$$	X
47 Tillicum Beach	7	59	40	WE	F		X		HSF	$$$	X
48 Whittaker Creek Recreation Site		31	32		NF		X		HFBL	$$	

35 Alder Dune

Location: About 6 miles north of Florence
Season: Year-round
Sites: 39 basic sites; no hookups
Maximum length: 45 feet
Facilities: Tables, grills, nonflush toilets, drinking water
Fee per night: $$$
Management: Siuslaw National Forest
Contact: (541) 902-8526 or (541) 271-6000; (877) 444-6777 for reservations (May 1–Sept 30); www.fs.usda.gov/recmain/siuslaw/recreation
Finding the campground: From the junction of US 101 and OR 126 in Florence, go 6.4 miles north on US 101. The campground is on the west side of the highway.
GPS coordinates: N44 04.129' / W124 06.087'

About the campground: This campground, with paved sites and roads, occupies a coastal forest of alders and conifers along Alder and Dune Lakes. Dune Lake is green and picturesque, with an irregular shoreline. Alder Lake has a marshy side arm and grassy spits, but its main body is larger and deeper than Dune Lake. Fishing, swimming, and canoeing are possible. Hiking trails pass through dunes and coastal forest and link the camp to Sutton Creek Recreation Area to the south. East off US 101, 1.6 miles south of camp, is the nature trail touring Darlingtonia Wayside. The trail visits a bog of rare cobra lilies (or pitcher plants), carnivores of the plant kingdom. They flower in May and June. Sutton Lake, slightly farther to the south, has a ramp for boating.

36 Baker Beach Recreation Site

Location: About 8 miles north of Florence
Season: Year-round
Sites: 4 basic sites; no hookups
Maximum length: 25 feet
Facilities: Tables, grills, nonflush toilets; no drinking water
Fee per night: $$
Management: Siuslaw National Forest
Contact: (541) 902-8526 or (541) 271-6000; www.fs.usda.gov/recmain/siuslaw/recreation
Finding the campground: From the junction of US 101 and OR 126 in Florence, go 7.6 miles north on US 101. Turn west onto Baker Beach Road; the recreation site is 0.4 mile ahead.
GPS coordinates: N44 05.253' / W124 07.104'
About the campground: Within sound of the surf, this campground, popular with equestrians, consists of a large gravel parking lot with sites fanning off into the edging shore pines and vegetated dunes. A trail crosses the dunes to the beach; be sure to keep to the trail. To protect the threatened snowy plover, the beach is closed behind the high tide line from March 15 through September 15.

37 Beachside State Recreation Area

Location: About 3 miles south of Waldport
Season: Mid-Mar–Oct
Sites: 32 hookup sites, 42 basic sites, 2 yurts; water and electric hookups
Maximum length: 30 feet
Facilities: Tables, grills, flush toilets, drinking water, showers
Fee per night: $$–$$$
Management: Oregon State Parks and Recreation Department
Contact: (541) 563-3220; (800) 452-5687 for reservations; www.oregon.gov/OPRD/PARKS/camping.shtml
Finding the campground: From the junction of OR 34 and US 101 in Waldport, go 3.4 miles south on US 101. The park is on the west side of the highway.
GPS coordinates: N44 22.863' / W124 05.321'

About the campground: This beach campground features private, well-shaded sites in a coastal pine–Sitka spruce forest. The understory salal and wax myrtle contribute to site privacy. The camp affords easy access to miles of broad, sandy beach and beautiful ocean. Traffic noise from US 101 carries to the sites closest to the highway. The hookup sites typically have longer parking spurs. Besides beachcombing, beach strolling, sunning, and surf play, campers can try their hands at clamming and crabbing in Alsea Bay or fishing for steelhead or salmon on the Alsea River, both north of the park. For trout fishing there is the Yachats River, to the south.

38 Blackberry

Location: About 17 miles east of Waldport
Season: Mid-May–Labor Day weekend
Sites: 32 basic sites; no hookups
Maximum length: 40 feet
Facilities: Tables, grills, nonflush toilets, drinking water, drift/car-top boat launch
Fee per night: $$
Management: Siuslaw National Forest
Contact: (541) 563-8400; (877) 444-6777 for reservations; www.fs.usda.gov/recmain/siuslaw/recreation
Finding the campground: The campground is south off OR 34, 17.1 miles east of Waldport.
GPS coordinates: N44 22.279' / W123 50.118'
About the campground: Overnighters will enjoy this beautiful riverside campground with paved parking pads, lots of open grass, and towering hemlocks, Sitka spruces, and Douglas firs. Bigleaf maples shade the Alsea River. Some sites directly overlook the river, but all lie within easy access of it. Fishing and relaxing are the primary draws to this campground, and the coast is only minutes away.

39 Cape Perpetua

Location: About 3 miles south of Yachats, 11 miles south of Waldport
Season: Mid-May–Sept
Sites: 38 basic sites; no hookups
Maximum length: 32 feet
Facilities: Tables, grills, flush toilets, drinking water, dump station
Fee per night: $$$
Management: Siuslaw National Forest
Contact: (541) 563-8400; (877) 444-6777 for reservations; www.fs.usda.gov/recmain/siuslaw/recreation
Finding the campground: The campground is east off US 101, 3.3 miles south of Yachats.
GPS coordinates: N44 16.901' / W124 06.286'
About the campground: This serene campground along Cape Creek charms guests with its grassy sites and framing wooded hillside. Footbridges span the creek to link the campground to a nature

trail, which leads to a 500-year-old Sitka spruce and the area's interpretive center. An underpass allows safe passage beneath US 101 to a trail system along the ragged seashore, which is punctuated by blowholes, high-splashing waves, chasms, and tide pools. A scenic drive or foot trail leads to the top of the headland for whale watching; longer trails explore ridges and the creek canyon. Captain James Cook named this headland Cape Perpetua in 1778.

40 Carl G. Washburne Memorial State Park

Location: About 14 miles north of Florence
Season: Year-round
Sites: 58 hookup sites, 7 walk-in tent sites, 2 yurts; water, electric, and sewer hookups
Maximum length: 45 feet
Facilities: Tables, grills, flush toilets, drinking water, showers, dump station across US 101
Fee per night: $$-$$$
Management: Oregon State Parks and Recreation Department
Contact: (541) 547-3416; www.oregon.gov/OPRD/PARKS/camping.shtml
Finding the campground: From US 101, 11.4 miles south of Yachats and 13.9 miles north of Florence, turn east for the park campground. The park's beach and day-use area are on the west side of the highway.
GPS coordinates: N44 09.698' / W124 06.783'
About the campground: Snuggled in a coastal forest with a lush understory that includes rhododendron blooms in early summer, this spacious campground offers a pleasing retreat that's perfect for relaxing. China and Blowout Creeks thread through the park. Elk and tide pools are possible nature discoveries. A trail from camp passes under US 101 for safe, convenient access to the beach; another trail links the park to Heceta Head Lighthouse. You can also drive the 2.1 miles south to this photogenic lighthouse. Sea Lion Caves, a popular private attraction featuring a Steller's sea lion rookery, is 3.2 miles south of the park.

41 Clay Creek Recreation Site

Location: About 28 miles southeast of Mapleton
Season: Memorial Day weekend–Sept
Sites: 21 basic sites; no hookups
Maximum length: 32 feet
Facilities: Tables, grills, nonflush toilets, drinking water, playground, ball field, horseshoe pits, cartop boat launch
Fee per night: $$
Management: Bureau of Land Management—Eugene District
Contact: (541) 683-6600; www.blm.gov/or/
Finding the campground: From OR 126, 12 miles east of Mapleton and 33 miles west of Eugene, turn south onto Siuslaw River Road. Travel 9.7 miles and bear left on Siuslaw River Access Road. Proceed another 6 miles and turn right to reach the entrance to the recreation site.

GPS coordinates: N43 54.244' / W123 34.257'

About the campground: Spacious sites with paved parking pads, mossy vine-maple tangles, and tall straight firs make up this camp area along Clay Creek and the Siuslaw River. The river flows broad, cloudy, and green and calls to anglers; check current fishing regulations before casting your line. A small swimming area invites you to cool off. The site's Clay Creek Trail ascends a ridge above camp to visit a remnant old-growth stand. From camp you cross the concrete bridge on Clay Creek Road and then cross over Clay Creek to begin the hike.

42 Harbor Vista

Location: In Florence
Season: Year-round
Sites: 38 hookup sites; water and electric hookups
Maximum length: 40 feet
Facilities: Tables, grills, flush and nonflush toilets, drinking water, showers, dump station, playground, vista shelter
Fee per night: $$$
Management: Lane County
Contact: (541) 682-2000, reservations accepted; www.lanecounty.org/departments/PW/Parks
Finding the campground: In Florence turn west off US 101 onto Heceta Beach Road and go 1.8 miles. Turn left onto Rhododendron Drive and proceed another 1.2 miles. Turn right onto Jetty Road North; the campground is on the left in 0.1 mile.

Alternatively, turn west off US 101 onto Thirty-fifth Street and go 0.9 mile. Turn right onto Rhododendron Drive, and proceed another 1.3 miles. Turn left onto Jetty Road North to reach the campground in 0.1 mile.

GPS coordinates: N44 00.956' / W124 07.495'
About the campground: This campground offers a quiet, clean, comfortable base from which to explore the area. Sites rest in coastal vegetation of shore pine, salal, rhododendron, and wax myrtle; some sites are more open than others. From the vista shelter you can see North Jetty and the Siuslaw River mouth. Outward explorations lead to ocean beaches, dunes, coastal lakes, and Old Town Florence.

43 Horse Creek Trailhead

Location: About 14 miles northeast of Florence
Season: Year-round
Sites: 10 basic sites; no hookups
Maximum length: 60 feet
Facilities: Tables, grills, nonflush toilets, corrals, hitching posts, horse loading ramp, stock water; no drinking water
Fee per night: Donation
Management: Siuslaw National Forest

Contact: (541) 902-8526 or (541) 271-6000; www.fs.usda.gov/recmain/siuslaw/recreation
Finding the campground: From US 101, 10.3 miles north of Florence and 0.5 mile south of Sea Lion Caves, turn east onto Horse Creek Road (FR 5800), which begins paved but becomes single-lane gravel with turnouts. Follow it 3.2 miles to campground.
GPS coordinates: N44 06.420' / W124 05.558'
About the campground: In a dense forest of tall Sitka spruce, this pleasant, isolated campground serves a burgeoning hiker/horse trail system that already encompasses 14 miles of trail through the coastal mountains. The camp is functional, clean, and comfortable, and the sites are well spaced for campers with horses.

44 Port of Siuslaw RV Park and Marina

Location: On the bay in Florence
Season: Year-round
Sites: 91 full and partial hookup sites, 13 basic sites; water, electric, sewer, and cable hookups
Maximum length: 40 feet
Facilities: Tables, flush toilets, drinking water, showers, laundry, dump station, boat launch, sport marina
Fee per night: $$$
Management: Port of Siuslaw
Contact: (541) 997-3040, reservations accepted; www.portofsiuslaw.com
Finding the campground: In Florence take the Old Town Loop off US 101 to First Street. The campground is at the corner of First and Harbor Streets, less than 0.25 mile off US 101.
GPS coordinates: N43 58.144' / W124 06.026'
About the campground: At the Port of Siuslaw, in the heart of Old Town Florence, campers have a choice between pleasant, shore pine–shaded lawn sites or the open, graveled sites directly over-looking the bay. This is an ideal base for outward explorations or simply planting yourself in camp. Easy walks lead to the marina and marine offerings and to the shops and eateries of Florence. The beach and dunes are just a short drive away. Boating, sportfishing, crabbing from the dock, and clamming in the mudflats are popular pursuits.

45 Rock Creek

Location: About 16 miles north of Florence
Season: Memorial Day–Sept
Sites: 15 basic sites; no hookups
Maximum length: 22 feet
Facilities: Tables, grills, nonflush toilets, drinking water
Fee per night: $$$
Management: Siuslaw National Forest
Contact: (541) 563-8400; www.fs.usda.gov/recmain/siuslaw/recreation

Finding the campground: From US 101, 9.7 miles south of Yachats and 15.6 miles north of Florence, turn east to enter campground.

GPS coordinates: N44 11.141' / W124 06.628'

About the campground: Gateway to Rock Creek Wilderness, this small campground sits where Rock Creek yawns to the ocean and the valley floor broadens into scenic meadows. Rock Creek is a beautiful, sparkling coastal water emerging from a forested canyon. An angler's path heads upstream from camp, providing the only access to the wilderness, but check current fishing regulations before fishing the creek. The path passes through old homestead meadows that are now frequented by elk. It is an easy jaunt from the campground to Cape Perpetua, Old Town Florence, and the northern reaches of Oregon Dunes National Recreation Area.

46 Sutton Creek Recreation Area

Location: About 5 miles north of Florence

Season: Year-round

Sites: 22 hookup sites, 55 basic sites; electric hookups only

Maximum length: 40 feet

Facilities: Tables, grills, flush toilets, drinking water, playground, boat launch (at Sutton Lake to the north)

Fee per night: $$$

Management: Siuslaw National Forest

Contact: (541) 902-8526 or (541) 271-6000; (877) 444-6777 for reservations (May 1–Sept 30); www.fs.usda.gov/recmain/siuslaw/recreation

Finding the campground: From the junction of US 101 and OR 126 in Florence, go 4.5 miles north on US 101. Turn west to enter Sutton Creek Recreation Area. The campground is located off the recreation area entrance road.

GPS coordinates: N44 03.273' / W124 06.425'

About the campground: This charming coastal campground is nestled among cedars, shore pines, hemlocks, and spruces along Sutton Creek. It extends a comfortable stay, with good site privacy and ample space. Parking spurs are paved. Area trails visit dune, ocean, estuary, and lake attractions. In camp, a short nature trail reveals a bog of carnivorous darlingtonia (or California pitcher plant). Darlingtonia Wayside, 0.1 mile north on US 101, offers another chance to view this rare plant. Sutton Lake draws boaters and anglers. Florence and the Oregon Dunes National Recreation Area are but a short drive south. Sea Lion Caves are 9 miles north on US 101.

47 Tillicum Beach

Location: About 5 miles south of Waldport

Season: Year-round

Sites: 7 hookup sites, 52 basic sites; water and electric hookups

Maximum length: 40 feet

Facilities: Tables, grills, flush toilets, drinking water

Fee per night: $$$
Management: Siuslaw National Forest
Contact: (541) 563-8400; (877) 444-6777 for reservations (available July–Labor Day); www
.fs.usda.gov/recmain/siuslaw/recreation
Finding the campground: From the junction of OR 34 and US 101 in Waldport, go 4.5 miles
south on US 101. Turn west to enter the campground.
GPS coordinates: N44 21.921' / W124 05.525'
About the campground: On a low bluff above the beach, a dense growth of low shore pines, salal,
evergreen huckleberry, and wax myrtle enfolds this campground. Sites closer to shore are more
exposed and receive more sun. Silvered snags and wind-sculpted spruce add interest to sunset
photography. Beach pursuits and visits to Cape Perpetua or Waldport further engage campers.

48 Whittaker Creek Recreation Site

Location: About 14 miles southeast of Mapleton
Season: Late May–Sept
Sites: 31 basic sites; no hookups
Maximum length: 32 feet
Facilities: Tables, grills, nonflush toilets, drinking water, horseshoe pits, drift/car-top boat launch
Fee per night: $$
Management: Bureau of Land Management—Eugene District
Contact: (541) 683-6600; www.blm.gov/or/
Finding the campground: From OR 126, 12 miles east of Mapleton and 33 miles west of Eugene,
turn south onto Siuslaw River Road. Go 1.5 miles and turn right onto Whittaker Creek Road. Go
another 0.2 mile; the entrance to the recreation site is on the right.
GPS coordinates: N43 59.159' / W123 39.764'
About the campground: This campground is bisected by Whittaker Creek, which houses an
experimental fish trap and is closed to fishing. Sites occupy either alder woodland or fir forest. The
close-by Siuslaw River suggests launching a drift boat or fishing, but check current fishing regulations first. This large coastal river flows broad, cloudy, and green. The interpretive Old Growth Ridge
National Recreation Trail begins in camp and climbs to a river overlook and an old-growth grove.

Reedsport Area

	Hookup Sites	Total Sites	Max. RV Length	Hookups	Toilets	Showers	Drinking Water	Dump Station	Recreation	Fee	Can Reserve
49 East Shore Recreation Site (Loon Lake)		6	40		NF				SFB	$$	
50 Loon Lake Recreation Site		60	40		F	X	X	X	SFBL	$$	
51 Smith River Falls Recreation Site		10	Small		NF				SF	None	
52 Vincent Creek Recreation Site		5	Small		NF					None	

49 East Shore Recreation Site (Loon Lake)

Location: About 21 miles southeast of Reedsport
Season: Memorial Day weekend–Oct
Sites: 6 basic sites; no hookups
Maximum length: 40 feet
Facilities: Tables, grills, nonflush toilets, boat dock; no drinking water
Fee per night: $$
Management: Bureau of Land Management–Coos Bay District
Contact: (541) 756-0100; www.blm.gov/or/
Finding the campground: From OR 38, 22.5 miles west of Elkton and 13 miles east of Reedsport, head south on winding Loon Lake Road to reach the recreation site in 7.5 miles.
GPS coordinates: N43 35.541' / W123 50.119'
About the campground: This small campground occupies a forested slope above Loon Lake; there is a separate day-use area across the road on the lakeshore. Fishing, boating, riding personal watercraft, and swimming are popular pursuits. A boat launch is located at Loon Lake Recreation Site.

50 Loon Lake Recreation Site

Location: About 20 miles southeast of Reedsport
Season: Memorial Day weekend–Sept
Sites: 52 basic sites, 8 tent sites; no hookups
Maximum length: 40 feet
Facilities: Tables, flush toilets, drinking water, showers, dump station, playground, boat launch, fish-cleaning station
Fee per night: $$
Management: Bureau of Land Management—Coos Bay District
Contact: (541) 756-0100; www.blm.gov/or/
Finding the campground: From OR 38, 22.5 miles west of Elkton and 13 miles east of Reedsport, head south on winding Loon Lake Road to reach the recreation site in 6.6 miles.
GPS coordinates: N43 35.851' / W123 50.964'
About the campground: Situated in a stately Douglas fir forest interspersed with bigleaf maples and coastal shrubs is this fully accommodating campground on Loon Lake. Although the terrain has a mild slope, campsite parking is level and paved. Guests have access to boating, fishing, swimming, and water-skiing on lovely Loon Lake. During the first week in August, the popular annual fishing derby is fun for the whole family.

51 Smith River Falls Recreation Site

Location: About 26 miles northeast of Reedsport
Season: Year-round
Sites: 10 basic sites; no hookups
Maximum length: Small units only
Facilities: Tables, grills, nonflush toilets; no drinking water
Fee per night: None
Management: Bureau of Land Management—Coos Bay District
Contact: (541) 756-0100; www.blm.gov/or/
Finding the campground: From US 101, 0.3 mile north of the Umpqua River bridge on the northern outskirts of Reedsport, turn east onto Smith River Road (CR 48) and go 25.3 miles. The recreation site is on the right.
GPS coordinates: N43 47.452' / W123 48.799'
About the campground: Located 0.2 mile upstream from Smith River Falls, this small, rustic campground occupies the terraces of a river slope. Alders grow toward the river; conifers shade the campsites. A few glorious old-growth trees tower above camp. Because of the short, uneven gravel or earthen parking pads and the sometimes-awkward approach to sites, this campground is better suited for tents or pickup campers. At Smith River Falls, rounded rock ledges part and fold the river, creating tiers of cascading water. Near the falls, flat-topped rocks appeal to sunbathers; elsewhere, potholes lend interest to the river rock. A fish enhancement project is located near the falls.

52 Vincent Creek Recreation Site

Location: About 29 miles northeast of Reedsport
Season: Year-round
Sites: 5 basic sites; no hookups
Maximum length: Small units only
Facilities: Tables, grills, nonflush toilets; no drinking water
Fee per night: None
Management: Bureau of Land Management—Coos Bay District
Contact: (541) 756-0100; www.blm.gov/or/
Finding the campground: From US 101, 0.3 mile north of the Umpqua River bridge at the northern outskirts of Reedsport, turn east onto Smith River Road (CR 48) and go 28.7 miles. The recreation site is on the right. The entry road travels past a guard station on its way into camp.
GPS coordinates: N43 47.587' / W123 46.568'
About the campground: This small, primitive, no-frills campground sits near the confluence of Vincent Creek and the Smith River. Alders and firs shade the river bench. The sites lack established parking pads, and you should be aware that rain-soaked ground can cause trouble for heavier vehicles.

Oregon Dunes National Recreation Area

	Hookup Sites	Total Sites	Max. RV Length	Hookups	Toilets	Showers	Drinking Water	Dump Station	Recreation	Fee	Can Reserve
53 Bluebill		18	30		NF		X		HF	$$$	
54 Carter Lake		23	35		F		X		HFBL	$$$	X
55 Driftwood II		67	40		F	X	X		FO	$$$	X
56 Eel Creek		52	30		F		X		H	$$$	X
57 Half Moon Bay		45	100		NF		X		FO	$$$	X
58 Horsfall		70	50		F	X	X		O	$$$	X
59 Horsfall Beach		34	50		F		X		HSFOR	$$$	
60 Jessie M. Honeyman Memorial State Park	168	355	60	WES	F	X	X	X	HSFBLO	$$-$$$	X
61 Lagoon		38	35		F		X		HF	$$$	
62 Riley Ranch	50	92	40	WE	F	X	X		FO	$$-$$$	
63 Salmon Harbor Marina (Middle Spit Self-Contained Camping)		166	40		F	X	X	X	FBL	$$	
64 Spinreel		36	40		F		X		O	$$$	
65 Tahkenitch		34	30		F		X		HFBL	$$$	X
66 Tahkenitch Landing		27	30		NF				FBL	$$	X
67 Tenmile Lake RV Park	45	45	40	WE	F	X	X	X	FBL	$$-$$$	
68 Tyee		14	22		NF		X		FBL	$$$	X
69 Umpqua Lighthouse State Park	20	44	45	WES	F	X	X		HSF	$$-$$$	X
70 Waxmyrtle		55	35		F		X		HFO	$$$	
71 Wild Mare Horse Camp		12	50		NF		X		HR	$$$	X
72 William M. Tugman State Park	94	94	50	WE	F	X	X	X	FBL	$$-$$$	X
73 Winchester Bay Marina RV Resort (formerly Salmon Harbor Marina RV Resort)	138	163	40	WESC	F	X	X	X	FBLC	$$$	X
74 Windy Cove	64	97	30	WESC	F	X	X		FBL	$$-$$$	X

Off-road vehicles at Spinreel Riding Area

53 Bluebill

Location: About 4 miles north of North Bend/Coos Bay
Season: May–Sept
Sites: 18 basic sites; no hookups
Maximum length: 30 feet
Facilities: Tables, grills, nonflush toilets, drinking water
Fee per night: $$$
Management: Siuslaw National Forest
Contact: (541) 271-6000; www.fs.usda.gov/recmain/siuslaw/recreation
Finding the campground: From US 101, 0.6 mile north of the Coos Bay Bridge, turn west toward Horsfall Dune and Beach. Go 1 mile and turn right on Horsfall Beach Road, reaching the campground in another 1.7 miles.
GPS coordinates: N43 27.015' / W124 15.714'
About the campground: This family campground near Bluebill Lake and seasonal ponds and lagoons has paved parking and at least partial shade afforded by the shore pines and myrtles.

Pussy willows and Indian plum grow in the wetlands. Bluebill Lake Trail offers an easy walk to and around the lake. Nearby off-highway-vehicle areas offer more boisterous pursuits.

54 Carter Lake

Location: About 8 miles south of Florence
Season: May–Sept
Sites: 23 basic sites; no hookups
Maximum length: 35 feet
Facilities: Tables, grills, flush toilets, drinking water, boat launch (0.4 mile south of campground)
Fee per night: $$$
Management: Siuslaw National Forest
Contact: (541) 271-6000; (877) 444-6777 for reservations; www.fs.usda.gov/recmain/siuslaw/recreation
Finding the campground: From the Siuslaw River bridge in Florence, drive 7.4 miles south on US 101. Turn west to reach the campground and Taylor Dunes Trailhead.
GPS coordinates: N43 51.533' / W124 08.700'
About the campground: Located next to an undisturbed dune field and mile-long Carter Lake, this campground particularly appeals to naturalists. A tall coastal forest intermingled with rhododendrons enfolds camp, but some highway noise carries across the lake. A 0.5-mile wheelchair-accessible trail travels through the dunes to Taylor Lake, while cedar posts guide hikers along a 1.5-mile route west across the open dunes to the beach. With off-highway vehicles prohibited on the dunes, hikers can discover nature's tracks and wind patterns in the sand. The mirror-black water of Carter Lake welcomes the use of small rowboats and rafts and calls to anglers.

55 Driftwood II

Location: About 8 miles south of Florence
Season: Year-round
Sites: 67 basic sites; no hookups
Maximum length: 40 feet
Facilities: Flush toilets, drinking water, showers, sand access point for off-highway vehicles (OHVs)
Fee per night: $$$
Management: Siuslaw National Forest
Contact: (541) 271-6000; (877) 444-6777 for reservations; www.fs.usda.gov/recmain/siuslaw/recreation
Finding the campground: From the Siuslaw River bridge in Florence, drive 6.8 miles south on US 101. Turn west into the Siltcoos Recreation Area to reach the campground in 1.2 miles.
GPS coordinates: N43 52.857' / W124 08.896'
About the campground: Used almost exclusively by OHV enthusiasts, this campground is more practical than scenic. It consists of a large paved parking area for vehicle camping; only a few areas among the edging shore pines are suitable for tents. Islands of shore pines also divide the

blocks of paved sites, lending modest shade and a sense of landscaping. One side of the OHV camp abuts the dunes—the primary draw for camp guests. Hiking, lake and ocean fishing, and beachcombing may also appeal to visitors.

56 Eel Creek

Location: About 10 miles south of Reedsport
Season: May–Nov
Sites: 52 basic sites; no hookups
Maximum length: 30 feet
Facilities: Tables, grills, flush toilets, drinking water
Fee per night: $$$
Management: Siuslaw National Forest
Contact: (541) 271-6000; (877) 444-6777 for reservations; www.fs.usda.gov/recmain/siuslaw/recreation
Finding the campground: The campground is west off US 101, about 10 miles south of Reedsport.
GPS coordinates: N43 35.370' / W124 11.225'
About the campground: This family campground sits in a reclaimed-dune forest and rich coastal thicket at the back of a picturesque dune field. Sites have paved parking and basic amenities; tree frogs and hummingbirds provide seasonal entertainment. Adjacent to camp and closed to motorized vehicles, Umpqua Scenic Dunes invite carefree wandering and nature study, with cedar posts to guide you across the dunes and through the deflation plain to the beach. Some dunes stretch 400 feet high. Eel Lake at William M. Tugman State Park, 1 mile to the north, offers fishing and boating (10 miles per hour maximum). To the south, Tenmile Lake offers bass fishing, speed boating, and waterskiing.

57 Half Moon Bay

Location: In Winchester Bay, about 5 miles south of Reedsport
Season: Year-round
Sites: 45 basic sites; no hookups
Maximum length: 100 feet, with many in excess of 50 feet
Facilities: Tables, grills, nonflush toilets, drinking water
Fee per night: $$$
Management: Douglas County Parks
Contact: (541) 271-5634; (541) 957-7001 for reservations (only a portion of the sites are reservable); www.co.douglas.or.us/parks
Finding the campground: From US 101 in Winchester Bay (3 miles south of Reedsport), turn west onto Salmon Harbor Drive. Continue 1.8 miles to the campground on the right.
GPS coordinates: N43 39.836' / W124 12.131'

About the campground: This popular off-highway-vehicle (OHV) camp sits adjacent to a staging area for Oregon Dunes National Recreation Area, offering a quick jump into the flying-sand fun. Its location also provides easy access to the coastal experience, be it beach lazing, surf or pier fishing, whale watching, or sightseeing. The flat camp has gravel roads and parking, with sites tucked among the coastal scrub, shore pines, spruce, and myrtle. The long sites, many of them pull-through, are ideal for OHV users. Personal shade sources make your time at camp more comfortable.

58 Horsfall

Location: About 3 miles north of North Bend/Coos Bay
Season: Year-round
Sites: 70 basic sites; no hookups
Maximum length: 50 feet
Facilities: Some tables and fire rings, flush toilets, drinking water, showers
Fee per night: $$$
Management: Siuslaw National Forest
Contact: (541) 271-6000; (877) 444-6777 for reservations; www.fs.usda.gov/recmain/siuslaw/recreation
Finding the campground: From US 101, 0.6 mile north of the Coos Bay Bridge, turn west toward Horsfall Dune and Beach. Go 1 mile and turn right onto Horsfall Beach Road, reaching the campground in another 0.5 mile.
GPS coordinates: N43 26.479' / W124 14.747'
About the campground: This campground features clusters of single paved sites rimmed by shore pines and coastal scrub and separated by meridians of natural vegetation. The camp provides a pleasant base for off-highway-vehicle enthusiasts—when they take a break from roving the dunes. There is direct dune access from camp.

59 Horsfall Beach

Location: About 5 miles north of North Bend/Coos Bay
Season: Year-round
Sites: 34 basic sites; no hookups
Maximum length: 50 feet
Facilities: Flush toilets, drinking water
Fee per night: $$$
Management: Siuslaw National Forest
Contact: (541) 271-6000; www.fs.usda.gov/recmain/siuslaw/recreation
Finding the campground: From US 101, 0.6 mile north of the Coos Bay Bridge, turn west toward Horsfall Dune and Beach. Go 1 mile and turn right on Horsfall Beach Road, reaching the campground at road's end in 2.3 miles.
GPS coordinates: N43 27.217' / W124 16.580'

About the campground: Primarily for off-highway-vehicle enthusiasts, this campground consists of a large, open paved area with numbered sites. A foredune separates the campground from the beach, but paths cross over it, allowing for wave play or surf fishing on the ocean shore. Horse trails extend south.

60 Jessie M. Honeyman Memorial State Park

Location: About 3 miles south of Florence
Season: Year-round
Sites: 168 full and partial hookup sites, 187 basic sites, 10 yurts; water, electric, and sewer hookups
Maximum length: 60 feet
Facilities: Tables, grills, flush toilets, drinking water, showers, dump station, boat launches, boat rentals, swimming beaches, playground, food concession
Fee per night: $$–$$$
Management: Oregon State Parks and Recreation Department
Contact: (541) 997-3641; (800) 452-5687 for reservations; www.oregon.gov/OPRD/PARKS/camping.shtml
Finding the campground: The campground is west off US 101, 2.5 miles south of the Siuslaw River bridge at the south end of Florence.
GPS coordinates: N43 55.441' / W124 06.685'
About the campground: This bustling campground receives some noise from the off-highway vehicles (OHVs) on the neighboring dunes, but mostly it offers a pleasant stay for active families. Sites are spacious and private. Hookup sites occupy a shore pine plain, while sites without hookups rest in the lovely tall forest of hemlocks, spruces, and towering rhododendrons. Campers have direct access to two freshwater coastal lakes: Cleawox (closer to camp) and Woahink (the larger of the two, across US 101). Nonmotorized boating only is allowed on Cleawox Lake; Woahink Lake serves larger, motorized boats. Both lakes welcome swimming. Dune play and OHV driving likewise engage campers.

61 Lagoon

Location: About 8 miles south of Florence
Season: Year-round
Sites: 38 basic sites; no hookups
Maximum length: 35 feet
Facilities: Tables, grills, flush toilets, drinking water
Fee per night: $$$
Management: Siuslaw National Forest
Contact: (541) 271-6000; www.fs.usda.gov/recmain/siuslaw/recreation
Finding the campground: From the Siuslaw River bridge in Florence, drive 6.8 miles south on US 101 and turn west into the Siltcoos Recreation Area. The campground is on the right in 0.8 mile.

Motor home in campground, Jessie M. Honeyman Memorial State Park

GPS coordinates: N43 52.804' / W124 08.524'

About the campground: Adjacent to a scenic black lagoon, this family campground occupies a semi-open coastal shore pine forest. Of the Siltcoos Recreation Area camps, this one sits farthest from the off-highway-vehicle (OHV) activity. Operation of OHVs in camp is prohibited. The natural offerings that engage guests include hiking the trails along the lagoon and the Siltcoos River or into Siltcoos Lake (the lake trailhead is across US 101 from the recreation area turnoff). Nature lovers may also seek out the section of beach near the river mouth that is off limits to OHVs.

62 Riley Ranch

Location: About 6 miles north of North Bend
Season: Year-round
Sites: 50 hookup sites, 42 basic sites, 2 cabins; water and electric hookups
Maximum length: 40 feet
Facilities: Tables, grills, flush toilets, drinking water, showers, fishing pond
Fee per night: $$–$$$
Management: Coos County
Contact: (503) 396-3121; www.co.coos.or.us/ccpark/parkslist.html
Finding the campground: From US 101, 6 miles north of the Coos Bay Bridge, turn west onto Riley Ranch Road to enter this county park campground. The turnoff is near milepost 227, west of the community of Hauser.
GPS coordinates: N43 31.100' / W124 13.246'
About the campground: This dunes area campground is still gaining its legs, but has already won a following. Off-highway-vehicle (OHV) enthusiasts base here. The camp has generous gravel pads to accommodate the sand-seeking guests. Some sites are tucked in the edge of coastal forest; others are more exposed. Butterfield Lake, adjacent to camp, is a coastal freshwater lake stocked with trout. Perch, crappie, and bass are other potential catches. In your outings away from camp, you'll find myrtlewood artists and the attractions of Coos Bay–North Bend and the Cape Arago coast. When development is complete, the park will serve both equestrian and OHV users.

63 Salmon Harbor Marina (Middle Spit Self-Contained Camping)

Location: In Winchester Bay, about 4 miles south of Reedsport
Season: Year-round
Sites: 166 RV sites, no tent sites; no hookups
Maximum length: 40 feet
Facilities: Small gazebo, some tables and barbecue stands, flush toilets, drinking water, pay showers, fee dump station, playground (at adjacent county park at far end of camp area), 2 boat launches, 850 boat slips, fish-cleaning station, boat wash, designated fishing and crabbing docks
Fee per night: $$

Management: Salmon Harbor
Contact: (541) 271-3407
Finding the campground: In Winchester Bay, 4 miles south of Reedsport, turn west off US 101 onto Salmon Harbor Drive. Continue 0.2 mile to the marina complex.
GPS coordinates: N43 40.669' / W124 10.810'
About the campground: Located 1 mile upstream from where the Umpqua River meets the ocean, this 5-acre open, paved camping area suits the nautical, the through-traveler, and those seeking a base from which to explore the coast. Gulls, seabirds, diving birds, and Canada geese share the bay location. The docks and boat moorings add atmosphere; sidewalks welcome morning and evening strolls along the marina. You may view recreational and working boats, along with a stern-wheeler. Area attractions include fishing charters, a commercial cannery, the dunes, Umpqua River Lighthouse, a vessel tour of the *Hero* at Reedsport, and Dean Creek Elk Viewing Site (east of Reedsport on OR 38).

64 Spinreel

Location: About 14 miles south of Reedsport
Season: Year-round
Sites: 36 basic sites; no hookups
Maximum length: 40 feet
Facilities: Tables, grills, flush toilets, drinking water
Fee per night: $$$
Management: Siuslaw National Forest
Contact: (541) 271-6000; www.fs.usda.gov/recmain/siuslaw/recreation
Finding the campground: From the junction of US 101 and OR 38 in Reedsport, go 13.4 miles south on US 101. Turn west onto Wildwood Drive; the campground is on the left in 0.3 mile.
GPS coordinates: N43 34.188' / W124 12.244'
About the campground: This campground provides off-highway-vehicle (OHV) access to the dunes and is located near a dune-vehicle rental for the curious who might wish to try the sport. Wide, paved sites suitable for OHVs serve campers; a backdrop of natural coastal shrubs and trees adds to the camp's ambience.

65 Tahkenitch

Location: About 12 miles south of Florence
Season: May–Sept
Sites: 34 basic sites; no hookups
Maximum length: 30 feet
Facilities: Tables, grills, flush toilets, drinking water, boat launch (on Tahkenitch Lake at Tahkenitch Landing, 0.2 mile north)
Fee per night: $$$
Management: Siuslaw National Forest

Contact: (541) 271-6000; (877) 444-6777 for reservations; www.fs.usda.gov/recmain/siuslaw/recreation

Finding the campground: From the Siuslaw River bridge in Florence, drive 12 miles south on US 101. Turn west to enter the campground.

GPS coordinates: N43 47.757' / W124 08.951'

About the campground: This coastal campground sits at the base of a forested dune. Its proximity to US 101 does mean some vehicle noise, but the traffic generally quiets by nightfall. From camp you may explore a natural dune area where off-highway vehicles are prohibited. It is ideal for enjoying a carefree romp, nature study, and photography. From camp the Tahkenitch Dunes Trail travels 2.75 miles through coastal woods, over dunes, and along the beach, passing Threemile Lake along the way. Anglers may try their luck at Threemile or Tahkenitch Lake or in the ocean surf.

66 Tahkenitch Landing

Location: About 12 miles south of Florence
Season: Year-round
Sites: 27 basic sites; no hookups
Maximum length: 30 feet
Facilities: Tables, grills, nonflush toilets, barrier-free dock, boat launch; no drinking water
Fee per night: $$
Management: Siuslaw National Forest
Contact: (541) 271-6000; (877) 444-6777 for reservations; www.fs.usda.gov/recmain/siuslaw/recreation
Finding the campground: From the Siuslaw River bridge in Florence, drive 11.8 miles south on US 101. Turn east to enter the campground.
GPS coordinates: N43 48.074' / W124 08.794'
About the campground: This attractive campground offers prized sites overlooking Tahkenitch Lake, a large coastal lake with mostly undeveloped shores. A forest frames the lake basin. At the day-use area, just below camp, you will find a rustic dock and boat ramp. The western arm of the lake is capped with lily pads. Ospreys soar over the lake and dive for fish, while geese plod along shore in search of handouts. On the west side of US 101, the Tahkenitch Dunes Trail travels 2.75 miles through woods, over dunes, and along the beach, passing Threemile Lake along the way.

67 Tenmile Lake RV Park

Location: About 12 miles northeast of North Bend
Season: Year-round
Sites: 45 hookup sites, small tent area; water and electric hookups
Maximum length: 40 feet
Facilities: Tables, grills, flush toilets, drinking water, showers, dump station; boat ramp, docks and beach at park's day-use area
Fee per night: $$–$$$

Management: Coos County

Contact: (503) 396-3121; www.co.coos.or.us/ccpark/parkslist.html

Finding the campground: From US 101, 10.5 miles south of Reedsport and 11.2 miles north of the Coos Bay Bridge, turn east onto Airport Way toward Lakeside and Tenmile Lakes Recreation Area. At the T-junction in 0.6 mile, turn right onto Eighth Street. Continue 0.3 mile, and turn left onto Park Avenue, following signs to the park. Enter the campground at road's end in 0.2 mile.

GPS coordinates: N43 34.417' / W124 10.207'

About the campground: This open camp, still in development, occupies a reclaimed spot that was largely open and paved. The camp has trimmed grass and tiny planted pines that have a long way to grow for shade, but lawn and shade trees are a short jaunt away at the park's day-use area. The big draws here are two sprawling, long-armed, shallow freshwater lakes—North and South Tenmile—which offer boating and fishing for bass, bluegill, catfish, and trout. The coast beckons with its usual lineup.

68 Tyee

Location: About 6 miles south of Florence

Season: May–Oct

Sites: 14 basic sites; no hookups

Maximum length: 22 feet

Facilities: Tables, grills, nonflush toilets, drinking water, boat launch

Fee per night: $$$

Management: Siuslaw National Forest

Contact: (541) 271-6000; (877) 444-6777 for reservations; www.fs.usda.gov/recmain/siuslaw/recreation

Finding the campground: From the Siuslaw River bridge in Florence, drive 5.5 miles south on US 101. Turn east onto Pacific Avenue, reaching the campground soon after taking the turn.

GPS coordinates: N43 52.992' / W124 07.297'

About the campground: Along the Siltcoos River sits this mostly wooded campground, although some sites nudge an open lawn that overlooks the glassy river. An attractive rockwork border can be found toward the river. Boating and fishing are the chief activities, with large, adjacent Siltcoos Lake hosting much of the fun. Vying for visitors' time are dune recreation and the area hiking trails at Siltcoos Recreation Area (to the south). The trails lead to Siltcoos Lake and along a lagoon and beach.

69 Umpqua Lighthouse State Park

Location: About 6 miles south of Reedsport

Season: Year-round

Sites: 20 hookup sites, 24 basic sites, 8 yurts, 2 cabins; water, electric, and sewer hookups

Maximum length: 45 feet

Facilities: Tables, grills, flush toilets, drinking water, showers

Fee per night: $$–$$$
Management: Oregon State Parks and Recreation Department
Contact: (541) 271-4118; (800) 452-5687 for reservations; www.oregon.gov/OPRD/PARKS/camping.shtml
Finding the campground: From the junction of US 101 and OR 38 in Reedsport, go south on US 101 for 5 miles. Turn west onto Umpqua Lighthouse Road, and continue 0.2 mile. Turn right to enter the campground in another 0.3 mile.
GPS coordinates: N43 39.581' / W124 11.578'
About the campground: This campground sits adjacent to the Umpqua River Lighthouse, built in 1894. Sites occupy a wooded slope above Lake Marie, a scenic coastal lake rimmed by forest and possessing dark, still reflections. Shrub divides, paved parking, and groomed personal spaces make the sites appealing. Trails and fishing at Lake Marie keep campers engaged at the park. Oregon Dunes, Reedsport, and Deans Creek Elk Viewing Site make worthwhile outings.

70 Waxmyrtle

Location: About 8 miles south of Florence
Season: June–Sept
Sites: 55 basic sites; no hookups
Maximum length: 35 feet
Facilities: Tables, grills, flush toilets, drinking water
Fee per night: $$$
Management: Siuslaw National Forest
Contact: (541) 271-6000; www.fs.usda.gov/recmain/siuslaw/recreation
Finding the campground: From the Siuslaw River bridge in Florence, drive 6.8 miles south on US 101. Turn west into Siltcoos Recreation Area. The campground is on the left in 0.9 mile, opposite a black lagoon.
GPS coordinates: N43 52.555' / W124 08.606'
About the campground: Along the Siltcoos River, this family campground features wooded sites in a setting of tall shore pines; privacy borders are shaped by the black huckleberries and wax myrtles. Although the driving of off-highway vehicles (OHVs) is prohibited in camp, OHV enthusiasts do have access to their "field of dreams" via a path that skirts camp. Hiking trails along the river and lagoon, a section of beach near the river mouth that is closed to OHVs, and a trail to Siltcoos Lake appeal to the foot-powered crowd.

71 Wild Mare Horse Camp

Location: About 4 miles north of North Bend/Coos Bay
Season: Year-round
Sites: 12 basic sites; no hookups
Maximum length: 50 feet
Facilities: Tables, grills, nonflush toilets, drinking water, rustic horse corrals

Fee per night: $$$
Management: Siuslaw National Forest
Contact: (541) 271-6000; (877) 444-6777 for reservations; www.fs.usda.gov/recmain/siuslaw/recreation
Finding the campground: From US 101, 0.6 mile north of the Coos Bay Bridge, turn west toward Horsfall Dune and Beach. Go 1 mile and turn right onto Horsfall Beach Road. Proceed 1.8 miles to the campground.
GPS coordinates: N43 27.100' / W124 16.153'
About the campground: Closed to off-highway vehicles, this campground exclusively serves equestrians. It accesses a network of fine horse trails through the dunes and scrub habitat and has well-spaced, substantial sites for comfort and ease of parking. Shore pines and coastal scrub surround and divide the sites. The North Bend/Coos Bay area suggests outings for services, coastal recreation, and perhaps an evening at the casino.

72 William M. Tugman State Park

Location: About 9 miles south of Reedsport
Season: Year-round
Sites: 94 hookup sites, 16 yurts; water and electric hookups
Maximum length: 50 feet
Facilities: Tables, grills, flush toilets, drinking water, showers, dump station, wheelchair-accessible fishing docks, boat launch
Fee per night: $$–$$$
Management: Oregon State Parks and Recreation Department
Contact: (541) 759-3604; (800) 452-5687 for reservations; www.oregon.gov/OPRD/PARKS/camping.shtml
Finding the campground: The campground is east off US 101, about 9 miles south of Reedsport.
GPS coordinates: N43 35.906' / W124 10.682'
About the campground: This landscaped campground and adjoining day-use area provide convenient boating and fishing access to Eel Lake, a big, scenic coastal lake. Visitors can also enjoy nearby Tenmile Lake, which allows faster boat speeds and is noted for its bass fishing. Other destinations include Umpqua Scenic Dunes—a natural dune area open for quiet exploration—and the coastal and inland attractions of the Reedsport area.

73 Winchester Bay Marina RV Resort (formerly Salmon Harbor Marina RV Resort)

Location: In Winchester Bay, about 4 miles south of Reedsport
Season: Year-round
Sites: 138 hookup sites, 25 tent sites; water, electric, sewer, and cable hookups, free wireless
Maximum length: 40 feet

Facilities: Flush toilets, drinking water, showers, dump station (at marina complex), laundry, playground, modem hookup at laundry; convenient access to 2 boat launches, 850 boat slips, fish-cleaning station, designated fishing and crabbing docks (at marina complex)
Fee per night: $$$
Management: Salmon Harbor
Contact: (541) 271-0287, reservations accepted; www.marinarvresort.com
Finding the campground: In Winchester Bay, 4 miles south of Reedsport, turn west off US 101 onto Salmon Harbor Drive. Continue 0.25 mile to reach the resort on the right.
GPS coordinates: N43 40.716' / W124 11.138'
About the campground: Upstream from where the Umpqua River meets the ocean, this attractive landscaped RV resort is surrounded on three sides by water. Lawn, shrubs, and native shore pines dress the grounds, and a mile-long paved pedestrian/bicycle trail encircles the resort. Campers enjoy a wide range of amenities and have convenient access to the marina and to the attractions of Reedsport and Winchester Bay.

74 Windy Cove

Location: In Winchester Bay, about 4 miles south of Reedsport
Season: Year-round
Sites: 64 hookup sites, 33 basic sites; water, electric, sewer, and cable hookups
Maximum length: 30 feet
Facilities: Tables, flush toilets, drinking water, showers, wireless (available), boat docks and launch (across road from park at Salmon Harbor Marina)
Fee per night: $$-$$$
Management: Douglas County
Contact: (541) 957-7001, reservations accepted; www.co.douglas.or.us/parks
Finding the campground: In Winchester Bay, 4 miles south of Reedsport, turn west off US 101 onto Salmon Harbor Drive. Continue 0.2 mile; the park is on the left, opposite Salmon Harbor Marina.
GPS coordinates: N43 40.519' / W124 10.961'
About the campground: At the foot of a forested hill, this 10-acre park encompasses a pair of landscaped camp areas. From camp, guests can easily access Salmon Harbor's fishing, boating, and sightseeing; explore Oregon Dunes National Recreation Area via foot or dune vehicle; visit Umpqua River Lighthouse; tour the *Hero* at Reedsport; or put a spotting scope on a bull elk at Dean Creek Elk Viewing Site (east of Reedsport along OR 38).

North Bend–Coos Bay Area

	Hookup Sites	Total Sites	Max. RV Length	Hookups	Toilets	Showers	Drinking Water	Dump Station	Recreation	Fee	Can Reserve
75 Bastendorff Beach County Park	74	99	50	WE	F	X	X	X	HSF	$$–$$$	
76 Charleston Marina RV Park	100	100	35	WESC	F	X	X	X	FBL	$$–$$$	X
77 Nesika County Park		20	Small		NF				F	$$	
78 Rooke-Higgins County Park		26	Small		NF				FBL	$$	
79 Sunset Bay State Park	63	129	45	WES	F	X	X		HSF	$$–$$$	X

75 Bastendorff Beach County Park

Location: Outside Charleston, about 10 miles west of North Bend/Coos Bay
Season: Year-round
Sites: 74 hookup sites, 25 basic sites, 2 cabins; water and electric hookups
Maximum length: 50 feet
Facilities: Tables, grills, flush toilets, drinking water, showers, dump station, playground, horseshoe pits, basketball court, fish-cleaning sink
Fee per night: $$–$$$
Management: Coos County
Contact: (541) 888-5353; www.co.coos.or.us/ccpark/parkslist.html
Finding the campground: From Charleston, 8 miles west of North Bend/Coos Bay, drive 1.6 miles west on Cape Arago Highway. Turn right at the sign for the county park; proceed about 0.2 mile more to reach the campground.
GPS coordinates: N43 20.481' / W124 20.847'
About the campground: This quiet county park encompasses 91 acres, with a long sandy beach and rich coastal woods. Natural thickets shape privacy borders between campsites. Despite the paved parking, some campsites are more level than others. The Cape Arago coast is famous for its cliffs, coves, and offshore rocks topped by seals and barking sea lions. South Slough National Estuarine Reserve, with its visitor center and hiking and canoe trails, offers an alternative outing.

76 Charleston Marina RV Park

Location: In Charleston, about 8 miles west of North Bend/Coos Bay
Season: Year-round
Sites: 100 hookup sites, tent area, 2 yurts; water, electric, sewer, and cable hookups

Maximum length: 35 feet

Facilities: Tables, flush toilets, drinking water, showers, dump station, laundry, playground, boat launch, crab-cooking area

Fee per night: $$-$$$

Management: Port of Coos Bay

Contact: (541) 888-9512, reservations accepted; www.charlestonmarina.com

Finding the campground: From Cape Arago Highway in Charleston, take Boat Basin Drive north for 0.2 mile. Turn right onto Kingfisher Drive to reach the marina RV park.

GPS coordinates: N43 20.657' / W124 19.527'

About the campground: This port campground consists of numbered, paved sites paired with gravel meridians and tables and a separate, grassy tent area. Raucous gulls contribute to the seaside ambience. Campers enjoy direct access to the bay and marina, where they can go boating, book a sportfishing charter, or try crabbing. Restaurants lie within walking distance, and the Cape Arago coast lays out a scenic drive.

77 Nesika County Park

Location: About 18 miles northeast of North Bend/Coos Bay

Season: Apr–Sept

Sites: 20 basic sites; no hookups

Maximum length: Best suited for smaller units

Facilities: Tables, fire rings, nonflush toilets; no drinking water

Fee per night: $$

Management: Coos County

Contact: (541) 396-3121

Finding the campground: From the Coos River Junction at the south end of Coos Bay, turn east off US 101 onto Sixth Avenue, following the signs for Allegany. Zigzag through the outskirts of town, and soon come out on Coos River Road. Remain on it all the way to Allegany (13.5 miles from US 101). From there follow the signs for Golden and Silver Falls State Park, continuing 4.2 miles east on East Fork Millicoma Road. The campground is on the right, 0.2 mile past the county park's day-use area. The route is winding and narrow.

GPS coordinates: N43 26.464' / W123 59.573'

About the campground: This attractive, rustic, linear campground occupies a low terrace along the East Fork Millicoma River and offers relatively spacious, private sites nestled in a forest of Douglas firs and myrtles. Thimbleberry and salmonberry abound in the understory. Most sites have gravel parking; a few are grassy. A stairway descends to the shallow Millicoma River, which courses over bedrock and is punctuated by low cascades. A 0.2-mile foot trail links the camp and day-use areas. Golden and Silver Falls State Park is located 6 miles east of here off Glenn Creek Road. Its short trails offer perspectives on a pair of 200-foot waterfalls.

78 Rooke-Higgins County Park

Location: About 9 miles east of Coos Bay
Season: Year-round
Sites: 26 basic sites; no hookups
Maximum length: Best suited for smaller units
Facilities: Tables, fire rings, nonflush toilets; no drinking water
Fee per night: $$
Management: Coos County
Contact: (541) 396-3121
Finding the campground: From the Coos River Junction at the south end of Coos Bay, turn east off US 101 onto Sixth Avenue, following the signs for Allegany. Zigzag through the outskirts of town, and soon come out on Coos River Road. Remain on it all the way to the park campground, 9.3 miles from US 101.
GPS coordinates: N43 24.264' / W124 03.827'
About the campground: Across the road from the tidewater-influenced Millicoma River, this campground spreads across a wooded flat at the foot of a forested slope. It offers a quiet, rustic camping experience. Fishing and drift boating or canoeing the sleepy Millicoma are common diversions. If you continue driving upstream past Allegany, you can visit Golden and Silver Falls State Park, with its pair of cool, shady waterfall glens.

79 Sunset Bay State Park

Location: About 12 miles southwest of North Bend/Coos Bay
Season: Year-round
Sites: 63 full and partial hookup sites, 66 basic sites, 8 yurts; water, electric, and sewer hookups
Maximum length: 45 feet
Facilities: Tables, grills, flush toilets, drinking water, showers, playground
Fee per night: $$–$$$
Management: Oregon State Parks and Recreation Department
Contact: (541) 888-4902; (800) 452-5687 for reservations; www.oregon.gov/OPRD/PARKS/camping.shtml
Finding the campground: From US 101 in North Bend/Coos Bay, go 12 miles southwest on Cape Arago Highway, following the signs to Charleston and the state park. The campground is on the left.
GPS coordinates: N43 19.862' / W124 22.224'
About the campground: This campground sits across the road from Sunset Bay, a scenic, quiet ocean cove that reflects the setting sun. The landscaped sites are closely spaced. Surf fishing and swimming are popular, and a segment of the Oregon Coast Trail follows the shoreline through the park, visiting eroded cliffs, the sculptured gardens at Shore Acres, and an overlook of an offshore reef where sea lions—and in recent years elephant seals—haul out. Shore Acres State Park and Simpson Reef Viewpoint may also be accessed via the Cape Arago Highway. Other possibilities for outings are South Slough National Estuarine Reserve and the Mill Casino.

Bandon-Port Orford Area

	Hookup Sites	Total Sites	Max. RV Length	Hookups	Toilets	Showers	Drinking Water	Dump Station	Recreation	Fee	Can Reserve
80 Boice-Cope County Park		34	40		F	X	X	X	HFBL	$$	
81 Bullards Beach State Park	185	193	60	WES	F	X	X	X	HSFBLR	$$$	X
82 Butler Bar		7	T		NF	X			F	None	
83 Cape Blanco State Park	53	61	65	WE	F	X	X	X	HSFR	$$-$$$	X
84 Edson Creek Recreation Site		27	40		NF	X			F	$	
85 Humbug Mountain State Park	32	94	55	WE	F	X	X	X	HSFC	$$-$$$	
86 Sixes River Recreation Site		19	Small		NF	X			F	$	

80 Boice-Cope County Park

Location: About 17 miles south of Bandon
Season: Year-round
Sites: 23 RV sites, 11 tent sites; no hookups
Maximum length: 40 feet
Facilities: Tables, grills, flush toilets, drinking water, showers, dump station, boat launch
Fee per night: $$
Management: Curry County
Contact: (541) 247-3306
Finding the campground: From downtown Bandon go 14.2 miles south on US 101. Turn west onto Floras Lake Loop Road, and proceed 1.1 miles. Turn right onto Curry CR 136, following the signs for a boat ramp. In another 1.3 miles bear left. Go 0.1 mile and turn right onto Boice-Cope Road. The campground is 0.3 mile ahead on the left; the boat ramp is just beyond the camp at road's end.
GPS coordinates: N42 54.115' / W124 30.133'
About the campground: Rimmed by Sitka spruces and shore pines, this crisp, clean campground occupies a groomed lawn above Floras Lake. The dunes and seashore are but a short walk beyond the picturesque lake, which attracts sailboarders, anglers, and migrating birds. A footbridge at the outlet leads to the dunes and the long, wild beach. Hikers must heed the protective closures for the snowy plover. Information about when and which areas are closed is posted at the bridge.

81 Bullards Beach State Park

Location: 2 miles north of Bandon
Season: Year-round
Sites: 185 full and partial hookup sites, 8 horse sites, 13 yurts; water, electric, and sewer hookups
Maximum length: 60 feet
Facilities: Tables, grills, flush toilets, drinking water, showers, dump station, playground, boat ramp, corrals at horse camp
Fee per night: $$$
Management: Oregon State Parks and Recreation Department
Contact: (541) 347-3501; (800) 452-5687 for reservations; www.oregon.gov/OPRD/PARKS/camping.shtml
Finding the campground: The campground is west off US 101, 2 miles north of Bandon.
GPS coordinates: N43 09.159' / W124 23.909'
About the campground: This large coastal campground with paved sites sits at the Coquille River mouth, in a protected area of shore pines and coastal thicket behind a beach foredune. Campers

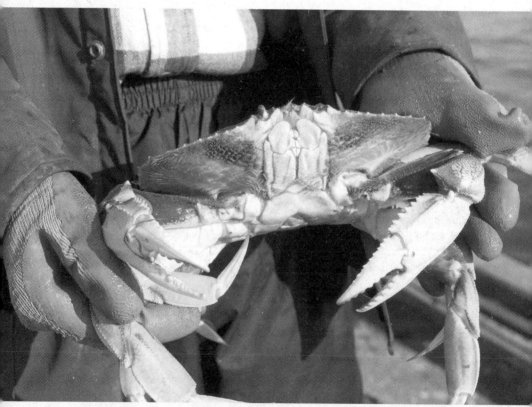

Dungeness crab caught off pier, Weber's Pier, Bandon

have access to hiking and horse trails, a long stretch of wild beach, jetty fishing, and the photogenic Coquille River Lighthouse, built in 1896. The adjoining Bandon Marsh Wildlife Refuge brings a bounty of birds to your doorstep. The shops and waterfront of Old Town Bandon invite investigation.

82 Butler Bar

Location: About 22 miles east of Port Orford
Season: Year-round
Sites: 7 basic sites; no hookups
Maximum length: Best suited for tents
Facilities: Tables and fire rings, nonflush toilet, drinking water (in summer)
Fee per night: None
Management: Siskiyou National Forest
Contact: (541) 439-6200; www.fs.usda.gov/recmain/rogue-siskiyou/recreation
Finding the campground: From US 101, about 3 miles north of Port Orford, turn east onto Elk River Road, which later becomes FR 5325. Follow the river upstream for 19 miles. Turn left onto FR 5201 and proceed 0.1 mile to the campground.
GPS coordinates: N42 43.540' / W124 16.274'
About the campground: This scenic, rustic campground sits on a forested bench above the Elk Wild and Scenic River. Grassy Knob Wilderness is its neighbor across the river. The Elk River is an enchantress, flowing blue-green. Because gorge walls often contain the river, the campground's easy river access is all the more prized.

83 Cape Blanco State Park

Location: About 9 miles north of Port Orford
Season: Year-round
Sites: 53 hookup sites, 8 horse sites, 4 cabins; water and electric hookups
Maximum length: 65 feet
Facilities: Tables, grills, flush toilets, drinking water, showers, dump station, corrals at horse camp
Fee per night: $$-$$$
Management: Oregon State Parks and Recreation Department
Contact: (541) 332-6774; (800) 452-5687 for reservations; www.oregon.gov/OPRD/PARKS/camping.shtml
Finding the campground: From Port Orford, go 4 miles north on US 101. Turn west onto Cape Blanco Road and follow it 5 miles to the park.
GPS coordinates: N42 49.974' / W124 33.098'
About the campground: Inland from the bluff, in a protective stand of trees, you will find this comfortable family campground. The horse camp occupies coastal grassland below. At this exciting, wild strip of Oregon coast, you can photograph the 1870 Cape Blanco Lighthouse, which braves wind and storm from atop the bluff, or tour the 1898 Hughes House, which sits above the

floodplain of the Sixes River. Beachcombers scour the black sands and gravels for prized, naturally polished agates, many of them golden in hue. Anglers fish for salmon on the Sixes River, and the Elk River is just a short drive away. The Oregon Coast Trail and the wild beach invite hiking. Equestrians enjoy 7 miles of horse trail and 150 acres of open riding range.

84 Edson Creek Recreation Site

Location: About 9 miles northeast of Port Orford
Season: Late May–Sept
Sites: 27 basic sites; no hookups
Maximum length: 40 feet
Facilities: Tables, grills, nonflush toilets, drinking water
Fee per night: $
Management: Bureau of Land Management—Coos Bay District
Contact: (541) 756-0100; www.blm.gov/or/
Finding the campground: From US 101, 5 miles north of Port Orford, turn east onto Sixes River Road. Continue 4.1 miles to reach campground on the left.
GPS coordinates: N42 48.915' / W124 24.626'
About the campground: This campground claims a grassy bench with myrtles and alders along Edson Creek, just above its confluence with the Sixes River. Campers can choose between sunny or shady locations. River fishing and coastal attractions are within convenient reach.

85 Humbug Mountain State Park

Location: 6 miles south of Port Orford
Season: Year-round
Sites: 32 hookup sites, 62 basic sites; water and electric hookups
Maximum length: 55 feet
Facilities: Tables, grills, flush toilets, drinking water, showers, dump station
Fee per night: $$–$$$
Management: Oregon State Parks and Recreation Department
Contact: (541) 332-6774; www.oregon.gov/OPRD/PARKS/camping.shtml
Finding the campground: The campground is east off US 101 (near milepost 307), 6 miles south of Port Orford.
GPS coordinates: N42 41.279' / W124 26.465'
About the campground: This campground occupies a scenic lawn and shore pine flat in the shadow of Humbug Mountain. Brush Creek serenades campers. Underpasses allow campers to safely access both the beach and the 3-mile trail to the top of the mountain. At the foot of the camp's eastern ridge, an abandoned section of Old Highway 101 welcomes exercise walks and jogs. You can also search for agates on shore, fish the nearby Elk and Sixes Rivers, or visit the harbor at Port Orford.

86 Sixes River Recreation Site

Location: About 16 miles northeast of Port Orford
Season: Late May–Sept
Sites: 19 basic sites; no hookups
Maximum length: Small units only
Facilities: Tables, grills, nonflush toilets, drinking water
Fee per night: $
Management: Bureau of Land Management–Coos Bay District
Contact: (541) 756-0100; www.blm.gov/or/
Finding the campground: From US 101, 5 miles north of Port Orford, turn east onto Sixes River Road and go 10.7 miles to reach this campground. The road narrows, becoming dirt for the final 0.5 mile. Be careful on the descent into camp.
GPS coordinates: N42 48.244' / W124 18.510'
About the campground: This restful, terraced campground occupies a slope above the beautiful Sixes River. Myrtles, alders, and maples frame and shade the sites, with a few fir trees lending punctuation. Fishing engages campers.

Coquille–Myrtle Point Area

	Hookup Sites	Total Sites	Max. RV Length	Hookups	Toilets	Showers	Drinking Water	Dump Station	Recreation	Fee	Can Reserve
87 Laverne County Park	46	76	40	WE	F, NF	X	X	X	SF	$$	
88 Park Creek Recreation Site		15	Small		NF					None	
89 Sturdivant City Park		9	25		F, NF		X		FBL	$$	

87 Laverne County Park

Location: About 14 miles northeast of Coquille
Season: Year-round
Sites: 46 hookup sites, 30 basic sites, 1 cabin; water and electric hookups
Maximum length: 40 feet
Facilities: Tables, grills, flush and nonflush toilets, drinking water, showers, dump station, playground
Fee per night: $$
Management: Coos County
Contact: (541) 396-2344; www.co.coos.or.us/ccpark/parkslist.html
Finding the campground: From OR 42 (Main Street) in Coquille, turn north onto North Central Boulevard and go 0.7 mile. Turn right and continue 13 miles on Coquille-Fairview Road to reach the camp on the right.
GPS coordinates: N43 15.478' / W124 01.683'
About the campground: This family campground occupies a 350-acre wooded flat above the North Fork Coquille River. Tall Douglas firs, myrtles, and mossy stumps contribute to the coolness and relaxation of camp; the remoteness helps ensure quiet. Fishing and swimming are popular pursuits.

88 Park Creek Recreation Site

Location: About 23 miles northeast of Coquille
Season: Late May–Sept
Sites: 15 basic sites; no hookups
Maximum length: Small units only
Facilities: Tables, grills/barbecues, nonflush toilets; no drinking water
Fee per night: None
Management: Bureau of Land Management—Coos Bay District
Contact: (541) 756-0100; www.blm.gov/or/
Finding the campground: From Coquille take Coquille-Fairview Road northeast 9 miles to Fairview. Turn south onto Fairview–Middle Creek Road, heading toward Dora. Go 3.8 miles and turn left onto Middle Creek Road, now proceeding toward Burnt Mountain Access Road and Park Creek. Continue 7.8 miles, bearing right at the fork to remain on Middle Creek Road. Go 2.4 miles more, turn right, and follow the paved single-lane entry road 0.2 mile into camp.
GPS coordinates: N43 14.751' / W123 53.783'
About the campground: The reward for the long, out-of-the-way drive is an attractive, remote forest campground. Cloaked in scenic, big, mossy maples and myrtles, the campground sits at the confluence of Park and Middle Creeks. If you do not require a lot of diversions to be content, this is the camp for you. Bring a soft pillow and a good book.

89 Sturdivant City Park

Location: In Coquille
Season: Year-round
Sites: 9 basic sites; no hookups
Maximum length: 25 feet
Facilities: Tables, fire rings, flush and nonflush toilets, drinking water, playground, ball field, horseshoe pits, boat launch and dock
Fee per night: $$
Management: City of Coquille
Contact: (541) 396-5131
Finding the campground: In Coquille turn south off OR 42 onto OR 42S, the Coquille-Bandon Highway. Cross the railroad tracks to enter the park on the right in 0.1 mile.
GPS coordinates: N43 10.517' / W124 11.970'
About the campground: Campsites dot a grassy bench at one edge of this recreational park on the Coquille River. Besides tables and fire rings, a few young planted trees contribute to sites. The river flows broad and slow. In Coquille you might want to check out the old-fashioned melodrama playing at the Sawdust Theater on summer Saturday nights.

Powers Area

	Hookup Sites	Total Sites	Max. RV Length	Hookups	Toilets	Showers	Drinking Water	Dump Station	Recreation	Fee	Can Reserve
90 Daphne Grove		14	35		NF				S	$	
91 Eden Valley		11	30		NF				C	None	
92 Island		5	T		NF					$	
93 Myrtle Grove		5	T		NF				S	None	
94 Powers County Park	40	70	40	WE	F	X	X	X	F	$$	
95 Rock Creek		7	Small		NF				HF	$	
96 Sru Lake (formerly Squaw Lake)		6	Small		NF				F	None	

90   Daphne Grove

Location: 14 miles south of Powers
Season: Year-round
Sites: 14 basic sites; no hookups
Maximum length: 35 feet
Facilities: Tables, fire rings, nonflush toilets, covered day-use shelter; no drinking water
Fee per night: $ (Memorial Day–Oct)
Management: Siskiyou National Forest
Contact: (541) 439-6200; www.fs.usda.gov/recmain/rogue-siskiyou/recreation
Finding the campground: From Powers go south toward Agness on Powers Road South/FR 33. The campground is on the right in 14 miles.
GPS coordinates: N42 44.135' / W124 03.319'
About the campground: This campground occupies a semi-open flat above the South Fork Coquille River. Live oak, maple, myrtle, tan oak, and conifer trees shape the setting. The campground has paved roads and parking. Although this stretch of the South Fork is closed to angling, the river still supplies a soothing hush and a place to cool your ankles.

91   Eden Valley

Location: About 30 miles southeast of Powers
Season: Year-round
Sites: 11 basic sites; no hookups
Maximum length: 30 feet

Facilities: Tables, grills, nonflush toilets; no drinking water
Fee per night: None
Management: Siskiyou National Forest
Contact: (541) 439-6200; www.fs.usda.gov/recmain/rogue-siskiyou/recreation
Finding the campground: From Powers go south toward Agness on Powers Road South/FR 33 for 16.1 miles. Turn left (east) onto FR 3348 and continue 13.6 miles to the campground, which is on the right off FR 280.
GPS coordinates: N42 48.508' / W123 53.407'
About the campground: East of Foggy Creek, this recreation area spans both sides of FR 3348. The camp has gravel roads and parking. The scenic, full Douglas fir forest contributes to a relaxing stay. If you are looking for some exercise, this campground sits along the Glendale to Powers Bicycle Recreation Area route.

92 Island

Location: About 16 miles south of Powers
Season: Year-round
Sites: 5 basic sites; no hookups
Maximum length: Suitable for tents only
Facilities: Tables, fire rings or grills, nonflush toilets; no drinking water
Fee per night: $ (Memorial Day–Oct)
Management: Siskiyou National Forest
Contact: (541) 439-6200; www.fs.usda.gov/recmain/rogue-siskiyou/recreation
Finding the campground: From Powers go south toward Agness on Powers Road South/FR 33 for 15.3 miles. Turn right onto FR 3300.490 to enter the campground.
GPS coordinates: N42 43.326' / W124 02.546'
About the campground: This small, developed campground offers a pleasant stay along the South Fork Coquille River. The camp has gravel roads and parking and an attractive woods setting. Rhododendrons complement the bountiful understory. Sites are partially shaded most of the day. Check regulations before fishing.

93 Myrtle Grove

Location: About 8 miles south of Powers
Season: Year-round
Sites: 5 tent sites; no hookups
Maximum length: Suitable for tents only
Facilities: Tables, fire rings, nonflush toilets; no drinking water
Fee per night: None
Management: Siskiyou National Forest
Contact: (541) 439-6200; www.fs.usda.gov/recmain/rogue-siskiyou/recreation

Finding the campground: From Powers head south on Powers Road South/FR 33 toward Agness. Go 8.4 miles to the campground on the right.

GPS coordinates: N42 47.135' / W124 01.471'

About the campground: Myrtles, maples, and a few firs shade this small, attractive campground along the South Fork Coquille River. Big boulders add to the character of the river. With the river closed to fishing, swimming and relaxing are the favored pastimes. Elk Creek Falls (the trailhead is 3 miles north of camp on FR 33) is worth the hike.

94 Powers County Park

Location: At the north end of Powers, about 19 miles southeast of Myrtle Point

Season: Year-round

Sites: 40 hookup sites, 30 tent sites, 1 cabin; water and electric hookups

Maximum length: 40 feet

Facilities: Tables, grills, flush toilets, drinking water, showers, dump station, playground, fish-cleaning station, horseshoe pits, sports courts and fields

Fee per night: $$

Management: Coos County

Contact: (541) 439-2791; www.co.coos.or.us/ccpark/parkslist.html

Finding the campground: From the Powers Junction on OR 42, 2.5 miles east of Myrtle Point, go 16.7 miles south to reach this park on the northern outskirts of Powers.

GPS coordinates: N42 53.574' / W124 04.777'

About the campground: Restful, spotlessly clean, and landscaped in native vegetation, this campground serves family campers well. Wake up to birdsong, and study the stars at night. A 30-acre pond at the park is stocked with trout and occasionally with surplus steelhead. There is ample room to roam, or you can just settle back and relax at your site.

95 Rock Creek

Location: About 18 miles south of Powers

Season: Year-round

Sites: 7 basic sites; no hookups

Maximum length: Best for small units

Facilities: Tables, grills, nonflush toilets; no drinking water

Fee per night: $ (Memorial Day–Oct)

Management: Siskiyou National Forest

Contact: (541) 439-6200; www.fs.usda.gov/recmain/rogue-siskiyou/recreation

Finding the campground: From Powers go 16.5 miles south on Powers Road South/FR 33. Turn southwest onto FR 3347 and continue 1 mile to the camp.

GPS coordinates: N42 42.461' / W124 03.598'

About the campground: This small campground along Rock Creek engages with its stand of old-growth firs intermingled with myrtles and tan oaks. Rock Creek rushes clear over rounded stones, collecting in a few deeper pools. Upstream from camp is the trailhead for the 1.2-mile trail to Azalea Lake. This 2-acre lake is stocked with trout and decorated in July by azalea blooms. Backtracking north on FR 33 to its junction with FR 3348 and then following FR 3348 east for 1.6 miles, will take you to the Coquille River Falls trailhead. The exciting falls is reached via a short, steep trail.

96   Sru Lake (formerly Squaw Lake)

Location: About 21 miles southeast of Powers
Season: Year-round
Sites: 6 basic sites; no hookups
Maximum length: Small units only
Facilities: Tables, grills, nonflush toilets; no drinking water
Fee per night: None
Management: Siskiyou National Forest
Contact: (541) 439-6200; www.fs.usda.gov/recmain/rogue-siskiyou/recreation
Finding the campground: From Powers go south on Powers Road South/FR 33 toward Agness. In 16.1 miles turn left (east) onto FR 3348; proceed 4 miles to FR 080. Turn right and continue 0.8 mile; the campground is on the left.
GPS coordinates: N42 43.839' / W124 00.371'
About the campground: The well-spaced campsites occupy the basin of Sru Lake, which is fringed by a remnant stand of old-growth trees. Alders and willows edge the lakeshore. Campers can choose between full or partial shade. But without developed parking pads, the sites are better suited for tent camping. You can try your luck at reeling in a lake trout for the evening meal, but be sure to check the regulations first.

Gold Beach–Agness Area

	Hookup Sites	Total Sites	Max. RV Length	Hookups	Toilets	Showers	Drinking Water	Dump Station	Recreation	Fee	Can Reserve
97 Foster Bar		8	26		F		X		HFBL	$$	
98 Huntley Park		70	40	F, NF	X	X			F	$$	
99 Lobster Creek		6	20		F		X		FBL	$$	
100 Quosatana		43	30		F		X	X	SFBL	$$	

97 Foster Bar

Location: About 34 miles northeast of Gold Beach
Season: Year-round; maintained May–Nov
Sites: 4 basic sites, 4 walk-in tent sites; no hookups
Maximum length: 26 feet
Facilities: Tables, grills, flush toilets, drinking water, boat ramp
Fee per night: $$
Management: Siskiyou National Forest
Contact: (541) 247-3600; www.fs.usda.gov/recmain/rogue-siskiyou/recreation
Finding the campground: From US 101 in Gold Beach, at the south end of the Patterson (Rogue River) Bridge, turn east onto Jerry's Flat Road/CR 595, which becomes FR 33 upon entering Siskiyou National Forest. Drive 30.5 miles and turn right (upstream) onto CR 375 toward Illahe and Foster Bar. Reach the camp and boat launch/takeout on the right in 3.5 miles.
GPS coordinates: N42 38.088' / W124 03.121'
About the campground: This casual, broad camp above the Rogue Wild and Scenic River serves river recreationists and escapists. An on-site host is on duty seasonally. Sites are dispersed across the dry meadow or at its treed edge. Floating and fishing the river and hiking the Rogue River Trail are popular pursuits. Agness—population "small"—welcomes with its general store and Agness-Illahe Museum (open seasonally).

Rogue Wild & Scenic River, Rogue-Coquille National Scenic Byway, Siskiyou National Forest

98 Huntley Park

Location: About 7 miles east of Gold Beach
Season: Year-round
Sites: 70 basic sites; no hookups
Maximum length: 40 feet
Facilities: Tables, fire rings, flush and nonflush toilets, drinking water, showers, horseshoe pits
Fee per night: $$
Management: Port of Gold Beach
Contact: (541) 247-9377
Finding the campground: From US 101 in Gold Beach, at the south end of the Patterson (Rogue River) Bridge, head east onto Jerry's Flat Road/CR 595. Go 6.9 miles; the campground is on the left.
GPS coordinates: N42 28.783' / W124 19.648'
About the campground: This Rogue River campground and adjoining picnic area enjoy a rich setting of myrtles and firs. Access to the Rogue is via the big gravel river bar. Sites closest to the water are more open. Quail coveys are common in camp, and deer are no strangers. Rogue River recreation, including salmon fishing and taking a jet boat tour, and sightseeing in the Gold Beach area will keep you entertained.

99 Lobster Creek

Location: About 9 miles northeast of Gold Beach
Season: Year-round
Sites: 3 basic sites, 3 tent sites, open camping on the gravel river bar; no hookups
Maximum length: 20 feet (for basic sites)
Facilities: Tables, grills, flush toilets, drinking water, boat launch; no facilities for gravel bar camping
Fee per night: $$ for sites; $ for open camping on gravel bar
Management: Siskiyou National Forest
Contact: (541) 247-3600; www.fs.usda.gov/recmain/rogue-siskiyou/recreation
Finding the campground: At the south end of the Patterson (Rogue River) Bridge in Gold Beach, turn east off US 101 onto Jerry's Flat Road, which becomes FR 33. Travel 9.3 miles to the campground on the left.
GPS coordinates: N42 30.127' / W124 17.754'
About the campground: Tucked away in a lush myrtle woodland is this small campground primarily for tent campers. A few sites are suitable for RVs, but most RVers choose to set up along the gravel bar for direct access to the lower Rogue River. Fishing and boating are key draws, but there are trails in the area to explore as well.

100 Quosatana

Location: About 14 miles northeast of Gold Beach
Season: Year-round
Sites: 43 basic sites; no hookups
Maximum length: 30 feet
Facilities: Tables, grills, flush toilets, drinking water, dump station, boat launch
Fee per night: $$
Management: Siskiyou National Forest
Contact: (541) 247-3600; www.fs.usda.gov/recmain/rogue-siskiyou/recreation
Finding the campground: At the south end of the Patterson (Rogue River) Bridge in Gold Beach, turn east off US 101 onto Jerry's Flat Road, which becomes FR 33. Travel 13.9 miles to the campground.
GPS coordinates: N42 29.863' / W124 13.954'
About the campground: This beautiful, sprawling campground claims a prized flat on the lower Rogue River. Campers can select from sites at the meadow's edge or within the tranquil myrtle grove. Seasonally the mature myrtles scent the air with their eucalyptus-like aroma. Photographers are attracted by the mossy multiple trunks. River access for fishing, boating, and swimming and an open, mowed field for sports engage guests, as does the camp's quiet. Deer and wild turkeys are campground interlopers.

Brookings Area

	Hookup Sites	Total Sites	Max. RV Length	Hookups	Toilets	Showers	Drinking Water	Dump Station	Recreation	Fee	Can Reserve
101 Alfred A. Loeb State Park	48	48	50	WE	F	X	X		HSFBL	$$-$$$	
102 Beachfront RV Park	93	123	40	WESC	F	X	X	X	FBL	$$-$$$	X
103 Harris Beach State Park	86	149	50	WESC	F	X	X	X	HSF	$$-$$$	X
104 Ludlum		7	20		F		X		SF	$$	
105 Winchuck		15	40		NF		X		HSF	None	

101 Alfred A. Loeb State Park

Location: Northeast of Brookings
Season: Year-round
Sites: 48 hookup sites, 3 cabins; water and electric hookups
Maximum length: 50 feet
Facilities: Tables, grills, flush toilets, drinking water, showers, boat ramp
Fee per night: $$-$$$
Management: Oregon State Parks and Recreation Department
Contact: (541) 469-2021; www.oregon.gov/OPRD/PARKS/camping.shtml
Finding the campground: From the junction of US 101 and North Bank Chetco River Road in Brookings, travel 8 miles northeast on North Bank Chetco River Road; the park is on the right.
GPS coordinates: N42 06.701' / W124 11.258'
About the campground: Situated along the north bank of the pristine Chetco River, this quiet campground occupies a scenic grove of old-growth myrtles intermixed with evergreens. The park's Riverside Trail journeys upstream along the steep riverbank to link up with the forest service's Redwood Nature Trail, which traverses the nation's northernmost redwood grove. A crosswalk links the two trails for a 2.5-mile round-trip hike. The big attraction though is fishing the Chetco River. And for sheer relaxation, how can you miss with such an inviting camp setting?

102 Beachfront RV Park

Location: In Brookings
Season: Year-round
Sites: 84 full hookup sites, 9 partial hookup sites, 17 basic sites, 13 tent sites; water, electric, sewer, and cable hookups; wireless access

Maximum length: 40 feet

Facilities: Tables, barbecues in tent area, flush toilets, drinking water, showers, laundry, dump station, restaurant, public boat launch, public pier for crabbing and fishing

Fee per night: $$–$$$

Management: Port of Brookings

Contact: (541) 469-5867; (800) 441-0856 for reservations; www.port-brookings-harbor.org or www.beachfrontrvpark.com

Finding the campground: From US 101 in Brookings, turn west onto Lower Harbor Road. Go 0.1 mile, bearing left at the junction. Proceed 0.8 mile and turn right onto Boat Basin Road to reach the park in another 0.1 mile.

GPS coordinates: N42 02.625' / W124 16.018'

About the campground: This RV park offers camping on an open, shadeless gravel flat overlooking the ocean. To the back of the campground is the harbor. The park is clean, orderly, and convenient. Ocean views, the sound of the surf, and the briny breeze together set the stage for your stay. Only at the tent area will you find a lawn and a few low shore pines. Beachcombing and jetty fishing for perch and fall salmon are among the popular pastimes. Along the harbor you will find fresh-fish sellers, seafood eateries, and fishing charters.

103 Harris Beach State Park

Location: In Brookings

Season: Year-round

Sites: 86 full and partial hookup sites, 63 basic sites, 6 yurts; water, electric, sewer, and cable hookups

Maximum length: 50 feet

Facilities: Tables, grills, flush toilets, drinking water, showers, dump station, playground

Fee per night: $$–$$$

Management: Oregon State Parks and Recreation Department

Contact: (541) 469-2021; (800) 452-5687 for reservations; www.oregon.gov/OPRD/PARKS/camping.shtml

Finding the campground: The campground is west off US 101, at the north end of Brookings.

GPS coordinates: N42 04.121' / W124 18.545'

About the campground: Occupying a prized coastal location, this developed campground sits back from the ocean in dense vegetation. A wildlife refuge on Goat Island, weathered cliffs, sea stacks, and a sandy beach are among its attractions. The Viewpoint Trail leads from camp to an overlook of a natural bridge. Sea- and shorebirds can animate the scene. To the north, Samuel H. Boardman State Park offers hiking, picnicking, quiet beaches, and ocean vistas. Fishing the Chetco River or visiting the shops and eateries of Brookings can help fill out an itinerary.

104 Ludlum

Location: About 14 miles southeast of Brookings
Season: Mid-May–Sept
Sites: 7 basic sites; no hookups
Maximum length: 20 feet
Facilities: Tables, grills, flush toilets, drinking water, Ludlum House (available for overnight rental; reservation required)
Fee per night: $$ (more for house rental)
Management: Siskiyou National Forest
Contact: (541) 412-6000; www.fs.usda.gov/recmain/rogue-siskiyou/recreation
Finding the campground: From the Chetco River bridge in Brookings, travel south on US 101 for 4.1 miles. Turn east onto Winchuck River Road (CR 896), which becomes FR 1107, and go 8 miles. Turn left onto FR 1108, following for 2 miles to Ludlum Recreation Area. Turn right to enter the campground; the rental house is reached by following the campground road.
GPS coordinates: N42 02.132' / W124 06.535'
About the campground: This quiet, remote forest campground adjacent to Wheeler Creek and the Winchuck River is within a half hour's drive of ocean beaches and northern California redwoods. When not relaxing along the waters, swimming, or fishing, campground guests can explore area trails, such as the Chimney Camp Trail along Wheeler Creek.

105 Winchuck

Location: About 12 miles southeast of Brookings
Season: May–Sept
Sites: 15 basic sites; no hookups
Maximum length: 40 feet
Facilities: Tables, grills, nonflush toilets, drinking water, wheelchair-accessible river access
Fee per night: None
Management: Siskiyou National Forest
Contact: (541) 412-6000; www.fs.usda.gov/recmain/rogue-siskiyou/recreation
Finding the campground: From the Chetco River bridge in Brookings, go south on US 101 for 4.1 miles. Turn east onto Winchuck River Road (CR 896), which becomes FR 1107, and travel 8 miles. Bear right, and proceed 0.1 mile to the campground, which straddles the road.
GPS coordinates: N42 01.171' / W124 06.351'
About the campground: The halves of this relaxing forest campground are wrapped in a bend of the sparkling green Winchuck River, another prized coastal waterway of incredible clarity. Crosswalks link the camp areas, and short trails explore along the river. Myrtles, tan oaks, alders, and mossy boulders and outcrops add to the river's soothing spell. Fishing and an upstream gravel-bar beach and swimming hole keep campers entertained.

Portland Area

At the confluence of the Willamette and Columbia Rivers, Portland, the "City of Roses," succeeds in blending culture, progress, industry, and nature into a very livable metropolis that is noted for its bridges and great beauty. The downtown district is vibrant and highly walkable, or visitors can hop on the Max-line or a Metro bus to get about town. City enticements include fine museums, theaters and concert halls, gardens, and the Portland Saturday Market, where artisans sell their creations. The acclaimed Oregon Zoo and Oregon Museum of Science and Industry (OMSI) have long been favorite destinations, and Forest Park is an unrivaled wilderness island within a city of this size. The trails that explore it are first-rate. Elsewhere, wetlands and estuarine lakes attract wildlife and naturalists.

Special events include the Rose Festival, with its Grand Floral Parade, Dragon Boat Races, and the arrival of the Festival Fleet; The Bite, an annual waterfront event at which local eateries serve up their specialties; the Brewer's Festival; and the sailing of the Christmas Ships. Restaurants cater to an array of ethnic tastes, street concerts enliven Pioneer Courthouse Square, and the Trail Blazers bring basketball fans to their feet at the Rose Garden. The waterfront invites sunset gazing and romancing.

Outside the metropolitan center, the pace slows. Images of farms and vineyards, the fir-clad Coast Range foothills, and the shores of the Columbia River provide a counterbalance to the hum of the city. U-pick farms and roadside stands parade a colorful assortment of fruits and vegetables. Hot-air balloons may draw eyes skyward, and abandoned railroad grades may suggest a hike or bicycle ride through the countryside.

The Portland area shares in the mild year-round climate of the Willamette Valley. Winds funneling out of the Columbia Gorge can invigorate senses. Summers are warm and inviting; spring and fall feature a mix of showers and sunshine; and winter brings rain interspersed with crisp, clear, cool days. You can also expect snow and ice for a day or two each winter—the perfect time to purchase a latte and curl up with a good book. With more bookstores per capita than any other US city, Portland is known as the "reading capital of the nation," and, like Seattle, Portland helped pioneer the specialty-coffee fad.

Tom McCall Waterfront Park from Steele Bridge, Portland

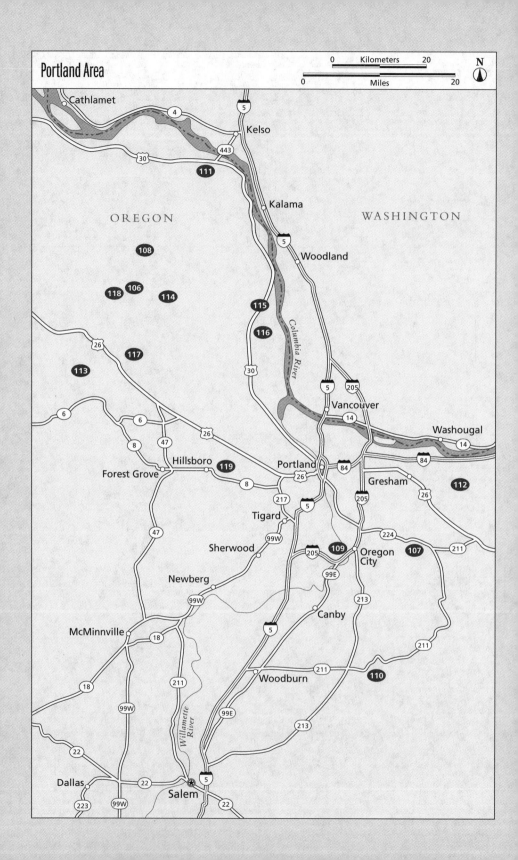

Portland Area

	Hookup Sites	Total Sites	Max. RV Length	Hookups	Toilets	Showers	Drinking Water	Dump Station	Recreation	Fee	Can Reserve
106 Anderson Park	19	19	40	WES	F	X	X	X	HFC	$$-$$$	X
107 Barton County Park	84	97	40	WE	F	X	X	X	SFBL	$$$	X
108 Big Eddy	35	35	40	WES	F	X	X	X	FBL	$$-$$$	X
109 Clackamette Park	35	35	40	WE	F		X	X	FBL	$$$	
110 Feyrer Memorial County Park	20	20	40	WE	F	X	X	X	FBL	$$$	
111 Hudson/Parcher County Park	26	35	40	WES	F	X	X	X		$$-$$$	X
112 Oxbow Regional Park		67	35		F	X	X		HSFBL	$$$	
113 Reehers Camp		16	40		NF		X		HR	$$	
114 Scaponia County Park		10	T, small		NF		X			$$	
115 Scappoose Bay Marine Park		Open	40		F		X		HFBL	$$	
116 Scappoose RV Park	6	11	40	WES	F	X	X	X		$$-$$$	
117 "Stub" Stewart State Park	93	114	50	WES	F	X	X		HRC	$$-$$$	X
118 Vernonia Airport Park		22	40		NF		X		F	$$	
119 Washington County FairPlex RV Park	14	14	30	WE		X	X			$$$	

106 Anderson Park

Location: In Vernonia, about 35 miles northwest of Portland
Season: Year-round
Sites: 19 hookup sites, open area for RVs or tents; water, electric, and sewer hookups
Maximum length: 40 feet
Facilities: Flush toilets, drinking water, showers, dump station, playground
Fee per night: $$-$$$
Management: City of Vernonia
Contact: (503) 429-5291 (city hall); (503) 429-2531 for reservations (park host); www.vernonia-or.gov/living/parks.asp
Finding the campground: From OR 47 in Vernonia, turn southeast onto Jefferson Avenue at the sign for Anderson Park. Proceed 0.2 mile to the park.
GPS coordinates: N45 51.364' / W123 11.557'
About the campground: This peaceful park and campground spreads along the north shore of the upper Nehalem River near the Rock Creek confluence. A scattering of big conifers lends shade to

the camp's open lawn. Campers have direct access to river fishing, with bass caught at nearby Vernonia Lake. Anderson Park holds the northern terminus of the 21-mile Banks–Vernonia State Trail. The first 7 miles of this rail trail are paved for family bike rides, hikes, or exercise walks. The park is at its busiest during Vernonia Days, the first weekend in August. Events celebrate the tradition of logging, and there is a small-town parade.

107 Barton County Park

Location: Near Barton, about 10 miles east of Oregon City
Season: May–Oct
Sites: 84 hookup sites, 13 basic sites; water and electric hookups
Maximum length: 40 feet
Facilities: Tables, grills, flush toilets, drinking water, showers, dump station, playground, horseshoe pits, sports fields, boat ramp (drift boat or raft)
Fee per night: $$$
Management: Clackamas County
Contact: (503) 742-4414, reservations accepted; www.co.clackamas.or.us/parks
Finding the campground: From OR 224 at Barton, 9 miles northwest of Estacada and 9.5 miles southeast of I-205 at exit 12 (north of Oregon City), head southwest on Bakers Ferry Road; it is signed for the park. Go 0.2 mile and bear left to enter the park.
GPS coordinates: N45 22.936' / W122 24.380'
About the campground: At this park on the Clackamas River, the campsites are either secluded in trees or lined up at the edge of the woods ringing a central lawn above the river. Big cottonwood, ash, and cedar trees contribute shade. The park is a popular river take-out point for rafters starting their float trip at Milo McIver State Park (located west of Estacada, off OR 224). Fishing and swimming are also popular, and there is a large riverside day-use area.

108 Big Eddy

Location: About 8 miles north of Vernonia
Season: Year-round
Sites: 14 full hookup sites, 21 water and electric sites; water, electric, and sewer hookups
Maximum length: 40 feet
Facilities: Tables, grills, flush toilets, drinking water, showers, dump station, volleyball net, playground, horseshoe pits, primitive boat ramp
Fee per night: $$–$$$
Management: Columbia County
Contact: (503) 397-2353; (503) 366-3984 for reservations; www.co.columbia.or.us/departments
Finding the campground: The park is west off OR 47, 7.8 miles north of Vernonia.
GPS coordinates: N45 55.904' / W123 09.712'

About the campground: This large, mostly shaded family campground sits where an eddy occurs along a snaking bend of the Nehalem River. Sites have gravel parking spurs. Ample lawn and tall firs and cedars contribute to the camp atmosphere, and alders and bigleaf maples grow riverside. The river is open to drift boats and canoes, and fishing is popular. Vernonia may beckon a visit, with its Banks–Vernonia State Trail, the Vernonia Days celebration in August, and the Columbia County Historical Museum.

109 Clackamette Park

Location: In Oregon City
Season: Year-round
Sites: 35 hookup sites; water and electric hookups
Maximum length: 40 feet
Facilities: Tables, flush toilets, drinking water, dump station, horseshoe pits, swings, skateboard area, boat launch
Fee per night: $$$
Management: Oregon City
Contact: (503) 496-1201; www.orcity.org/parksandrecreation
Finding the campground: From I-205 take exit 9 at Oregon City and head north on McLoughlin Boulevard. Proceed about 0.1 mile and turn west into this park on the river.
GPS coordinates: N45 22.264' / W122 36.323'
About the campground: On the Willamette River at the Clackamas River confluence, this park is popular with boaters and anglers. Salmon, shad, and sturgeon provide the action. The camp itself is mostly a gravel flat, with a few big cottonwoods along the river. Oregon City is home to the historic McLoughlin House. Because of his key role in Oregon's settlement, Dr. John McLoughlin has been dubbed the "Father of Oregon."

110 Feyrer Memorial County Park

Location: About 2 miles southeast of Molalla and 40 miles south of Portland
Season: May–Sept
Sites: 20 hookup sites; water and electric hookups
Maximum length: 40 feet
Facilities: Tables, grills, flush toilets, drinking water, showers, dump station, playground, horseshoe pits, sports fields, boat ramp for raft or drift boats
Fee per night: $$$
Management: Clackamas County
Contact: (503) 742-4414; www.co.clackamas.or.us/parks
Finding the campground: From OR 211 at the east side of Molalla, turn south onto South Mathias Road and go 0.3 mile. Bear left (east) onto Feyrer Park Road; continue 1.5 miles to reach the park's campground on the left. The boat ramp is on the right.
GPS coordinates: N45 08.329' / W122 32.116'

About the campground: This park on the Molalla River offers both camping and day use. The campsites have paved parking and sit back from the day-use area at the edge of a mature, mixed forest with an effusive understory. Family recreation, fishing, and wading entertain campers. The Molalla River flows shallow over a rocky bed, with cobble bars and a forested far shore.

111 Hudson/Parcher County Park

Location: About 4 miles west of Rainier
Season: Year-round
Sites: 15 full hookup sites, 11 partial hookup sites, 9 tent sites; water, electric, and sewer hookups
Maximum length: 40 feet
Facilities: Tables, fire pits, flush toilets, drinking water, showers, dump station, playground, ball fields
Fee per night: $$–$$$
Management: Columbia County
Contact: (503) 397-2353; (503) 366-3984 for reservations; www.co.columbia.or.us/departments
Finding the campground: From Rainier go west on US 30 for 3.1 miles. Turn left (south) onto Larson Road, reaching the park in another 0.8 mile.
GPS coordinates: N46 05.402' / W122 59.723'
About the campground: This relaxing family park on a grassy flat enjoys shade from the mature conifer and deciduous trees. Preacher Creek, which threads through the park and supports native trout, is closed to fishing. The campground supplies a convenient stopover for US 30 travelers passing between Portland and the coast. It also lies within easy reach of the Columbia River, where you can indulge in boating, windsurfing, and fishing.

112 Oxbow Regional Park

Location: About 8 miles east of Gresham
Season: Year-round unless river is high; gates locked at sunset
Sites: 67 basic sites; no hookups
Maximum length: 35 feet
Facilities: Tables, flush toilets, drinking water, showers, playground, horseshoe pits, boat ramp; no pets allowed
Fee per night: $$$
Management: Metro Regional Parks and Greenspaces
Contact: (503) 797-1850; www.oregonmetro.gov
Finding the campground: From I-205 in Portland, go east on Division Street and Oxbow Parkway, following signs 13 miles to the park.
GPS coordinates: N45 29.798' / W122 17.461'
About the campground: This park, cupped in a horseshoe bend of the Sandy Wild and Scenic River, encompasses 1,000 wooded acres to explore. You can fish, swim, canoe, raft, or go drift boating in

the Sandy River. The campsites rest mainly in second-growth forest within an easy walk of the river. Areas of old-growth forest also remain in the park, contributing to the diversity of birds and other wildlife. Footpaths travel Alder Ridge, the bend of the river, and the river flat. A popular 10-mile float trip begins at this park and ends at Lewis and Clark State Park, which is south off I-84 east of Troutdale. Fall visitors sometimes are treated to the natural spectacle of spawning chinook salmon.

113 Reehers Camp

Location: About 25 miles northwest of Hillsboro
Season: Mid-May–Sept
Sites: 10 horse campsites, 6 basic sites; no hookups
Maximum length: 40 feet
Facilities: Tables, grills, nonflush toilets, drinking water, picnic shelter, site horse corrals, manure bin
Fee per night: $$
Management: Tillamook State Forest
Contact: (503) 357-2191; www.oregon.gov/ODF/tillamookstateforest/Recreation.shtml
Finding the campground: From the Timber Junction on US 26, 8 miles northwest of the intersection of US 26 and OR 47, drive south on Timber Road for 3.1 miles. Turn right (west) onto Northwest Cochran Road, which is signed for the campground. This road begins paved but becomes gravel surfaced. Follow it for 2.5 miles; turn left to enter the campground. A trailhead and day-use area sit 0.2 mile farther west.
GPS coordinates: N45 42.417' / W123 20.104'
About the campground: This roomy, well-developed camp, with separate equestrian and traditional family campsites, occupies a one-time compound of the Civilian Conservation Corps. The camp rests within a short trail distance of the Nehalem River in deep woods of lovely big Douglas firs, bigleaf maples, vine maples, and alders. Trails extend outward from camp. The Triple C Trail heads north off Cochran Road across from the day-use trailhead parking lot. By going south on the Gales Creek Trail, you'll reach Gales Creek Forest Camp in 9 miles.

114 Scaponia County Park

Location: About 10 miles northeast of Vernonia, 15 miles west of Scappoose
Season: May–Dec, winter camping weather dependent
Sites: 10 basic sites; no hookups
Maximum length: Best for tents and small units
Facilities: Tables, grills, nonflush toilets, drinking water
Fee per night: $$
Management: Columbia County
Contact: (503) 397-2353; www.co.columbia.or.us/departments
Finding the campground: From Vernonia travel 5 miles north on OR 47. Turn east onto Scappoose-Vernonia Road to reach the park on the right in another 5.2 miles.
GPS coordinates: N45 50.681' / W123 05.737'

About the campground: This small, rustic wayside campground rests in a second-growth forest along the slow-moving, creek-size East Fork Nehalem River. Although the quiet is occasionally broken by the sound of traffic, the park promotes relaxation. It has informal parking and shady lawn sites. In fall, hunters use the camp as a base.

115 Scappoose Bay Marine Park

Location: About 2 miles southwest of St. Helens
Season: Year-round
Sites: Self-contained RV camping; no hookups
Maximum length: 40 feet
Facilities: Flush toilets, drinking water, pump-out station, three-lane boat launch, marina, moorage, picnic shelter, kayak rental
Fee per night: $$
Management: Port of St. Helens
Contact: (503) 397-2888
Finding the campground: From US 30, 5 miles northwest of Scappoose and 1.5 miles southeast of St. Helens city center, turn east onto Millard Road. Go 0.3 mile and turn right onto Old Portland Road. Continue 0.4 mile to the park on the left.
GPS coordinates: N45 49.696' / W122 50.298'
About the campground: This 23-acre facility on the Columbia River features a well-kept marina and allows self-contained, dry camping in the parking area. Some large oaks dot the grassy perimeter of the "camp." This is primarily a boater's access on Scappoose Bay, which feeds into Multnomah Channel on the Columbia River. Nature trails allow you to stretch your legs.

116 Scappoose RV Park

Location: About 2 miles north of Scappoose
Season: Year-round
Sites: 6 full hookup sites, 1 basic site, 4 tent sites; water, electric, and sewer hookups
Maximum length: 40 feet
Facilities: Tables, grills, flush toilets, drinking water, showers, dump station, playground, covered picnic site
Fee per night: $$–$$$
Management: Columbia County
Contact: (503) 397-2353; www.co.columbia.or.us/departments
Finding the campground: From Scappoose go 1.5 miles northwest on US 30. Turn east onto West Lane Road at the sign for the park. Continue 0.6 mile and turn left onto North Honeyman Road. Go 0.1 mile to enter the park on the right.
GPS coordinates: N45 46.678' / W122 51.907'
About the campground: This small, well-kept park is located near the rural airport and surrounded by open fields. Despite some noise from a nearby gravel operation, the sites are pleasant, with

lawn and full shade from the park's mature firs and bigleaf maples. Scappoose celebrates Airport Appreciation Day in June and the Sauerkraut Festival in October.

117 "Stub" Stewart State Park

Location: About 31 miles west of Portland
Season: Year-round
Sites: 78 hookup sites, 15 hookup sites with horse corrals, 21 walk-in tent sites, 15 cabins; water, electric, and sewer hookups
Maximum length: 50 feet
Facilities: Tables, grills, flush toilets, drinking water, showers, wireless (available), vending machines
Fee per night: $$–$$$
Management: Oregon State Parks and Recreation Department
Contact: (503) 324-0606; (800) 452-5687 for reservations; www.oregon.gov/OPRD/PARKS/camping.shtml
Finding the campground: From the junction of US 26 and OR 47 west of Portland, head north on OR 47 for 4.1 mile. Turn east, following signs for the park. Reach the welcome center in 0.7 mile and the named campgrounds in 0.9 mile.
GPS coordinates: N45 44.220' / W123 11.485'
About the campground: This sweeping park and camp facility offers a full recreation menu with trails for hiking, cycling, and horseback riding; heights for viewing; and second-growth fir-alder woods and canyons for nature study. More than 20 miles of trails web the park's 1,673 acres, including part of the Banks–Vernonia rail trail. An eighteen-hole disc golf course or a three-hole traditional golf course will challenge your aim. For the former, bring your own discs and score cards. The park's location in the coastal foothills means winter can bring days of ice and snow; come prepared.

118 Vernonia Airport Park

Location: About 4 miles southwest of Vernonia
Season: Year-round
Sites: 22 basic sites, no hookups
Maximum length: 40 feet
Facilities: Tables, grills, nonflush toilets, drinking water, playground
Fee per night: $$
Management: City of Vernonia
Contact: (503) 429-5291; www.vernonia-or.gov/living/parks.asp
Finding the campground: From OR 47, 12.7 miles north of US 26 and 2 miles south of Vernonia, turn west onto Timber Road at the park sign. Go 1.1 miles, turn right onto Airport Road, and continue following the signs 0.4 mile to the park.
GPS coordinates: N45 51.006' / W123 14.575'

Rolling vine-clad hills in Oregon's wine country

About the campground: Near the small rural airport, this campground occupies a mixed conifer and maple and alder setting along the Nehalem River. Sites have gravel parking. Fishing and wading are possible pastimes, along with hiking or cycling the Banks–Vernonia rail trail, which has marked trailheads off OR 47 and in Vernonia.

119 Washington County FairPlex RV Park

Location: In Hillsboro
Season: Closed to the public July and Aug; otherwise open as space allows
Sites: 14 RV hookup sites (self-contained only), no tent sites; water and electric hookups
Maximum length: 30 feet
Facilities: Drinking water, showers
Fee per night: $$$
Management: Washington County
Contact: (503) 648-1416 (call ahead; sometimes closed for seasonal events); www.faircomplex.com
Finding the campground: From Cornell Road in Hillsboro, turn south at the FairPlex entrance, across from the Portland Hillsboro Airport.
GPS coordinates: N45 31.833' / W122 56.797'
About the campground: This small overnight facility, which primarily serves fairground participants and through-travelers, is an extension of the main fairground's parking lot. The side-by-side sites are numbered, and all require backing in toward a mesh fence. But the camp does overlook an area of lawn and conifers.

Mount Hood and the Columbia River Gorge

Two striking geographic features shape this region. The first is Mount Hood, the tallest, most famous, and most climbed peak in the Oregon Cascades. At a height of 11,235 feet, it reigns above a prized wilderness, sweeping forests, high mountain lakes, and wild and scenic waterways. The second feature is the Columbia River Gorge, the picturesque divide between Oregon and Washington recognized as a national scenic area. The Oregon side of the gorge has more than a dozen major waterfalls streaking its 3,000-foot cliffs. The stiff winds that funnel through the gorge challenge sailboarders to ride the choppy Columbia River.

Uniting the dynamic duo is the Mount Hood–Columbia Gorge Scenic Loop. This sightseeing drive begins along the river and follows I-84 and the Historic Columbia River Highway east from Troutdale to the city of Hood River. From there the tour continues south on OR 35 and west on US 26 to Gresham. In Gresham the tour heads north on 242nd Avenue to return to I-84 and Troutdale.

Historically the Columbia River supported Native American fishing camps, carried Lewis and Clark and the Corps of Discovery west to the Pacific Ocean, and tested the mettle of the Oregon Trail pioneers in the years before Barlow Road provided an overland route around Mount Hood to the Willamette Valley. Mount Hood has long been an explorer's landmark, adventurer's challenge, and artist's inspiration.

Spectacular scenery and outstanding outdoor recreation are common to both areas. Overall, the Columbia River Gorge is the better suited of the two for car touring, with its many waterfalls, apple and cherry orchards, museums, the Bonneville Dam fish hatchery and fish-counting station, the stern-wheeler tour, and historic train rides. But the outdoor enthusiast is not overlooked. The gorge serves up hiking, salmon and sturgeon fishing, windsurfing, and boating. Mount Hood caters to an active crowd, with mountain climbing, downhill and cross-country skiing, snowboarding,

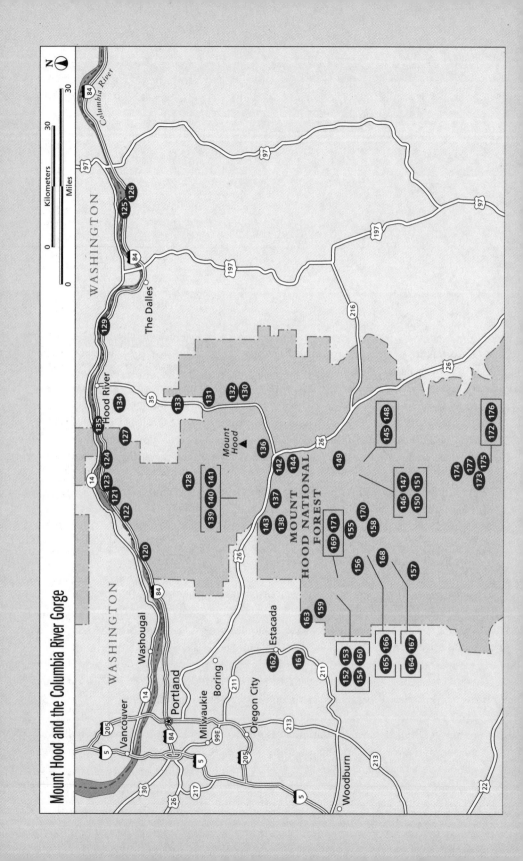

Mount Hood and the Columbia River Gorge

snowmobiling, fishing, hiking, golfing, and huckleberry picking. Mount Hood is also one of the few areas in the country to offer summer downhill skiing.

Both areas have historic lodges, wonderful campgrounds, and superb vistas. While both are popular playgrounds for the Portland metropolitan area, they still hold places for quiet reflection and unspoiled wilds.

At Mount Hood and the Columbia River Gorge, you can enjoy all four seasons. At the higher elevations you will find comfortable summer temperatures and winter snow. Generally, the lower elevations remain mild most of the year, with the drier eastern part of the gorge heating up in summer. In summer the gorge funnels ocean-cooled west winds; in winter it channels icy east winds. While subfreezing temperatures can make for treacherous gorge travel, they transform the waterfalls into frozen art. Rain, though, is the more common winter signature, both in the gorge and at the lower mountain elevations.

Cascade Locks–Multnomah Falls Area

	Hookup Sites	Total Sites	Max. RV Length	Hookups	Toilets	Showers	Drinking Water	Dump Station	Recreation	Fee	Can Reserve
120 Ainsworth State Park	45	51	60	WES	F	X	X	X	H	$$-$$$	
121 Cascade Locks Marine Park	10	15	40	WE	F	X	X	X	FBL	$$-$$$	
122 Eagle Creek		16	20		F		X		H	$$	
123 Herman Creek Horse Camp		7	20		NF		X		HR	$$	
124 Wyeth		14	30		F				H	$$	

120 Ainsworth State Park

Location: About 9 miles west of Cascade Locks
Season: Mid-Mar-Oct
Sites: 45 hookup sites, 6 walk-in tent sites; water, electric, and sewer hookups
Maximum length: 60 feet
Facilities: Tables, grills, flush toilets, drinking water, showers, dump station
Fee per night: $$-$$$
Management: Oregon State Parks and Recreation Department
Contact: (503) 695-2301; www.oregon.gov/OPRD/PARKS/camping.shtml
Finding the campground: Take exit 35 off I-84, 35 miles east of Portland and 9 miles west of Cascade Locks. On the south side of the freeway, follow the Historic Columbia River Highway west for 0.6 mile to the park entrance on the left.
GPS coordinates: N45 35.713' / W122 03.113'
About the campground: The developed campsites rest in close proximity to one another, separated by small divides of nonnative landscaping, but they serve as a convenient base for exploring the area. The Columbia River Gorge has a wealth of vistas, natural attractions, trails, and history. Driving west on the Historic Columbia River Highway opens the doorway to discovery. By following the Gorge Trail, which skirts camp, you may visit Oneonta Gorge and Ponytail, Horsetail, and Triple Falls. Autumn visitors to Multnomah Falls can spy spawning salmon in Multnomah Creek below the falls. At 620 feet, Multnomah Falls is the fourth-tallest falls in the nation; its historic lodge—with visitor center, gift shop, and restaurant—is a popular stop.

121 Cascade Locks Marine Park

Location: In Cascade Locks
Season: Year-round
Sites: 10 hookup sites, 5 basic sites; water and electric hookups

Motor home at Multnomah Falls, Columbia River Gorge National Scenic Area

Maximum length: 40 feet
Facilities: Tables, flush toilets, drinking water, showers, dump station, playground, gift shop, boat ramp, fish-cleaning station, small marina
Fee per night: $$–$$$
Management: Port of Cascade Locks
Contact: (541) 374-8619; www.portofcascadelocks.org
Finding the campground: From I-84 eastbound take exit 44 for Cascade Locks. Head 0.5 mile east on Wanapa Street; turn north at the sign for the marine park.

The exit from I-84 westbound is also labeled exit 44. From here, though, follow Wanapa Street west through town to the signed turnoff for the marine park. An underpass with a 12-foot height and 20-foot width clearance leads into the park.
GPS coordinates: N45 40.042' / W121 53.756'
About the campground: This convenient overnight spot in the Columbia River Gorge is located within the marine park, just above the boat launch area. It has developed parking pads and groomed lawns. Its central location is ideal if you want to explore the gorge. Within the marine park you can fish for salmon or sturgeon, tour the Cascade Locks Historical Museum, or book a trip on the Columbia River stern-wheeler.

122 Eagle Creek

Location: About 3 miles west of Cascade Locks
Season: Mid-May–Sept
Sites: 16 basic sites; no hookups
Maximum length: 20 feet
Facilities: Tables, grills, flush toilets, drinking water
Fee per night: $$
Management: Columbia River Gorge National Scenic Area
Contact: (541) 308-1700; www.fs.usda.gov/recmain/crgnsa/recreation
Finding the campground: From I-84 eastbound take exit 41 to the campground.

If you are traveling westbound from Cascade Locks, follow I-84 west to the Bonneville Dam exit (exit 40) and get onto I-84 heading east. Take exit 41 and proceed to the campground.
GPS coordinates: N45 38.563' / W121 55.489'
About the campground: Tucked away on a wooded hillside above Eagle Creek is this small, family campground—the first USDA Forest Service campground in the nation. The popular Eagle Creek Trail extends upstream from the camp, stringing past picturesque waterfalls to enter the Mark O. Hatfield Wilderness Area. Other trails trace the southern wall of the gorge or top hills for vistas. In fall, salmon migrate up the gravelly bed of Eagle Creek, sometimes drawing a following of bald eagles (hence the creek's name). Next door to the campground is the Cascade Salmon Fish Hatchery, but it is not set up for visitors. However, Bonneville Dam, to the west, has a visitor center with fish-viewing windows as well as a fish hatchery.

123 Herman Creek Horse Camp

Location: About 2 miles east of Cascade Locks
Season: Mid-May–Oct
Sites: 7 basic sites; no hookups
Maximum length: 20 feet
Facilities: Tables, grills, nonflush toilets, drinking water, hitching rails
Fee per night: $$
Management: Columbia River Gorge National Scenic Area
Contact: (541) 308-1700; www.fs.usda.gov/recmain/crgnsa/recreation
Finding the campground: At the east end of Cascade Locks, take Forest Lane east for 1.7 miles, quickly crossing to the south side of I-84. Past the Herman Creek Work Center, turn right for the campground and trailhead.
GPS coordinates: N45 40.977' / W121 50.522'
About the campground: Located east of Herman Creek in a low-elevation forest, this small, basic camp facility can accommodate stock. The trail up Herman Creek into the Mark O. Hatfield Wilderness begins on the west side of camp and ascends to Wahtum Lake, the Pacific Crest National Scenic Trail (PCT), and a host of other trail connections. Individuals with horses can transport them across the Bridge of the Gods into Washington to follow the PCT north; parking is at the north end of the bridge. The camp also serves fishing enthusiasts.

124 Wyeth

Location: About 8 miles east of Cascade Locks
Season: May–Oct
Sites: 14 basic sites; no hookups
Maximum length: 30 feet
Facilities: Tables, grills, flush toilets; no drinking water
Fee per night: $$
Management: Columbia River Gorge National Scenic Area
Contact: (541) 308-1700; www.fs.usda.gov/recmain/crgnsa/recreation
Finding the campground: From I-84, 7 miles east of Cascade Locks, take exit 51 and follow Wyeth Road east along the south side of the freeway to the campground in 0.5 mile.
GPS coordinates: N45 41.305' / W121 46.309'
About the campground: This mostly forested campground along Gorton Creek has paved roads and site parking, with ample spacing between the sites. Small firs and bigleaf maples offer shade. By this point, the Columbia River Gorge is beginning to transition out of the thick woods at its west end to the grassland steppes at its east end. You can access the Gorge and Wyeth Trails from camp. Small cascades and falls contribute to the character of Gorton Creek. The Wyeth area was an early Oregon Territory settlement, a Civilian Conservation Corps Camp in the 1930s, and a Conscientious Objector camp in the 1940s.

The Dalles–Hood River Area

	Hookup Sites	Total Sites	Max. RV Length	Hookups	Toilets	Showers	Drinking Water	Dump Station	Recreation	Fee	Can Reserve
125 Celilo Park		Open	40	F			X		SFBL	None	
126 Deschutes River State Recreation Area	33	58	50	WE	F	X	X		HFBLRC	$$–$$$	X
127 Kingsley County Park		23	T, small		NF		X		FBLO	$$	
128 Lost Lake		129	32		NF	X	X	X	HFLR	$$$	X
129 Memaloose State Park	44	110	60	WES	F	X	X	X		$$	X
130 Nottingham		23	32		NF				HF	$$	
131 Routson County Park		10	T		F		X		HF	$$	
132 Sherwood		14	16		NF				HF	$$	
133 Toll Bridge County Park	62	80	40	WES	F	X	X	X	F	$$–$$$	X
134 Tucker County Park	14	94	30	W	F	X	X		HF	$$	
135 Viento State Park	56	74	30	WE	F	X	X		H	$$	

125 Celilo Park

Location: About 15 miles east of The Dalles
Season: Year-round
Sites: Open camping; no hookups
Maximum length: 40 feet
Facilities: Flush toilets, drinking water, playground, boat launch
Fee per night: None
Management: US Army Corps of Engineers
Contact: (541) 506-7819; www.nwp.usace.army.mil
Finding the campground: From I-84, 12 miles east of The Dalles, take exit 97. The park is located on the north side of the freeway.
GPS coordinates: N45 39.006' / W120 57.654'
About the campground: This Columbia River park doubles as a campground, with RVs setting up in the parking area and tents pitched on the lawns. Respect the designated day-use area. Boating, fishing, and windsurfing are the river recreations. Cross-river views are of the grassy hills and cliffs of Washington. Mature shade trees offer escape from the sun.

126 Deschutes River State Recreation Area

Location: About 18 miles east of The Dalles
Season: Year-round
Sites: 33 hookup sites, 25 basic sites; water and electric hookups
Maximum length: 50 feet
Facilities: Tables, grills, flush toilets, drinking water, showers, boat launch (on opposite shore of river), Oregon Trail exhibit
Fee per night: $$–$$$
Management: Oregon State Parks and Recreation Department
Contact: (541) 739-2322; (800) 452-5687 for reservations; www.oregon.gov/OPRD/PARKS/camping.shtml
Finding the campground: From I-84, 12 miles east of The Dalles, take exit 97. Travel east along the south side of the freeway for 3 miles; the park is on the right.
GPS coordinates: N45 37.980' / W120 54.516'
About the campground: The campground's highly appealing tree-shaded lawn faces out on the Deschutes Wild and Scenic River, just upstream from its confluence with the Columbia River. The camp is an oasis in an arid canyon of sagebrush and basalt. There is direct river access from camp, as well as foot trails that traverse both shores. A bike trail likewise explores the canyon. The Deschutes offers world-class fishing, attracting fly fishers from around the world, and the river is equally popular with boaters and floaters. A public launch is located across the river at Heritage Landing, a day-use area. Come with binoculars for birding.

127 Kingsley County Park

Location: On Upper Green Point Reservoir, about 12 miles southwest of Hood River
Season: Apr–Oct
Sites: 23 basic sites; no hookups
Maximum length: Small units; best for tents
Facilities: Tables, fire rings, nonflush toilets, drinking water (bring some with you in case pump fails), boat launch and dock near dam
Fee per night: $$
Management: Hood River County
Contact: (541) 387-6889; www.co.hood-river.or.us
Finding the campground: From US 30 (Oak Street) in Hood River, head south on Thirteenth Street for 0.7 mile. Merge onto Twelfth Street, which later becomes Tucker Road. Go another 3.4 miles, taking several turns to remain on Tucker Road/OR 281. Turn right onto Portland Drive and go 2 miles, entering the community of Oak Grove. In Oak Grove briefly head left only to immediately bear right onto Binns Hill Road. Follow it 0.3 mile to Kingsley Road; turn left and continue 5.9 miles to the park. At the park the roads change to dirt.
GPS coordinates: N45 38.417' / W121 40.426'
About the campground: This park offers open, primitive camping in the select-cut fir forest along the east bank of Upper Green Point Reservoir. Parking is what you can make of it. This

moderate-size reservoir welcomes boating (5 miles per hour) and fishing. The park's biggest appeal, though, is to off-highway vehicle enthusiasts, with multiple area routes to explore.

128 Lost Lake

Location: On Lost Lake, about 33 miles southwest of Hood River
Season: May–Oct
Sites: 120 basic sites, 3 group sites, 6 horse sites, 7 cabins, 6 rooms; no hookups
Maximum length: 32 feet
Facilities: Tables, grills, nonflush toilets, drinking water, showers, dump station, boat rental, boat ramp (nonmotorized boating), fish-cleaning stations, barrier-free trails, corrals
Fee per night: $$$
Management: Mount Hood National Forest; operated by Lost Lake Resort Inc.
Contact: (541) 352-6002; (541) 386-6366, resort and reservations; www.fs.usda.gov/recmain/mthood/recreation and for resort: www.lostlakeresort.org

Mt. Hood and Lost Lake, Mt. Hood National Forest

Finding the campground: From OR 35, about 14 miles south of the town of Hood River and 0.5 mile north of the community of Mount Hood, turn west onto Woodworth Road. Follow it 2.1 miles to Dee Highway/OR 281. Turn right, head 4 miles north to the old mill town of Dee, and cross the river bridge. Keep left to follow Lost Lake Road/FR 13 the remaining 13.4 miles to the recreation area.
GPS coordinates: N45 29.657' / W121 48.956'
About the campground: Although it takes a bit of navigating to get here, Lost Lake and its outdoor playground more than satisfy. The 240-acre triangular lake offers quiet boating, fine fishing, and one of the best clear-day views of Mount Hood to be had anywhere. Old-growth forest and bountiful rhododendrons shape glorious realms to explore by trail or savor at camp. Set back from shore, the wooded camp is highly attractive and well ordered, with paved roads and parking. The concessionaire has designated sites by party size and number of vehicles. Some sites occupy a split level, with the tables and grills on a different terrace than the parking. Trails explore the lakeshore, old-growth grove, Lost Lake Butte, and the Old Skyline route. The Old-Growth Trail and the eastern part of the Lakeshore Trail are barrier-free, with long stretches of boardwalk.

129 Memaloose State Park

Location: 11 miles west of The Dalles
Season: Mid-Mar–Oct
Sites: 44 hookup sites, 66 basic sites; water, electric, and sewer hookups
Maximum length: 60 feet
Facilities: Tables, grills, flush toilets, drinking water, showers, dump station
Fee per night: $$
Management: Oregon State Parks and Recreation Department
Contact: (541) 478-3008; (800) 452-5687 for reservations; www.oregon.gov/OPRD/PARKS/camping.shtml
Finding the campground: The campground is north off I-84, 11 miles west of The Dalles, with westbound access only.
GPS coordinates: N45 41.801' / W121 20.739'
About the campground: This park takes the name of a Columbia River island that was used by Native Americans as a sacred burial ground and was flooded with the damming of the river. The landscaped camp rests above the river and below the freeway; planted shade trees bring added comfort to a stay. With no river access at the park, visitors must seek their entertainment away from the campground. The Columbia Gorge welcomes fishing, hiking, boating, windsurfing, and sightseeing. Historic The Dalles and its Columbia Gorge Discovery Center warrant a look.

130 Nottingham

Location: About 27 miles south of Hood River
Season: Late May–mid-Oct
Sites: 23 basic sites; no hookups
Maximum length: 32 feet

Facilities: Tables, grills, nonflush toilets; no drinking water
Fee per night: $$
Management: Mount Hood National Forest
Contact: (541) 352-6002; www.fs.usda.gov/recmain/mthood/recreation
Finding the campground: The campground is west off OR 35, 26.3 miles south of Hood River and 12.3 miles north of the junction of US 26 and OR 35.
GPS coordinates: N45 22.065' / W121 34.196'
About the campground: This family campground rests in open conifer forest along the East Fork Hood River, which originates on Mount Hood. Special fishing regulations apply to the river. Area trails travel along the river and climb to Badger Creek Wilderness. Mount Hood sightseeing is popular, with Cloud Cap and Timberline within reasonable distances of the camp. Pioneer Woman's Grave and a segment of the Oregon Trail can be found near the junction of US 26 and OR 35.

131 Routson County Park

Location: About 21 miles south of Hood River
Season: Apr–Oct
Sites: 10 tent sites; no hookups
Maximum length: Suitable for tents only
Facilities: Some tables and some grills, flush toilets, drinking water
Fee per night: $$
Management: Hood River County
Contact: (541) 387-6889; www.co.hood-river.or.us
Finding the campground: The campground is east off OR 35, 20.7 miles south of Hood River. A narrow gravel road overhung by trees leads into camp.
GPS coordinates: N45 26.857' / W121 34.832'
About the campground: Despite the running-water facilities, the sites themselves are primitive and random. They occupy a stand of tall firs set back from the racing, glacier-born East Fork Hood River; special fishing regulations apply. Although small RV units could park on the earthen flat, the entrance road's blind access, overhanging limbs, and tight turnaround at camp make this park better suited to tent campers.

132 Sherwood

Location: About 25 miles south of Hood River
Season: May–mid-Oct
Sites: 14 basic sites; no hookups
Maximum length: 16 feet
Facilities: Tables, grills, nonflush toilets; no drinking water
Fee per night: $$
Management: Mount Hood National Forest
Contact: (541) 352-6002; www.fs.usda.gov/recmain/mthood/recreation

Finding the campground: The campground is west off OR 35, 24.6 miles south of Hood River. **GPS coordinates:** N45 23.689' / W121 34.238'

About the campground: This campground on the East Fork Hood River offers a pleasant forest stay, with access to fishing and hiking, but its proximity to OR 35 brings with it some traffic sounds. Special fishing regulations apply to protect salmon and steelhead. Trails travel along the river and upstream along Cold Spring Creek, which flows into the river north of camp. Tamanawas Falls—an elegant waterfall with lacy streamers tumbling 100 feet over a basalt cliff—puts an exclamation mark on the journey up Cold Spring Creek.

133 Toll Bridge County Park

Location: About 15 miles south of Hood River
Season: Apr–Oct
Sites: 20 full hookup sites, 42 partial hookup sites, 15 tent sites, 3 group sites; water, electric, and sewer hookups
Maximum length: 40 feet
Facilities: Tables, grills, flush toilets, drinking water, showers, dump station
Fee per night: $$–$$$
Management: Hood River County
Contact: (541) 352-5522 for information and reservations; www.co.hood-river.or.us
Finding the campground: From Hood River go 15 miles south on OR 35. Turn right (west) onto Toll Bridge Road; continue 0.3 mile to the campground on the right.
GPS coordinates: N45 31.171' / W121 34.169'
About the campground: This campground and its large, adjacent day-use area sit along the East Fork Hood River, which originates on Mount Hood. The full-hookup sites occupy parklike grounds, with lawns shaded by pines and firs. Elsewhere the campsites are tucked into semi-open, mixed woods, with tree species common to both eastern and western Oregon. Fishing and sightseeing in the orchard country of Hood River County may provide amusement. In Parkdale you may wish to visit the Hutson Museum, with its Native American, pioneer, and gemstone collections.

134 Tucker County Park

Location: About 5 miles south of Hood River
Season: Apr–Oct
Sites: 14 hookup sites, 80 basic sites; water hookups
Maximum length: 30 feet
Facilities: Tables, grills, flush toilets, drinking water, showers, playground, horseshoe pits
Fee per night: $$
Management: Hood River County
Contact: (541) 387-6889; www.co.hood-river.or.us
Finding the campground: From US 30 in Hood River, go 0.7 mile south on Thirteenth Street. Merge onto Twelfth Street, which later becomes Tucker Road. Travel 4.3 miles, taking several turns

to remain on Tucker Road/OR 281 South. Bear right at Parkdale-Dee Junction and go 0.4 mile to enter the park on the right.

GPS coordinates: N45 39.082' / W121 33.802'

About the campground: You will find this family campground in an open, mostly natural forest setting of ponderosa pines and oaks above the Hood River. Noisy and turbulent, the river courses past camp; a short nature trail provides access and views. Wood ducks may sometimes be seen along the waterway. The camp lies within convenient reach of the Columbia River Gorge to the north. Lost Lake can be reached by traveling south and west via OR 281 (Hood River Highway) and FR 13.

135 Viento State Park

Location: 8 miles west of Hood River

Season: Mid-Mar–Oct

Sites: 56 hookup sites, 18 basic sites; water and electric hookups

Maximum length: 30 feet

Facilities: Tables, grills, flush toilets, drinking water, showers

Fee per night: $$

Management: Oregon State Parks and Recreation Department

Contact: (541) 374-8811; www.oregon.gov/OPRD/PARKS/camping.shtml

Finding the campground: The park is located off I-84, 8 miles west of Hood River. The primary campground is on the north side of the freeway; tent camping is on the south side.

GPS coordinates: N45 41.860' / W121 40.053'

About the campground: Just off the interstate, this tidy campground among the maples and oaks is convenient for both through-travelers and visitors to the Columbia River Gorge National Scenic Area. The separate tent area occupies natural woodland. Possible excursions include visits to Bonneville Dam, Cascade Locks, and the Washington shore; waterfall viewing along the Old Scenic Highway; and windsurfing at Koberg Beach in Hood River. For hiking head to Starvation Creek State Park (2 miles west), where trails climb to Mount Defiance and the heights of the gorge. Trails also begin off the Old Scenic Highway.

Zigzag–Government Camp Area

	Hookup Sites	Total Sites	Max. RV Length	Hookups	Toilets	Showers	Drinking Water	Dump Station	Recreation	Fee	Can Reserve
136 Alpine		16	16		NF		X		H	$$$	
137 Camp Creek		25	22		NF		X		HFR	$$-$$$	X
138 Green Canyon		15	22		NF				HSF	$$-$$$	
139 Lost Creek		15	22		NF		X		HF	$$-$$$	X
140 McNeil		34	22		NF				H	$$	
141 Riley Horse Camp		14	16		NF				HR	$$	X
142 Still Creek		27	16		NF		X		H	$$-$$$	X
143 Tollgate		15	16		NF		X		HFR	$$-$$$	X
144 Trillium Lake		57	40		NF		X		HSFBL	$$-$$$	X

136 Alpine

Location: About 4 miles north of Government Camp
Season: June–Labor Day
Sites: 16 tent sites; no hookups
Maximum length: 16 feet, best suited for tents
Facilities: Tables, grills, nonflush toilets, drinking water
Fee per night: $$$
Management: Mount Hood National Forest
Contact: (503) 622-3191; www.fs.usda.gov/recmain/mthood/recreation
Finding the campground: From US 26 east of Government Camp, turn north onto Timberline Road. Continue 4.5 miles to reach the campground.
GPS coordinates: N45 19.226' / W121 42.329'
About the campground: This lofty camp puts you in an alpine meadow and fir-hemlock setting just below timberline on Mount Hood. Mount Hood offers year-round skiing and snowboarding and is one of the most climbed peaks in the country. The superb Timberline Trail encircles the mountain, and you can visit historic Timberline Lodge, noted for its stone masonry and woodwork. Because the camp appeals to snowboarders, it tends to be livelier than other area campgrounds.

137 Camp Creek

Location: About 5 miles east of Zigzag
Season: Mid-May–Labor Day
Sites: 25 basic sites; no hookups
Maximum length: 22 feet
Facilities: Tables, grills, nonflush toilets, drinking water
Fee per night: $$–$$$
Management: Mount Hood National Forest
Contact: (503) 622-3191; (877) 444-6777 for reservations; www.fs.usda.gov/recmain/mthood/recreation
Finding the campground: The campground is south off US 26, 19.2 miles east of Sandy and 2.6 miles east of Rhododendron.
GPS coordinates: N45 18.220' / W121 51.908'
About the campground: In a deep, old-growth forest alongside sparkling Camp Creek sits this inviting campground, which makes an ideal base for exploring the Mount Hood area. The camp oozes charm with its many big trees and rich greenery. A small tributary through camp supports bountiful skunk cabbage, pungent in spring. The sites have defined, surfaced parking and are well spaced for comfort. Creek fishing, hiking, and sightseeing may pull you away from camp. The Pioneer Bridle Trail parallels US 26 at the north side of the campground, following the route of the Oregon Trail. Little Zigzag Falls and Flag Mountain Trails are not far from camp.

138 Green Canyon

Location: About 5 miles south of Zigzag
Season: Mid-May–Labor Day
Sites: 15 basic sites; no hookups
Maximum length: 22 feet
Facilities: Tables, grills, nonflush toilets; no drinking water
Fee per night: $$–$$$
Management: Mount Hood National Forest
Contact: (503) 622-3191; www.fs.usda.gov/recmain/mthood/recreation
Finding the campground: From US 26 at Zigzag, go south on Salmon River Road/FR 2618 for 4.5 miles; the campground is on the right.
GPS coordinates: N45 16.977' / W121 56.587'
About the campground: On an old-growth-forested flat along the Salmon Wild and Scenic River, you will find this quiet campground, where you can either retreat from the flurry of activity around Mount Hood or join right in. The Mount Hood area welcomes fishing, hiking, berry picking, sightseeing, history tracking, and summer skiing. Near camp, trails parallel the Salmon River in both directions; the upstream hike enters the Salmon-Huckleberry Wilderness. The more challenging Green Canyon Way Trail begins across the road from camp and strikes straight uphill into the wilderness. The Salmon River offers catch-and-release fishing only.

139 Lost Creek

Location: About 7 miles northeast of Zigzag
Season: Late May–Labor Day
Sites: 10 wheelchair-accessible basic sites, 5 pack-in/roll-in wheelchair sites, 1 yome (cross between tent and cabin); no hookups
Maximum length: 22 feet
Facilities: Tables, grills, nonflush toilets, drinking water (The entire campground is wheelchair accessible.)
Fee per night: $$–$$$
Management: Mount Hood National Forest
Contact: (503) 622-3191; (877) 444-6777 for reservations; www.fs.usda.gov/recmain/mthood/recreation
Finding the campground: From US 26 at Zigzag, turn north onto East Lolo Pass Road (FR 18) and go 4.2 miles. Turn right onto FR 1825; follow it for another 2.7 miles to the campground on the right.
GPS coordinates: N45 22.927' / W121 50.179'
About the campground: In a picturesque mountain hemlock forest sits this accessible campground with its level and paved sites. Lost Creek lends a soothing backdrop, and rhododendrons seasonally color the scene. A fine interpretive trail begins at camp and explores the immediate area. Fishing also provides entertainment.

140 McNeil

Location: About 5 miles northeast of Zigzag
Season: Late May–Labor Day
Sites: 34 basic sites; no hookups
Maximum length: 22 feet
Facilities: Tables, grills, nonflush toilets; no drinking water
Fee per night: $$
Management: Mount Hood National Forest
Contact: (503) 622-3191; www.fs.usda.gov/recmain/mthood/recreation
Finding the campground: From US 26 at Zigzag, turn north onto East Lolo Pass Road (FR 18) and go 4.2 miles. Turn right onto FR 1825 and go 0.8 mile; the campground is on the left.
GPS coordinates: N45 23.109' / W121 52.045'
About the campground: This camp above the Sandy River sits in an open lodgepole pine forest on Old Maid Flat—a lahar (volcanic flow of mud and debris) from Mount Hood's active days. Sites are for the most part sunny and dry. The camp has a difficult river access but is within reach of the Mount Hood Wilderness trails and lies just off the 70-mile Mount Hood Loop Drive. The auto tour loop travels East Lolo Pass Road (paved and gravel) to the north side of the mountain, passes through Dee and Parkdale, and then follows OR 35 south and US 26 west to complete the cinch around Mount Hood.

141 Riley Horse Camp

Location: About 5 miles northeast of Zigzag
Season: Late May–Labor Day
Sites: 14 basic sites; no hookups
Maximum length: 16 feet
Facilities: Tables, grills, nonflush toilets, horse corrals, hitching rails; no drinking water
Fee per night: $$
Management: Mount Hood National Forest
Contact: (503) 622-3191; (877) 444-6777 for reservations; www.fs.usda.gov/recmain/mthood/recreation
Finding the campground: From US 26 at Zigzag, turn north onto East Lolo Pass Road (FR 18) and go 4.1 miles. Turn right onto FR 1825, go 1.1 miles, and then turn right onto FR 1825.382 to reach the campground.
GPS coordinates: N45 22.927' / W121 51.658'
About the campground: This quiet camp rests in a mixed conifer forest at the western foot of Mount Hood, just outside Mount Hood Wilderness Area. Equestrians find easy access to trails that enter the wilderness and link up with the Pacific Crest Trail. Lost Creek flows past the camp, and the sites are mostly shaded.

142 Still Creek

Location: About 1 mile southeast of Government Camp
Season: June–Labor Day
Sites: 27 basic sites; no hookups
Maximum length: 16 feet
Facilities: Tables, grills, nonflush toilets, drinking water
Fee per night: $$–$$$
Management: Mount Hood National Forest
Contact: (503) 622-3191; (877) 444-6777 for reservations; www.fs.usda.gov/recmain/mthood/recreation
Finding the campground: From Government Camp go 0.5 mile east on US 26. Turn south onto FR 2650; continue 0.3 mile to the campground.
GPS coordinates: N45 17.745' / W121 44.216'
About the campground: This peaceful camp along Still Creek offers comfortable, well-spaced sites in a rich forest of hemlock and fir with a huckleberry and mixed shrub understory. At the south end of camp is the Old Barlow Road, which you can follow west on foot across Still Creek; a cedar post at the road's start indicates you are on the actual Oregon Trail. By driving 0.4 mile east on Old Barlow Road, you will find Summit Meadows and a pioneer grave. Fishing and quiet boating are possible at Trillium Lake, only 2 miles east; a day-use fee is charged.

143 Tollgate

Location: 3 miles east of Zigzag
Season: Mid-May–Labor Day
Sites: 15 basic sites; no hookups
Maximum length: 16 feet
Facilities: Tables, grills, nonflush toilets, drinking water, rustic picnic shelter
Fee per night: $$–$$$
Management: Mount Hood National Forest
Contact: (503) 622-3191; (877) 444-6777 for reservations; www.fs.usda.gov/recmain/mthood/recreation
Finding the campground: The campground is south off US 26, 17 miles east of Sandy and 0.4 mile east of Rhododendron.
GPS coordinates: N45 19.317' / W121 54.397'
About the campground: Despite its proximity to US 26, this cozy campground occupies a lovely forested flat of mature firs and cedars above the Zigzag River. The campsites have defined, surfaced parking, but a few are awkward to get into with longer vehicles because of the angle of

Picnic shelter at Tollgate Campground, Mt. Hood National Forest

approach and the many trees. A rustic picnic shelter and remnant mossy fireplaces lend charm. East of the campground you will find the historic tollgate on Old Barlow Road, which was part of the Oregon Trail. This interpretive site can be reached via the Pioneer Bridle Trail, at the north end of camp, or via US 26. Special fishing rules apply to the river.

144 Trillium Lake

Location: About 3 miles southeast of Government Camp, on Trillium Lake
Season: June–mid-Oct, dependent on snow
Sites: 57 basic sites; no hookups
Maximum length: 40 feet
Facilities: Tables, grills, nonflush toilets, drinking water, boat launch, fishing pier
Fee per night: $$–$$$
Management: Mount Hood National Forest
Contact: (503) 622-3191; (877) 444-6777 for reservations; www.fs.usda.gov/recmain/mthood/recreation
Finding the campground: From Government Camp travel 1.7 miles east on US 26. Turn south onto FR 2656 and proceed 1.4 miles; the campground is on the right.
GPS coordinates: N45 16.247' / W121 44.106'
About the campground: This campground occupies a rich, diverse forest along the east shore of Trillium Lake, which rests in the shadow of Mount Hood. Lodgepole pine, cedar, fir, mountain hemlock, rhododendron, and bear grass weave an enchanting backdrop. Campers enjoy superb views and photographic opportunities, with a direct view of Mount Hood from the dam. The quiet mountain lake welcomes family recreation with nonmotorized boating, fishing, and hiking on a lakeside trail.

Timothy Lake Area

	Hookup Sites	Total Sites	Max. RV Length	Hookups	Toilets	Showers	Drinking Water	Dump Station	Recreation	Fee	Can Reserve
145 Clackamas Lake		46	32		NF		X		HFR	$$-$$$	X
146 Gone Creek		50	32		NF		X		HFBL	$$	X
147 Hoodview		43	32		NF		X		HFBL	$$	X
148 Joe Graham Horse Camp		14	28		NF		X		HFR	$$$	X
149 Little Crater Lake		16	22		NF		X		H	$$	X
150 Oak Fork		47	32		NF		X		HFBL	$$	X
151 Pine Point		25	32		NF		X		HFBL	$$-$$$	X

145 Clackamas Lake

Location: About 20 miles south of Government Camp
Season: Late May–Labor Day
Sites: 46 basic sites (horses allowed in sites 1–19); no hookups
Maximum length: 32 feet
Facilities: Tables, grills, nonflush toilets, drinking water, hitching posts, pioneer cabin monument
Fee per night: $$-$$$
Management: Mount Hood National Forest
Contact: (503) 622-3191; (877) 444-6777 for reservations; www.fs.usda.gov/recmain/mthood/recreation
Finding the campground: From Government Camp travel 11.5 miles southeast on US 26. Turn right onto paved FR 42 (Skyline Road) and follow it 8.6 miles. Turn left, continuing 0.1 mile to the campground on the left.
GPS coordinates: N45 05.745' / W121 44.890'
About the campground: This campground occupies a mixed forest at the upper edge of Clackamas Meadow, site of the historic Miller Cabin. A boardwalk from camp leads to tiny Clackamas Lake, which feeds into the scenic Oak Grove Fork of the Clackamas River. Springs percolate up through the sandy bottom of this shallow lake. Outings from camp may include visits to Timothy Lake and the Clackamas Historic Ranger Station. The nearby Miller Trail leads to the Pacific Crest Trail.

146 Gone Creek

Location: On Timothy Lake, about 21 miles south of Government Camp
Season: Late May–Labor Day
Sites: 50 basic sites; no hookups
Maximum length: 32 feet
Facilities: Tables, grills, nonflush toilets, drinking water, boat launch
Fee per night: $$
Management: Mount Hood National Forest
Contact: (503) 622-3191; (877) 444-6777 for reservations; www.fs.usda.gov/recmain/mthood/recreation
Finding the campground: From Government Camp travel 11.5 miles southeast on US 26. Turn right onto paved FR 42 (Skyline Road) and follow it for 8.3 miles. Turn right onto FR 57; proceed 1.6 miles to the campground on right.
GPS coordinates: N45 06.748' / W121 46.529'
About the campground: This campground on the south shore of man-made Timothy Lake sits in mixed-age conifer forest with several older firs and hemlocks towering above camp. Most sites receive partial shade. Mount Hood is visible across the reservoir. Camp stays generally include boating (10 miles per hour maximum), fishing, or hiking the Timothy Lake Trail.

147 Hoodview

Location: On Timothy Lake, about 22 miles south of Government Camp
Season: Late May–Labor Day
Sites: 43 basic sites; no hookups
Maximum length: 32 feet
Facilities: Tables, grills, nonflush toilets, drinking water, boat launch
Fee per night: $$
Management: Mount Hood National Forest
Contact: (503) 622-3191; (877) 444-6777 for reservations; www.fs.usda.gov/recmain/mthood/recreation
Finding the campground: From Government Camp travel 11.5 miles southeast on US 26. Turn right onto paved FR 42 (Skyline Road) and follow it for 8.3 miles. Turn right onto FR 57; proceed 2.6 miles to the campground on the right.
GPS coordinates: N45 06.475' / W121 47.515'
About the campground: On the south shore of man-made Timothy Lake, this campground boasts some big firs and mountain hemlocks in its mixed-age forest that offers good shade. In early summer rhododendron pompoms decorate camp. Premium-priced sites overlook the lake, with Mount Hood viewed from shore. Boating (10 miles per hour maximum), fishing, and the 13-mile Timothy Lake Trail, which circles the lake, keep campers occupied.

148 Joe Graham Horse Camp

Location: About 19 miles south of Government Camp
Season: June–Sept
Sites: 14 basic sites; no hookups
Maximum length: 28 feet
Facilities: Tables, grills, nonflush toilets, drinking water, corrals
Fee per night: $$$
Management: Mount Hood National Forest
Contact: (503) 622-3191; (877) 444-6777 for reservations; www.fs.usda.gov/recmain/mthood/recreation
Finding the campground: From Government Camp travel 11.5 miles southeast on US 26. Turn right onto paved FR 42 (Skyline Road) and follow it 7.2 miles. Turn left onto FR 021 for the horse camp.
GPS coordinates: N45 06.029' / W121 44.803'
About the campground: Adjacent to the Oak Grove Fork Clackamas River and picturesque Clackamas Meadow, this campground for the exclusive use of equestrians rests in an old-growth forest of fir and hemlock. The camp has large pole corrals and spacious sites to accommodate horse trailers and camp vehicles. It offers a peaceful, attractive stay and affords access to area horse and hiking trails and fishing.

149 Little Crater Lake

Location: On Little Crater Lake, about 18 miles south of Government Camp
Season: June–Labor Day
Sites: 16 basic sites; no hookups
Maximum length: 22 feet
Facilities: Tables, grills, nonflush toilets, drinking water, paved trail to Little Crater Lake
Fee per night: $$
Management: Mount Hood National Forest
Contact: (503) 622-3191; (877) 444-6777 for reservations; www.fs.usda.gov/recmain/mthood/recreation
Finding the campground: From Government Camp go 11.5 miles southeast on US 26. Turn right onto paved FR 42 (Skyline Road) and follow it 4.1 miles. Turn right onto paved FR 58, heading toward High Rock. Continue 2.3 miles and turn left to enter the camp.
GPS coordinates: N45 08.903' / W121 44.740'
About the campground: Little Crater Lake, the star attraction of this camp, is an artesian-fed lake of dazzling color. Though only an acre in size, the lake is 45 feet deep. The water is 34 degrees Fahrenheit, and its clarity reveals silvery logs on the lake bottom. The lake's rustic viewing platform is just a pleasant meadow walk from camp; meadow wildlife sightings are common. Lupine, gentian, and false hellebore sprinkle color in the meadow. For longer adventures, an earthen trail beyond the lake links up with the Pacific Crest Trail in 0.5 mile. The campground itself is tucked in forest and has gravel parking spurs.

150 Oak Fork

Location: On Timothy Lake, about 21 miles south of Government Camp
Season: Late May–mid-Oct
Sites: 47 basic sites; no hookups
Maximum length: 32 feet
Facilities: Tables, grills, nonflush toilets, drinking water, boat launch, dock
Fee per night: $$
Management: Mount Hood National Forest
Contact: (503) 622-3191; (877) 444-6777 for reservations; www.fs.usda.gov/recmain/mthood/recreation
Finding the campground: From Government Camp go 11.5 miles southeast on US 26. Turn right onto paved FR 42 (Skyline Road) and follow it for 8.3 miles. Turn right onto FR 57 and proceed 1.4 miles; the campground is on the right.
GPS coordinates: N45 06.907' / W121 46.284'
About the campground: On the southeast shore of Timothy Lake, these campsites sit slightly back from the reservoir's edge in a rich atmosphere of full shade. The camp offers sites with lake views, gravel parking (some pull-through), and a recreational lineup that includes boating (10 miles per hour maximum), fishing, and hiking the Timothy Lake Trail or the Miller Trail, which also visits the lake area.

151 Pine Point

Location: On Timothy Lake, about 23 miles south of Government Camp
Season: Late May–Labor Day
Sites: 13 single basic sites, 8 double sites, 4 group sites; no hookups
Maximum length: 32 feet
Facilities: Tables, grills, nonflush toilets, drinking water, boat launch
Fee per night: $$–$$$
Management: Mount Hood National Forest
Contact: (503) 622-3191; (877) 444-6777 for reservations; www.fs.usda.gov/recmain/mthood/recreation
Finding the campground: From Government Camp go 11.5 miles southeast on US 26. Turn right onto paved FR 42 (Skyline Road) and follow it for 8.3 miles. Turn right onto FR 57 and proceed 3.2 miles; the campground is on the right.
GPS coordinates: N45 06.789' / W121 47.987'
About the campground: This campground occupies a second-growth forest on the southwest shore of Timothy Lake, a man-made lake with gravelly sand beaches. Timber cutting has left a patchwork on the enfolding hills; younger forest rims the lake. Located near the dam, this campground offers semi-open sites with gravel parking pads (some pull-through). Several sites have lake views. Boating is kept to 10 miles per hour maximum to preserve the quiet. Fishing or hiking along the Timothy Lake Trail also engages campers.

Estacada-Clackamas River Area

	Hookup Sites	Total Sites	Max. RV Length	Hookups	Toilets	Showers	Drinking Water	Dump Station	Recreation	Fee	Can Reserve
152 Armstrong		11	16		NF		X		FB	$$	X
153 Carter Bridge		15	28		NF				FBL	$$	
154 Fish Creek		24	16		NF		X		FB	$$	X
155 Hideaway Lake		9	16		NF				HFB	$$	
156 Indian Henry		86	36		F		X		HFB	$$	X
157 Kingfisher		23	36		NF		X		F	$$	X
158 Lake Harriet		13	30		NF		X		FBL	$$	X
159 Lazy Bend		21	24		F		X		FB	$$	X
160 Lockaby		30	16		NF		X		FBL	$$	X
161 Metzler County Park	60	70	35	WE	F	X	X	X	HSF	$$$	X
162 Milo McIver State Park	44	53	50	WE	F	X	X	X	HFBLRC	$$	X
163 Promontory Park		50	35		F	X	X		FBL	$$-$$$	X
164 Raab		26	22		NF				SF	$$	X
165 Rainbow		17	24		NF				HF	$$	X
166 Ripplebrook		13	16		NF				F	$$	X
167 Riverford		10	16		NF				F	$$	
168 Riverside		16	22		NF		X		HF	$$	X
169 Roaring River		14	16		NF		X		HF	$$	X
170 Shellrock Creek		7	16		NF				HF	$$	
171 Sunstrip		9	18		NF				HB	$$	X

152 Armstrong

Location: About 14 miles southeast of Estacada
Season: May–Sept
Sites: 11 basic sites; no hookups
Maximum length: 16 feet
Facilities: Tables, grills, nonflush toilets, drinking water
Fee per night: $$
Management: Mount Hood National Forest
Contact: (503) 630-6861; (877) 444-6777 for reservations; www.fs.usda.gov/recmain/mthood/recreation

Finding the campground: From Estacada go 14.1 miles southeast on OR 224; the campground is on the right.

GPS coordinates: N45 09.713' / W122 09.129'

About the campground: Part of the Clackamas Wild and Scenic River lineup of campgrounds, this facility offers gravel site parking in a setting of young cedar and maple trees. It sits at the foot of a slope near a bridge and has a grassy bank for easy river access.

153 Carter Bridge

Location: About 14 miles southeast of Estacada

Season: May–Sept

Sites: 15 basic sites; no hookups

Maximum length: 28 feet

Facilities: Tables, grills, nonflush toilets; no drinking water

Fee per night: $$

Management: Mount Hood National Forest

Contact: (503) 630-6861; www.fs.usda.gov/recmain/mthood/recreation

Finding the campground: From Estacada go 13.6 miles southeast on OR 224; the campground is on the left.

GPS coordinates: N45 10.056' / W122 09.365'

About the campground: Sitting in a young forest of cedar, maple, and alder, this Clackamas River camp still enjoys a nice amount of shade. The camp is just downstream from a whitewater launch site and, like most of its overnight counterparts, offers river fishing.

154 Fish Creek

Location: About 14 miles southeast of Estacada

Season: May–Sept

Sites: 24 basic sites; no hookups

Maximum length: 16 feet

Facilities: Tables, grills, nonflush toilets, drinking water

Fee per night: $$

Management: Mount Hood National Forest

Contact: (503) 630-6861; (877) 444-6777 for reservations; www.fs.usda.gov/recmain/mthood/recreation

Finding the campground: From Estacada go 14.2 miles southeast on OR 224. Turn right onto Fish Creek Road to enter the campground.

GPS coordinates: N45 09.534' / W122 09.179'

About the campground: This campground claims an attractive forested bench along the Clackamas River. Rhododendrons seasonally color the campground. For most visitors fishing is the river's primary allure, with fly rods the chosen arsenal. Early in the year, kayaking and rafting bring their own following to the river.

155 Hideaway Lake

Location: On Hideaway Lake, about 41 miles southeast of Estacada
Season: Mid-June–Sept
Sites: 9 basic sites; no hookups
Maximum length: 16 feet
Facilities: Tables, grills, nonflush toilets; no drinking water
Fee per night: $$
Management: Mount Hood National Forest
Contact: (503) 630-6861; www.fs.usda.gov/recmain/mthood/recreation
Finding the campground: From Estacada go 25 miles southeast on OR 224 and continue east on FR 57 for another 7.4 miles. Turn left onto FR 58, go 3.1 miles, and again turn left onto FR 5830. Proceed 5.3 miles more; turn left to reach the camp in 0.2 mile.
GPS coordinates: N45 07.402' / W121 57.999'
About the campground: This rustic camp, best suited for tents, provides access to an idyllic 12-acre lake tucked away in a hemlock-fir forest. Thirty feet deep, Hideaway Lake naturally produces both rainbow and brown trout. Because the thick vegetation limits shore access, inflatable fishing tubes and rafts serve anglers well. Hikers can trace the Shellrock Trail from the northwest shore of Hideaway Lake to Rock Lakes Basin Loop. This all-day hike or backpack visits additional remote lakes, which offer solitude and fishing. Serene Lake is the largest of the hike-to lakes.

156 Indian Henry

Location: About 21 miles southeast of Estacada
Season: Mid-May–Sept
Sites: 86 basic sites; no hookups
Maximum length: 36 feet
Facilities: Tables, grills, flush toilets, drinking water
Fee per night: $$
Management: Mount Hood National Forest
Contact: (503) 630-6861; (877) 444-6777 for reservations; www.fs.usda.gov/recmain/mthood/recreation
Finding the campground: From Estacada go 20.5 miles southeast on OR 224. Bear right onto FR 4620 just before the bridge. Continue 0.6 mile to the campground on the left; the Clackamas River Trail is on the right.
GPS coordinates: N45 06.487' / W122 04.565'
About the campground: This Clackamas River campground offers paved sites in a tall forest of hemlock, cedar, and fir. Hazardous tree removal has temporarily altered the forest's settled look and opened its cathedral. Across from camp you can access the 8-mile river trail; midway along it, a side spur takes you to the long plummet of Pup Falls. Fishing and rafting are primary river pursuits.

157 Kingfisher

Location: About 34 miles southeast of Estacada
Season: Late May–Sept
Sites: 23 basic sites; no hookups
Maximum length: 36 feet
Facilities: Tables, grills, nonflush toilets, drinking water
Fee per night: $$
Management: Mount Hood National Forest
Contact: (503) 630-6861; (877) 444-6777 for reservations; www.fs.usda.gov/recmain/mthood/recreation
Finding the campground: From Estacada go 25 miles southeast on OR 224 to its junction with FR 57 and FR 46. Bear right onto FR 46 and travel 3.5 miles. Turn right onto FR 63 and continue 3.5 miles. Turn right onto FR 70 toward Bagby Hot Springs; follow it 1.7 miles to reach the campground on the left.
GPS coordinates: N44 58.625' / W122 05.466'
About the campground: This forest campground sits along the Hot Springs Fork Collawash River and is the closest developed campground to Bagby Hot Springs. Beautiful old-growth firs and cedars and a vibrant midstory contribute to the camp's invitation. Gravel bars give anglers access to the river and their chosen sport.

158 Lake Harriet

Location: On Lake Harriet, about 32 miles southeast of Estacada
Season: May–Sept
Sites: 13 basic sites; no hookups
Maximum length: 30 feet
Facilities: Tables, grills, nonflush toilets, drinking water
Fee per night: $$
Management: Mount Hood National Forest
Contact: (503) 630-6861; (877) 444-6777 for reservations; www.fs.usda.gov/recmain/mthood/recreation
Finding the campground: From Estacada go 25 miles southeast on OR 224 to its junction with FR 57 and FR 46. Bear left onto FR 57 and travel 6.3 miles. Turn left onto gravel FR 4630; continue 1.1 miles to the campground.
GPS coordinates: N45 04.396' / W121 57.524'
About the campground: This campground occupies the alder-and-fir perimeter of a large, dirt parking flat where the Oak Grove Fork Clackamas River feeds into man-made Lake Harriet. The elongated reservoir sits at the foot of steep forested hillsides. A sandy boat ramp in the camp allows you to launch a rowboat or raft for fishing. No motors are allowed on the lake.

159 Lazy Bend

Location: About 9 miles southeast of Estacada
Season: May–mid-Oct
Sites: 21 basic sites; no hookups
Maximum length: 24 feet
Facilities: Tables, grills, flush toilets, drinking water
Fee per night: $$
Management: Mount Hood National Forest
Contact: (503) 630-6861; (877) 444-6777 for reservations; www.fs.usda.gov/recmain/mthood/recreation
Finding the campground: From Estacada go 9.3 miles southeast on OR 224; the campground is on the right.
GPS coordinates: N45 11.452' / W122 12.494'
About the campground: On the Clackamas Wild and Scenic River, this campground has paved site parking in a rich setting of firs, maples, and alders. Cascaras, filberts, and vine maples fill out the midstory. The steep, forested slope across from camp adds to the naturalness of the setting. An informal riverside path heading upstream from camp serves anglers.

160 Lockaby

Location: 14 miles southeast of Estacada
Season: May–Sept
Sites: 30 basic sites; no hookups
Maximum length: 16 feet
Facilities: Tables, grills, nonflush toilets, drinking water
Fee per night: $$
Management: Mount Hood National Forest
Contact: (503) 630-6861; (877) 444-6777 for reservations; www.fs.usda.gov/recmain/mthood/recreation
Finding the campground: From Estacada go 14 miles southeast on OR 224; the campground is on the left.
GPS coordinates: N45 09.921' / W122 09.170'
About the campground: This campground is just upstream from a raft put-in site on the Clackamas River. It occupies a narrow forest corridor of cedars, maples, dogwoods, and alders. Several sites sit a few strides off the campground road but are close to the river. The Clackamas is a popular fishing water and provides a relaxing backdrop to a stay.

161 Metzler County Park

Location: About 6 miles southwest of Estacada
Season: May–Sept
Sites: 60 hookup sites, 10 basic sites; water and electric hookups
Maximum length: 35 feet
Facilities: Tables, barbecues, flush toilets, drinking water, showers, dump station, playground, ball fields, horseshoe pits
Fee per night: $$$
Management: Clackamas County
Contact: (503) 742-4414, reservations accepted; online reservations: http://reservations .clackamas.us/; www.co.clackamas.or.us/parks
Finding the campground: From the junction of OR 211 and OR 224 in south Estacada, go 3.7 miles south on OR 211. Turn right (west) onto South Tucker/South Springwater Road and continue 0.6 mile. Turn left onto Metzler Park Road to make a steep descent into the park. Turn right for the campground in 1.8 miles.
GPS coordinates: N45 13.701' / W122 21.949'
About the campground: Ideal for family getaways, this charming county park rests along Clear Creek, where three swimming holes keep campers cool in summer and brook trout provide sport for fishing enthusiasts. The rustic basic sites, which sit closer to the creek, are shaded by cedar, fir, and maple trees. The hookup sites sit farther back in younger woods. A nature trail suggests a stroll.

162 Milo McIver State Park

Location: About 4 miles west of Estacada
Season: Mid-Mar–Oct
Sites: 44 hookup sites, 9 basic sites; water and electric hookups
Maximum length: 50 feet
Facilities: Tables, grills, flush toilets, drinking water, showers, dump station, disc golf, boat launch, fish hatchery, picnic shelters
Fee per night: $$
Management: Oregon State Parks and Recreation Department
Contact: (503) 630-7150; (800) 452-5687 for reservations; www.oregon.gov/OPRD/PARKS/ camping.shtml
Finding the campground: From the junction of OR 211 and OR 224 in Estacada, go 1 mile south on OR 211. Turn right (west) onto South Hayden Road and proceed 1.3 miles. Turn right onto South Springwater Road and continue 1.2 miles to reach the park entrance on the right. Follow the signs into the campground.
GPS coordinates: N45 17.783' / W122 21.363'
About the campground: Along the Clackamas River, this large state park features both groomed and natural areas. In addition to its developed, wooded campground, it has sweeping grassy picnic areas dotted with shade trees and riparian woods crisscrossed by hiking and equestrian trails.

Wildlife sightings add to the enjoyment, while a bike path offers another way to see the park. The disc golf course covers a good-size area, but fishing, boating, and rafting remain top draws.

163 Promontory Park

Location: At North Fork Reservoir, 6 miles southeast of Estacada
Season: Mid-May–mid-Sept
Sites: 50 basic sites, 13 yomes (cross between tent and cabin); no hookups
Maximum length: 35 feet
Facilities: Tables, grills, flush toilets, drinking water, showers, camp store, playground, children's fishing pond, boat moorage, boat rental, launch, docks
Fee per night: $$; $$$ for yomes
Management: Portland General Electric
Contact: (503) 630-7229 (for information and reservations); www.portlandgeneral.com/parks
Finding the campground: From the junction of OR 211 and OR 224 in south Estacada, go east on OR 224 for 6.1 miles. Turn right to enter the park and then make a quick left. Follow signs through the park to the campground.
GPS coordinates: N45 13.352' / W122 14.635'
About the campground: This campground provides access to 350-acre North Fork Reservoir, a popular place for boating and fishing, and to 1-acre Small Fry Lake, a stocked fishing pond where youngsters can catch a two-fish daily limit. The developed sites sit fairly close together in a forest of tall Douglas fir. A few sites overlook the steep bank to the long, narrow reservoir.

164 Raab

Location: About 29 miles southeast of Estacada
Season: Mid-May–early Sept
Sites: 26 basic sites; no hookups
Maximum length: 22 feet
Facilities: Tables, grills, nonflush toilets; no drinking water
Fee per night: $$
Management: Mount Hood National Forest
Contact: (503) 630-6861; (877) 444-6777 for reservations; www.fs.usda.gov/recmain/mthood/recreation
Finding the campground: From Estacada go 25 miles southeast on OR 224 to its junction with FR 57 and FR 46. Bear right onto FR 46 and go 3.5 miles. Turn right onto FR 63; the campground is on the right in 0.7 mile.
GPS coordinates: N45 01.355' / W122 04.172'
About the campground: On a bluff above the Collawash River, this campground is framed by rhododendrons and tall firs and cedars. A wire-mesh fence separates the campground from the edge of the bluff; below are enticing green pools. If you follow the fence upstream, it leads to an outcrop

overlooking a stretch of rushing river, but there is no access here. Farther upstream, a gravel bar provides river access.

165 Rainbow

Location: About 25 miles southeast of Estacada
Season: Mid-May–early Sept
Sites: 17 basic sites; no hookups
Maximum length: 24 feet
Facilities: Tables, grills, nonflush toilets; no drinking water
Fee per night: $$
Management: Mount Hood National Forest
Contact: (503) 630-6861; (877) 444-6777 for reservations; www.fs.usda.gov/recmain/mthood/recreation
Finding the campground: From Estacada go 25 miles southeast on OR 224 to its junction with FR 57 and FR 46. Bear right onto FR 46; the campground is on the right in less than 0.1 mile.
GPS coordinates: N45 04.572' / W122 02.708'
About the campground: This campground basks in a multistory forest along the Oak Grove Fork Clackamas River, above its confluence with the main stem Clackamas River. The forest is visually rich with Douglas fir, cedar, moss-festooned bigleaf maple, vine maple, hazel, and an understory floral mosaic. Some sites rest along the river. The Riverside Trail travels along both waterways and through old-growth forest, passing between Rainbow and Riverside Campgrounds. Fishing is popular.

166 Ripplebrook

Location: About 26 miles southeast of Estacada
Season: Mid-May–early Sept
Sites: 13 basic sites; no hookups
Maximum length: 16 feet
Facilities: Tables, grills, nonflush toilets; no drinking water
Fee per night: $$
Management: Mount Hood National Forest
Contact: (503) 630-6861; (877) 444-6777 for reservations; www.fs.usda.gov/recmain/mthood/recreation
Finding the campground: From Estacada go almost 25 miles southeast on OR 224; turn left to enter the campground. The turn is just before the junction of OR 224 and FR 57 and FR 46.
GPS coordinates: N45 04.813' / W122 02.502'
About the campground: This campground stretches for more than 0.25 mile along the Oak Grove Fork Clackamas River. Due to its linear design, a number of sites offer fine river views. Douglas fir, cedar, and bigleaf maple trees shade the campsites; the understory explodes with greenery. Fishing or exploring the prized area hiking trails engage visitors.

167 Riverford

Location: About 29 miles southeast of Estacada
Season: Mid-May–early Sept
Sites: 7 basic sites, 3 walk-in tent sites; no hookups
Maximum length: 16 feet
Facilities: Tables, grills, nonflush toilets; no drinking water
Fee per night: $$
Management: Mount Hood National Forest
Contact: (503) 630-6861; www.fs.usda.gov/recmain/mthood/recreation
Finding the campground: From Estacada go 25 miles southeast on OR 224 to its junction with FR 57 and FR 46. Bear right onto FR 46 and go 3.6 miles; the campground is on the right. (The campground entrance is 0.1 mile past the junction with FR 63.)
GPS coordinates: N45 01.968' / W122 03.552'
About the campground: This small, remote campground occupies a low bluff above the Clackamas Wild and Scenic River. Many of the sites offer river views, and a mixed-age woods supplies shade. The pleasant retreat serves fishing enthusiasts. Off FR 63 you can locate the trailheads to Bagby Hot Springs and Bull of the Woods Wilderness.

168 Riverside

Location: About 28 miles southeast of Estacada
Season: Mid-May–early Sept
Sites: 10 basic sites, 6 walk-in tent sites; no hookups
Maximum length: 22 feet
Facilities: Tables, grills, nonflush toilets, drinking water
Fee per night: $$
Management: Mount Hood National Forest
Contact: (503) 630-6861; (877) 444-6777 for reservations; www.fs.usda.gov/recmain/mthood/recreation
Finding the campground: From Estacada go 25 miles southeast on OR 224 to its junction with FR 57 and FR 46. Bear right onto FR 46 and go 2.9 miles; the campground is on the right.
GPS coordinates: N45 02.619' / W122 03.721'
About the campground: This campground rests on a low bluff above the main stem Clackamas Wild and Scenic River. Some sites overlook the water; others are wrapped in glorious forest. Grassy flats claim forest openings. The campground has a paved road and parking pads. Birds enliven the canopy with movement and song, and wily trout beckon anglers. The Riverside Trail, with its old-growth trees, invites a stroll.

169 Roaring River

Location: About 17 miles southeast of Estacada
Season: Late May–early Sept
Sites: 14 basic sites; no hookups
Maximum length: 16 feet
Facilities: Tables, grills, nonflush toilets, drinking water
Fee per night: $$
Management: Mount Hood National Forest
Contact: (503) 630-6861; (877) 444-6777 for reservations; www.fs.usda.gov/recmain/mthood/recreation
Finding the campground: From Estacada go 16.5 miles southeast on OR 224; the campground is on the left.
GPS coordinates: N45 09.502' / W122 06.901'
About the campground: This campground has access to two federally designated Wild and Scenic Rivers. It sits across the road from the Clackamas River, while the picturesque Roaring River races along the campground's western edge. The facility primarily serves tent campers, with its sites tucked among the old-growth cedars and firs and moss-draped maples. The Roaring River Trail climbs away from camp; for fishing, the Clackamas River is the better bet.

170 Shellrock Creek

Location: About 33 miles southeast of Estacada
Season: Mid-June–early Sept
Sites: 7 basic sites; no hookups
Maximum length: 16 feet
Facilities: Tables, grills, nonflush toilets; no drinking water
Fee per night: $$
Management: Mount Hood National Forest
Contact: (503) 630-6861; www.fs.usda.gov/recmain/mthood/recreation
Finding the campground: From Estacada go 25 miles southeast on OR 224 to its junction with FR 57 and FR 46. Bear left onto FR 57 and go 7.3 miles. Turn left onto FR 58 and proceed 0.4 mile; the campground is on the left.
GPS coordinates: N45 05.089' / W121 55.348'
About the campground: This small overnight facility is best suited for tent camping. It rests along picturesque Shellrock Creek in a forest of big firs and cedars interspersed with yew trees and rhododendrons. Sites receive a mix of sun and shade. Parking is along the widened, gravel road shoulder; some sites have better tent flats than others. From this quiet camp you may fish or hike the 0.5-mile Pacific Yew Trail, which starts near the bridge but can be overgrown.

171 Sunstrip

Location: About 17 miles southeast of Estacada
Season: May–Sept
Sites: 9 basic sites; no hookups
Maximum length: 18 feet
Facilities: Tables, grills, nonflush toilets; no drinking water
Fee per night: $$
Management: Mount Hood National Forest
Contact: (503) 630-6861; (877) 444-6777 for reservations; www.fs.usda.gov/recmain/mthood/recreation
Finding the campground: From Estacada go 17.1 miles southeast on OR 224; the campground is on the right.
GPS coordinates: N45 09.050' / W122 06.388'
About the campground: This small Clackamas River campground is nestled in the shoreline forest of maple, fir, and hemlock. A few sites overlook the river. Across from camp rises a steep canyon slope. Fishing is the primary pursuit.

Olallie Lake Scenic Area

	Hookup Sites	Total Sites	Max. RV Length	Hookups	Toilets	Showers	Drinking Water	Dump Station	Recreation	Fee	Can Reserve
172 Camp Ten		10	16		NF				HFB	$$	
173 Lower Lake		8	16		NF				HF	$$	
174 Olallie Meadows		7	16		NF				HR	$$	
175 Paul Dennis		17	16		NF				HFB	$$	
176 Peninsula		35	24		NF				HFB	$$	
177 Triangle Lake Equestrian Camp		8	30		NF				HR	$$	

172 Camp Ten

Location: On Olallie Lake, about 39 miles northeast of Detroit
Season: Mid-June–Sept
Sites: 10 basic sites; no hookups
Maximum length: 16 feet
Facilities: Tables, grills, nonflush toilets; no drinking water
Fee per night: $$
Management: Mount Hood National Forest
Contact: (503) 630-6861; www.fs.usda.gov/recmain/mthood/recreation
Finding the campground: From OR 22 in Detroit, head northeast on FR 46 for 25 miles. Turn east onto FR 4690 and follow it for 8.1 miles. (The route changes to gravel after 6 miles.) Turn right onto gravel FR 4220 for Olallie Lake Scenic Area. Continue for 6.2 miles; the campground is on the left.
GPS coordinates: N44 48.179' / W121 47.324'
About the campground: On the southwest shore of Olallie Lake, this campground has closely spaced sites in a forest of lichen-festooned mountain hemlock and spruce. Parking can be restrictive in some areas. A few sites overlook Olallie Lake, a beautiful, big high-mountain lake that pairs with an Olallie Butte view. A hiking trail encircles Olallie Lake but requires a walk along the road on the lake's west shore. The huckleberry bushes draw berry pickers in late summer. Fishing and nonmotorized boating keep campers on the go.

173 Lower Lake

Location: Near Lower Lake, about 38 miles northeast of Detroit
Season: Mid-June–Sept
Sites: 8 basic sites; no hookups
Maximum length: 16 feet
Facilities: Tables, grills, nonflush toilets; no drinking water
Fee per night: $$
Management: Mount Hood National Forest
Contact: (503) 630-6861; www.fs.usda.gov/recmain/mthood/recreation
Finding the campground: From OR 22 in Detroit, head northeast on FR 46 for 25 miles. Turn east onto FR 4690 and follow it for 8.1 miles. (The route changes to gravel after 6 miles.) Turn right onto gravel FR 4220 for Olallie Lake Scenic Area. Continue for 4.5 miles; the campground is on the right.
GPS coordinates: N44 49.393' / W121 47.857'
About the campground: In a mountain forest of spruce, fir, pine, and hemlock, this campground offers a quiet retreat. A talus slope abuts one site. A 0.5-mile trail leads from camp to the scenery, fishing, and huckleberry and blueberry patches at Lower Lake. From the fork in the trail beyond Lower Lake, you can walk 1 mile to Fish Lake, snuggled in a deep, treed basin. Or you can hike 3 miles to Red Lake, passing a string of lakes en route.

174 Olallie Meadows

Location: About 35 miles northeast of Detroit
Season: Mid-June–Sept
Sites: 7 basic sites, 1 rental cabin; no hookups
Maximum length: 16 feet
Facilities: Tables, grills, nonflush toilet; no drinking water
Fee per night: $$
Management: Mount Hood National Forest
Contact: (503) 630-6861; www.fs.usda.gov/recmain/mthood/recreation
Finding the campground: From OR 22 in Detroit, head northeast on FR 46 for 25 miles. Turn east on FR 4690 and follow it for 8.1 miles. (The route changes to gravel after 6 miles.) Turn right onto gravel FR 4220 toward Olallie Lake Scenic Area. The campground is on the left in another 1.4 miles.
GPS coordinates: N44 51.470' / W121 46.383'
About the campground: Lodgepole pine and spruce enclose this campground and rustic cabin at the edge of picturesque Olallie Meadows—a rich, moist, textured meadow of grasses, wildflowers, and blueberries. You can sometimes spy deer or sandhill cranes in the lea. Views include Olallie, Sisi, and Badger Buttes. Horses may be tethered to horse trailers at camp, but the animals are not allowed in the meadow. The trail to Russ Lake begins at camp and passes two other mountain lakes along the way. Come prepared for mosquitoes. The forest service is considering making this an overflow camp facility, so you might be directed first to one of the other camps.

175 Paul Dennis

Location: On Olallie Lake, about 39 miles northeast of Detroit
Season: Mid-June–Sept
Sites: 17 basic sites; no hookups
Maximum length: 16 feet
Facilities: Tables, grills, nonflush toilets; no drinking water
Fee per night: $$
Management: Mount Hood National Forest
Contact: (503) 630-6861; www.fs.usda.gov/recmain/mthood/recreation
Finding the campground: From OR 22 in Detroit, head northeast on FR 46 for 25 miles. Turn east onto FR 4690 and follow it for 8.1 miles. (The route changes to gravel after 6 miles.) Turn right onto gravel FR 4220 toward Olallie Lake Scenic Area. Continue 5.2 miles and turn left to reach the campground in 0.25 mile.
GPS coordinates: N44 48.634' / W121 47.208'
About the campground: On the northeast shore of Olallie Lake, next door to rustic Olallie Lake Resort, a setting of lodgepole pines and mountain hemlocks enfolds this campground. Dwarf huckleberry and bear grass spread between the trees. Some sites overlook the big mountain lake, but all lie within easy access of the lake for fishing, nonmotorized boating, and admiring. A lakeshore trail nearly circles the lake and provides access to trails into Olallie Lake Scenic Area.

176 Peninsula

Location: On Olallie Lake, about 40 miles northeast of Detroit
Season: Mid-June–Sept
Sites: 35 basic sites; no hookups
Maximum length: 24 feet
Facilities: Tables, grills, nonflush toilets; no drinking water
Fee per night: $$
Management: Mount Hood National Forest
Contact: (503) 630-6861; www.fs.usda.gov/recmain/mthood/recreation
Finding the campground: From OR 22 in Detroit, head northeast on FR 46 for 25 miles. Turn east onto FR 4690 and follow it for 8.1 miles. (The route changes to gravel after 6 miles.) Turn right onto gravel FR 4220 toward Olallie Lake Scenic Area. Reach the campground on the left in 6.6 miles.
GPS coordinates: N44 48.138' / W121 47.010'
About the campground: This campground occupies a high-elevation forest on a peninsula of beautiful, blue Olallie Lake. Some sites look out on the lake and the towering profile of Olallie Butte. Huckleberry picking, hiking, fishing, and quiet boating are favorite pastimes at and near camp.

177 Triangle Lake Equestrian Camp

Location: About 35 miles northeast of Detroit
Season: Mid-June–Sept
Sites: 8 basic sites; no hookups
Maximum length: 30 feet
Facilities: Tables, grills, nonflush toilets, corrals; no drinking water
Fee per night: $$
Management: Mount Hood National Forest
Contact: (503) 630-6861; www.fs.usda.gov/recmain/mthood/recreation
Finding the campground: From OR 22 in Detroit, head northeast on FR 46 for 25 miles. Turn east onto FR 4690 and follow it for 8.1 miles. (The route changes to gravel after 6 miles.) Turn right onto gravel FR 4220 toward Olallie Lake Scenic Area. The campground is on the right in 2.1 miles.
GPS coordinates: N44 51.009' / W121 46.585'
About the campground: For the exclusive use of equestrians, this campground offers tranquil sites in a setting of lodgepole pines and mountain hemlocks. Long gravel parking pads accommodate both camp vehicles and horse trailers. Within Olallie Lake Scenic Area, equestrians find a variety of trails open to riding, but the short trail to shallow, marshy Triangle Lake is off-limits to horses. Fishing, quiet boating, and berry picking can fill out a stay.

Willamette Valley and Western Cascades Slope

Between the Cascade Mountains and the Coast Range stretches the broad, fertile Willamette Valley fed by the Willamette River, which originates high in the snowy Cascades. The rich soil and mild climate of the Willamette Valley inspired thousands of families in the mid-1800s to make the grueling, 2,000-mile overland journey west on the Oregon Trail. The allure of fertile soil was the rival of gold, which fed the California gold rush at about the same time.

The valley is prime wildlife habitat; common sightings include Canada geese, ospreys, bald eagles, herons, deer, and the state animal—the beaver. The valley is also a critical migration and wintering spot on the Pacific Flyway. One of the best and most relaxing ways to watch wildlife is from a raft. The Willamette River was seemingly made for a lazy float trip. You may contact an outfitter, or pick up the *Willamette River Recreation Guide* from the Oregon State Parks and Recreation Department or a local visitor center. This brochure, complete with a river trail map, shows put-in and take-out spots, mileages, and approximate river flow and float times. Hiking trails offer another way to enjoy the valley scenery and wildlife—but learn what poison oak looks like and where it grows. Paved trails along river greenways serve cyclists, wheelchair users, exercise walkers, joggers, and families pushing baby strollers.

You need not get your hands dirty to share in the land's bounty. Roadside produce stands teem with baskets, lugs, and bins of fresh fruits, vegetables, and nuts. The many varieties astound and the tastes tantalize. But if you are a hands-on person, there are also plenty of U-pick farms. The Willamette Valley is noted for its fine berries and Pinot Noir grapes. Throughout the valley, award-winning wineries open their tasting rooms to the public.

Back roads will take you past covered bridges, river ferries, tulip fields, Christmas tree farms, golf courses, fishing waters, and blackberry brambles. At the heart of the valley, along the busy artery of I-5, are the region's two major cities: Salem, the state

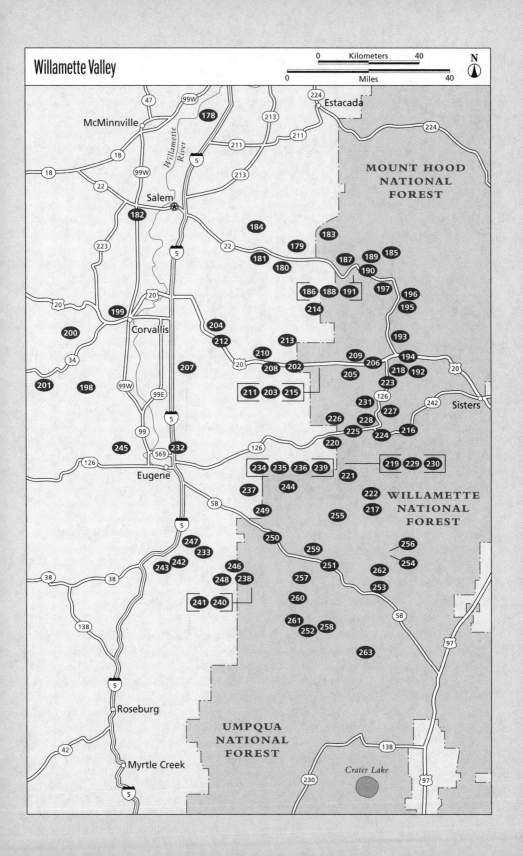

Royal Anne cherries, Marion County

capital, and Eugene, a university town. Smaller farm and forest towns extend yesteryear charm.

The mild Willamette Valley climate allows year-round recreation, if you do not mind braving the occasional rainstorm. Winter visitors should bring a full suit of rain gear and a sunny disposition. Summer days bask in sunlight, with temperatures climbing into the 90s, but humidity is seldom a problem.

This region also encompasses the western slope of the central Cascade Mountain Range, which makes up the Willamette River watershed. It brings together the spectacular scenery and recreational lineup of the upper Willamette, Santiam, and McKenzie River drainages. Among the attractions are scenic byways, hiking trails, old-growth forest, sterling waterfalls, and prized waters for fishing, canoeing, speed boating, and water-skiing. Winter sports expand the offering. But whether you are working up a sweat or simply kicking back at camp, the mountain offering is top-notch.

The Cascades experience four distinct seasons, with the lower elevations remaining mild year-round. Winter rain typically claims the lower flanks, changing to snow before the passes and upper mountain reaches. Mixed conditions characterize spring and fall, and afternoon thunderstorms are possible in summer.

Salem Area

	Hookup Sites	Total Sites	Max. RV Length	Hookups	Toilets	Showers	Drinking Water	Dump Station	Recreation	Fee	Can Reserve
178 Champoeg State Park	79	85	50	WES	F	X	X	X	HFBC	$$–$$$	X
179 Elkhorn Valley Recreation Site		23	18		NF		X		SF	$$	
180 Fisherman's Bend Recreation Site	49	54	40	WES	F	X	X	X	HFBL	$$–$$$	X
181 John Neal Memorial Park	10	23	60	W	F	X	X		FBL	$$$	X
182 Polk County Fairgrounds	100	100	40	WE	F	X	X	X		$$	
183 Shady Cove		13	16		NF				HSF	$	
184 Silver Falls State Park	47	99	60	WE	F	X	X	X	HSRC	$$–$$$	X

178 Champoeg State Park

Location: About 30 miles north of Salem
Season: Year-round
Sites: 12 full hookup sites, 67 partial hookup sites, 6 walk-in tent sites, 6 yurts, 6 cabins; water, electric, and sewer hookups
Maximum length: 50 feet
Facilities: Tables, grills, flush toilets, drinking water, showers, dump station, dock, visitor center, museum, picnic pavilions, amphitheater for history pageant and other events, disc golf
Fee per night: $$–$$$
Management: Oregon State Parks and Recreation Department
Contact: (503) 678-1251; (800) 452-5687 for reservations; www.oregon.gov/OPRD/PARKS/camping.shtml
Finding the campground: From exit 278 on I-5, 5 miles south of Wilsonville, head west on Ehlen Road/Yergen Road. Go 3.6 miles and turn right onto Case Road, which later merges into Champoeg Road (bearing left). Go 5.8 miles to enter the park on the right. The route is signed.
GPS coordinates: N45 15.006' / W122 52.763'
About the campground: This park captivates with Willamette Valley charm: sweeping green pastures, picturesque oaks, the sleepy Willamette River, and a comfortable, clean camp. The park sits where Oregon's first provisional government—the Northwest's first pro-American government—took flight. This area was also a Native American hunting and gathering camp, a fur-trading post, and a steamboat landing. Interpretive signs and the visitor center relate these tales. For the active the park offers a 10-mile bicycle path, 1.5 miles of riverside hiking trail, fishing, and birding. The park is well located for exploring the valley back roads and visiting U-pick farms or for taking in the attractions of Portland.

179 Elkhorn Valley Recreation Site

Location: About 30 miles east of Salem
Season: Memorial Day weekend–Labor Day
Sites: 23 basic sites; no hookups
Maximum length: 18 feet
Facilities: Tables, grills, nonflush toilets, drinking water
Fee per night: $$
Management: Salem District Bureau of Land Management
Contact: (503) 375-5646; www.blm.gov/or/
Finding the campground: From OR 22 at Mehama, 22 miles east of Salem, turn northeast onto North Fork Road/FR 2209, signed for Little North Fork Recreation Area. Go 8.4 miles; the campground is on the left.
GPS coordinates: N44 47.980' / W122 27.244'
About the campground: This pleasant camp occupies an old-growth forest along the clear, blue-green Little North Fork Santiam River. Pastimes include relaxation, swimming, fishing, and walking short trails along the river. The camp is a jumping-off point to a host of area trails that follow the river, pass swimming holes, and lead into the prized forest and mountain settings of Opal Creek Scenic Recreation Area. A nearby golf course suggests an alternative means of whiling away the day.

180 Fisherman's Bend Recreation Site

Location: 28 miles east of Salem
Season: May–Oct
Sites: 20 full hookup sites, 29 partial hookup sites, 5 tent sites, 2 cabins; water, electric, and sewer hookups
Maximum length: 40 feet
Facilities: Tables, grills, flush toilets, drinking water, showers, dump station, playground, ball fields and courts, horseshoes, boat launch (drift boats or rafts), barrier-free trail and fishing dock for individuals with disabilities
Fee per night: $$–$$$
Management: Salem District Bureau of Land Management
Contact: (503) 375-5646 or (503) 897-2406; (877) 444-6777 for reservations; www.blm.gov/or/
Finding the campground: From OR 22, 28 miles east of Salem and 1.6 miles west of Mill City, turn south to enter the recreation site and campground.
GPS coordinates: N44 45.396' / W122 31.003'
About the campground: This large but friendly and welcoming campground and day-use area sits beside the North Santiam River, a popular waterway for fishing, rafting, and drift boating. The camp occupies a wooded flat, and the good-size sites allow for comfort and privacy. A network of trails explores the riparian habitat. Great blue herons, mergansers, kingfishers, nighthawks, and ospreys travel the river corridor.

181 John Neal Memorial Park

Location: In Lyons, about 25 miles east of Salem
Season: Mid-Apr–Sept
Sites: 10 hookup sites, 13 basic sites, group sites; water hookups
Maximum length: 60 feet
Facilities: Tables, grills, flush toilets, drinking water, showers, playground, ball field, horseshoe pits, launch for drift boat or raft
Fee per night: $$$
Management: Linn County
Contact: (541) 967-3917, reservations accepted; www.co.linn.or.us/parks
Finding the campground: From OR 22, 22 miles east of Salem and 7.7 miles west of Mill City, turn south onto OR 226 and go 0.9 mile. Continue east off OR 226 on Main Street for 0.5 mile. Turn left onto Thirteenth Street to enter the park in 0.6 mile.
GPS coordinates: N44 46.997' / W122 36.489'
About the campground: Convenient for OR 22 travelers, this quiet campground claims a low bluff above the North Santiam River, a popular waterway for rafting and fishing. A natural forest of cedar, fir, maple, and alder complements the camp setting.

182 Polk County Fairgrounds

Location: In Rickreall, about 11 miles southwest of Salem
Season: Year-round; reserved for county fair participants in Aug
Sites: 100 hookup sites, dry camping, tent camping on open lawn; water and electric hookups
Maximum length: 40 feet
Facilities: Flush toilets, drinking water, showers, dump station, playground
Fee per night: $$
Management: Polk County
Contact: (503) 623-3048; www.co.polk.or.us/fair
Finding the campground: From Salem go 10 miles west on OR 22. Turn south onto OR 99W and go 0.8 mile, passing through Rickreall. The fairgrounds are on the left.
GPS coordinates: N44 55.528' / W123 13.682'
About the campground: Within the parking lot for the main fairgrounds, you will find these paved and gravel sites. Power poles signal the hookup sites; tent camping is on the lawn. The area is shadeless but convenient for travelers and fairground attendees and participants. Next door is Nesmith County Park, with its picnic tables and inviting lawn and shade trees. Area wineries may suggest touring. U-pick farms suggest another way to spend time.

183 Shady Cove

Location: About 41 miles east of Salem
Season: Year-round
Sites: 13 basic sites; no hookups
Maximum length: 16 feet
Facilities: Tables, grills, nonflush toilets; no drinking water
Fee per night: $
Management: Willamette National Forest
Contact: (503) 854-3366; www.fs.usda.gov/recmain/willamette/recreation
Finding the campground: From OR 22 at Mehama, about 22 miles east of Salem, turn northeast at the sign for Little North Fork Recreation Area. Travel 19 miles on North Fork Road/FR 2209 and FR 2207 to reach this campground at Shady Cove Bridge. The route begins paved, changing to gravel.
GPS coordinates: N44 50.728' / W122 18.010'
About the campground: Serving anglers and hikers, this campground occupies a richly forested flat above the Little North Santiam River at Shady Cove Bridge. Because the road into camp is twisting and sometimes rough, this facility is best suited for tent camping or small RVs. The Little North Fork Santiam River Trail is located across the river from camp; other area trails enter Opal Creek Scenic Recreation Area. Inviting green pools on the Little North Santiam River attract swimmers to this canyon.

184 Silver Falls State Park

Location: About 28 miles east of Salem
Season: Year-round
Sites: 47 hookup sites, 46 basic sites, 6 horse campsites, 14 cabins; water and electric hookups
Maximum length: 60 feet
Facilities: Tables, grills, flush toilets, drinking water, showers, dump station, nature center, play area, swimming pond, corrals at horse camp
Fee per night: $$–$$$
Management: Oregon State Parks and Recreation Department
Contact: (503) 873-8681; (800) 452-5687 for reservations; www.oregon.gov/OPRD/PARKS/camping.shtml
Finding the campground: From OR 22, 12 miles east of Salem, take the exit for Silver Falls State Park. Follow OR 214 northeast for 15.5 miles to the park. OR 214 follows a weaving course, but signs mark the junctions.
GPS coordinates: N44 52.147' / W122 39.073'
About the campground: Located in the Cascade foothills along Silver Creek, this picturesque family park boasts ten major waterfalls. You can visit each via the Trail of Ten Falls hiking loop, which offers a unique perspective as it passes above, below, and behind the droplet curtains. Falls viewing is also available from the picnic area, from the drive-to overlooks, or by walking short distances on the trail. Elsewhere, bicycle trails and horse trails explore the wooded park, with its areas of old-growth and mature second-growth forest. The tidy campground is set apart from the day-use bustle. The comfortable sites are easy to access, and campers can choose between sun and shade. Howard Creek Horse Camp serves equestrians.

Detroit Lake Area

	Hookup Sites	Total Sites	Max. RV Length	Hookups	Toilets	Showers	Drinking Water	Dump Station	Recreation	Fee	Can Reserve
185 Breitenbush		30	24		NF		X		HF	$$	X
186 Cove Creek		65	40		F	X	X		SFBL	$$	X
187 Detroit Lake State Recreation Area	178	311	60	WES	F	X	X		SFBL	$$–$$$	X
188 Hoover		37	40		F, NF		X		HFSBL	$$–$$$	X
189 Humbug		21	30		NF		X		HF	$$	
190 Santiam Flats		32	40		NF		X		FBL	$$	
191 Southshore		32	30		NF		X		HFSBL	$$	

185 Breitenbush

Location: About 9 miles northeast of Detroit
Season: Mid-May–mid-Sept
Sites: 30 basic sites; no hookups
Maximum length: 24 feet
Facilities: Tables, grills, nonflush toilets, drinking water
Fee per night: $$
Management: Willamette National Forest
Contact: (503) 854-3366; (877) 444-6777 for reservations; www.fs.usda.gov/recmain/willamette/recreation
Finding the campground: From OR 22 at the west end of Detroit, turn north onto FR 46 and go 9.1 miles; the campground is on the right.
GPS coordinates: N44 46.836' / W121 59.441'
About the campground: Hemlocks, cedars, and vine maples envelop this attractive camp along the Breitenbush River. The pristine river is framed by overhanging trees and the greenery of its banks. Campers can fish or hike the nearby South Breitenbush Gorge Trail, which passes through old-growth forest and along a rocky chasm that pinches the South Fork into a fury of rushing water. The trailhead is off FR 4685, northeast of camp. The campground is also near the private, alternative-lifestyle Breitenbush Hot Springs.

186 Cove Creek

Location: On Detroit Lake, about 6 miles south of Detroit
Season: Mid-May–Sept
Sites: 65 basic sites; no hookups
Maximum length: 40 feet
Facilities: Tables, grills, flush toilets, drinking water, coin-operated showers, boat launch, dock
Fee per night: $$
Management: Willamette National Forest
Contact: (503) 854-3366; (877) 444-6777 for reservations; www.fs.usda.gov/recmain/willamette/recreation
Finding the campground: From Detroit go 2.9 miles east on OR 22. Turn right (south) onto Blowout Road/FR 10 and continue 3.5 miles; the campground is on the right.
GPS coordinates: N44 42.728' / W122 09.472'
About the campground: On the south shore of Detroit Lake, this large, comfortable campground offers great access to the reservoir's full lineup of fun: fishing, boating, swimming, sailing, water-skiing, and just relaxing beside the glistening water. The camp claims a gentle, evergreen-clad slope and offers paved roads and parking and running-water amenities. For hiking, the Stahlman Point Lookout Trail begins off Blowout Road, 0.1 mile south of the campground turnoff.

187 Detroit Lake State Recreation Area

Location: On Detroit Lake, 2 miles southwest of Detroit
Season: Mid-Mar–Oct
Sites: 178 full and partial hookup sites, 133 basic sites; water, electric, and sewer hookups
Maximum length: 60 feet
Facilities: Tables, grills, flush toilets, drinking water, showers, boat moorage, launch, accessible fishing dock, swimming beach, sport courts, store
Fee per night: $$–$$$
Management: Oregon State Parks and Recreation Department
Contact: (503) 854-3346; (800) 452-5687 for reservations; www.oregon.gov/OPRD/PARKS/camping.shtml
Finding the campground: This campground is located on the north shore of Detroit Lake, off OR 22, 2 miles west of Detroit and 50 miles east of Salem.
GPS coordinates: N44 43.736' / W122 10.534'
About the campground: At this large, developed campground, welcoming fir-forested sites provide a base for recreation at Detroit Lake, a huge reservoir within the North Santiam River Canyon. Some sites overlook the water. Lake recreation includes everything from fishing to waterskiing, making the lake and the state park popular summer destinations.

188 Hoover

Location: On Detroit Lake, about 4 miles southeast of Detroit
Season: Mid-Apr–Sept
Sites: 37 basic sites; no hookups
Maximum length: 40 feet
Facilities: Tables, grills, flush and nonflush toilets, drinking water, boat launch, barrier-free trail, wheelchair-accessible fishing platforms, 200-foot-long pier
Fee per night: $$–$$$
Management: Willamette National Forest
Contact: (503) 854-3366; (877) 444-6777 for reservations; www.fs.usda.gov/recmain/willamette/recreation
Finding the campground: From Detroit go east on OR 22 for 2.8 miles. Turn right onto Blowout Road/FR 10 and continue 0.8 mile; the campground entrance is on the right.
GPS coordinates: N44 42.757' / W122 07.371'
About the campground: On the North Santiam River arm of Detroit Lake, a rich Douglas fir forest shades this campground while the understory greenery pleases the eye. Campsites are well spaced for privacy and comfort, but the water sports are likely to keep you away from camp. Fishing, boating, swimming, and waterskiing vie for your time. The 0.3-mile Hoover Nature Trail loops through forest. The lower leg of the loop is wheelchair-accessible and leads to fishing platforms.

189 Humbug

Location: About 4 miles northeast of Detroit
Season: Early May–Sept
Sites: 21 basic sites; no hookups
Maximum length: 30 feet
Facilities: Tables, grills, nonflush toilets, drinking water
Fee per night: $$
Management: Willamette National Forest
Contact: (503) 854-3366; www.fs.usda.gov/recmain/willamette/recreation
Finding the campground: From OR 22 at the west end of Detroit, turn north onto FR 46. Continue 4.4 miles; the campground is on the right.
GPS coordinates: N44 46.253' / W122 04.624'
About the campground: At this Breitenbush River campground, you will find fairly spacious sites in a semi-open conifer forest rimmed by old-growth trees. The Humbug Flat Trail leaves from camp, passing above the river through bountiful rhododendrons and varied forest. Steep angler paths plunge toward fishing holes. The river flows clear as it riffles over rounded cobbles. Anglers can also try fishing from the dam, the shore, or a boat on Detroit Lake, a short drive to the south.

190 Santiam Flats

Location: On Detroit Lake, about 3 miles east of Detroit
Season: Year-round
Sites: 32 basic sites; no hookups
Maximum length: 40 feet
Facilities: Tables, fire rings, nonflush toilets, drinking water (seasonally), primitive boat launch
Fee per night: $$
Management: Willamette National Forest
Contact: (503) 854-3366; www.fs.usda.gov/recmain/willamette/recreation
Finding the campground: From OR 22, 2.5 miles east of Detroit, turn south into this campground on the lake.
GPS coordinates: N44 42.698' / W122 06.955'
About the campground: This campground occupies a flat that had long been used by the public for camping and accessing Detroit Lake. Order now has been established with defined sites and reduced numbers. But the original appeal remains intact: fishing and boating Detroit Lake.

191 Southshore

Location: On Detroit Lake, about 7 miles south of Detroit
Season: Mid-May–mid-Sept
Sites: 32 basic sites; no hookups
Maximum length: 30 feet
Facilities: Tables, grills, nonflush toilets, drinking water, boat launch, dock
Fee per night: $$
Management: Willamette National Forest
Contact: (503) 854-3366; www.fs.usda.gov/recmain/willamette/recreation
Finding the campground: From Detroit go 2.9 miles east on OR 22. Turn right (south) onto Blow-out Road/FR 10 and continue 4.2 miles; the campground is on the right.
GPS coordinates: N44 42.332' / W122 10.575'
About the campground: On the south shore of Detroit Lake—a huge reservoir open to recreation—this campground occupies a shady mixed-conifer forest. Together with its lush understory, the forest setting is almost as recommending as the lake. All campsites have paved parking, though some sites are not as level as others. Swimming, fishing, boating, waterskiing, and sailing keep lakegoers happy. For hiking, the Stahlman Point Lookout Trail is not far from camp.

Marion Forks Area

	Hookup Sites	Total Sites	Max. RV Length	Hookups	Toilets	Showers	Drinking Water	Dump Station	Recreation	Fee	Can Reserve
192 Big Lake and Big Lake West		60	35		F, NF		X		HFBL	$$	X
193 Big Meadows Horse Camp		9	36		NF		X		HR	$$	
194 Lost Lake		15	16		NF				F	$	
195 Marion Forks		8	30		NF				HF	$$	
196 Riverside		37	24		NF		X		F	$$	X
197 Whispering Falls		16	30		NF		X		F	$$	

192 Big Lake and Big Lake West

Location: On Big Lake, about 26 miles southeast of Marion Forks
Season: July–Oct
Sites: 49 basic sites (Big Lake), 11 walk-in tent sites (Big Lake West); no hookups
Maximum length: 35 feet
Facilities: Tables, grills, flush and nonflush toilets (nonflush only at Big Lake West), drinking water (Big Lake only), boat ramp
Fee per night: $$
Management: Willamette National Forest
Contact: (541) 822-3381; (877) 444-6777 for Big Lake Campground reservations; www.fs.usda.gov/recmain/willamette/recreation
Finding the campground: From US 20 at Santiam Pass, about 22 miles southeast of Marion Forks, turn south onto Big Lake Road/FR 2690. Continue about 4 miles to these campgrounds.
GPS coordinates: N44 22.651' / W121 52.253'
About the campgrounds: The primary campground occupies the north shore of Big Lake, while the walk-in tent sites line the west shore. Big Lake is an aptly named natural lake below Hayrick and Hoodoo Buttes. Mount Washington adds to skyline views. Sites are nestled in a high-elevation forest of firs, hemlocks, and lodgepole pines. A few snags on the west shore have been carved with totems. The lake offers fishing, swimming, boating, and waterskiing, as well as canoeing along the scalloped shoreline. Area trails visit Patjens Lakes and Mount Washington Wilderness Area.

193 Big Meadows Horse Camp

Location: About 10 miles south of Marion Forks
Season: Mid-July–Oct
Sites: 9 basic sites; no hookups
Maximum length: 36 feet
Facilities: Tables, grills, nonflush toilets, drinking water, corrals, hitching posts, loading ramps, stock watering trough
Fee per night: $$
Management: Willamette National Forest
Contact: (503) 854-3366; www.fs.usda.gov/recmain/willamette/recreation
Finding the campground: From OR 22, 27 miles east of Detroit and 5.6 miles west of Santiam Junction (the junction of OR 22 and US 20), turn north onto FR 2267. Go 0.9 mile and turn left onto FR 2257; enter the campground on the left in 0.5 mile.
GPS coordinates: N44 29.669' / W121 59.020'
About the campground: Established for equestrians, this campground rests in a welcoming forest of mixed firs, spruce, and mountain hemlock. Pole fencing defines the campground roadways and site turnouts. Each site is paired with a four-stall corral. Deer sometimes visit the vacant stalls, seeking hay. Horse trails head out from camp. If you plan to enter Mount Jefferson Wilderness Area, be sure to obtain a wilderness permit. Huckleberry picking is a seasonal diversion.

194 Lost Lake

Location: About 2 miles east of Santiam Junction
Season: July–Nov
Sites: 15 basic sites; no hookups
Maximum length: 16 feet
Facilities: Tables, grills, nonflush toilets; no drinking water
Fee per night: $
Management: Willamette National Forest
Contact: (541) 822-3381; www.fs.usda.gov/recmain/willamette/recreation
Finding the campground: From the junction of US 20, OR 22, and OR 126 (Santiam Junction), go east on US 20/OR 126 for 1.8 miles; turn north into campground.
From Santiam Pass drive 4.5 miles west on US 20/OR 126 to the camp turnoff.
GPS coordinates: N44 25.901' / W121 54.736'
About the campground: At this rustic campground, sites string along the west and north shore of Lost Lake, which trends to marsh by late summer. Birding, fishing, and relaxing at camp are popular pursuits. Although the campground's proximity to the highway can be loud, the convenience is ideal for through-travel and for road trips to Sisters, the McKenzie and Metolius Wild and Scenic Rivers, the area scenic byways, and Clear Lake.

195 Marion Forks

Location: In Marion Forks
Season: Year-round
Sites: 8 basic sites; no hookups
Maximum length: 30 feet
Facilities: Tables, grills, nonflush toilets; no drinking water
Fee per night: $$
Management: Willamette National Forest
Contact: (541) 854-3366; www.fs.usda.gov/recmain/willamette/recreation
Finding the campground: The camp sits northeast off OR 22 at Marion Forks, 16 miles southeast of Detroit. A sign for the hatchery and forest camp marks the turn.
GPS coordinates: N44 36.648' / W121 56.827'
About the campground: Neighboring the Marion Forks Fish Hatchery, this quiet campground lines the south shore of sparkling Marion Creek. The formalized, attractive sites are nicely shaded; pole fencing at camp protects the creek bank. The creek is not one for fishing, but it lends a pleasant voice to camp. Area trails lead to Independence Rock, Marion Lake, and the backcountry lakes and wilds of Mount Jefferson Wilderness Area.

196 Riverside

Location: About 3 miles north of Marion Forks
Season: Mid-May–Sept
Sites: 37 basic sites; no hookups
Maximum length: 24 feet
Facilities: Tables, grills, nonflush toilets, drinking water
Fee per night: $$
Management: Willamette National Forest
Contact: (503) 854-3366; (877) 444-6777 for reservations; www.fs.usda.gov/recmain/willamette/recreation
Finding the campground: The campground is west off OR 22, 13.5 miles southeast of Detroit.
GPS coordinates: N44 38.546' / W121 56.753'
About the campground: In a full, multistory forest, this campground stretches along the shore of the North Santiam River. In spring rhododendron and dogwood blooms dress up the midstory. Sparkling, clear, and green, the river courses over bedrock and seduces anglers. Some sites overlook the river; all sites have surfaced parking.

197 Whispering Falls

Location: About 8 miles northwest of Marion Forks
Season: Mid-May–Sept
Sites: 16 basic sites; no hookups
Maximum length: 30 feet
Facilities: Tables, grills, nonflush toilets, drinking water
Fee per night: $$
Management: Willamette National Forest
Contact: (503) 854-3366; www.fs.usda.gov/recmain/willamette/recreation
Finding the campground: The campground is west off OR 22, 8 miles southeast of Detroit.
GPS coordinates: N44 41.297' / W122 00.626'
About the campground: This forest campground offers a picturesque stay on the North Santiam River. It takes its name from the gentle-voiced tributary waterfall across the river from camp. A full forest and lush understory contribute to the beauty and privacy of the campsites. An abrupt bank separates much of the campground from the river, but the River Trail leads to a shoreline access for fishing and river admiring.

Corvallis Area

	Hookup Sites	Total Sites	Max. RV Length	Hookups	Toilets	Showers	Drinking Water	Dump Station	Recreation	Fee	Can Reserve
198 Alsea Falls Recreation Site		16	30		NF		X		HSF	$$	
199 Benton Oaks RV Park and Campground	28	28	60	WESC	F	X	X	X	HC	$$$	X
200 Marys Peak		6	T		NF				H	$$	
201 Salmonberry County Park		28	40		F	X	X		FBL	$$$	

198 Alsea Falls Recreation Site

Location: About 29 miles southwest of Corvallis
Season: Late-May–Sept
Sites: 16 basic sites; no hookups
Maximum length: 30 feet
Facilities: Tables, grills, nonflush toilets, drinking water
Fee per night: $$
Management: Salem District Bureau of Land Management
Contact: (503) 375-5646; www.blm.gov/or/
Finding the campground: From Corvallis go 16 miles south on OR 99W. Turn right (west) at the sign for Alpine and Alsea Falls and drive 12.9 miles, passing through the town of Alpine, to reach the campground. The road is paved and graveled and follows part of the Alsea Falls National Backcountry Byway.
GPS coordinates: N44 19.250' / W123 29.228'
About the campground: Mossy old stumps and moist pockets of skunk cabbage accent the forest of tall firs and alders that envelops this camp on the South Fork Alsea River. Sites are spacious and relaxing. From the bridge at camp, trails head down river 0.5 mile to Alsea Falls. You can extend the hike another mile to Green Peak Falls: Opposite the developed shore, continue downstream from Alsea Falls to McBee Park (a rustic campground), and then hike upstream along Peak Creek to this unexpected waterfall. Green Peak Falls is 50 feet tall and twice as wide.

199 Benton Oaks RV Park and Campground

Location: In Corvallis
Season: Year-round
Sites: 28 hookup sites; open tent camping (Memorial Day–Labor Day); water, electric, sewer, and cable hookups
Maximum length: 60 feet
Facilities: Flush toilets, drinking water, showers, dump station, laundry, wireless (available)
Fee per night: $$$ (higher rates in effect for weekends of Oregon State University home games)
Management: Benton County
Contact: (541) 766-6521 (information and reservations); www.bentoncountyfair.net/oaks/
Finding the campground: From US 20 at the west end of Corvallis, go north on 53rd Street for 1 mile to reach the fairgrounds on the left.
GPS coordinates: N44 34.027' / W123 18.881'
About the campground: This camp area at the fairgrounds exists primarily to serve fair participants during events, but it also provides travelers with a convenient base for exploring the Corvallis area. Attractions include the Willamette River, the valley U-pick farms, the Bald Hill Trails, William L. Finley National Wildlife Refuge, Oregon State University, and Peavy Arboretum. Sites have paved parking, some pull-through. Oaks nudge to the campground, and a neighboring farm opens views to the coastal hills.

200 Marys Peak

Location: About 25 miles southwest of Corvallis
Season: Mid-May–Nov, unless snow necessitates road closure
Sites: 6 tent sites; no hookups
Maximum length: Suitable for tents only
Facilities: Tables, grills, nonflush toilets; no drinking water
Fee per night: $$
Management: Siuslaw National Forest
Contact: (541) 563-8400; www.fs.usda.gov/recmain/siuslaw/recreation
Finding the campground: From OR 34, 10 miles west of Philomath, turn north onto Marys Peak Road. Proceed 9 miles; the campground entrance is on the right.
GPS coordinates: N44 30.596' / W123 33.652'
About the campground: Just below the summit of Marys Peak, this tiny campground along Parker Creek occupies a semi-open stand of small noble firs. The Meadows Edge Trail skirts the campground to explore the fuller noble fir forest and open meadow of the upper mountain reaches. Other trails travel the east and north flanks of Marys Peak, the highest peak in the Coast Range. The mountain is noted for wildflowers, winter snow play, and its views that stretch from the Pacific Ocean to the Cascades. The popular destination is still wild enough for deer and bobcats to be seen.

201　Salmonberry County Park

Location: About 30 miles southwest of Corvallis
Season: Mid-May–mid-Oct
Sites: 13 basic sites, 15 tent sites; no hookups
Maximum length: 40 feet
Facilities: Tables, grills, flush toilets, drinking water, showers, drift/car-top boat launch, barrier-free trail
Fee per night: $$$
Management: Benton County
Contact: (541) 766-6871; www.co.benton.or.us/parks/
Finding the campground: From OR 34, 6.4 miles west of Alsea and 32 miles east of Waldport, turn south onto Salmonberry Road. Continue 0.3 mile to enter the park on the left.
GPS coordinates: N44 20.596' / W123 41.125'
About the campground: On an attractive flat above the quiet-flowing Alsea River, this campground has sites with gravel pads edging a large, central lawn. Alders shape the camp perimeter. Each site has been constructed to serve wheelchair users, with easy access to tables and grills. A 700-foot cinder-grade gravel trail provides barrier-free access from the camp to the river. Fishing and drift boating are popular pursuits. This camp conveniently serves travelers passing between the Willamette Valley and the coast.

Lebanon–Sweet Home Area

	Hookup Sites	Total Sites	Max. RV Length	Hookups	Toilets	Showers	Drinking Water	Dump Station	Recreation	Fee	Can Reserve
202 Cascadia State Park		25	35		F		X		HSF	$$	
203 Fernview		11	22		NF		X		HSF	$$	
204 Gill's Landing	21	21	60	WESCI	F	X	X	X	FBL	$$$	X
205 House Rock		17	22		NF		X		HSF	$$	X
206 Lost Prairie		10	24		NF		X		H	$$	
207 Pioneer Park		10	35		NF		X			$$	
208 River Bend County Park	74	84	60	WE	F	X	X	X	SFB	$$$	X
209 Sevenmile Horse Camp		4	40		NF				HR	NWF Pass	
210 Sunnyside County Park	132	165	40	WE	F	X	X	X	SFBL	$$$	X
211 Trout Creek		23	32		NF		X		HSF	$$	X
212 Waterloo County Park	100	120	40	WE	F	X	X	X	SFBL	$$$	X
213 Whitcomb Creek County Park		39	30		NF		X		SFBL	$$$	X
214 Yellowbottom		22	20		NF		X		HSF	$$	
215 Yukwah		20	32		NF		X		HSF	$$	

202 Cascadia State Park

Location: 14 miles east of Sweet Home
Season: May–Sept
Sites: 25 basic sites; no hookups
Maximum length: 35 feet
Facilities: Tables, grills, flush toilets, drinking water, horseshoe pits, sports field
Fee per night: $$
Management: Oregon State Parks and Recreation Department
Contact: (541) 367-6021; www.oregon.gov/OPRD/PARKS/camping.shtml
Finding the campground: The campground sits north off US 20, 14 miles east of Sweet Home.
GPS coordinates: N44 23.995' / W122 28.816'
About the campground: In the South Santiam River Valley, you will find this pleasant camp with paved roads and parking, ample lawn, and shade trees. Although the sites sit fairly close together, they enjoy a natural habitat. Trout fishing on the river and hiking the 0.75-mile trail to Soda Creek Falls top the list of things to do. Foster Reservoir lies west of camp for boating and fishing; Menagerie Wilderness is east of the park for more serious hiking.

South Santiam River, Over the River and Through the Woods Scenic Byway, Willamette National Forest

203 Fernview

Location: 24 miles east of Sweet Home
Season: May–Sept
Sites: 9 basic sites, 2 tent sites; no hookups
Maximum length: 22 feet
Facilities: Tables, grills, nonflush toilets, drinking water
Fee per night: $$
Management: Willamette National Forest
Contact: (541) 367-5168; www.fs.usda.gov/recmain/willamette/recreation
Finding the campground: From Sweet Home drive 24 miles east on US 20; turn south into the campground.
GPS coordinates: N44 24.170' / W122 18.158'
About the campground: This campground on the south bank of the South Santiam River oozes with tranquility. A rich vine maple midstory creates an attractive canopy over the individual sites; towering hemlocks and firs deepen the shade. The South Santiam River consists of rushing stretches, deep pools for swimming or fishing, gravel bars, and outcrops. The campground is within easy reach of hiking trails to Rooster Rock (in the Menagerie Wilderness), House Rock, Iron Mountain, and the Old Santiam Wagon Road.

204 Gill's Landing

Location: In Lebanon
Season: Year-round; winter use for self-contained units only
Sites: 21 hookup sites; water, electric, sewer, cable, and Internet hookups
Maximum length: 60 feet
Facilities: Tables, grills, flush toilets, drinking water, showers, dump station, boat launch, dock, swimming area; playground, horseshoe pits, and ball field at neighboring River Park
Fee per night: $$$
Management: City of Lebanon
Contact: (541) 258-4917 (information and reservations); www.ci.lebanon.or.us/
Finding the campground: From Main Street in the center of Lebanon, go east on Grant Street to reach the park in 0.7 mile.
GPS coordinates: N44 32.347' / W122 53.508'
About the campground: This relaxing park offers a pleasant stay beside the South Fork Santiam River. The full-service campground has developed parking spaces in a wooded setting. Grassy areas also invite repose. Trails lead from the camp to the river for fishing access; the river boasts excellent trout, salmon, and steelhead fishing. Sand is brought in annually for the swimming area.

205 House Rock

Location: About 28 miles east of Sweet Home
Season: May–Sept
Sites: 12 basic sites, 5 tent sites; no hookups
Maximum length: 22 feet
Facilities: Tables, grills, nonflush toilets, drinking water
Fee per night: $$
Management: Willamette National Forest
Contact: (541) 367-5168; (877) 444-6777 for reservations; www.fs.usda.gov/recmain/willamette/recreation
Finding the campground: From Sweet Home drive 27 miles east on US 20. Turn south onto gravel Latiwi Creek Road/FR 2044, and proceed about 1 mile to the campground.
GPS coordinates: N44 23.549' / W122 14.706'
About the campground: Bigleaf maples, alders, cedar, firs, and hemlocks weave a rich canopy of shade for this campground at the confluence of Latiwi and Sheep Creeks. Because the sites lack long parking pads or pull-throughs, camping here is better suited to tents or small rigs. Fishing and area trails may coax guests away from the comfort of camp. House Rock, Old Santiam Wagon Road, Iron Mountain, and Rooster Rock are possible hikes in the area.

206 Lost Prairie

Location: 40 miles east of Sweet Home
Season: Late May–Sept
Sites: 2 basic sites, 8 walk-in tent sites; no hookups
Maximum length: 24 feet
Facilities: Tables, grills, nonflush toilets, drinking water
Fee per night: $$
Management: Willamette National Forest
Contact: (541) 367-5168; www.fs.usda.gov/recmain/willamette/recreation
Finding the campground: This campground sits south off US 20, 40 miles east of Sweet Home and 4.2 miles west of the junction of US 20 and OR 126.
GPS coordinates: N44 24.188' / W122 04.670'
About the campground: This campground enjoys a meadow and forest setting along Hackleman Creek. The walk-in sites are set back among the firs and spruce, just strides from the paved parking area. Wildflowers sprinkle the meadow. Just west of camp is the Hackleman Trail Old Growth Grove.

207 Pioneer Park

Location: In Brownsville
Season: Mid-Apr–mid-Oct
Sites: 4 basic sites, 6 walk-in tent sites; no hookups
Maximum length: 35 feet
Facilities: Tables, fire rings, nonflush toilets, drinking water, ball fields, horseshoe pits, dining pavilion, amphitheater
Fee per night: $$
Management: City of Brownsville
Contact: (541) 466-5666; www.ci.brownsville.or.us/park
Finding the campground: From the junction of Main Street and Park Avenue in Brownsville, go 0.1 mile west on Park Avenue to the campground.
GPS coordinates: N44 23.572' / W122 59.362'
About the campground: This rather informal campground sits at one end of the park in a grove of mature bigleaf maples. The park occupies a bend in the Calapooya River and offers river access. Campers also have access to historic Brownsville, with its lovely old homes, museums, and antiques shops.

208 River Bend County Park

Location: About 9 miles east of Sweet Home
Season: Apr–Nov
Sites: 74 hookup sites, 10 basic sites, 2 cabins; water and electric hookups
Maximum length: 60 feet
Facilities: Tables, grills, flush toilets, drinking water, showers, dump station, picnic shelter, playground, softball field
Fee per night: $$$
Management: Linn County
Contact: (541) 967-3917, reservations accepted; www.co.linn.or.us/parks
Finding the campground: From the junction of US 20 and OR 228 in Sweet Home, head east on US 20 for about 9 miles. The campground is on the north side of US 20, about 3 miles east of the Quartzville Road turnoff.
GPS coordinates: N44 24.402' / W122 34.159'
About the campground: Nestled in a bend on the South Santiam River, this campground offers a relaxing and attractive stay in a woodsy/semi-open setting. Sites are well spaced for privacy and have long, developed parking spurs. Fishing and floating the river bend are popular entertainments. People can put in with their rafts or inner tubes at the upper end of the camp and take out at the lower end.

209 Sevenmile Horse Camp

Location: About 32 miles east of Sweet Home
Season: Year-round, dependent on snow
Sites: 4 basic sites; no hookups
Maximum length: 40 feet
Facilities: Tables, grills, nonflush toilets, corrals, manure bin, water for stock; no drinking water
Fee per night: Northwest Forest Pass required
Management: Willamette National Forest
Contact: (541) 367-5168; www.fs.usda.gov/recmain/willamette/recreation
Finding the campground: From US 20, 32 miles east of Sweet Home and 12.7 west of the junction of US 20 and OR 126, turn south onto FR 024, which angles east below US 20. Go 0.3 mile to the campground.
GPS coordinates: N44 23.030' / W122 12.758'
About the campground: In a lovely, tall Cascade forest, this restful, serviceable horse camp has gravel roads and parking, four well-spaced sites, and a broad central staging area. It provides access to the historic Old Santiam Wagon Road, with a 14-mile ride east to Fish Lake Guard Station (off OR 126) and a 7-mile ride west to Mountain House.

210 Sunnyside County Park

Location: About 7 miles northeast of Sweet Home
Season: Apr–early Nov
Sites: 132 hookup sites, 10 basic sites, 23 adjoined-use sites; water and electric hookups
Maximum length: 40 feet
Facilities: Tables, grills, flush toilets, drinking water, showers, dump station, playground, boat dock, launch, moorage, stocked fishing ponds, fish-cleaning station, horseshoe pits, volleyball
Fee per night: $$$
Management: Linn County
Contact: (541) 967-3917, reservations accepted; www.co.linn.or.us/parks
Finding the campground: From Sweet Home go 5.5 miles east on US 20. Turn north onto Quartzville Road, a BLM Backcountry Byway, heading toward Green Peter Reservoir. Go 1.4 miles to enter the county park on the right.
GPS coordinates: N44 25.663' / W122 36.622'
About the campground: This tidy, attractive campground occupies a vast, trimmed lawn with cottonwoods and some planted pines and maples for pockets of shade. It sits between a forested ridge and Foster Reservoir and near a pair of big ponds with stark shores. The campground has paved roads and parking pads. Foster and Green Peter Reservoirs invite lake recreation. Blackberry bushes bordering Quartzville Road invite berry pickers to stain their fingers and perhaps collect enough for a pie.

211 Trout Creek

Location: 21 miles east of Sweet Home
Season: May–Oct
Sites: 23 basic sites; no hookups
Maximum length: 32 feet
Facilities: Tables, grills, nonflush toilets, drinking water
Fee per night: $$
Management: Willamette National Forest
Contact: (541) 367-5168; (877) 444-6777 for reservations; www.fs.usda.gov/recmain/willamette/recreation
Finding the campground: The campground is south off US 20, 21 miles east of Sweet Home.
GPS coordinates: N44 23.854' / W122 20.924'
About the campground: This South Santiam River campground offers swimming, fishing, and a pleasant stay in a natural woodland setting, but there is some road noise. Some sites overlook the river; others offer great privacy. The multistory forest with its many dogwoods is especially appealing early in the camping season. Area trails enter Menagerie Wilderness or travel along Falls Creek to Soapgrass Mountain and Gordon Lakes. From the Trout Creek Trailhead, across the road from camp, a short spur leads to an elk-viewing platform. The main trail journeys through wilderness to Rooster Rock.

212 Waterloo County Park

Location: About 9 miles northwest of Sweet Home
Season: Year-round
Sites: 100 hookup sites, 20 basic sites; water and electric hookups
Maximum length: 40 feet
Facilities: Tables, grills, flush toilets, drinking water, showers, dump station, playground, disc golf, beach area, boat launch, shelter
Fee per night: $$$
Management: Linn County
Contact: (541) 967-3917, reservations accepted; www.co.linn.or.us/parks
Finding the campground: From the junction of US 20 and OR 228 in Sweet Home, follow US 20 west for 8.4 miles. Turn right (north) onto Waterloo Drive at the sign for the park. Go 1 mile, passing through the community of Waterloo, and turn right into the park. The campground is at the end of the park road.
GPS coordinates: N44 29.434' / W122 49.229'
About the campground: This extensive riverside campground fronts the broad and glassy South Santiam River and enjoys a relaxing valley location. Sweeping lawns, shade-providing oaks and maples, and browsing deer lend to the idyllic scene. Cottonwoods grow along the river. The park offers room to roam, but beware of poison oak. The river is open to boating, swimming, and fishing. Blackberry brambles hold tasty summer bites, if you can navigate the thorns.

213 Whitcomb Creek County Park

Location: On Green Peter Reservoir, about 17 miles northeast of Sweet Home
Season: Mid-Apr–late Sept
Sites: 39 basic sites; no hookups
Maximum length: 30 feet
Facilities: Tables, grills, nonflush toilets, drinking water, boat dock, launch
Fee per night: $$$
Management: Linn County
Contact: (541) 967-3917, reservations accepted; www.co.linn.or.us/parks
Finding the campground: From Sweet Home go 5.5 miles east on US 20. Turn north onto Quartz-ville Road, a BLM Backcountry Byway, heading toward Green Peter Reservoir. Go 11.1 miles and turn right into the county park. Continue 0.6 mile to enter the campground on the right; the boat ramp and picnic area are straight ahead.
GPS coordinates: N44 29.109' / W122 30.356'
About the campground: You will find this campground on the Whitcomb Creek Arm of Green Peter Reservoir, a popular place for speed boating, fishing, and swimming. In this terraced park, the spacious sites enjoy deep forest shade; some sites are more level than others. Should the campground fill, owners of self-contained units can take advantage of dispersed camping along the widened road shoulder of the reservoir outside the park.

214 Yellowbottom

Location: About 29 miles northeast of Sweet Home
Season: Late May–Labor Day
Sites: 22 basic sites; no hookups
Maximum length: 20 feet
Facilities: Tables, grills, nonflush toilets, drinking water
Fee per night: $$
Management: Salem District Bureau of Land Management
Contact: (503) 375-5646; www.blm.gov/or/
Finding the campground: From Sweet Home go 5.5 miles east on US 20. Turn north onto Quartz-ville Road, a BLM Backcountry Byway, heading toward Green Peter Reservoir. Continue 23.7 miles and turn left into the campground.
GPS coordinates: N44 35.341' / W122 22.324'
About the campground: This highly attractive campground is set in a stand of magnificent old-growth trees interwoven with vine maples, rhododendrons, cascaras, and yews. Across the road are a picnic area and an access trail to Quartzville Creek, a wild and scenic waterway that engages with boulders, gravel bars, and gorgeous swimming holes. Sunbathing, swimming, and fishing are popular pursuits. At camp, Rhododendron Flat Loop offers a 1.2-mile hike.

215 Yukwah

Location: About 22 miles east of Sweet Home
Season: May–Oct
Sites: 20 basic sites; no hookups
Maximum length: 32 feet
Facilities: Tables, grills, nonflush toilets, drinking water, fishing platform
Fee per night: $$
Management: Willamette National Forest
Contact: (541) 367-5168; www.fs.usda.gov/recmain/willamette/recreation
Finding the campground: The campground is south off US 20, 21.5 miles east of Sweet Home.
GPS coordinates: N44 23.951' / W122 20.319'
About the campground: This neighbor to Trout Creek Campground offers a similar stay on the South Santiam River, with perhaps a few stouter firs in camp. The forested sites radiate from the campground loop road, an arrangement that allows for plenty of privacy. A 0.25-mile trail provides river access.

Blue River-McKenzie Bridge Area

	Hookup Sites	Total Sites	Max. RV Length	Hookups	Toilets	Showers	Drinking Water	Dump Station	Recreation	Fee	Can Reserve
216 Alder Springs		6	T		NF				H	None	
217 Box Canyon Horse Camp		13	30		NF				HR	None	
218 Coldwater Cove		35	30		NF		X		HFBL	$$	X
219 Cougar Crossing		11	25		NF				HSFB	$$	
220 Delta		38	36		NF		X		HSFB	$$	X
221 French Pete		17	30		NF		X		HSF	$$	
222 Frissell Crossing		12	36		NF		X		HF	$$	
223 Ice Cap Creek		22	22		F				HFB	$$	
224 Limberlost		12	16		NF				F	$$	
225 McKenzie Bridge		20	35		NF		X		FBL	$$	X
226 Mona		23	36		F		X		SFBL	$$	X
227 Olallie		17	35		NF		X		HFBL	$$	X
228 Paradise		64	40		F, NF		X		HFBL	$$	X
229 Slide Creek		16	40		NF		X		SFBL	$$	X
230 Sunnyside		13	T		NF				SFB	$$	
231 Trail Bridge		46	45		F, NF		X		HFBL	$$	

216 Alder Springs

Location: About 15 miles east of the community of McKenzie Bridge
Season: Maintained June–Sept
Sites: 6 tent sites; no hookups
Maximum length: Suitable for tents only
Facilities: Tables, grills, nonflush toilets; no drinking water
Fee per night: None
Management: Willamette National Forest
Contact: (541) 822-3381; www.fs.usda.gov/recmain/willamette/recreation
Finding the campground: From McKenzie Bridge go 4.6 miles east on OR 126. Turn right (east) onto OR 242; the campground is on the left in 10.4 miles.
GPS coordinates: N44 10.646' / W121 54.812'
About the campground: On McKenzie Pass Scenic Byway, you will find this tiny camp in the firs opposite the trailhead to Linton Lake. Other trails in the area visit Proxy Falls and Scott Mountain. The byway, which passes between Three Sisters and Mount Washington Wilderness Areas, is a

photographer's dream, with striking images of lava, forest, lakes, and volcanoes. Dee Wright Observatory, a medieval-looking outpost atop a lava flow at McKenzie Pass, delivers a unique perspective on the neighborhood and is itself a photo subject.

217 Box Canyon Horse Camp

Location: About 30 miles southeast of the community of Blue River
Season: June–Nov, dependent on snow
Sites: 13 basic sites; no hookups
Maximum length: 30 feet
Facilities: Tables, grills, nonflush toilets, corrals, water trough for stock; no drinking water
Fee per night: None
Management: Willamette National Forest
Contact: (541) 822-3381; www.fs.usda.gov/recmain/willamette/recreation
Finding the campground: From the Blue River Junction on OR 126, drive east on OR 126 about 5 miles. Turn south onto FR 19 (Aufderheide Forest Drive), heading toward Cougar Reservoir. In 0.2 mile turn right to remain on FR 19. The camp is west off FR 19 in another 25.4 miles.
GPS coordinates: N43 54.270' / W122 05.052'
About the campground: This peaceful camp at the forested foot of Chucksney Mountain provides a pleasant overnight base for equestrians. Tall firs, rhododendrons, and ferns dress up the camp. Across the road are a historic guard station and an attractive meadow swath; interpretive panels along FR 19 introduce the area history. Trails from camp travel to Chucksney Mountain and into the Three Sisters Wilderness Area.

218 Coldwater Cove

Location: On Clear Lake, 18 miles northeast of the community of McKenzie Bridge
Season: Mid-June–mid-Oct
Sites: 35 basic sites; no hookups
Maximum length: 30 feet
Facilities: Tables, grills, nonflush toilets, drinking water, boat launch (nonmotorized boating)
Fee per night: $$
Management: Willamette National Forest
Contact: (541) 822-3381; (877) 444-6777 for reservations; www.fs.usda.gov/recmain/willamette/recreation
Finding the campground: From OR 126, 18 miles northeast of McKenzie Bridge, turn east at the campground sign.
GPS coordinates: N44 21.992' / W121 59.338'
About the campground: This camp occupies the forested shore at the southeast corner of Clear Lake—a frigid, spring-fed natural lake at the head of the McKenzie Wild and Scenic River. A lava flow dotted by vine maples abuts the fir-shaded camp. Because of the sloping shore, some sites are more level than others. Ringing the lake, a superb trail visits Great Spring (source of the icy

Hiker bridge on the Clear Lake Trail, Willamette National Forest

water), forest and lava flow, and rustic Clear Lake Resort, where rowboats may be rented. Another exceptional trail explores downstream along the exciting river, passing Sahalie and Koosah Falls, both of which have drive-to viewing areas. Fishing, rowing the length of the lake, and watching ospreys dive for fish are popular pastimes.

219 Cougar Crossing

Location: On Cougar Reservoir, about 14 miles southeast of the community of Blue River
Season: Year-round
Sites: 11 basic sites; no hookups
Maximum length: 25 feet
Facilities: Tables, grills, nonflush toilets; no drinking water
Fee per night: $$
Management: Willamette National Forest
Contact: (541) 822-3381; www.fs.usda.gov/recmain/willamette/recreation
Finding the campground: From the Blue River Junction on OR 126, drive east on OR 126 about 5 miles. Turn south onto FR 19 (Aufderheide Forest Drive), heading toward Cougar Reservoir. In 0.2 mile turn right to remain on FR 19. The camp is on the right in 9.3 miles, just after you cross the reservoir bridge.
GPS coordinates: N42 17.171' / W120 38.379'
About the campground: This small camp, which sits near the reservoir bridge and an information kiosk on Aufderheide Forest Drive, offers camping at the head of Cougar Reservoir. The sites have graveled parking and are open or partially shaded in a leafy setting dispersed with a few firs. Early in the year the camp is actually on the reservoir. But as the lake water recedes in summer, the camp overlooks the stark reservoir basin and the South Fork McKenzie River. Reservoir recreation—boating, fishing, swimming, and waterskiing—and Terwilliger Hot Springs, a fee area 2.2 miles north of the camp on FR 19, fill out campers' itineraries.

220 Delta

Location: About 5 miles east of the community of Blue River
Season: May–late Oct
Sites: 38 basic sites; no hookups
Maximum length: 36 feet
Facilities: Tables, grills, nonflush toilets, drinking water
Fee per night: $$
Management: Willamette National Forest
Contact: (541) 822-3381; (877) 444-6777 for reservations; www.fs.usda.gov/recmain/willamette/recreation
Finding the campground: From the Blue River Junction on OR 126, drive east on OR 126 about 5 miles. Turn south onto FR 19 (Aufderheide Forest Drive), heading toward Cougar Reservoir. Go 0.2 mile; turn right to reach the campground in another 0.9 mile.

GPS coordinates: N44 09.778' / W122 16.440'

About the campground: This quiet, old-growth-forested campground occupies a delta formed by the main stem and the South Fork McKenzie River. Firs, cedars, and hemlocks tower over camp; enormous stumps, logs, dogwoods, and ferns add to the enchantment. The sites are spacious and well spaced; some are reservable. The barrier-free Delta Nature Trail begins at the end of the campground loop. Fishing, rafting on the McKenzie River, sightseeing along Aufderheide Scenic Drive, and boating on Cougar Reservoir are other diversions.

221 French Pete

Location: About 15 miles southeast of the community of Blue River
Season: Mid-May–mid-Sept
Sites: 17 basic sites; no hookups
Maximum length: 30 feet
Facilities: Tables, grills, nonflush toilets, drinking water
Fee per night: $$
Management: Willamette National Forest
Contact: (541) 822-3381; www.fs.usda.gov/recmain/willamette/recreation
Finding the campground: From the Blue River Junction on OR 126, drive east on OR 126 about 5 miles. Turn south onto FR 19 (Aufderheide Forest Drive), heading toward Cougar Reservoir. In 0.2 mile turn right to remain on FR 19. The camp is on the right in another 10.6 miles.
GPS coordinates: N44 02.519' / W122 12.474'
About the campground: In an old-growth setting along the South Fork McKenzie River, this linear campground is a gateway to the popular French Pete Trail. This canyon trail wins over hikers with its prized old-growth forest and sparkling creek. Engaging pools suggest a summer cool-off. Other area trails explore peaks and drainages. You may also fish, recreate on Cougar Reservoir downstream from camp, and soak in Terwilliger Hot Springs, a fee area 3.5 miles to the north.

222 Frissell Crossing

Location: About 26 miles southeast of the community of Blue River
Season: Mid-May–mid-Sept
Sites: 12 basic sites; no hookups
Maximum length: 36 feet
Facilities: Tables, grills, nonflush toilets, drinking water
Fee per night: $$
Management: Willamette National Forest
Contact: (541) 822-3381; www.fs.usda.gov/recmain/willamette/recreation
Finding the campground: From the Blue River Junction on OR 126, drive east on OR 126 about 5 miles. Turn south onto FR 19 (Aufderheide Forest Drive), heading toward Cougar Reservoir. In 0.2 mile turn right to remain on FR 19. The camp is on the left in another 21 miles.
GPS coordinates: N43 57.514' / W122 05.008'

About the campground: This campground occupies an old-growth stand along the South Fork McKenzie River, just upstream from its confluence with the Roaring River. If you continue south past camp a short distance on FR 19, you will be able to view the Roaring River, a fast-plunging river of white bubbles fanning the lush greenery at its sides. The campground appeals to anglers, hikers, and camp "slugs." The ancient trees, lovely undergrowth, and hush of the river together shape a soothing backdrop for your stay. Trails lead upstream along the South Fork and a side creek.

223 Ice Cap Creek

Location: 17 miles northeast of the community of McKenzie Bridge
Season: Late May–mid-Sept
Sites: 14 basic sites, 8 tent sites; no hookups
Maximum length: 22 feet
Facilities: Tables, grills, flush toilets, waterfall viewing area; no drinking water
Fee per night: $$
Management: Willamette National Forest
Contact: (541) 822-3381; www.fs.usda.gov/recmain/willamette/recreation
Finding the campground: The campground is west off OR 126, 17 miles northeast of McKenzie Bridge.
GPS coordinates: N44 20.514' / W122 00.036'
About the campground: This camp in a fir-and-cedar woods along the McKenzie Wild and Scenic River provides access to the waterfall viewing platforms upstream from camp and to Carmen Reservoir downstream. The sites are spaced for comfort and privacy, but RVers may need to shop around for the most level site. Three viewpoints present the beauty and surge of 63-foot Koosah Falls; equally impressive Sahalie Falls is a short hike farther upstream. Trails travel both sides of the river, allowing a loop between the upper bridge and Carmen Reservoir. Fishing and quiet boating are available at the reservoir and Clear Lake, or you can fish the river.

224 Limberlost

Location: About 6 miles east of the community of McKenzie Bridge
Season: Late May–Sept
Sites: 10 basic sites, 2 tent sites; no hookups
Maximum length: 16 feet
Facilities: Tables, grills, nonflush toilets; no drinking water
Fee per night: $$
Management: Willamette National Forest
Contact: (541) 822-3381; www.fs.usda.gov/recmain/willamette/recreation
Finding the campground: From McKenzie Bridge go 4.6 miles east on OR 126. Turn right (east) onto OR 242; the campground is on the left in 1.4 miles.
GPS coordinates: N44 10.443' / W122 03.220'

About the campground: This cozy, rustic campground above Lost Creek sits at the lower end of McKenzie Pass Scenic Byway (OR 242). The entire byway is usually open by July and remains open through October, allowing for the viewing of fall colors. Lava flows, cinder cones, craters, and the magnificent presence of Three Sisters and Mount Washington, along with their respective wilderness areas, recommend the byway. Tall, straight trees enfold the closely spaced sites. Pockets of skunk cabbage accent the banks of the deep, clear creek. Area trails visit Proxy Falls, Linton Lake, and Scott Mountain and travel along the Upper McKenzie River.

225 McKenzie Bridge

Location: Less than 1 mile west of the community of McKenzie Bridge
Season: Late Apr–late Sept
Sites: 20 basic sites; no hookups
Maximum length: 35 feet
Facilities: Tables, grills, nonflush toilets, drinking water, primitive boat launch for drift boats and rafts
Fee per night: $$
Management: Willamette National Forest
Contact: (541) 822-3381; (877) 444-6777 for reservations; www.fs.usda.gov/recmain/willamette/recreation
Finding the campground: The campground is south off OR 126, 8.7 miles east of Blue River and 0.4 mile west of McKenzie Bridge.
GPS coordinates: N44 10.552' / W122 10.474'
About the campground: Campers here can enjoy the fun and relaxation afforded by the McKenzie River. The camp occupies a full second-growth forest of firs, cedars, and western hemlocks, with a vibrant understory. Many sites overlook the river; all have gravel parking and are well spaced. River rafting, fishing, and reclining at camp are popular.

226 Mona

Location: On Blue River Reservoir, about 7 miles northeast of the community of Blue River
Season: Mid-May–early Sept
Sites: 23 basic sites; no hookups
Maximum length: 36 feet
Facilities: Tables, grills, flush toilets, drinking water, boat launch (en route to camp)
Fee per night: $$
Management: Willamette National Forest
Contact: (541) 822-3381; (877) 444-6777 for reservations; www.fs.usda.gov/recmain/willamette/recreation
Finding the campground: From the Blue River Junction on OR 126, go 2.7 miles east on OR 126. Turn north onto FR 15 for Blue River Reservoir. Go 3.8 miles, crossing over an arm of the reservoir, and follow the long entrance road into camp.

GPS coordinates: N44 12.170' / W122 15.812'
About the campground: This campground overlooks Blue River Reservoir from a forested plateau. A few old-growth monarchs rise among the otherwise second-growth trees. The camp is well laid out for comfort, with both pull-through and back-in camp spaces. Roads and parking are paved. The large lake is open to fishing, swimming, boating, and waterskiing.

227 Olallie

Location: 11 miles northeast of the community of McKenzie Bridge
Season: Late Apr–late Oct
Sites: 17 basic sites; no hookups
Maximum length: 35 feet
Facilities: Tables, grills, nonflush toilets, drinking water, boat launch (drift boat or raft)
Fee per night: $$
Management: Willamette National Forest
Contact: (541) 822-3381; (877) 444-6777 for reservations; www.fs.usda.gov/recmain/willamette/recreation
Finding the campground: The campground is west off OR 126, 11 miles northeast of McKenzie Bridge.
GPS coordinates: N44 15.422' / W122 02.404'
About the campground: This terraced campground sits at the confluence of Olallie Creek and the McKenzie Wild and Scenic River. The sites are spacious and occupy a semi-open forest setting; several sites have river views. The McKenzie River National Recreation Trail travels the opposite shore and can be accessed off Deer Creek Road (FR 2654), downstream from camp. Fishing, rafting, and drift boating are popular diversions.

228 Paradise

Location: About 4 miles east of the community of McKenzie Bridge
Season: Mid-May–late Oct
Sites: 64 basic sites; no hookups
Maximum length: 40 feet
Facilities: Tables, grills, flush and nonflush toilets, drinking water, primitive boat launch for rafts
Fee per night: $$
Management: Willamette National Forest
Contact: (541) 822-3381; (877) 444-6777 for reservations; www.fs.usda.gov/recmain/willamette/recreation
Finding the campground: From McKenzie Bridge go 3.8 miles east on OR 126; turn left to enter the campground.
GPS coordinates: N44 11.059' / W122 05.425'
About the campground: One of a handful of idyllic McKenzie River campgrounds, this facility serves rafters, anglers, and hikers. The McKenzie National Recreation Trail follows the Wild and Scenic River

upstream some 24 miles to Clear Lake and its headwater spring, passing Sahalie and Koosah Falls en route. If your time is limited and your feet are unwilling, you can also reach the lake and falls via OR 126. Sites have paved parking and sit in a rich, multistory old-growth forest.

229 Slide Creek

Location: On Cougar Reservoir, about 15 miles southeast of the community of Blue River
Season: May–Sept
Sites: 16 basic sites; no hookups
Maximum length: 40 feet
Facilities: Tables, grills, nonflush toilets, drinking water, paved boat launch
Fee per night: $$
Management: Willamette National Forest
Contact: (541) 822-3381; (877) 444-6777 for reservations; www.fs.usda.gov/recmain/ willamette/recreation
Finding the campground: From the Blue River Junction on OR 126, drive east on OR 126 about 5 miles. Turn south onto FR 19 (Aufderheide Forest Drive), heading toward Cougar Reservoir. In 0.2 mile bear right to remain on FR 19, following it another 9.3 miles. Upon crossing the reservoir bridge, turn left onto gravel FR 500, which heads north along the east shore. Continue 1.4 miles to the campground on the left.
GPS coordinates: N44 04.558' / W122 13.532'
About the campground: This popular east-shore campground is located where Slide Creek feeds into Cougar Lake. The attractive, long, green lake invites fishing, swimming, boating, and water-skiing. The canyon's ragged skyline and steep walls, rocky and forested, add to the setting. The campsites have developed, off-shoulder parking and are shaded by firs, maples, and dogwoods. Trailheads and a popular hot springs area lie within short drives of the camp.

230 Sunnyside

Location: On Cougar Reservoir, about 15 miles southeast of the community of Blue River
Season: Mid-May–Sept
Sites: 13 tent sites; no hookups
Maximum length: Suitable for tents only
Facilities: Tables, grills, nonflush toilets; no drinking water
Fee per night: $$
Management: Willamette National Forest
Contact: (541) 822-3381; www.fs.usda.gov/recmain/willamette/recreation
Finding the campground: From the Blue River Junction on OR 126, drive east on OR 126 about 5 miles. Turn south onto FR 19 (Aufderheide Forest Drive), heading toward Cougar Reservoir. In 0.2 mile bear right to remain on FR 19, following it another 9.3 miles. Upon crossing the reservoir bridge, turn left onto gravel FR 500. Proceed about 0.8 mile to the campground on the left. The entry road to the camp is steep.

GPS coordinates: N44 03.857' / W122 13.346'

About the campground: On the east shore of Cougar Reservoir, this improved dispersed camp offers gravel parking spurs, basic amenities, and shade for comfort. Boaters typically put in at Slide Creek Campground, just to the north, then moor their boats along shore here at Sunnyside. The lake invites fishing, swimming, boating, and waterskiing. Trailheads and a hot springs area are but short drives away.

231 Trail Bridge

Location: On Trail Bridge Reservoir, 13 miles northeast of the community of McKenzie Bridge
Season: Late Apr–mid-Oct
Sites: 19 basic sites, 27 walk-in tent sites; no hookups
Maximum length: 45 feet
Facilities: Tables, grills, flush and nonflush toilets, drinking water, boat launch
Fee per night: $$
Management: Willamette National Forest
Contact: (541) 822-3381; www.fs.usda.gov/recmain/willamette/recreation
Finding the campground: The campground is west off OR 126, 13 miles northeast of McKenzie Bridge.
GPS coordinates: N44 16.813' / W122 02.891'

About the campground: This campground offers forested tent sites along Trail Bridge Reservoir, where the McKenzie River is harnessed for power generation. Additional RV camping is available on the open flat alongside the reservoir. The reservoir offers fishing and boating. There is also convenient access to the McKenzie River National Recreation Trail and to the McKenzie Pass–Santiam Pass Scenic Byway, a loop drive following OR 126, US 20, and OR 242. The forest service and the Eugene Water and Electric Board have a planned reconstruction slated for this camp, which will include an extended closure. Call to be sure the campground is open, or be ready to camp elsewhere in the area.

Eugene-Cottage Grove Area

	Hookup Sites	Total Sites	Max. RV Length	Hookups	Toilets	Showers	Drinking Water	Dump Station	Recreation	Fee	Can Reserve
232 Armitage County Park	32	32	60	WESC	F		X		FBL	$$$	X
233 Baker Bay		49	50		F, NF	X	X	X	SFBL	$$$	X
234 Bedrock		15	30		NF				HF	$$	
235 Big Pool		5	T		NF		X		HF	$$	
236 Broken Bowl		16	20		F		X		HF	$$	
237 Cascara-Fall Creek State Recreation Site		47	45		NF		X		SFBL	$$	
238 Cedar Creek		9	16		NF		X		HSF	$$	
239 Dolly Varden		5	T		NF				HF	$$	
240 Hobo Camp		5	16		NF				HF	None	
241 Lund Park		10	16		NF				HF	$	
242 Pine Meadows		92	50		F	X	X	X	FBL	$$	X
243 Primitive		15	50		NF		X		FBL	$$	X
244 Puma		11	25		NF		X		HF	$$	
245 Richardson County Park	88	88	60	WE	F	X	X	X	SFBL	$$$	X
246 Rujada		12	22		F, NF		X		HF	$$	
247 Schwartz		82	50		F	X	X	X	FB	$$	X
248 Sharps Creek Recreation Site		10	25		NF		X		SF	$	
249 Winberry		6	14		NF		X		HF	$	

232   Armitage County Park

Location: About 5 miles north of Eugene
Season: Year-round
Sites: 32 hookup RV/tent sites; water, electric, sewer, and cable hookups
Maximum length: 60 feet, with most over 50 feet
Facilities: Tables, grills, flush toilets, drinking water, wireless, horseshoe pits, volleyball court, boat ramp
Fee per night: $$$
Management: Lane County Parks
Contact: (541) 682-2000, reservations accepted; www.co.lane.or.us/departments/PW/Parks/

Finding the campground: From I-5 take exit 199 and head west into Coburg, following signs for the park. In 0.8 mile turn left onto Willamette Street, which later becomes Coburg Road. Continue 2.5 miles, entering the park on the right.

From I-5 in Eugene take exit 195 toward Florence and Junction City, following the Belt Line Highway west. In about 1 mile take the Coburg exit. Drive north 1.8 miles on Coburg Road to reach the campground on the left.

GPS coordinates: N44 06.655' / W123 03.017'

About the campground: Along the McKenzie River, this clean, convenient, landscaped camp serves river enthusiasts, interstate through-travelers, and Willamette Valley and Eugene excursionists. The park's fenced off-leash-dog area is popular with pooch owners and, judging by the tail wags, pooches. But noise from the interstate and railroad can disturb sleep.

233 Baker Bay

Location: On Dorena Lake, about 7 miles east of Cottage Grove
Season: Mid-Apr–mid-Oct
Sites: 49 basic sites; no hookups
Maximum length: 50 feet
Facilities: Tables, grills, flush and nonflush toilets, drinking water, showers, dump station, play structure, volleyball court, swimming area, boat rental, boat launch, dock, food concession
Fee per night: $$$
Management: Lane County
Contact: (541) 942-7669 (concessionaire) or (541) 682-2000 (Lane County Parks), reservations accepted; www.co.lane.or.us/departments/PW/Parks/
Finding the campground: From I-5 at Cottage Grove, take exit 174 and go east on Row River Road for 4.4 miles. Bear right onto South Shore Road, following signs toward Dorena Lake. Continue 2.7 miles; turn left for the campground.
GPS coordinates: N43 46.303' / W122 56.154'
About the campground: This campground and day-use recreation area faces Baker Bay, part of man-made Dorena Lake, which is contained in an attractive basin of rolling, wooded hills. The recreation area welcomes with lawn, shade trees, and an accent of charismatic big oaks. From the fir-and-oak grove of camp, most sites offer lake glimpses. Because this is a bustling recreation water on summer weekends, midweek visits promise greater calm. Waterskiing, strolling along the shoreline, and taking a walk or bicycle ride on nearby Row River Rail Trail are possible diversions.

234 Bedrock

Location: About 16 miles northeast of Lowell
Season: Late May–mid-Sept
Sites: 9 basic sites, 6 tent sites; no hookups
Maximum length: 30 feet
Facilities: Tables, grills, nonflush toilets; no drinking water
Fee per night: $$
Management: Willamette National Forest
Contact: (541) 782-2283; www.fs.usda.gov/recmain/willamette/recreation
Finding the campground: From OR 58, 13 miles east of I-5 and 23 miles west of Oakridge, turn north onto Jasper-Lowell Road. Drive 2.8 miles, following the signs to Unity. Turn right onto Big Fall Creek Road for Winberry and North Shore; go 0.4 mile. Bear left to remain on Big Fall Creek Road for another 13.8 miles. Enter the campground on the left.
GPS coordinates: N43 58.335' / W122 32.743'
About the campground: Although fire a decade ago and windfalls have opened the cathedral, the understory shows resilient, vibrant growth. Fall Creek National Recreation Trail, which can be accessed at the camp, allows for hikes along the creek in either direction. Nearby nature trails, fishing, and engaging in the recreation at Fall Creek Reservoir expand the offering.

235 Big Pool

Location: About 14 miles northeast of Lowell
Season: Mid-May–mid-Sept
Sites: 5 tent sites; no hookups
Maximum length: Suitable for tents only
Facilities: Tables, grills, nonflush toilets, drinking water
Fee per night: $$
Management: Willamette National Forest
Contact: (541) 782-2283; www.fs.usda.gov/recmain/willamette/recreation
Finding the campground: From OR 58, 13 miles east of I-5 and 23 miles west of Oakridge, turn north onto Jasper-Lowell Road. Drive 2.8 miles, following the signs to Unity. Turn right onto Big Fall Creek Road toward Winberry and North Shore; go 0.4 mile. Bear left to remain on Big Fall Creek Road. Proceed another 10.9 miles to the campground on the right.
GPS coordinates: N43 57.962' / W122 35.874'
About the campground: Sandwiched between the road and Fall Creek, this tiny camp rests in a lush low-elevation Douglas fir forest. The Fall Creek National Recreation Trail (NRT) travels the opposite shore of Fall Creek but can be easily accessed in either direction from camp. To the east, Johnny Creek and Clark Creek Nature Trails connect with the NRT and appeal in their own rights. You may also fish or take in the recreation at Fall Creek Reservoir.

236 Broken Bowl

Location: About 13 miles northeast of Lowell
Season: Late May–mid-Sept
Sites: 6 basic sites, 10 tent sites; no hookups
Maximum length: 20 feet
Facilities: Tables, grills, flush toilets, drinking water
Fee per night: $$
Management: Willamette National Forest
Contact: (541) 782-2283; www.fs.usda.gov/recmain/willamette/recreation
Finding the campground: From OR 58, 13 miles east of I-5 and 23 miles west of Oakridge, turn north onto Jasper-Lowell Road. Drive 2.8 miles, following the signs to Unity. Turn right onto Big Fall Creek Road toward Winberry and North Shore; go 0.4 mile. Bear left to remain on Big Fall Creek Road. Continue 10.2 miles to the campground.
GPS coordinates: N43 57.745' / W122 36.596'
About the campground: This campground and day-use area along Fall Creek has a lush, low-elevation setting of Douglas fir and western hemlock and provides access to Fall Creek National Recreation Trail, as well as water play in the creek. A paved trail from the day-use area leads to Fall Creek.

237 Cascara–Fall Creek State Recreation Site

Location: On Fall Creek Reservoir, about 10 miles northeast of Lowell
Season: May–Sept
Sites: 42 basic sites, 5 walk-in tent sites; no hookups
Maximum length: 45 feet
Facilities: Tables, grills, nonflush toilets, drinking water, swimming beach, improved boat ramp, dock
Fee per night: $$
Management: Oregon State Parks and Recreation Department
Contact: (541) 937-1173; www.oregon.gov/OPRD/PARKS/camping.shtml
Finding the campground: From OR 58, 13 miles east of I-5 and 23 miles west of Oakridge, turn north onto Jasper-Lowell Road. Drive 2.8 miles, following the signs to Unity. Turn right onto Big Fall Creek Road toward Winberry and North Shore; go 0.4 mile. Bear left to remain on Big Fall Creek Road; continue 7.2 miles. Turn right onto Peninsula Road; proceed 0.3 mile to the campground entrance on the right.
GPS coordinates: N43 58.300' / W122 40.007'
About the campground: Along Fall Creek Reservoir, this comfortable campground tucked amid firs, alders, and a tangled understory offers sites that are either fully shaded or receive a mix of sun and shade. The sites have gravel parking. Campers enjoy convenient access to the reservoir for fishing and boating. A designated area serves swimmers.

238 Cedar Creek

Location: 23 miles east of Cottage Grove
Season: Late May–Sept
Sites: 9 basic sites; no hookups
Maximum length: 16 feet
Facilities: Tables, grills, nonflush toilets, drinking water
Fee per night: $$
Management: Umpqua National Forest
Contact: (541) 767-5000; www.fs.usda.gov/recmain/umpqua/recreation
Finding the campground: From I-5 at Cottage Grove, take exit 174 and go east on Row River Road, which later becomes Brice Creek Road (FR 22), for 23 miles. The campground is on the north side of Brice Creek Road.
GPS coordinates: N43 40.220' / W122 42.401'
About the campground: At the foot of the Calapooya Mountains, this small campground enjoys a rich, low-elevation forest and overlooks scenic Brice Creek, a clear stream punctuated by cascades and pools. A pedestrian bridge over the creek accesses the historic 5.5-mile Brice Creek Trail, which offers a fine tour along the creek and through old-growth stands; it is open to hiking and mountain bike riding. A spur and a loop option off the Brice Creek Trail add waterfall views on Trestle Creek, but these trails are open to hiking only. The pools of the creek may inspire you to swim or dance a fly line.

239 Dolly Varden

Location: About 12 miles northeast of Lowell
Season: Mid-May–Sept
Sites: 5 tent sites; no hookups
Maximum length: Suitable for tents only
Facilities: Tables, grills, nonflush toilets; no drinking water
Fee per night: $$
Management: Willamette National Forest
Contact: (541) 782-2283; www.fs.usda.gov/recmain/willamette/recreation
Finding the campground: From OR 58, 13 miles east of I-5 and 23 miles west of Oakridge, turn north onto Jasper-Lowell Road. Drive 2.8 miles, following the signs to Unity. Turn right onto Big Fall Creek Road toward Winberry and North Shore; go 0.4 mile. Bear left to remain on Big Fall Creek Road. Continue 9.7 miles to reach the campground.
GPS coordinates: N43 57.760' / W122 36.977'
About the campground: Like its counterparts farther upstream, this Fall Creek campground has a rich forest setting. It sits next to the lower trailhead for the 14-mile Fall Creek National Recreation Trail (NRT), which pursues the creek upstream, sometimes tracing the canyon slope. The NRT can be fragmented for more manageable short hikes, or you can walk the Johnny Creek and Clark Creek Nature Trails (both short drives east of camp). The recreation at Fall Creek Reservoir is also within a reasonable reach of camp.

240 Hobo Camp

Location: About 26 miles east of Cottage Grove
Season: Late May–Sept, with reduced service in off-season
Sites: 5 basic sites; no hookups
Maximum length: 16 feet
Facilities: Tables, grills, nonflush toilets; no drinking water
Fee per night: None
Management: Umpqua National Forest
Contact: (541) 767-5000; www.fs.usda.gov/recmain/umpqua/recreation
Finding the campground: From I-5 at Cottage Grove, take exit 174 and go east on Row River Road, which later becomes Brice Creek Road (FR 22), for 25.3 miles. The camp straddles FR 22.
GPS coordinates: N43 38.810' / W122 40.219'
About the campground: This small fine campground offers a trio of sites best suited for tents or small units above Brice Creek, with two additional sites for bigger units on the opposite side of this quiet forest road. Shading the camp are tall firs, interspersed with cedars and bigleaf maples. Area trails visit Trestle Creek and Parker Creek Falls, Adams Mountain, and the banks of Brice Creek.

241 Lund Park

Location: About 25 miles east of Cottage Grove
Season: Mid-May–mid-Nov
Sites: 8 basic sites, 2 walk-in tent sites; no hookups
Maximum length: 16 feet
Facilities: Tables, grills, nonflush toilets; no drinking water
Fee per night: $
Management: Umpqua National Forest
Contact: (541) 767-5000; www.fs.usda.gov/recmain/umpqua/recreation
Finding the campground: From I-5 at Cottage Grove, take exit 174 and go east on Row River Road, which later becomes Brice Creek Road (FR 22), for 24.8 miles. The camp is on the north side of FR 22.
GPS coordinates: N43 39.062' / W122 40.727'
About the campground: This campground occupies a forest terrace above Brice Creek. Historically the site was a miners' wayside between Cottage Grove and the Bohemia Mining Area. It grew to include a hotel, post office, dam, and powerhouse by the early 1900s. Now, quiet prevails. Shaded by fir and bigleaf maple, the camp has gravel roads and site parking. Nearby hiking trails lead to Trestle Creek and Parker Creek Falls and to area mountains. The Brice Creek Trail, which follows along the creek for 5.5 miles, is open to hiking and mountain biking.

242 Pine Meadows

Location: On Cottage Grove Lake, about 7 miles south of Cottage Grove
Season: Late May–mid-Sept
Sites: 92 basic sites; no hookups
Maximum length: 50 feet
Facilities: Tables, fire rings, flush toilets, drinking water, showers, dump station, playground, nearby boat launch
Fee per night: $$
Management: US Army Corps of Engineers
Contact: (541) 942-5631; (877) 444-6777 for reservations; www.nwp.usace.army.mil/recreation/
Finding the campground: From I-5 south of Cottage Grove, take exit 170 and follow London Road south along the east side of the freeway for 3 miles. Turn left onto Cottage Grove Reservoir Road and go another 2.5 miles; the campground is on the right.
GPS coordinates: N43 42.018' / W123 03.518'
About the campground: This large, developed campground stretches along a fair piece of the eastern shore of Cottage Grove Lake, a large valley reservoir. The camp has a city park atmosphere, with lovely, groomed lawns and shading pines and firs. An open, grassy meadow extends between camp and the man-made lake. The campground has paved parking, with some pull-through sites available. The reservoir offers fishing, boating, and waterskiing, but late in the year, the water can be drawn down. Boaters access the lake at Wilson Creek Day Use, 0.6 mile south of camp.

243 Primitive

Location: On Cottage Grove Lake, about 8 miles south of Cottage Grove
Season: Late May–early Sept
Sites: 15 basic sites; no hookups
Maximum length: 50 feet
Facilities: Tables, fire rings, nonflush toilets, drinking water, nearby boat launch
Fee per night: $$
Management: US Army Corps of Engineers
Contact: (541) 942-5631; (877) 444-6777 for reservations (through the Pine Meadows listing); www.nwp.usace.army.mil/recreation/
Finding the campground: From I-5 south of Cottage Grove, take exit 170 and follow London Road south along the east side of the freeway for 3 miles. Turn left onto Cottage Grove Reservoir Road and go 3 miles to the campground on the right.
GPS coordinates: N43 41.725' / W123 03.902'
About the campground: These primitive campsites are scattered across a broad meadow dotted by trees and wildflowers on the east shore of Cottage Grove Lake. A few sites sit closer to the open, grassy shore. Geese, ducks, and herons are camp companions. The reservoir hosts fishing, boating, and waterskiing, with access at Wilson Creek Day Use, 0.1 mile south of camp.

244 Puma

Location: About 18 miles northeast of Lowell
Season: Late May–Sept
Sites: 8 basic sites, 3 tent sites; no hookups
Maximum length: 25 feet
Facilities: Tables, grills, nonflush toilets, drinking water
Fee per night: $$
Management: Willamette National Forest
Contact: (541) 782-2283; www.fs.usda.gov/recmain/willamette/recreation
Finding the campground: From OR 58, 13 miles east of I-5 and 23 miles west of Oakridge, turn north onto Jasper-Lowell Road. Drive 2.8 miles, following the signs to Unity. Turn right onto Big Fall Creek Road toward Winberry and North Shore and go 0.4 mile. Bear left to remain on Big Fall Creek Road. Continue 15.4 miles to the campground.
GPS coordinates: N43 58.625' / W122 31.072'
About the campground: At this Fall Creek campground, the sites sit fairly close to one another, but the forest setting is appealing. Fall Creek National Recreation Trail leads hikers through the canyon, while the creek welcomes water play.

245 Richardson County Park

Location: On Fern Ridge Lake, about 20 miles northwest of Eugene
Season: Mid-Apr–mid-Oct
Sites: 88 hookup sites; water and electric hookups
Maximum length: 60 feet
Facilities: Tables, grills, flush toilets, drinking water, showers, dump station, playground, volleyball courts, horseshoe pits, swimming area, dock, launch, marina with 286 mooring slips, concession stand
Fee per night: $$$
Management: Lane County
Contact: (541) 682-2000 or (541) 935-2005, reservations accepted; www.co.lane.or.us/departments/PW/Parks/
Finding the campground: From OR 126 at Veneta (about 15 miles west of Eugene), turn north onto Territorial Road. Go 4.7 miles and turn right onto Clear Lake Road. The park is 0.2 mile ahead.
GPS coordinates: N44 06.959' / W123 18.824'
About the campground: Covering 157 acres on the northwest shore of Fern Ridge Lake (a large valley reservoir), this park has ample room to explore. The campground has a dual personality, with some sites in the valley trees and others spread across the groomed lawns dotted with planted conifers. You will find paved roads and parking pads, as well as several pull-through sites. The park has areas for sunning or resting in the shade, romping, swimming, boating, and fishing.

246 Rujada

Location: About 20 miles east of Cottage Grove
Season: Late May–mid-Sept
Sites: 12 basic sites; no hookups
Maximum length: 22 feet
Facilities: Tables, grills, flush and nonflush toilets, drinking water, softball field and horseshoe pits at picnic area
Fee per night: $$
Management: Umpqua National Forest
Contact: (541) 767-5000; www.fs.usda.gov/recmain/umpqua/recreation
Finding the campground: From I-5 in Cottage Grove, take exit 174 and go east on Row River Road for 18.3 miles. Turn left onto Layng Creek Road (FR 17); continue 1.8 miles to the campground and picnic area.
GPS coordinates: N43 42.408' / W122 44.576'
About the campground: This pleasant campground sits along Layng Creek in a rich, varied forest with towering hemlocks and firs. The sites are roomy and well spaced, with tent pads and adequate parking. The 1.5-mile Swordfern Trail begins at the picnic area parking lot and travels through lovely forest along Layng Creek.

247 Schwartz

Location: About 5 miles east of Cottage Grove
Season: Late Apr–late Sept
Sites: 82 basic sites; no hookups
Maximum length: 50 feet
Facilities: Tables, grills, flush toilets, drinking water, showers, dump station, playground, horseshoe pits
Fee per night: $$
Management: US Army Corps of Engineers
Contact: (541) 942-5631; (877) 444-6777 for reservations; ww.nwp.usace.army.mil/recreation/
Finding the campground: From I-5 in Cottage Grove, take exit 174 and go east on Row River Road for 4.4 miles. Bear right onto South Shore Road, following the signs for Dorena Lake. Continue 0.4 mile to the campground.
GPS coordinates: N43 47.053' / W122 57.603'
About the campground: This quiet Row River Valley campground stretches below the dam of Dorena Lake. The river camp occupies a grassy meadow, with shading maples, firs, oaks, and cottonwoods. An ash swale contributes to the overall setting. The facility has paved roads and parking and convenient access to fishing and boating on Dorena Lake. The area's Row River Rail Trail attracts hikers and bicyclists.

248 Sharps Creek Recreation Site

Location: About 18 miles southeast of Cottage Grove
Season: Late May–Sept
Sites: 10 basic sites; no hookups
Maximum length: 25 feet
Facilities: Tables, grills, nonflush toilets, drinking water (hand pump on Sharps Creek Road)
Fee per night: $
Management: Bureau of Land Management—Eugene District
Contact: (541) 683-6600; www.blm.gov/or/
Finding the campground: From I-5 in Cottage Grove, take exit 174 and go east on Row River Road for about 15 miles. Turn right (south) onto Sharps Creek Road; proceed 3.2 miles to the campground entrance on the right.
GPS coordinates: N43 39.704' / W122 48.384'
About the campground: This small camp among tall, second-growth firs sits across the road from Sharps Creek and a handful of picnic sites atop the bluff. In this lightly traveled area, the campground remains relatively quiet; a neighboring field adds to its calm. Scenic Sharps Creek unites sparkling waters, gravel banks, and deep blue-green pools cupped in rocky outcrops. One particularly deep pool fashions a fine swimming hole.

249 Winberry

Location: About 12 miles northeast of Lowell
Season: Late May–early Sept
Sites: 2 basic sites, 4 tent sites; no hookups
Maximum length: Small units only (14 feet)
Facilities: Tables, grills, nonflush toilets, drinking water
Fee per night: $
Management: Willamette National Forest
Contact: (541) 782-2283; www.fs.usda.gov/recmain/willamette/recreation
Finding the campground: From OR 58, 13 miles east of I-5 and 23 miles west of Oakridge, turn north onto Jasper-Lowell Road. Drive 2.8 miles, following the signs to Unity. Turn right onto Big Fall Creek Road toward Winberry and North Shore; go 0.4 mile. Turn right onto Winberry Creek Road (FR 1802); proceed 9 miles to the campground on the right.
GPS coordinates: N43 54.083' / W122 36.977'
About the campground: Along the shore of crystalline Winberry Creek, this quiet camp is ideal for tenters. Tall firs, scenic bigleaf maples, and an effusive understory of vine maple, hazel, thimbleberry, and cascara decorate its grounds. The campground offers fishing; hiking is available nearby. A 1-mile trail leads to Station Butte (consult your Willamette National Forest map).

Oakridge Area

	Hookup Sites	Total Sites	Max. RV Length	Hookups	Toilets	Showers	Drinking Water	Dump Station	Recreation	Fee	Can Reserve
250 Black Canyon		72	38		NF		X		HSFBL	$$	X
251 Blue Pool		24	20		NF		X		F	$$	
252 Campers Flat		5	18		NF		X		HF	$$	
253 Gold Lake		21	24		NF		X		HFBL	$$	
254 Islet		55	30		NF		X		HSBL	$$	
255 Kiahanie		19	24		NF		X		F	$$	
256 North Waldo		58	30		NF		X		HSBL	$$	
257 Packard Creek		35	28		NF		X		SFBL	$$	X
258 Sacandaga		16	24		NF		X		HF	$	
259 Salmon Creek Falls		15	20		NF		X		SF	$$	
260 Sand Prairie		21	28		F, NF				HF	$$	
261 Secret		6	24		NF				SF	$$	
262 Shadow Bay		92	32		NF		X		HSBL	$$	X
263 Timpanogas Lake		10	24		NF		X		HFB	$	

250 Black Canyon

Location: 6 miles west of Oakridge
Season: Late May–late Sept
Sites: 59 basic sites, 13 tent sites; no hookups
Maximum length: 38 feet
Facilities: Tables, grills, nonflush toilets, drinking water, interpretive site, boat ramp (canoes and motor boats)
Fee per night: $$
Management: Willamette National Forest
Contact: (541) 782-2283; (877) 444-6777 for reservations; www.fs.usda.gov/recmain/willamette/recreation
Finding the campground: The campground is north off OR 58, 6 miles west of Oakridge and 22 miles east of Eugene.
GPS coordinates: N43 48.364' / W122 33.937'
About the campground: This camp claims a fir-cedar flat where the Middle Fork Willamette River bends to meet the upper end of Lookout Point Reservoir. The improved sites have level asphalt parking and enjoy the peace and shade that come from a mature forest setting. The designated

tent sites have tent pads to ease the job of setting up camp. Rainbow and cutthroat trout challenge the skills of anglers, while the Black Canyon Nature Trail offers a 1-mile interpretive walk through the forest. Reservoir activities include boating, fishing, swimming, and waterskiing.

251 Blue Pool

Location: 9 miles east of Oakridge
Season: May–mid-Sept
Sites: 19 basic sites, 5 walk-in tent sites; no hookups
Maximum length: 20 feet
Facilities: Tables, grills, nonflush toilets, drinking water
Fee per night: $$
Management: Willamette National Forest
Contact: (541) 782-2283; www.fs.usda.gov/recmain/willamette/recreation
Finding the campground: The campground is south off OR 58, 9 miles east of Oakridge.
GPS coordinates: N43 42.572' / W122 17.889'
About the campground: A mixed forest of fir, cedar, maple, and alder and a lush understory surround this campground. The well-spaced, private sites, some overlooking Salt Creek, have paved parking. Salt Creek provides a soothing backdrop and welcomes fishing. A 14-mile road trip upstream leads to the Salt Creek Falls Viewing Area, which features the 286-foot namesake waterfall, the second tallest in the state. At the developed viewing area, picnicking and hiking extend the recreation. Several paths double as cross-country ski trails in winter.

252 Campers Flat

Location: About 23 miles south of Oakridge
Season: Late May–mid-Sept
Sites: 5 basic sites; no hookups
Maximum length: 18 feet
Facilities: Tables, grills, nonflush toilets, drinking water
Fee per night: $$
Management: Willamette National Forest
Contact: (541) 782-2283; www.fs.usda.gov/recmain/willamette/recreation
Finding the campground: From OR 58, 2 miles east of Oakridge, turn south onto Kitson Springs Road toward Hills Creek Reservoir. Go 0.5 mile and turn right onto FR 21. Continue 20 miles; the campground is on the right.
GPS coordinates: N43 30.077' / W122 24.763'
About the campground: This small campground along the Middle Fork Willamette River features semi-open sites in a setting of cedars and cottonwoods. The river rushes past camp and shows sections of riffles and a deep pool bounded by rock outcroppings. Rainbow and cutthroat trout may tug at your fishing line here, so may suckers. An interpretive sign in camp identifies a portion of the old Oregon Central Military Wagon Road. Hikers can access the Middle Fork Trail near camp

or pick up the 4.1-mile Youngs Rock Trail across the road from the campground entrance. The Youngs Rock Trail is popular with mountain bikers.

253 Gold Lake

Location: On Gold Lake, about 28 miles southeast of Oakridge
Season: July–mid-Oct, dependent on snow
Sites: 21 basic sites; no hookups
Maximum length: 24 feet
Facilities: Tables, grills, nonflush toilets, drinking water, boat launch for nonmotorized boating, wheelchair-accessible canoe dock, picnic shelter
Fee per night: $$
Management: Willamette National Forest
Contact: (541) 782-2283; www.fs.usda.gov/recmain/willamette/recreation
Finding the campground: From OR 58, 26 miles east of Oakridge and 0.6 mile west of Willamette Pass, turn north onto gravel FR 500; continue 2 miles to the campground.
GPS coordinates: N43 37.795' / W122 03.005'
About the campground: This attractive, popular campground is located along Gold Lake, a 100-acre, 25-foot-deep mountain lake in an alpine forest setting of true fir, spruce, white pine, and mountain hemlock. Huckleberry and mountain ash further adorn camp and shore. The lake outlet has its own charm, with its deep-grass banks, alder clumps, and aquatic wildflowers. The outlet bridge bisects the camp, which has gravel parking, a few pull-through sites, and some lakeside sites. Only fly fishing and nonmotorized boating are allowed on the lake. Trailheads at and near camp open the door to neighboring high lakes and peaks for anyone willing to put boot leather to trail. Some paths double as cross-country ski trails.

254 Islet

Location: On Waldo Lake, about 36 miles east of Oakridge
Season: Mid-July–Sept
Sites: 55 basic sites; no hookups
Maximum length: 30 feet
Facilities: Tables, grills, nonflush toilets, drinking water, boat launch
Fee per night: $$
Management: Willamette National Forest
Contact: (541) 782-2283; www.fs.usda.gov/recmain/willamette/recreation
Finding the campground: From OR 58, 23 miles southeast of Oakridge, turn north onto FR 5897 toward Waldo Lake. Go 11 miles and continue left on FR 5898 toward North Waldo and Islet Campgrounds. Islet Campground is ahead in 1.5 miles.
GPS coordinates: N43 44.954' / W122 00.376'
About the campground: This campground rests near the north end of Waldo Lake, a large, natural mountain lake acclaimed as one of the clearest lakes in the world. The sites sit back from the

sandy shore in a forest of hemlocks and firs. Islet Point protrudes 0.1 mile into the lake and gives the camp its name. Benches at the end of the point encourage meditation and sunset gazing. The Shoreline Trail strings 1 mile between Islet and North Waldo Campgrounds. A longer trail system encircles the entire lake and branches off into Waldo Lake Wilderness. Canoeing and swimming further engage guests. Be sure to pack insect repellent—mosquitoes breed in the snowmelt pools and can be bothersome much of the summer.

255 Kiahanie

Location: About 22 miles northeast of Oakridge
Season: Late May–Sept
Sites: 19 basic sites; no hookups
Maximum length: 24 feet
Facilities: Tables, grills, nonflush toilets, drinking water
Fee per night: $$
Management: Willamette National Forest
Contact: (541) 782-2283; www.fs.usda.gov/recmain/willamette/recreation
Finding the campground: From OR 58 at the western outskirts of Oakridge, turn north at the sign for Westfir. From Westfir go east on Aufderheide Memorial Drive (FR 19) for 19.7 miles; the camp-ground is on the left.
GPS coordinates: N43 53.118' / W122 15.391'
About the campground: Along the scenic byway, this camp occupies a mostly uncut forest beside the North Fork Willamette Wild and Scenic River. The camp has a diverse canopy of fir, cedar, hemlock, yew, vine maple, alder, and bigleaf maple. Bountiful greenery, huge stumps, and the crystalline river complete the camp's welcoming calm. The camp has gravel roads and parking and provides river access for fly fishing. Native fish test anglers' skills.

256 North Waldo

Location: On Waldo Lake, about 35 miles east of Oakridge
Season: Mid-July–mid-Oct
Sites: 58 basic sites; no hookups
Maximum length: 30 feet
Facilities: Tables, grills, nonflush toilets, drinking water, boat launch
Fee per night: $$
Management: Willamette National Forest
Contact: (541) 782-2283; www.fs.usda.gov/recmain/willamette/recreation
Finding the campground: From OR 58, 23 miles southeast of Oakridge, turn north onto FR 5897 toward Waldo Lake and go 11 miles. Turn left onto FR 5898 toward North Waldo and Islet Camp-grounds; continue 0.4 mile. Turn right onto FR 5895 and travel 0.5 mile more to the campground.
GPS coordinates: N43 45.619' / W122 00.242'

Waldo Lake, Willamette National Forest

About the campground: This popular campground rests in a high-elevation forest at the north end of Waldo Lake, a 10-square-mile natural lake that lacks a permanent inlet. This helps make it one of the purest lakes in the world, although it's not great for fishing. The deep water off the camp's boat launch is perfect for sailboats. Hiking trails starting from camp include the 21-mile Waldo Lake Trail and the 1-mile Shoreline Trail to Islet Campground. Mosquitoes can be annoying; pack repellent.

257 Packard Creek

Location: On Hills Creek Reservoir, about 9 miles southeast of Oakridge
Season: Late Apr–Sept
Sites: 35 basic sites; no hookups
Maximum length: 28 feet
Facilities: Tables, grills and barbecues, nonflush toilets, drinking water, boat launch, 2 fishing docks (1 barrier free), swimming area, sites with individual docks, 2 picnic shelters
Fee per night: $$
Management: Willamette National Forest
Contact: (541) 782-2283; (877) 444-6777 for reservations; www.fs.usda.gov/recmain/willamette/recreation
Finding the campground: From OR 58, 2 miles east of Oakridge, turn south onto Kitson Springs Road toward Hills Creek Reservoir and go 0.5 mile. Turn right onto FR 21 and follow it 6 miles to the campground entrance on the left.
GPS coordinates: N43 40.261' / W122 25.913'
About the campground: This accommodating camp on Hills Creek Reservoir offers forested sites that sit fairly close together. Water sports are the primary draw, keeping visitors at the reservoir much of the day. Boating, fishing, swimming, and waterskiing are all popular. Expect the camp to fill on summer weekends and holidays. There is a short lakeshore trail at camp. Beware of poison oak when venturing off trails and roads.

258 Sacandaga

Location: About 27 miles south of Oakridge
Season: Late May–Sept
Sites: 16 basic sites; no hookups
Maximum length: 24 feet
Facilities: Tables, grills or barbecues, nonflush toilets, drinking water
Fee per night: $
Management: Willamette National Forest
Contact: (541) 782-2283; www.fs.usda.gov/recmain/willamette/recreation
Finding the campground: From OR 58, 2 miles east of Oakridge, turn south onto Kitson Springs Road toward Hills Creek Reservoir and go 0.5 mile. Turn right onto FR 21; follow it 24.6 miles to the campground entrance on the right.

GPS coordinates: N43 29.792' / W122 19.784'

About the campground: This campground occupies a mixed forest on a bluff above the Middle Fork Willamette River. The rush of the river echoes through the canyon and contributes to the peacefulness of camp. A trail leads to a bench seat with a river canyon view. Other paths lead down to the river, should you want to fish or admire the water and rugged riverbank. For longer hikes, the Middle Fork Willamette Trail can be accessed from the entrance road into camp.

259 Salmon Creek Falls

Location: About 5 miles east of Oakridge
Season: Late Apr–mid-Sept
Sites: 15 basic sites; no hookups
Maximum length: 20 feet
Facilities: Tables, grills, nonflush toilets, drinking water
Fee per night: $$
Management: Willamette National Forest
Contact: (541) 782-2283; www.fs.usda.gov/recmain/willamette/recreation
Finding the campground: From OR 58 at Oakridge, turn north at the light onto Crestview Street toward Oakridge Business District. Go 0.2 mile and turn right onto First Street, which becomes FR 24. Continue 4.9 miles to the campground on the right.
GPS coordinates: N43 45.742' / W122 22.459'
About the campground: A full, mature forest of conifers and deciduous trees shrouds this campground above Salmon Creek and Salmon Creek Falls. Bountiful flora adds to the loveliness of camp. Salmon Creek rushes through a tight canyon as it nears the falls and then cascades over 10-foot ledges and sloping bedrock. The viewing area for the falls is at the day-use area. Besides admiring and photographing the falls, you may fish, swim, or kayak.

260 Sand Prairie

Location: About 14 miles south of Oakridge
Season: Late May–Sept
Sites: 21 basic sites; no hookups
Maximum length: 28 feet
Facilities: Tables, grills and barbecues, flush and nonflush toilets; no drinking water
Fee per night: $$
Management: Willamette National Forest
Contact: (541) 782-2283; www.fs.usda.gov/recmain/willamette/recreation
Finding the campground: From OR 58, 2 miles east of Oakridge, turn south onto Kitson Springs Road toward Hills Creek Reservoir and go 0.5 mile. Turn right onto FR 21; follow it 11 miles to the campground on the right.
GPS coordinates: N43 36.012' / W122 27.172'

About the campground: This campground along the Middle Fork Willamette River is nicely forested and has well-spaced sites for comfort. The setting blends towering evergreens and a leafy midstory; the dogwoods are especially pretty when in bloom. The camp marks the start of the 27-mile Middle Fork Trail, the river offers trout fishing, and the upper end of Hills Creek Reservoir is within a short drive of the camp.

261 Secret

Location: About 22 miles south of Oakridge
Season: Late May–Sept
Sites: 6 basic sites; no hookups
Maximum length: 24 feet
Facilities: Tables, grills and barbecues, nonflush toilets; no drinking water
Fee per night: $$
Management: Willamette National Forest
Contact: (541) 782-2283; www.fs.usda.gov/recmain/willamette/recreation
Finding the campground: From OR 58, 2 miles east of Oakridge, turn south onto Kitson Springs Road toward Hills Creek Reservoir and go 0.5 mile. Turn right onto FR 21; follow it 19 miles to the campground on the right.
GPS coordinates: N43 30.866' / W122 26.504'
About the campground: This campground along the Middle Fork Willamette River feels pleasantly isolated, and its sites are nicely forested. The river's riffles and deep pools draw anglers and summer visitors seeking a refreshing dip. A nice pool is just upstream from camp. Cottonwoods reign along the river.

262 Shadow Bay

Location: On Waldo Lake, about 32 miles east of Oakridge
Season: Mid-July–Sept
Sites: 92 basic sites; no hookups
Maximum length: 32 feet
Facilities: Tables, grills, nonflush toilets, drinking water, boat launch (0.5 mile from camp)
Fee per night: $$
Management: Willamette National Forest
Contact: (541) 782-2283; (877) 444-6777 for reservations; www.fs.usda.gov/recmain/willamette/recreation
Finding the campground: From OR 58, 23 miles southeast of Oakridge, turn north onto FR 5897 toward Waldo Lake and go 6.6 miles. Take the left turn for Shadow Bay Campground, entering the campground in about 2 miles.
GPS coordinates: N43 41.804' / W122 02.562'
About the campground: On an attractive large bay at the south end of Waldo Lake, this campground occupies a moist forest that supports abundant foliage but also provides habitat for pesky

mosquitoes. Be sure to bring repellent. The camp offers access to the Shoreline Trail and has a designated swimming area. The sites rest in a mixed-age forest set back from Waldo Lake, Shadow Bay, and a small lily pond. Boats on the lake are restricted to a maximum speed of 10 miles per hour.

263 Timpanogas Lake

Location: On Timpanogas Lake, about 45 miles southeast of Oakridge
Season: Aug–mid-Oct
Sites: 10 basic sites; no hookups
Maximum length: 24 feet
Facilities: Tables, grills, nonflush toilets, drinking water
Fee per night: $
Management: Willamette National Forest
Contact: (541) 782-2283; www.fs.usda.gov/recmain/willamette/recreation
Finding the campground: From OR 58, 2 miles east of Oakridge, turn south onto Kitson Springs Road toward Hills Creek Reservoir and go 0.5 mile. Turn right onto FR 21; follow it 32 miles. Turn left onto FR 2154; proceed another 10 miles or so to the campground on the left.
GPS coordinates: N43 24.631' / W122 06.954'
About the campground: Situated below the Cascade Crest in the Oregon Cascades Recreation Area, this campground is one of the most enchanting spots in the state, but it is guarded by mosquitoes until late summer. The spacious, well-forested sites sit near the lovely blue platter of Timpanogas Lake. Forest, meadow, and rugged slope rim the lake, which is open to nonmotorized boating and fishing. Trails explore the lakeshore and visit Indigo Lake, another high-mountain jewel along which pikas and pine martens dwell. Huckleberry bushes weighted with berries attract pickers, and photographers find plenty of subject matter.

Southern Oregon

The southern region of the state features the spectacular Umpqua and Rogue River drainages, Crater Lake National Park, the wildlife havens of the Klamath Basin, and the rugged wilds and botanical diversity of the Siskiyou Mountains. It encompasses parts of six national forests: Siskiyou, Umpqua, Rogue River, Winema, Fremont, and Deschutes. Campers here will find superb opportunities for outdoor recreation and wildlife observation, but they will also be treated to cultural offerings, including the Shakespeare Festival in Ashland and the Favell Museum in Klamath Falls.

This is "Jefferson State" country. For decades the residents of southern Oregon and northern California have advocated creation of a new state as a way to gain a stronger

Motor home at Diamond Lake, Rogue-Umpqua National Scenic Byway, Umpqua National Forest

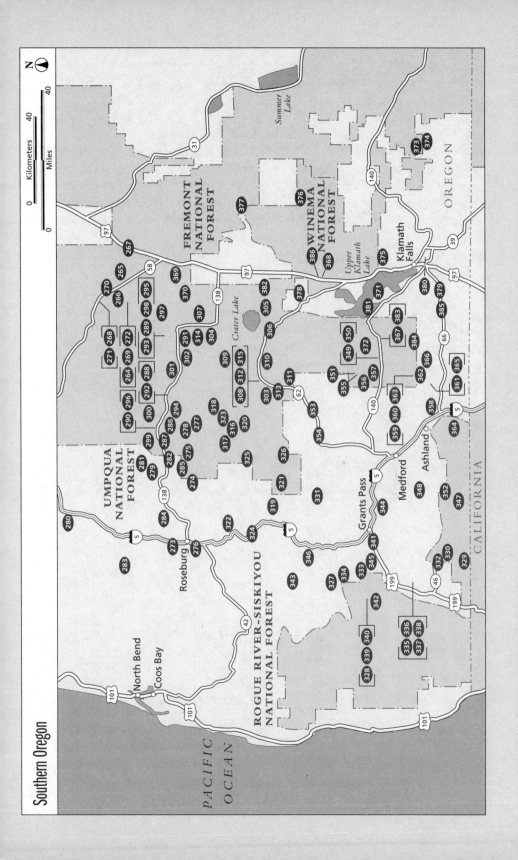

Southern Oregon

political voice. While they have not succeeded, they continue to maintain their separatist mindset. The major towns of this region are Roseburg, Grants Pass, Medford, Ashland, and Klamath Falls, but much of southern Oregon is lightly inhabited.

The weather can vary greatly in this diverse region. The southern valleys threaded by I-5 typically have mild, wet winters punctuated by a few snowstorms that can close the freeway. Summers are hot and dry. The mountains experience four seasons, with some slopes harboring stubborn snowfields that linger well into summer. The Crater Lake area often has snowbanks over 6 feet high when the summer travel season gets under way. Weather in the Klamath Basin is temperamental and varies from season to season. Winters can be relatively snow free and cold or so snowbound that you need snowshoes or cross-country skis to enjoy it. Summers are generally warm and dry. Mosquitoes can be annoying, especially in the high lakes region and around the lakes and marshes of Klamath Basin.

Odell and Crescent Lakes Area

	Hookup Sites	Total Sites	Max. RV Length	Hookups	Toilets	Showers	Drinking Water	Dump Station	Recreation	Fee	Can Reserve
264 Contorta Flat		18	35		NF				SFB	$$	
265 Crescent Creek		9	50		NF		X		F	$$	
266 Crescent Lake		46	50		NF		X		HSFBL	$$	
267 Cy Bingham County Park		10	30		NF				FC	None	
268 Princess Creek		32	50		NF				SFBL	$$	
269 Spring		73	50		NF		X		HSFBL	$$	
270 Sunset Cove		20	50		NF		X		SFBL	$$	
271 Trapper Creek		29	40		NF		X		HSFBL	$$	X
272 Whitefish Horse Camp		17	30		NF		X		HFBR	$$	X

264 Contorta Flat

Location: On Crescent Lake, about 11 miles southwest of the town of Crescent Lake
Season: Mid-May–Sept
Sites: 13 basic sites, 5 tent sites; no hookups
Maximum length: 35 feet
Facilities: Tables, fire rings, nonflush toilets; no drinking water
Fee per night: $$
Management: Deschutes National Forest
Contact: (541) 433-3200; www.fs.usda.gov/recmain/centraloregon/recreation
Finding the campground: From the small community of Crescent Lake on OR 58, turn south onto paved FR 60 and go 2.3 miles. Turn right to remain on FR 60 and continue 7.7 miles. Turn left onto FR 280, following it 0.8 mile to the campground at road's end. The last 2 miles are on gravel.
GPS coordinates: N42 38.485' / W121 52.450'
About the campground: On the south shore of Crescent Lake, this campground occupies a flat of lodgepole pines. Views include Diamond Peak and Red Top Mountain. The lodgepole pines (*Pinus contorta*), which lend the area its name, grow tall and thin, offering little shade. Afternoon winds and early-summer mosquitoes are common, but the area offers fishing, swimming, sailboarding, and sailing. Trails can be found in the nearby Diamond Peak Wilderness and Oregon Cascades Recreation Area.

265 Crescent Creek

Location: About 7 miles southeast of the town of Crescent Lake
Season: Mid-May–Sept
Sites: 9 basic sites; no hookups
Maximum length: 50 feet
Facilities: Tables, grills, nonflush toilets, drinking water
Fee per night: $$
Management: Deschutes National Forest
Contact: (541) 433-3200; www.fs.usda.gov/recmain/centraloregon/recreation
Finding the campground: From Crescent Lake drive 3.4 miles east on OR 58. Turn left onto Crescent Cutoff Road (FR 61); go 3.3 miles and turn right into camp. Because the sign for the campground is easy to miss, look for the entrance 0.1 mile past the intersection of FR 61 and FR 46.
GPS coordinates: N43 29.827' / W121 50.540'
About the campground: This lightly used camp occupies a forest flat of lodgepole and ponderosa pines along Crescent Creek, a wild and scenic waterway. Bunchgrass, wildflowers, and arid shrubs spread between the sites. In this dry terrain, campers need to be extra careful with campfires. The creek flows deep and clear between banks of shrubs and willows, offering anglers a challenge. An access path leads from camp to creek.

266 Crescent Lake

Location: On Crescent Lake, about 3 miles southeast of the town of Crescent Lake
Season: Year-round, dependent on snow
Sites: 46 basic sites, 3 yurts; no hookups
Maximum length: 50 feet
Facilities: Tables, grills, nonflush toilets, drinking water, boat launch, dock
Fee per night: $$
Management: Deschutes National Forest
Contact: (541) 433-3200; (877) 444-6777 for yurt reservations; www.fs.usda.gov/recmain/centraloregon/recreation
Finding the campground: From the small community of Crescent Lake on OR 58, turn south onto paved FR 60. Go 2.3 miles; turn right and remain on FR 60 another 0.4 mile. Turn left to enter the campground.
GPS coordinates: N43 30.083' / W121 58.494'
About the campground: At the north end of Crescent Lake sits this developed campground with paved interior roads and gravel parking. Firs and lodgepole pines shade the terraced camp. Some sites overlook the water; the upper sites may require more leveling. The lake is open to swimming, fishing, boating, sailing, sailboarding, and waterskiing. Winter brings its own fun. The Fawn Lake Trail starts off the campground entrance road.

267 Cy Bingham County Park

Location: In Crescent
Season: Mar–Nov, dependent on weather
Sites: 10 basic sites; no hookups
Maximum length: 30 feet
Facilities: Some tables and grills, nonflush toilets; no drinking water
Fee per night: None
Management: Klamath County
Contact: (541) 883-5121; www.klamathcounty.org/depts/cdd/parks/
Finding the campground: From US 97 in Crescent, head west on the Crescent Cutoff Road for 0.1 mile. Turn right and go a few hundred feet to the campground entrance on the left.
GPS coordinates: N43 27.947' / W121 42.040'
About the campground: Named for an early forester, this convenient, no-frills camp is just off US 97 and close to the Little Deschutes River. The camp occupies a lodgepole pine flat. Logs outline the earthen sites, each of which has a table and/or grill. River access is across the road, and a bike path parallels the Crescent Cutoff Road.

268 Princess Creek

Location: On Odell Lake, about 6 miles northwest of the town of Crescent Lake
Season: May–Sept
Sites: 32 basic sites; no hookups
Maximum length: 50 feet
Facilities: Tables, grills, nonflush toilets, boat launch, dock, ample boat parking; no drinking water
Fee per night: $$
Management: Deschutes National Forest
Contact: (541) 433-3200; www.fs.usda.gov/recmain/centraloregon/recreation
Finding the campground: The campground is south off OR 58, 5.6 miles northwest of Crescent Lake and 0.8 mile east of Willamette Pass.
GPS coordinates: N43 35.162' / W122 00.535'
About the campground: This camp is spread along the north shore of Odell Lake. You can see Diamond Peak across the water. Great concentrations of hemlock, along with fir and spruce, shade the camp and protect it from the lake's notorious afternoon winds. The camp has a paved road, gravel parking, and comfortable sites, but it also has traffic noise from OR 58 during the day. The lake is prized for its boating, fishing, and swimming. Bald eagles and ospreys also fish this 6-mile-long natural lake.

269 Spring

Location: On Crescent Lake, about 9 miles southwest of the town of Crescent Lake
Season: Mid-May–Sept
Sites: 68 basic sites, 5 tent sites; no hookups
Maximum length: 50 feet
Facilities: Tables, grills, nonflush toilets, drinking water, boat launch, dock
Fee per night: $$
Management: Deschutes National Forest
Contact: (541) 433-3200; www.fs.usda.gov/recmain/centraloregon/recreation
Finding the campground: From the community of Crescent Lake on OR 58, go south 2.3 miles on paved FR 60. Turn right to remain on FR 60 for another 5.8 miles. Turn left and proceed 0.6 mile to the campground.
GPS coordinates: N43 27.734' / W122 01.144'
About the campground: This is a developed campground on the south shore of Crescent Lake, a large lake on the outskirts of the Diamond Peak Wilderness. Sites have gravel parking and basic amenities and are partially shaded by lodgepole pines. Campers enjoy access to the lake for fishing, swimming, boating, waterskiing, sailboarding, and sailing and to Diamond Peak Wilderness for hiking. A trailhead 0.3 mile west of camp accesses the Oregon Cascades Recreation Area. Lake visitors should come prepared for mosquitoes at the start of summer.

270 Sunset Cove

Location: On Odell Lake, about 3 miles northwest of the town of Crescent Lake
Season: May–mid-Oct
Sites: 20 basic sites; no hookups
Maximum length: 50 feet
Facilities: Tables, grills, nonflush toilets, drinking water, boat launch, dock, wheelchair-accessible jetty for fishing, fish-cleaning station
Fee per night: $$
Management: Deschutes National Forest
Contact: (541) 433-3200; www.fs.usda.gov/recmain/centraloregon/recreation
Finding the campground: The campground is south off OR 58, 4.7 miles east of Willamette Pass and 2.8 miles west of Crescent Lake Junction.
GPS coordinates: N43 33.748' / W121 57.785'
About the campground: This Odell Lake campground is situated in an evergreen forest punctuated by old-growth trees. Its location on the east shore provides front-row seating for sunset viewing, but it also puts you in the path of strong afternoon winds if you venture out of tree cover. Nonetheless, the fishing, boating, swimming, and attractive setting overrule the wind factor, and sailboarders seem more than satisfied with the location's "drawback."

271 Trapper Creek

Location: On Odell Lake, about 9 miles northwest of the town of Crescent Lake
Season: June–mid-Oct
Sites: 29 basic sites; no hookups
Maximum length: 40 feet
Facilities: Tables, grills, nonflush toilets, drinking water, boat launch, small dock
Fee per night: $$
Management: Deschutes National Forest
Contact: (541) 433-3200; (877) 444-6777 for reservations; www.fs.usda.gov/recmain/centraloregon/recreation
Finding the campground: From OR 58, 0.5 mile east of Willamette Pass and 7 miles west of Crescent Lake Junction, turn south onto Odell Lake West Access Road (FR 5810). Go 2 miles; turn left for the campground.
GPS coordinates: N43 35.050' / W122 02.746'
About the campground: On the west shore of Odell Lake, along pretty Trapper Creek, this popular campground is tucked in a fir-and-spruce forest, where huckleberries claim the understory. A paved road connects the sites, most of which have full shade and are protected from the wind. A few sites overlook Odell Lake, an enormous mountain lake that offers fine views, first-rate fishing, superb boating, and swimming. If you want a change of pace, the Yoran Lake Trail starts near camp.

272 Whitefish Horse Camp

Location: Near Crescent Lake, about 7 miles south of the town of Crescent Lake
Season: June–Sept
Sites: 17 basic sites; no hookups
Maximum length: 30 feet
Facilities: Tables, grills, nonflush toilets, drinking water, corrals
Fee per night: $$
Management: Deschutes National Forest
Contact: (541) 433-3200; (877) 444-6777 for reservations; www.fs.usda.gov/recmain/centraloregon/recreation
Finding the campground: From the community of Crescent Lake on OR 58, head south on paved FR 60 for 2.3 miles. Turn right to remain on FR 60; continue 4.4 miles to the campground entrance on the right.
GPS coordinates: N43 28.364' / W122 01.981'
About the campground: This campground is for the exclusive use of equestrians. It is highly functional, with ample space between the sites and long, gravel parking pads. Corral size determines the difference in site pricing. The horse camp is set back in a lodgepole pine forest across the road from Crescent Lake, giving visitors the best of two worlds: the quiet of the forest and the recreation of the lake. Nearby day-use areas provide access to the lake. Horse trails leave camp to enter Diamond Peak Wilderness.

Roseburg Area

	Hookup Sites	Total Sites	Max. RV Length	Hookups	Toilets	Showers	Drinking Water	Dump Station	Recreation	Fee	Can Reserve
273 Amacher Park	20	30	35	WES	F	X	X		FBL	$$-$$$	
274 Cavitt Creek Recreation Site		10	30		NF		X		S	$	
275 Coolwater		7	24		NF		X		F	$$	
276 Douglas County Fairgrounds RV Park	50	50	40	WE	F	X	X	X		$$$	
277 Hemlock Lake		13	35		NF				HFBL	$$	
278 Lake in the Woods		11	35		F		X		HF	$$	
279 Millpond Recreation Site		12	30		F, NF		X		SF	$$	
280 Pass Creek County Park	30	30	42	WES	F	X	X		F	$$-$$$	
281 Rock Creek Recreation Site		17	30		NF		X		SF	$$	
282 Susan Creek Recreation Site		29	30		F	X	X		HFB	$$	
283 Tyee		15	40		NF		X		SF	$$	
284 Whistler's Bend Park		23	30		F, NF	X	X		HSFBL	$$	
285 Wolf Creek		8	30		F		X		HSF	$$	

273 Amacher Park

Location: About 3 miles north of Roseburg
Season: Apr–Oct
Sites: 20 hookup sites, 10 basic sites; water, electric, and sewer hookups
Maximum length: 35 feet
Facilities: Tables, flush toilets, drinking water, showers, boat launch
Fee per night: $$–$$$ (cash only)
Management: Douglas County
Contact: (541) 957-7001; www.co.douglas.or.us/parks
Finding the campground: Take exit 129 off I-5; head south along the east side of the freeway for 0.5 mile. Turn right to pass under the bridge supports and enter the park.
GPS coordinates: N43 16.936' / W123 21.581'
About the campground: This attractive but somewhat noisy park is located along the North Umpqua River and below the freeway and a rail line. The campground has beautiful lawns and big shade trees, and the North Umpqua seldom disappoints anglers and boaters. Any swimming is at your own risk. Look for a beautiful myrtle grove near the day-use area.

274 Cavitt Creek Recreation Site

Location: About 26 miles east of Roseburg
Season: Mid-May–early Oct
Sites: 10 basic sites; no hookups
Maximum length: 30 feet
Facilities: Tables, grills, nonflush toilets, drinking water
Fee per night: $
Management: Roseburg District Bureau of Land Management
Contact: (541) 440-4930; www.blm.gov/or/
Finding the campground: From Roseburg drive 16.4 miles east on OR 138 to Glide. Turn south onto Little River Road (CR 17) and go 6.6 miles. Turn right onto Cavitt Creek Road. Pass through the covered bridge and continue another 3.2 miles to arrive at the campground.
GPS coordinates: N43 12.024' / W123 01.391'
About the campground: This popular, primitive campground sits above Cavitt Creek in a Douglas fir forest threaded with vine maples and ocean spray. A paved path links the camp with a day-use area and leads to a creek overlook and a stairway to an inviting swimming hole that is fed by a 5-foot cascade.

275 Coolwater

Location: About 33 miles east of Roseburg
Season: Late May–Oct
Sites: 7 basic sites; no hookups
Maximum length: 24 feet
Facilities: Tables, grills, nonflush toilets, drinking water
Fee per night: $$
Management: Umpqua National Forest
Contact: (541) 496-3532; www.fs.usda.gov/recmain/umpqua/recreation
Finding the campground: From Roseburg drive 16.4 miles east on OR 138 to Glide. Turn south onto Little River Road (CR 17/FR 27); continue 16.1 miles to the campground.
GPS coordinates: N43 13.910' / W122 52.362'
About the campground: This camp along the Little River enjoys a quiet setting of evergreens and maples. Camp guests may fish or frolic on the river or take a drive. Just 5.6 miles northwest of camp on Little River Road, a 1-mile trail leads through old-growth splendor to Wolf Creek Falls.

276 Douglas County Fairgrounds RV Park

Location: In Roseburg
Season: Year-round, except during the county fair the second week in Aug
Sites: 50 hookup sites; water and electric hookups
Maximum length: 40 feet
Facilities: Some tables, flush toilets, drinking water, showers, dump station
Fee per night: $$$
Management: Douglas County
Contact: (541) 957-7010; www.co.douglas.or.us/dcfair/rvpark.html
Finding the campground: From I-5 at the south end of Roseburg, take exit 123 to reach the fairgrounds on the east side of the freeway.
GPS coordinates: N43 11.599' / W123 21.598'
About the campground: This clean, serviceable RV park is convenient for those attending fairground events and for travelers on I-5. Sites have gravel pads with lawn meridians on which to place your chair. A few mature trees provide shade, and the younger, planted trees promise more shade in the future. Also on the fairgrounds is the fine Douglas County Museum of History and Natural History.

277 Hemlock Lake

Location: On Hemlock Lake, about 47 miles east of Roseburg
Season: June–Oct
Sites: 10 basic sites, 3 tent sites; no hookups
Maximum length: 35 feet
Facilities: Tables, grills, nonflush toilets, boat launch; no drinking water
Fee per night: $$
Management: Umpqua National Forest
Contact: (541) 496-3532; www.fs.usda.gov/recmain/umpqua/recreation
Finding the campground: From Roseburg go 16.4 miles east on OR 138 to Glide. Turn south onto Little River Road (CR 17/FR 27) and follow the signs for Hemlock Lake. After 29.6 miles turn right off FR 27 onto FR 2700.495; continue 0.7 mile to the campground.
GPS coordinates: N43 11.390' / W122 42.298'
About the campground: You will find this pleasant campground on a fir-covered slope above the dam that forms Hemlock Lake. The man-made lake is the chief draw, inviting fishing and nonmotorized boating. If you prefer to hike, trails travel along the lake and visit Yellow Jacket Glade. Wildflower meadows and stands of old-growth trees complement the trails.

278 Lake in the Woods

Location: About 42 miles east of Roseburg
Season: Late May–Oct
Sites: 10 basic sites, 1 tent site; no hookups
Maximum length: 35 feet
Facilities: Tables, grills, flush toilets, drinking water
Fee per night: $$
Management: Umpqua National Forest
Contact: (541) 496-3532; www.fs.usda.gov/recmain/umpqua/recreation
Finding the campground: From Roseburg go 16.4 miles east on OR 138 to Glide. Turn south onto Little River Road (CR 17/FR 27); continue 26 miles to the campground on the right.
GPS coordinates: N43 12.983' / W122 43.330'
About the campground: This out-of-the-way campground offers a shady retreat in an old-growth forest at the edge of Lake in the Woods—a former swamp, horse pasture, and now lake. The shallow lake wears a cap of lilies and a ring of cattails, while rhododendron bushes decorate the forest. A restored historic cabin sits beside the lake. Seventy-foot Yakso Falls and 80-foot Hemlock Falls are only short hikes away.

279 Millpond Recreation Site

Location: About 27 miles northeast of Roseburg
Season: May–mid-Oct
Sites: 12 basic sites; no hookups
Maximum length: 30 feet
Facilities: Tables, grills, flush and nonflush toilets, drinking water, horseshoe pits, playing field, barrier-free trail along the creek, picnic pavilion
Fee per night: $$
Management: Bureau of Land Management—Roseburg District
Contact: (541) 440-4930; www.blm.gov/or/
Finding the campground: From OR 138, 22.4 miles east of Roseburg (about 6 miles east of Glide), turn left (northeast) onto Rock Creek Road. Continue 5 miles to the camp.
GPS coordinates: N43 22.801' / W122 57.020'
About the campground: The sites of this Rock Creek campground are distributed among second-growth trees and abundant groundcover. The riprap along the creek creates areas of deeper, faster water; there is one pool suitable for swimming. Rock Creek Fish Hatchery, near the junction of OR 138 and Rock Creek Road, is open year-round. You can view juvenile, fingerling, and brood fish, including chinook and coho salmon, steelhead, and rainbow trout.

280 Pass Creek County Park

Location: About 40 miles north of Roseburg
Season: Year-round
Sites: 30 hookup sites, open area for tent camping; water, electric, and sewer hookups
Maximum length: 42 feet
Facilities: Tables, grills, flush toilets, drinking water, showers, playground, laundry
Fee per night: $$–$$$
Management: Douglas County
Contact: (541) 957-7001; www.co.douglas.or.us/parks
Finding the campground: From exit 163 on I-5, 10 miles south of Cottage Grove, follow frontage Curtin Park Road north along the west side of the freeway into the park.
GPS coordinates: N43 43.519' / W123 12.404'
About the campground: This clean, attractive 23-acre park is sandwiched between Pass Creek and the freeway on the east and a rail line on the west. Sites have paved parking, and shrub dividers contribute to privacy. Mature conifer and deciduous trees lend shade. A man-made pond is available for fishing; it supports crappie, bass, bluegill, and some trout. Geese make themselves at home at a small wildlife sanctuary in the park.

281 Rock Creek Recreation Site

Location: About 29 miles northeast of Roseburg
Season: Late May–Sept
Sites: 17 basic sites; no hookups
Maximum length: 30 feet
Facilities: Tables, grills, nonflush toilets, drinking water, site cabinets
Fee per night: $$
Management: Bureau of Land Management—Roseburg District
Contact: (541) 440-4930; www.blm.gov/or/
Finding the campground: From OR 138, 22.4 miles east of Roseburg (about 6 miles east of Glide), turn left (northeast) onto Rock Creek Road. Continue 6.6 miles to the camp entrance.
GPS coordinates: N45 13.361' / W121 22.915'
About the campground: This campground offers a relaxing stay along Rock Creek. Second-growth firs and cedars join bigleaf maples and alders in providing shade for the sites, which are roomy and comfortable. Rock Creek flows wide and shallow, with a few deeper pools for wading. The camp is just a short drive from the Umpqua River, where you can hike, fly-fish, raft, kayak, or sightsee.

282 Susan Creek Recreation Site

Location: About 30 miles east of Roseburg
Season: May–Sept
Sites: 29 basic sites; no hookups
Maximum length: 30 feet
Facilities: Tables, grills, flush toilets, drinking water, showers, barrier-free trails, wildlife viewing platform
Fee per night: $$
Management: Bureau of Land Management—Roseburg District
Contact: (541) 440-4930; www.blm.gov/or/
Finding the campground: The campground is south off OR 138, 29.5 miles east of Roseburg and 12.5 miles east of Glide.
GPS coordinates: N43 17.795' / W122 53.634'
About the campground: This attractive, popular campground, which overlooks the North Umpqua River, was designed to be accessible and convenient for individuals with disabilities. The sites rest in a soothing setting of mature trees along the Wild and Scenic River, which is open to fly fishing, rafting, and kayaking. A magnificent 79-mile trail follows the river from its headwaters high in the Cascades to the Swiftwater Trailhead, west of camp. At Susan Creek Recreation Site, short trails lead to the river and a watchable wildlife platform. Others link the camp to the day-use area, visit 50-foot Susan Creek Falls, and pass rock mounds presumed made by Native American youths during vision quests.

283 Tyee

Location: About 23 miles northwest of Roseburg
Season: Mid-Mar–late Nov
Sites: 15 basic sites; no hookups
Maximum length: 40 feet
Facilities: Tables, grills, nonflush toilets, drinking water, horseshoe pits
Fee per night: $$
Management: Bureau of Land Management—Roseburg District
Contact: (541) 440-4930; www.blm.gov/or/
Finding the campground: From I-5 at Sutherlin, take exit 136 and go west on OR 138 for 10.6 miles. Cross the river bridge; continue 0.2 mile to Bullock Road. Turn right and follow Bullock Road 0.3 mile to the campground on the right.
GPS coordinates: N43 29.118' / W123 29.059'
About the campground: On a plateau above the Umpqua River, a day-use area divides the campground. A mix of fir, cedar, maple, vine maple, and dogwood lend full shade. Leafy shrubs contribute privacy to the already well-spaced sites. A paved path travels the length of the rim and offers views of the river, while stairs descend to a river access. Anglers find sport but should check current regulations before casting a line.

284 Whistler's Bend Park

Location: About 15 miles northeast of Roseburg
Season: Apr–Oct, dependent on conditions
Sites: 23 basic sites, 2 yurts; no hookups
Maximum length: 30 feet
Facilities: Tables, grills, flush and nonflush toilets, drinking water, showers, playground (at day-use area), disc golf, boat launch
Fee per night: $$
Management: Douglas County
Contact: (541) 673-4863; www.co.douglas.or.us/parks
Finding the campground: From Roseburg go east on OR 138 for 12 miles. Turn left (north) onto Whistler's Park Road and go 2.7 miles. Enter the county park and follow the signs to the campground.
GPS coordinates: N43 18.992' / W123 12.974'
About the campground: This 148-acre park tucked in a bend of the North Umpqua River provides campers with ample room to roam. Because it is managed as a wildlife refuge, the park offers opportunities to watch birds and wildlife, including the rare Columbia white-tailed deer. The rustic camp blends with its oak woodland and riverbank setting. The parking is paved. In spring, camas and iris adorn the natural grasses. The river captivates with its blue-green clarity and recreation. As always, be sure to check current fishing regulations. A river trail invites exercise, but beware of poison oak when exploring.

285 Wolf Creek

Location: About 28 miles east of Roseburg
Season: Late May–Sept
Sites: 5 basic sites, 3 tent sites; no hookups
Maximum length: 30 feet
Facilities: Tables, grills, flush toilets, drinking water; volleyball, horseshoe pits, and playing field at day-use area
Fee per night: $$
Management: Umpqua National Forest
Contact: (541) 496-3532; www.fs.usda.gov/recmain/umpqua/recreation
Finding the campground: From Roseburg go 16.4 miles east on OR 138 to Glide. Head south on Little River Road (CR 17/FR 27); continue 11.7 miles to the campground on the right.
GPS coordinates: N43 14.338' / W122 56.150'
About the campground: This campground along the Little River offers closely spaced sites in a second-growth forest. A nature trail makes a loop through the mixed-tree setting; you can access it at the camp or via the bridge over the river at the day-use area. If you drive 1.2 miles west of camp, you can walk the 1-mile Wolf Creek Trail, which crosses the crescent-shaped bridge over the Little River to tour a classic low-elevation forest en route to Wolf Creek Falls. The trail halts at an outcrop with an impressive view of the 80-foot upper-falls segment; below the viewpoint is the lower chute.

Steamboat–Lemolo Lake Area

	Hookup Sites	Total Sites	Max. RV Length	Hookups	Toilets	Showers	Drinking Water	Dump Station	Recreation	Fee	Can Reserve
286 Apple Creek		8	22		NF				HF	$$	
287 Bogus Creek		15	35		F		X		SFBL	$$	
288 Boulder Flat		9	24		NF				HSFBL	$$	
289 Bunker Hill		8	22		NF				HFB	$$	
290 Canton Creek		5	22		F		X		S	$$	
291 Clearwater Falls		12	25		NF					$$	
292 Eagle Rock		25	30		NF				HF	$$	
293 East Lemolo		15	22		NF				FBL	$$	
294 Horseshoe Bend		24	35		F		X		HSFBL	$$	
295 Inlet		14	25		NF				HFB	$$	
296 Island		7	20		NF				SFB	$$	
297 Kelsay Valley Trailhead Camp		16	20		NF				HFR	$$	
298 Poole Creek		59	35		NF		X		HSFBL	$$	
299 Scaredman Creek Recreation Site		10	25		NF		X		S	None	
300 Steamboat Falls		10	20		NF				S	$$	
301 Toketee		32	30		NF				HFBL	$$	
302 Whitehorse Falls		5	25		NF					$$	

286 Apple Creek

Location: About 5 miles east of Steamboat
Season: Late May–Sept
Sites: 8 basic sites; no hookups
Maximum length: 22 feet
Facilities: Tables, grills, nonflush toilets; no drinking water
Fee per night: $$
Management: Umpqua National Forest
Contact: (541) 496-3532; www.fs.usda.gov/recmain/umpqua/recreation
Finding the campground: The campground is south off OR 138, 4.5 miles east of Steamboat and 25.5 miles east of Glide.
GPS coordinates: N43 18.311' / W122 40.585'
About the campground: This campground rests on a forested bench below OR 138 and along the prized North Umpqua River. The camp is shaded by a mix of conifer and deciduous trees and has a luxuriant understory. Hikers will find the Panther Trailhead for the 79-mile North Umpqua

National Recreation Trail just west of the campground turnoff: Follow FR 4714 south across the river bridge to the trailhead. The trail follows the river and climbs to the upper canyon.

287 Bogus Creek

Location: 4 miles west of Steamboat
Season: Late May–Oct
Sites: 15 basic sites; no hookups
Maximum length: 35 feet
Facilities: Tables, grills, flush toilets, drinking water, raft launch
Fee per night: $$
Management: Umpqua National Forest
Contact: (541) 496-3532; www.fs.usda.gov/recmain/umpqua/recreation
Finding the campground: The campground is north off OR 138, 4 miles west of Steamboat and about 17 miles east of Glide.
GPS coordinates: N43 19.475' / W122 47.964'
About the campground: Across OR 138 from the North Umpqua River and a public river access, this campground sits in a restful forest setting beside Bogus Creek. Douglas firs dominate the landscape, and the sites are well spaced for comfort. The river is within easy striking distance for rafting, kayaking, and fly fishing. About 1 mile west is the Wright Creek Trailhead for the North Umpqua National Recreation Trail.

288 Boulder Flat

Location: 16 miles east of Steamboat
Season: May–Oct
Sites: 9 basic sites; no hookups
Maximum length: 24 feet
Facilities: Tables, grills, nonflush toilets, raft launch; no drinking water
Fee per night: $$
Management: Umpqua National Forest
Contact: (541) 496-3532; www.fs.usda.gov/recmain/umpqua/recreation
Finding the campground: The campground is north off OR 138, 16 miles east of Steamboat and 37 miles east of Glide.
GPS coordinates: N43 18.197' / W122 31.661'
About the campground: This campground, with its well-spaced sites, occupies a fir-and-maple flat on the North Umpqua River across from the Boulder Creek confluence. There is direct access to the river for fishing and rafting. The camp also lies within reach of the North Umpqua National Recreation Trail (accessed via Marsters Bridge to the west or near Soda Springs Dam 2 miles to the east) and the Boulder Creek Trail (also reached near Soda Springs Dam).

289 Bunker Hill

Location: On Lemolo Lake, about 60 miles east of Glide
Season: Mid-May–Oct
Sites: 8 basic sites; no hookups
Maximum length: 22 feet
Facilities: Tables, grills, nonflush toilets; no drinking water
Fee per night: $$
Management: Umpqua National Forest
Contact: (541) 498-2531; www.fs.usda.gov/recmain/umpqua/recreation
Finding the campground: From OR 138, 54 miles east of Glide, turn north onto FR 2610 (Birds Point Road), signed for Lemolo Lake. Go 3 miles to a junction; proceed straight on FR 2610 for another 2.5 miles. Turn right onto FR 2612 and go 0.6 mile; turn right to enter the campground.
GPS coordinates: N43 19.144' / W122 11.285'
About the campground: Below forested Bunker Hill on the northwest shore of man-made Lemolo Lake sits this small, rustic campground ideally suited for tents. You may spot bald eagles soaring over camp. Fishing and hiking are popular pastimes here; boating access is available elsewhere on the lake. Look for the North Umpqua National Recreation Trail near the intersection of FR 2610 and FR 2612. OR 138 is part of the Rogue-Umpqua Scenic Byway, should you get the itch to sightsee.

290 Canton Creek

Location: Less than 1 mile northeast of Steamboat
Season: May–Oct
Sites: 5 basic sites; no hookups
Maximum length: 22 feet
Facilities: Tables, grills, flush toilets, drinking water
Fee per night: $$
Management: Umpqua National Forest
Contact: (541) 496-3532; www.fs.usda.gov/recmain/umpqua/recreation
Finding the campground: From OR 138 in Steamboat, 21 miles east of Glide, go 0.3 mile north on FR 38 (Steamboat Creek Road). The campground is on the right.
GPS coordinates: N43 20.895' / W122 43.779'
About the campground: This small, lightly used campground is best suited for tent camping. It occupies a low bluff above Steamboat Creek near the Canton Creek confluence and is a popular place to swim in summer. Firs, maples, alders, and cedars shade the sites. A day-use area claims the upper end of the camp, and a memorial honors three Douglas County law enforcement officers who lost their lives in a helicopter crash nearby. Both Steamboat and Canton Creeks are closed to angling to protect spawning steelhead and salmon, but the North Umpqua River is open for catch-and-release fly fishing. Steamboat Falls, upstream from the camp via FR 38, is worth visiting and photographing; in the fall look for spawning chinooks.

291 Clearwater Falls

Location: About 52 miles east of Glide
Season: June–Oct, dependent on weather
Sites: 12 basic sites; no hookups
Maximum length: 25 feet
Facilities: Tables, grills, nonflush toilets; no drinking water
Fee per night: $$
Management: Umpqua National Forest
Contact: (541) 498-2531; www.fs.usda.gov/recmain/umpqua/recreation
Finding the campground: The western half of the campground sits south off OR 138, 51.5 miles east of Glide. The eastern half is reached by traveling another 1.2 miles east on OR 138, turning right (south) onto FR 4785, and then heading right (west) on Trap Creek Loop. Enter the campground in 0.8 mile.
GPS coordinates: N43 14.892' / W122 13.889'
About the campground: Parted by Clearwater Creek and its waterfall, this campground and its day-use area offer forest relaxation and falls viewing. The western campsites occupy a slope of old-growth Douglas firs and mountain hemlocks and have better access to waterfall viewing. The eastern sites are more open, sitting along the quiet water at the head of the falls. Because of some awkward approaches, the campground is best suited for small units and tent camping. From OR 138 you can reach additional waterfalls, as well as trails and Toketee, Lemolo, and Diamond Lakes.

292 Eagle Rock

Location: About 12 miles east of Steamboat
Season: Late May–Sept
Sites: 25 basic sites; no hookups
Maximum length: 30 feet
Facilities: Tables, grills, nonflush toilets; no drinking water
Fee per night: $$
Management: Umpqua National Forest
Contact: (541) 496-3532; www.fs.usda.gov/recmain/umpqua/recreation
Finding the campground: The campground is north off OR 138, 11.5 miles east of Steamboat and 32.5 miles east of Glide.
GPS coordinates: N43 17.740' / W122 33.200'
About the campground: This campground on the North Umpqua Wild and Scenic River has paved roads and parking. Sites are well spaced along a forested flat. Some are fully shaded by firs; others receive a mixture of sun and shade. The landmark outcrop known as Eagle Rock overlooks this part of the river. Hikers can access the North Umpqua National Recreation Trail at Marsters Bridge to the west. OR 138 serves up a scenic river drive for those who prefer to save their boot leather.

293 East Lemolo

Location: On Lemolo Lake, about 60 miles east of Glide
Season: Mid-May–Oct
Sites: 15 basic sites; no hookups
Maximum length: 22 feet
Facilities: Tables, grills, nonflush toilets, primitive boat launch; no drinking water
Fee per night: $$
Management: Umpqua National Forest
Contact: (541) 498-2531; www.fs.usda.gov/recmain/umpqua/recreation
Finding the campground: From OR 138, 54 miles east of Glide, turn north onto FR 2610 toward Lemolo Lake and go 3 miles. Turn right onto FR 2614 and go 2.2 miles. Turn left onto gravel FR 2614.430; proceed 0.3 mile to the camp at road's end.
GPS coordinates: N43 18.640' / W122 10.226'
About the campground: This camp overlooks the east shore of Lemolo Lake, a reservoir harnessing the North Umpqua River. The earthen sites are tucked among tightly clustered lodgepole pines. Because the camp is small, most sites offer views of the lake; some are right on the lakeshore. Forested Bunker Hill is visible across the water. Boating is a popular pastime, as is fishing for kokanee salmon and rainbow and brown trout.

294 Horseshoe Bend

Location: About 8 miles east of Steamboat
Season: Late May–late Sept
Sites: 24 basic sites; no hookups
Maximum length: 35 feet
Facilities: Tables, grills, flush toilets, drinking water, raft put-in
Fee per night: $$
Management: Umpqua National Forest
Contact: (541) 496-3532; www.fs.usda.gov/recmain/umpqua/recreation
Finding the campground: From OR 138, 7.5 miles east of Steamboat, turn south at the sign for Horseshoe Bend Campground, Raft Launch, and North Umpqua Trail. Go 0.1 mile; turn right onto FR 4750 and drive another 0.8 mile to the camp.
GPS coordinates: N43 17.341' / W122 37.660'
About the campground: This facility consists of three camp flats: Beaver, Deer, and Otter. Deer Flat is for groups and must be reserved in advance. For wheelchair-accessible sites and accommodations, go to Beaver Flat. The single-party campsites have paved parking and are nestled in the woods along the North Umpqua River. The riffles and pools of the river invite fishing, hiking, and rafting. You will find a river access trail in Otter Flat. From the Horseshoe Bend Raft Put-in, it is a 2- to 3-hour float to Gravel Bin Takeout, 6.7 miles downstream. The North Umpqua National Recreation Trail follows the river on the opposite shore; you can access it by backtracking 0.8 mile on FR 4750 and driving across the one-lane bridge to the trailhead.

295 Inlet

Location: On Lemolo Lake, about 60 miles east of Glide
Season: Mid-May–Oct
Sites: 14 basic sites; no hookups
Maximum length: 25 feet
Facilities: Tables, grills, nonflush toilets; no drinking water
Fee per night: $$
Management: Umpqua National Forest
Contact: (541) 498-2531; www.fs.usda.gov/recmain/umpqua/recreation
Finding the campground: From OR 138, 54 miles east of Glide, turn north onto FR 2610 toward Lemolo Lake. Go 3 miles to a junction; turn right onto FR 2614. Go 2.6 miles more to the campground entrance on the right.
GPS coordinates: N43 18.731' / W122 09.271'
About the campground: This campground sits across the road from the east shore of Lemolo Lake at the point where the North Umpqua River feeds into the reservoir. Lupine and paintbrush adorn the floor of the lodgepole pine forest. The camp has gravel roads and parking and offers convenient lake access for fishing. The North Umpqua National Recreation Trail passes nearby.

296 Island

Location: 1 mile east of Steamboat
Season: Year-round
Sites: 7 basic sites; no hookups
Maximum length: 20 feet
Facilities: Tables, grills, nonflush toilets; no drinking water
Fee per night: $$
Management: Umpqua National Forest
Contact: (541) 496-3532; www.fs.usda.gov/recmain/umpqua/recreation
Finding the campground: The campground is south off OR 138, 1 mile east of Steamboat.
GPS coordinates: N43 20.335' / W122 43.366'
About the campground: This campground is cut into a slope between OR 138 and the North Umpqua Wild and Scenic River, a blue-ribbon fly-fishing stream that has attracted the likes of author Zane Grey. Firs, maples, dogwoods, and the song of the river add to the camp's appeal. When river levels are adequate, you can make a 2- to 3-hour float trip between Horseshoe Bend Raft Put-in (6.5 miles east on OR 138) and Gravel Bin Raft Takeout (0.2 mile west of camp).

297 Kelsay Valley Trailhead Camp

Location: About 62 miles east of Glide
Season: Mid-May–Sept, dependent on weather
Sites: 16 basic sites (1 site with corral); no hookups
Maximum length: 20 feet
Facilities: Tables, grills, nonflush toilets, corral, hitching posts; no drinking water
Fee per night: $$
Management: Umpqua National Forest
Contact: (541) 498-2531; www.fs.usda.gov/recmain/umpqua/recreation
Finding the campground: From OR 138, 56 miles east of Glide, turn north onto gravel FR 60 (Windigo Pass Road) and go 4.5 miles. Turn right onto red-dirt FR 6000.958; follow it 1.5 miles to the campground and trailhead. You bypass a 2-site camp en route.
GPS coordinates: N43 19.086' / W122 05.812'
About the campground: This campground is designed to serve both families and equestrian campers. Several site spurs are long enough to accommodate horse trailers. The camp rests in a lodgepole pine forest on the outskirts of a wildflower-spangled high meadow threaded by Bradley Creek, a tributary of the North Umpqua River. Hiker/horse trails travel the area. If you follow the North Umpqua Trail upstream, you will eventually reach the river's headwaters, Maidu Lake, on the Cascade Crest. Come prepared for mosquitoes.

298 Poole Creek

Location: On Lemolo Lake, about 58 miles east of Glide
Season: Mid-May–Oct
Sites: 59 basic sites; no hookups
Maximum length: 35 feet
Facilities: Tables, grills, nonflush toilets, drinking water, boat launch, dock
Fee per night: $$
Management: Umpqua National Forest
Contact: (541) 498-2531; www.fs.usda.gov/recmain/umpqua/recreation
Finding the campground: From OR 138, 54 miles east of Glide, turn north onto FR 2610 toward Lemolo Lake. Go 3 miles to a junction; proceed straight on FR 2610 for another 1 mile to the campground entrance on the right.
GPS coordinates: N43 18.722' / W122 11.799'
About the campground: This campground sits in a dry forest of lodgepole pines, Shasta red firs, and mountain hemlocks on the western shore of Lemolo Lake, which captures the North Umpqua River as it descends from the Cascade Crest. Boating is a chief draw, as is fishing for kokanee salmon and eastern brook, rainbow, and German brown trout. Hiking trails and a designated swimming beach provide other diversions. Waterskiing is allowed on part of the lake.

299 Scaredman Creek Recreation Site

Location: About 4 miles north of Steamboat
Season: Year-round; maintained May–Sept
Sites: 8 basic sites, 2 tent sites; no hookups
Maximum length: 25 feet
Facilities: Tables, grills, nonflush toilets, drinking water (summer only)
Fee per night: None
Management: Bureau of Land Management—Roseburg District
Contact: (541) 440-4930; www.blm.gov/or/
Finding the campground: From OR 138 at Steamboat, 21 miles east of Glide, head northeast on FR 38 (Steamboat Creek Road) for 0.5 mile. Turn left onto Canton Creek Road; continue 3.5 miles to the campground on the right.
GPS coordinates: N43 22.807' / W122 45.665'
About the campground: You will find this quiet campground in a tall stand of Douglas firs along Canton Creek, downstream from the confluence with Scaredman Creek. Although Canton Creek is closed to fishing, the creek's beauty still engages as it riffles over gravel beds and pinches into green pools. This camp is ideal for relaxing or exploring the North Umpqua River corridor.

300 Steamboat Falls

Location: About 6 miles northeast of Steamboat
Season: June–Nov
Sites: 7 basic sites, 3 tent sites; no hookups
Maximum length: 20 feet
Facilities: Tables, grills, nonflush toilets; no drinking water
Fee per night: $$
Management: Umpqua National Forest
Contact: (541) 496-3532; www.fs.usda.gov/recmain/umpqua/recreation
Finding the campground: From OR 138 in Steamboat, 21 miles east of Glide, go northeast 5.5 miles on FR 38 (Steamboat Creek Road). Turn right onto FR 3810; continue 0.6 mile to the campground entrance.
GPS coordinates: N43 22.382' / W122 38.486'
About the campground: This campground lines a forested bench along Steamboat Creek at Steamboat Falls, a dazzling, multidirectional tiered waterfall that spans the 70- to 100-foot breadth of the creek. A fish ladder helps salmon bypass the falls as they migrate upstream. Because the creek is a critical spawning ground for salmon and steelhead trout, it and its tributaries are closed to fishing.

301 Toketee

Location: On Toketee Lake, about 43 miles east of Glide
Season: Year-round, weather permitting
Sites: 32 basic sites; no hookups
Maximum length: 30 feet
Facilities: Tables, grills, nonflush toilets, boat launch, dock; no drinking water
Fee per night: $$
Management: Umpqua National Forest
Contact: (541) 498-2531; www.fs.usda.gov/recmain/umpqua/recreation
Finding the campground: From OR 138, 41 miles east of Glide, turn north onto FR 34 (Toketee-Rigdon Road). Go 0.3 mile and turn left to remain on FR 34. Continue 1.2 miles to the campground on the right.
GPS coordinates: N43 16.411' / W122 24.334'
About the campground: This restful camp is located along the upper North Umpqua River, where it feeds into man-made Toketee Lake. The river resembles a sparkling, creek-size ribbon as it races past camp. Cedars and alders frame the waterway and shade the campsites. The camp has gravel roads and earthen parking, as well as an adjacent boat launch. Campers can boat and fish the reservoir. The North Umpqua National Recreation Trail passes next to camp, and the Toketee Lake Trail can be found along FR 34, 0.5 mile south of the camp entrance.

302 Whitehorse Falls

Location: About 48 miles east of Glide
Season: June–Oct
Sites: 5 basic sites; no hookups
Maximum length: 25 feet
Facilities: Tables, grills, nonflush toilets; no drinking water
Fee per night: $$
Management: Umpqua National Forest
Contact: (541) 498-2531; www.fs.usda.gov/recmain/umpqua/recreation
Finding the campground: The campground is north off OR 138, 48 miles east of Glide.
GPS coordinates: N43 14.822' / W122 18.283'
About the campground: This tiny, lightly used campground rests in a stand of old-growth Douglas firs above the Clearwater River and Whitehorse Falls. Rhododendrons and chinquapins complement the towering trees. At the camp's small picnic area, a viewing platform overlooks the 12-foot falls. A stair-step series of small cascades precedes the falls, and a deep, tranquil pool collects the plummeting water before it continues downstream. Additional falls along OR 138 may suggest outings, as will Toketee, Lemolo, and Diamond Lakes.

Crater Lake–Diamond Lake Area

	Hookup Sites	Total Sites	Max. RV Length	Hookups	Toilets	Showers	Drinking Water	Dump Station	Recreation	Fee	Can Reserve
303 Abbott Creek		25	40		NF		X		F	$$	
304 Broken Arrow		134	32		F	X	X	X	HSFBLC	$$	
305 Crater Lake National Park: Lost Creek		16	T		NF		X			$$	
306 Crater Lake National Park: Mazama		200	30		F	X	X	X	H	$$$	X
307 Diamond Lake		238	35		F	X	X	X	HSFBLC	$$-$$$	X
308 Farewell Bend		61	40		F		X		HF	$$	
309 Hamaker		10	30		NF		X		HF	$$	
310 Huckleberry Mountain		25	16		NF					None	
311 Mill Creek		10	25		NF				F	$	
312 Natural Bridge		17	30		NF				HF	$$	
313 River Bridge		11	25		NF				HF	$	
314 Thielsen View		60	35		NF		X		HSFBLC	$$	
315 Union Creek		78	30		NF		X		HF	$$	

303 Abbott Creek

Location: About 10 miles north of Prospect
Season: Mid-May–Oct
Sites: 25 basic sites; no hookups
Maximum length: 40 feet
Facilities: Tables, grills, nonflush toilets, drinking water
Fee per night: $$
Management: Rogue River National Forest
Contact: (541) 560-3400; www.fs.usda.gov/recmain/rogue-siskiyou/recreation
Finding the campground: From OR 62, 6.2 miles north of Prospect and 6.3 miles south of the junction of OR 62 and OR 230, turn west onto FR 68. Go 3.6 miles to reach the campground on the left.
GPS coordinates: N42 52.904' / W122 30.475'
About the campground: This camp flat beside Abbott Creek presents a mosaic of open meadow, clustered shrubs, and pocket groves of pines, firs, and deciduous trees. There are sites to appeal to the sun seeker, the shade lover, and even the undecided. The camp is quiet and rustic and offers access to the creek at several points. Because the creek is small, youngsters can fish and explore without getting into too much trouble.

304 Broken Arrow

Location: On Diamond Lake
Season: Mid-May–Labor Day Weekend
Sites: 130 basic sites, 4 group campsites; no hookups
Maximum length: 32 feet
Facilities: Tables, grills, flush toilets, drinking water, showers, dump station, barrier-free facilities
Fee per night: $$
Management: Umpqua National Forest
Contact: (541) 498-2531; (877) 444-6777, reservations accepted for a few sites; www.fs.usda .gov/recmain/umpqua/recreation
Finding the campground: From OR 138, 80 miles east of Roseburg, turn west onto Diamond Lake Loop (FR 4795) for the north entry to Diamond Lake Recreation Area. At 0.3 mile keep left and continue for another 2.9 miles. Turn right for the south shore attractions, reaching Broken Arrow on the left in 0.5 mile.
GPS coordinates: N43 08.095' / W122 08.327'
About the campground: Tucked away from shore in the lodgepole pines, this camp shared by humans, jays, and golden-mantled squirrels sits at the southeastern corner of Diamond Lake. The center of activity is the natural lake, which covers more than 3,000 acres. It offers year-round fun, taking you from goggles and swimsuits to snowshoes and mittens. During the camping season, swimming, boating, and fishing for rainbow trout are all popular. Five boat ramps serve lake users. Next to camp, South Shore Picnic Area has a designated swimming beach. A paved pedestrian-and-bicycle trail travels the shoreline; nearby hiking trails lead to Teal and Horse Lakes, Silent Creek, and Mount Bailey.

305 Crater Lake National Park: Lost Creek

Location: About 3 miles southeast of Crater Lake
Season: Mid-July–early Oct, dependent on weather
Sites: 16 tent sites; no hookups
Maximum length: Suitable for tents only
Facilities: Tables, grills, nonflush toilets, drinking water
Fee per night: $$; national park vehicle entry fee ($$) good for 7 days
Management: National Park Service
Contact: (541) 594-3000; www.nps.gov/crla
Finding the campground: From the Rim Drive Junction at the south end of Crater Lake, near Crater Lake National Park Headquarters, follow the rim loop counterclockwise. Go about 8 miles on East Rim Drive. Turn right toward the Pinnacles and Lost Creek Campground; continue 3 miles to the camp entrance on the right.
GPS coordinates: N42 52.739' / W122 02.330'
About the campground: Next to Sand Creek Canyon, en route to the Pinnacles, this campground threaded by Lost Creek occupies a quiet, shady stand of lodgepole pines. While the camp is removed from the main bustle, it is still within easy reach of the 33-mile Rim Drive, with its

Wizard Island, Crater Lake National Park

viewpoints, trailheads, and sightseeing opportunities. The camp is also just a short drive from the Pinnacles, an intriguing canyon of sandcastle-like volcanic fumaroles, which beg to be visited and photographed. The Pinnacles are one of nature's art galleries.

306 Crater Lake National Park: Mazama

Location: About 4 miles south of Crater Lake
Season: July–mid-Sept
Sites: 200 basic sites; no hookups
Maximum length: 30 feet
Facilities: Tables, grills, flush toilets, drinking water, showers, dump station, laundry, food service
Fee per night: $$$; national park vehicle entry fee ($$) good for 7 days
Management: National Park Service
Contact: (541) 594-3000; (888) 774-2728 for reservations; www.nps.gov/crla

Finding the campground: This campground is located east off the south entrance road to Crater Lake National Park, 0.1 mile north of the south entrance station off OR 62 and 3.5 miles south of Rim Drive.

GPS coordinates: N42 52.047' / W122 09.959'

About the campground: On a plateau of lodgepole pines above the picturesque, deeply eroded drainage of Annie Creek sits this campground at the gateway to Crater Lake National Park. Crater Lake was formed some 7,700 years ago when the ancient volcano Mount Mazama collapsed and filled with water to form the deepest lake in the United States and one of the clearest lakes in the world. The 33-mile Rim Drive explores the crater, with stops for hikes, sightseeing, and photography. The lake's color explores uncommon shades of blue. From camp, the Annie Creek Trail descends to the wildflower-spangled banks of Annie Creek. Other park trails top the caldera peaks for panoramic views of the caldera, lake, and Cascades. A narrated boat tour (a fee attraction) leaves from Cleetwood Cove. To board the boat, you must hike 1.1 miles and descend 700 feet in elevation from the rim trailhead to the cove.

307 Diamond Lake

Location: On Diamond Lake
Season: Mid-May–Oct, dependent on weather
Sites: 238 basic sites; no hookups
Maximum length: 35 feet
Facilities: Tables, grills, flush toilets, drinking water, showers, dump station, barrier-free facilities, 2 boat ramps, fish-cleaning station, visitor information station (across road from camp)
Fee per night: $$–$$$
Management: Umpqua National Forest
Contact: (541) 498-2531; (877) 444-6777 for reservations; www.fs.usda.gov/recmain/umpqua/recreation
Finding the campground: From OR 138, 80 miles east of Roseburg, turn west onto Diamond Lake Loop (FR 4795) for the north entry to Diamond Lake Recreation Area. At 0.3 mile keep left; continue 2.2 miles to the campground.
GPS coordinates: N43 10.068' / W122 07.958'
About the campground: Just off the Rogue-Umpqua Scenic Byway, along the east shore of 3,000-acre Diamond Lake, you will find this camping "metropolis." It is surrounded by the Mount Thielsen Wilderness, Oregon Cascades Recreation Area, and the Umpqua National Forest. Recreation on the lake includes fishing, swimming, and boating. A paved pedestrian-and-bicycle trail travels the lakeshore, and the local hiking options range from short nature trails to the interstate Pacific Crest National Scenic Trail. A full-service lakeside resort with boat and sports equipment rentals is just a short hop away.

308 Farewell Bend

Location: About 12 miles north of Prospect
Season: Mid-May–Oct
Sites: 61 basic sites; no hookups
Maximum length: 40 feet
Facilities: Tables, grills, flush toilets, drinking water, playground
Fee per night: $$
Management: Rogue River National Forest
Contact: (541) 560-3400; www.fs.usda.gov/recmain/rogue-siskiyou/recreation
Finding the campground: The campground is west off OR 62, 12.2 miles north of Prospect and 0.3 mile south of the junction of OR 62 and OR 230.
GPS coordinates: N42 54.971' / W122 26.102'
About the campground: This pleasant, popular campground is contained by a scenic bend of the Upper Rogue River. A few pine trees rise among the Douglas firs and hemlocks of camp. The sites have trampled earthen floors, but the perimeters burst with greenery. The river courses over bedrock, except where a gorge squeezes it into a 4- to 5-foot-wide chute. The campground is ideal for relaxing at the river or for sightseeing, with Crater Lake National Park, Diamond Lake Recreation Area, and the Upper Rogue River–Union Creek country all nearby. Superior hiking trails follow Union Creek and the Upper Rogue River.

309 Hamaker

Location: About 26 miles north of Prospect
Season: Mid-May–Oct
Sites: 10 basic sites; no hookups
Maximum length: 30 feet
Facilities: Tables, grills, nonflush toilets, drinking water
Fee per night: $$
Management: Rogue River National Forest
Contact: (541) 560-3400; www.fs.usda.gov/recmain/rogue-siskiyou/recreation
Finding the campground: From the junction of OR 62 and OR 230, 12.5 miles north of Prospect, head north on OR 230 for 12.2 miles. Turn right (east) onto gravel FR 6530. Go 0.6 mile and bear right onto FR 6530.900. Proceed another 0.8 mile to the campground.
GPS coordinates: N43 03.405' / W122 19.762'
About the campground: This idyllic campground occupies a forested bench overlooking the Rogue Wild and Scenic River as it threads out of Crater Lake National Park. Gorgeous old-growth Shasta red firs and Douglas firs rise above camp. The setting is perfect for lounging, but anglers in pursuit of wily trout can try their luck negotiating the shrubs of the riverbanks. Hikers might check out a segment of the Upper Rogue Trail, which pursues this prized waterway downstream from Crater Rim Viewpoint (north on OR 230) to Lost Creek Reservoir (southwest of Prospect). Reach the trail upstream from camp at the barricaded river bridge that is open to pedestrians only.

310 Huckleberry Mountain

Location: About 22 miles northeast of Prospect
Season: Mid-June–Oct, dependent on weather
Sites: 25 basic sites; no hookups
Maximum length: 16 feet
Facilities: Tables, fire rings, nonflush toilets; no drinking water
Fee per night: None
Management: Rogue River National Forest
Contact: (541) 560-3400; www.fs.usda.gov/recmain/rogue-siskiyou/recreation
Finding the campground: From the junction of OR 62 and OR 230, 12.5 miles north of Prospect, head east on OR 62 for 5.7 miles. Turn south onto gravel FR 60 at the sign for the campground near milepost 63. Follow FR 60, which is narrow, winding, and steep, for 4.2 miles to the campground.
GPS coordinates: N42 52.643' / W122 20.222'
About the campground: Because its access road is so steep and narrow, this rustic mountaintop camp is best suited to small units. The sites are widespread for ample privacy, but they lack formal parking. Old-growth Shasta red firs, meadows of false hellebore, and huckleberry flats compose the setting. In late summer, as the berries ripen, you may encounter folks with buckets swinging from their belts and blue stains on their fingertips. This serene retreat also appeals to wildlife.

311 Mill Creek

Location: About 3 miles north of Prospect
Season: Mid-May–Oct
Sites: 10 basic sites; no hookups
Maximum length: 25 feet
Facilities: Tables, grills, nonflush toilets; no drinking water
Fee per night: $
Management: Rogue River National Forest
Contact: (541) 560-3400; www.fs.usda.gov/recmain/rogue-siskiyou/recreation
Finding the campground: From Prospect go 2 miles north on OR 62. Turn right (east) onto FR 6200.030 and go 1 mile. Turn left onto FR 6200.035 to the campground.
GPS coordinates: N42 47.731' / W122 28.075'
About the campground: This tiny, creekside camp is set among old-growth firs, with a midstory tangle of dogwood, maple, and chinquapin. It offers a quiet base from which to explore the Upper Rogue River Area.

Rogue Wild and Scenic River, Rogue-Umpqua National Scenic Byway, Rogue River National Forest

312 Natural Bridge

Location: About 10 miles north of Prospect
Season: Mid-May–Oct
Sites: 17 basic sites; no hookups
Maximum length: 30 feet
Facilities: Tables, grills and rock fireplaces, nonflush toilets; no drinking water
Fee per night: $$
Management: Rogue River National Forest
Contact: (541) 560-3400; www.fs.usda.gov/recmain/rogue-siskiyou/recreation
Finding the campground: From OR 62, about 10 miles north of Prospect and 2.8 miles south of the junction of OR 62 and OR 230, head west on FR 6200.300 toward Natural Bridge. Go 0.4 mile and bear right for the campground. Left leads to the parking for Natural Bridge Viewpoint.
GPS coordinates: N42 53.546' / W122 27.791'
About the campground: Set back from OR 62, this quiet campground covers a large forested flat along the Rogue River. It offers spacious sites, many of them riverside. Firs, pines, hemlocks, and dogwoods shade the camp. Fishing, hiking, and sightseeing along the Rogue River lure guests. The Rogue Gorge Trail passes through camp, while the Upper Rogue National Recreation Trail traces the opposite bank of the Rogue River. You can access the Upper Rogue Trail via the footbridge to Natural Bridge Viewpoint. The viewpoint is worth the short walk to see the spectacular basalt gorge, where a lava tube swallows the river whole, only to spit it out 200 feet downstream.

313 River Bridge

Location: About 5 miles north of Prospect
Season: Mid-May–Oct
Sites: 11 basic sites; no hookups
Maximum length: 25 feet
Facilities: Tables, grills, nonflush toilets; no drinking water
Fee per night: $
Management: Rogue River National Forest
Contact: (541) 560-3400; www.fs.usda.gov/recmain/rogue-siskiyou/recreation
Finding the campground: From Prospect go 4 miles north on OR 62. Turn left (west) onto gravel FR 6210 and go 0.9 mile to the campground on the right.
GPS coordinates: N42 49.303' / W122 29.612'
About the campground: This small camp occupies a forest flat set back from the Rogue Wild and Scenic River where it takes a wide bend. Tall firs and hemlocks, along with a leafy midstory, create nearly full shade. The river and Upper Rogue National Recreation Trail are just steps away from your RV or tent. Riffles occasionally break the glassy surface of the river. A lava outcrop reveals a ropelike pattern and allows for bank fishing.

314 Thielsen View

Location: On Diamond Lake
Season: Mid-May–mid-Oct
Sites: 60 basic sites; no hookups
Maximum length: 35 feet
Facilities: Tables, grills, nonflush toilets, drinking water, boat ramps
Fee per night: $$
Management: Umpqua National Forest
Contact: (541) 498-2531; www.fs.usda.gov/recmain/umpqua/recreation
Finding the campground: From OR 138, 80 miles east of Roseburg, turn west onto Diamond Lake Loop (FR 4795) for the north entrance to Diamond Lake Recreation Area. At 0.3 mile go right; continue another 3 miles to the camp.
GPS coordinates: N43 10.068' / W122 10.037'
About the campground: At the foot of Mount Bailey on the west shore of Diamond Lake, this campground offers a comfortable stay and a magnificent view of Mount Thielsen. The campsites rest in a mixed forest of pine and fir. Historically the lake has been stocked, and the blue expanse offers ample room to troll. Bicyclists can ride an 11-mile paved trail around the lake; hikers can choose from a plethora of destinations in Mount Thielsen Wilderness, Oregon Cascades Recreation Area, and Umpqua National Forest.

315 Union Creek

Location: In the community of Union Creek, about 11 miles north of Prospect
Season: Mid-May–Oct
Sites: 78 basic sites; no hookups
Maximum length: 30 feet
Facilities: Tables, grills, nonflush toilets, drinking water
Fee per night: $$
Management: Rogue River National Forest
Contact: (541) 560-3400; www.fs.usda.gov/recmain/rogue-siskiyou/recreation
Finding the campground: The campground is west off OR 62, 11.2 miles north of Prospect and 1.3 miles south of the junction of OR 62 and OR 230.
GPS coordinates: N42 54.505' / W122 26.967'
About the campground: This engaging camp straddles Union Creek at its confluence with the Upper Rogue River. The sites are well spaced, cozy, and private. Trails explore both banks of the creek and the east shore of the river, but to access the Upper Rogue National Recreation Trail on the west shore, you will need to drive 1.5 miles south to Natural Bridge Campground and Viewpoint Parking and hike the pedestrian bridge over the river. Hiking, fishing, sightseeing, and nature study are area pursuits. Among the outstanding features are old-growth trees, dogwood blooms in spring, and dramatic unions of volcanic outcrop and racing water.

Myrtle Creek Area

	Hookup Sites	Total Sites	Max. RV Length	Hookups	Toilets	Showers	Drinking Water	Dump Station	Recreation	Fee	Can Reserve
316 Ash Flat		4	35		NF					$$	
317 Boulder Creek		7	22		NF		X		S	$$	
318 Camp Comfort		5	22		NF				S	$$	
319 Chief Miwaleta County Park	20	27	40	WES	NF		X		FBL	$$-$$$	X
320 Cover		7	22		NF					$$	
321 Devils Flat		3	22		NF				H	$$	
322 Millsite RV Park	11	11	50	WESC	F	X	X	X		$$$	
323 South Umpqua Falls		20	35		NF				S	$$	
324 Charles V. Stanton Park	20	40	45	WES	F	X	X	X	FBL	$$-$$$	X
325 Three C Rock		5	35		NF				F	$$	
326 Threehorn		5	22		NF					$$	

316 Ash Flat

Location: About 51 miles east of the town of Myrtle Creek
Season: Year-round
Sites: 4 basic sites; no hookups
Maximum length: 35 feet
Facilities: Tables, grills, nonflush toilets; no drinking water
Fee per night: $$
Management: Umpqua National Forest
Contact: (541) 825-3100; www.fs.usda.gov/recmain/umpqua/recreation
Finding the campground: From OR 227 in Tiller, go northeast on South Umpqua River Scenic Route (FR 28) for 17.4 miles. The campground is on the right.
GPS coordinates: N43 02.716' / W122 43.941'
About the campground: This tiny cluster of overnight sites in the upper South Umpqua River corridor rests in a tall fir setting where the trees have height but are small in diameter. The camp has gravel roads and site parking, and users can easily access the recreation and sights of the river corridor. Hiking and mountain biking are popular pursuits.

317 Boulder Creek

Location: About 50 miles east of the town of Myrtle Creek
Season: May–Oct
Sites: 7 basic sites; no hookups
Maximum length: 22 feet
Facilities: Tables, grills, nonflush toilets, drinking water
Fee per night: $$
Management: Umpqua National Forest
Contact: (541) 825-3100; www.fs.usda.gov/recmain/umpqua/recreation
Finding the campground: From OR 227 in Tiller, go northeast on South Umpqua River Scenic Route/FR 28 for 13.6 miles. The campground is on the right.
GPS coordinates: N43 03.244' / W122 46.639'
About the campground: This campground rests in a full conifer-maple forest along the South Umpqua River. Boulder Creek flows into the river at the upper end of camp. Paths to the river are a little rough but passable. They allow you to view the river and cool your ankles, but the river is closed to fishing. Waterfalls farther upstream might be worth a visit: Campbell Falls is 0.8 mile northeast; South Umpqua Falls is 6.1 miles northeast.

318 Camp Comfort

Location: About 60 miles east of the town of Myrtle Creek
Season: May–Oct
Sites: 5 basic sites; no hookups
Maximum length: 22 feet
Facilities: Tables, grills, nonflush toilets; no drinking water
Fee per night: $$
Management: Umpqua National Forest
Contact: (541) 825-3100; www.fs.usda.gov/recmain/umpqua/recreation
Finding the campground: From OR 227 at Tiller, go northeast on South Umpqua River Scenic Route/FR 28 for 26 miles. The campground entrance is on the right.
GPS coordinates: N43 06.364' / W122 35.684'
About the campground: This attractive camp is nestled in a grove of old-growth trees. Sugar pines, firs, hemlocks, and cedars scratch the sky; rhododendrons and vine maples fill out the midstory. A steep slope separates the camp from the South Umpqua River, but you can reach the river via the 0.25-mile, barrier-free Camp Comfort Trail. Because the end of this trail is relatively steep and topped with loose gravel, wheelchair users will probably want to turn around sooner. The trail leads through lovely woods, offers river overlooks, and ends where the Castle Rock and Black Rock Forks combine to form the river. Downstream from the confluence is a swimming hole, but be careful of the rock ledges along the sides of the pool. You can also take a 6.3-mile drive downstream to view South Umpqua Falls, a combination bedrock waterslide and broken-ledge chute.

319 Chief Miwaleta County Park

Location: On Galesville Reservoir, 9 miles east of Azalea
Season: Year-round
Sites: 20 hookup sites, 4 basic sites, 3 walk-in tent sites, 3 cabins; water, electric, and sewer hookups
Maximum length: Several sites in excess of 40 feet
Facilities: Tables, grills, nonflush toilets, drinking water, boat ramp
Fee per night: $$–$$$
Management: Douglas County Parks
Contact: (541) 837-3302 for information, (541) 957-7001 for reservations (only a few sites are reservable); www.co.douglas.or.us/parks
Finding the campground: From I-5 take exit 88 for Azalea and Galesville Reservoir. Travel east on Upper Cow Creek Road for 8 miles, turning right into the campground.
GPS coordinates: N42 51.074' / W123 09.779'
About the campground: This camp offers paved roads and parking among the tall, thin firs of Galesville Reservoir, a popular wet playground. Ferns, dry grass, and chinquapin spread beneath the trees. Small landscape islands and meridians define the RV sites in this compact shoreline campground. The tent area is tucked in forest. Boat and shore fishing for bluegill, large- and small-mouth bass, trout, and more keep anglers busy. Shallow water snags are part of the reservoir's character. Umpqua National Forest beckons with hiking trails.

320 Cover

Location: About 50 miles east of the town of Myrtle Creek
Season: May–Oct
Sites: 7 basic sites; no hookups
Maximum length: 22 feet
Facilities: Tables, grills, nonflush toilets; no drinking water
Fee per night: $$
Management: Umpqua National Forest
Contact: (541) 825-3100; www.fs.usda.gov/recmain/umpqua/recreation
Finding the campground: From OR 227 at Tiller, go northeast on South Umpqua River Scenic Route for 5 miles. Continue east on FR 29 for about 12 miles to the campground.
GPS coordinates: N42 58.549' / W122 41.311'
About the campground: This camp along Jackson Creek offers sites in a semi-open setting of Douglas firs and bigleaf maples, with alders growing toward the creek. Tiny Jackson Creek is a scenic complement to your stay as it courses over bedrock and gravel.

321 Devils Flat

Location: About 40 miles southeast of the town of Myrtle Creek
Season: May–Oct
Sites: 3 basic sites; no hookups
Maximum length: 22 feet
Facilities: Tables, grills, nonflush toilets; no drinking water
Fee per night: $$
Management: Umpqua National Forest
Contact: (541) 825-3100; www.fs.usda.gov/recmain/umpqua/recreation
Finding the campground: From I-5 take the Azalea exit (exit 88) and go east on CR 36 (Upper Cow Creek Road) for 17 miles. The campground is on the left.
GPS coordinates: N42 49.048' / W123 01.588'
About the campground: Just upstream from Cow Creek Falls, at the foot of a steep slope, this little-used campground straddles the road at the historic Devils Flat Guard Station. The circa 1915 ranger cabin still stands. The camp has a gravel road and open grassy sites ringed by cedars and ponderosa pines. From the guard station you can access the Cow Creek Falls and Devils Flat Trails. Because the camp is just 10 miles upstream from Galesville Reservoir (which captures Cow Creek), you can participate in the reservoir recreation as well.

322 Millsite RV Park

Location: In the city of Myrtle Creek
Season: Year-round
Sites: 11 hookup or tent sites (tents must be pitched on parking pads not on lawn); water, electric, sewer, and cable hookups
Maximum length: 50 feet
Facilities: Tables, flush toilets, drinking water, showers, dump station, ball field
Fee per night: $$$
Management: City of Myrtle Creek
Contact: (541) 863-3171; www.cityofmyrtlecreek.com
Finding the campground: From I-5 take exit 108 and go east into Myrtle Creek. At the west end of town, turn right (south) onto Southwest Fourth Avenue. Proceed 0.2 mile to this RV park at the far edge of the city park.
GPS coordinates: N43 01.467' / W123 17.622'
About the campground: This is a tidy, convenient little oasis on the I-5 corridor. The sites have paved parking, grassy meridians with tables, and the open park at their back. Campers can choose between sun and partial shade, but trains passing on a close-by track can rattle you from your slumber.

323 South Umpqua Falls

Location: About 53 miles east of the town of Myrtle Creek
Season: May–Oct
Sites: 20 basic sites; no hookups
Maximum length: 35 feet
Facilities: Tables, grills, nonflush toilets; no drinking water
Fee per night: $$
Management: Umpqua National Forest
Contact: (541) 825-3100; www.fs.usda.gov/recmain/umpqua/recreation
Finding the campground: From OR 227 in Tiller, go northeast on South Umpqua River Scenic Route (FR 28) for about 19.7 miles. The campground is on the left.
GPS coordinates: N43 03.299' / W122 41.386'
About the campground: This camp occupies a broad trimmed-grass meadow–and–forest edge flat 0.1 mile downstream from the popular South Umpqua River Falls attraction and playground, which hums with activity on warm summer days. Sites closer to the treed edge receive some shade, the others require you bring your own shade source.

324 Charles V. Stanton Park

Location: About 8 miles south of the town of Myrtle Creek, 2 miles north of Canyonville
Season: Year-round
Sites: 20 hookup sites, 20 basic sites; water, electric, and sewer hookups
Maximum length: 45 feet
Facilities: Tables, barbecues (at non-hookup sites only), flush toilets, drinking water, showers, dump station, playground, gravel-bar boat launch
Fee per night: $$–$$$
Management: Douglas County
Contact: (541) 957-7001, reservations accepted; www.co.douglas.or.us/parks
Finding the campground: From I-5 southbound take exit 101. Go 1 mile south along the frontage road on the east side of the freeway to the park.

From I-5 northbound take exit 99. Go 1 mile north on the east frontage road to the park.
GPS coordinates: N42 56.792' / W123 17.534'
About the campground: Along the South Umpqua River on the east side of I-5 is this attractive 22-acre campground shaded by mature firs and oaks. The lower camp flat contains the non-hookup sites and is closer to the river. All sites have paved parking. Beyond the camp are open lawns for those who want to romp or play. Fishing is popular; so too is the Indian casino, Seven Feathers, in Canyonville.

325 Three C Rock

Location: About 38 miles east of the town of Myrtle Creek
Season: Year-round
Sites: 5 basic sites; no hookups
Maximum length: 35 feet
Facilities: Tables, grills, nonflush toilets; no drinking water
Fee per night: $$
Management: Umpqua National Forest
Contact: (541) 825-3100; www.fs.usda.gov/recmain/umpqua/recreation
Finding the campground: From OR 227 in Tiller, go northeast on South Umpqua River Scenic Route/FR 28 for 4.7 miles. The campground is on the right.
GPS coordinates: N42 57.824' / W122 53.291'
About the campground: This small campground along the South Umpqua River harkens to the Civilian Conservation Corps camp that occupied this site in the 1930s. The camp rests in fir-pine forest with dry understory of grasses and Queen Anne's lace and tangles of blackberry. Sites receive a mix of sun and shade; the parking pads and road are gravel. Area trails call campers forth.

326 Threehorn

Location: About 50 miles southeast of the town of Myrtle Creek
Season: Year-round
Sites: 5 basic sites; no hookups
Maximum length: 22 feet
Facilities: Tables, grills, nonflush toilets; no drinking water
Fee per night: $$
Management: Umpqua National Forest
Contact: (541) 825-3100; www.fs.usda.gov/recmain/umpqua/recreation
Finding the campground: The campground is east off OR 227, 13 miles south of Tiller and 14.7 miles north of Shady Cove.
GPS coordinates: N42 48.191' / W122 52.062'
About the campground: This small, primitive campground is tucked in a stand of big, attractive sugar pines, cedars, and firs just off OR 227. It offers a relaxing, shady stay or a convenient overnight stop for people traveling this isolated highway. Sites have gravel parking; some are more level than others.

Grants Pass–Cave Junction Area

	Hookup Sites	Total Sites	Max. RV Length	Hookups	Toilets	Showers	Drinking Water	Dump Station	Recreation	Fee	Can Reserve
327 Alameda County Park		34	40		NF		X	X	FBL	$$	X
328 Big Pine		12	20		NF		X		H	$	
329 Bolan Lake		12	15		NF				HSFBL	$	
330 Cave Creek		18	16		NF		X		H	$$	
331 Elderberry Flat		11	30		NF				0	None	
332 Grayback		39	35		NF		X		F	$$	
333 Griffin County Park	15	19	40	WES	F	X	X	X	FBL	$$-$$$	X
334 Indian Mary County Park	58	92	40	WES	F	X	X	X	FBL	$$-$$$	X
335 Lake Selmac County Park: Eagle Loop		14	T		NF		X		SFB	$$	X
336 Lake Selmac County Park: Heron and Teal Loops		19	T		NF		X		HSFBL	$$	X
337 Lake Selmac County Park: Mallard Loop	15	31	40	WES	F	X	X		HSFBLR	$$-$$$	X
338 Lake Selmac County Park: Osprey Loop	21	35	40	WES	F	X	X	X	SFBL	$$-$$$	X
339 Sam Brown		19	24		NF		X		H	$	
340 Sam Brown Horse Camp		7	24		NF		X		HR	$	
341 Schroeder County Park	29	49	40	WES	F, NF	X	X		SFBL	$$-$$$	X
342 Secret Creek		4	T		NF					None	
343 Skull Creek		5	30		NF				F	None	
344 Valley of the Rogue State Park	147	168	75	WE	F	X	X	X	HF	$$-$$$	X
345 Whitehorse County Park	8	42	40	WE	F	X	X		SFBL	$$-$$$	X
346 Wolf Creek County Park	17	32	30	WE	NF		X	X	H	$$-$$$	X

327 Alameda County Park

Location: About 25 miles northwest of Grants Pass
Season: Year-round (dry camping in winter)
Sites: 34 basic sites, 1 yurt; no hookups
Maximum length: 40 feet
Facilities: Tables, grills, nonflush toilets, drinking water (except during winter), dump station, boat ramp

Fee per night: $$

Management: Josephine County

Contact: (541) 474-5285; (800) 452-5687 for reservations; www.co.josephine.or.us

Finding the campground: From I-5 north of Grants Pass, take exit 61 and go 3.6 miles northwest to Merlin. From there proceed west for 14.3 miles on Merlin–Galice Road, passing through Galice to reach this county campground on the right.

GPS coordinates: N42 36.349' / W123 34.870'

About the campground: This campground occupies a large flat along the Rogue Wild and Scenic River. Random oaks and ponderosa pines along with a few madrones shade the mostly earthen flat. This is a popular fishing and summer river recreation site. Camp guests can take advantage of the outfitter trips for rafting or fishing or the shuttle services offered along Merlin–Galice Road. Superb riverside hiking trails lie within short drives of camp.

328 Big Pine

Location: About 30 miles west of Grants Pass

Season: May–Oct

Sites: 12 basic sites; no hookups

Maximum length: 20 feet

Facilities: Tables, grills and barbecues, nonflush toilets, drinking water, playground, horseshoe pits

Fee per night: $

Management: Siskiyou National Forest

Contact: (541) 471-6500; www.fs.usda.gov/recmain/rogue-siskiyou/recreation

Finding the campground: From I-5 north of Grants Pass, take exit 61 and go 3.6 miles northwest to Merlin. From there proceed west 8.6 miles on Merlin–Galice Road. Turn south onto FR 25 toward Big Pine and Briggs Valley, and continue 11.9 miles. The campground is on the right.

GPS coordinates: N42 27.432' / W123 40.665'

About the campground: This fine family campground is stretched across a forested flat along the banks of Myers Creek. Some magnificent firs and pines tower above the camp; vine maples and filberts fill out the midstory. The campsites have earthen parking, and a rustic split-rail fence frames the camp meadow. You can follow a nature trail to explore the forest and visit the area's champion ponderosa pine. Big Pine shoots 250 feet skyward and has a diameter of almost 6 feet. Also from camp, spur trails lead to the longer trails that traverse the valleys of Taylor and Briggs Creeks.

329 Bolan Lake

Location: About 30 miles southeast of Cave Junction

Season: July–Oct, dependent on weather

Sites: 12 basic sites; no hookups

Maximum length: 15 feet

Facilities: Some tables and fire rings, nonflush toilets; no drinking water

Fee per night: $

Management: Siskiyou National Forest

Contact: (541) 592-4000; www.fs.usda.gov/recmain/rogue-siskiyou/recreation

Finding the campground: From the junction of US 199 and OR 46 in Cave Junction, go south on US 199 for 6.4 miles. Turn east onto Waldo Road (a scenic byway), heading toward Takilma and Happy Camp. Go 4.8 miles to a four-way intersection; proceed straight (the road name changes to Happy Camp Road). Continue 12.4 miles and turn left at a sign for the campground, now on gravel FR 4812. Go 4.1 miles to a three-way junction; proceed straight for Bolan Lake on FR 040 (likely unlabeled). Remain on FR 040 as it skirts below the north face of Bolan Mountain to enter the campground in 1.6 miles.

GPS coordinates: N42 01.417' / W123 27.578'

About the campground: This primitive campground is spread along the northern half of 15-acre Bolan Lake, a cold, deep mountain lake that occupies a forest and meadow at the foot of Bolan Mountain. The campground is beautiful and, despite its remoteness, very popular on weekends. A small gravel beach, trout fishing, and nonmotorized boating are the lake attractions. Trails from camp explore the lakeshore and ascend to Bolan Mountain Lookout.

330 Cave Creek

Location: About 15 miles east of Cave Junction

Season: Mid-May–mid-Sept

Sites: 18 basic sites; no hookups

Maximum length: 16 feet

Facilities: Tables, fire pits, nonflush toilets, drinking water

Fee per night: $$

Management: Siskiyou National Forest

Contact: (541) 592-4000; www.fs.usda.gov/recmain/rogue-siskiyou/recreation

Finding the campground: From the junction of US 199 and OR 46 at Cave Junction, go east on OR 46/FR 46 for 15.3 miles. The campground entrance is on the right. (No trailers may proceed past Grayback Campground, which is 11.1 miles east of Cave Junction.)

GPS coordinates: N42 06.880' / W123 25.869'

About the campground: Along Cave Creek stretches this linear, open-forest campground that provides convenient access to Oregon Caves National Monument (reached via trail or road). The monument offers guided underground tours and has fine nature trails that tie into the more extensive trail network of the region. A record-size Douglas fir is one of the hiking destinations. The cool of the cave is especially inviting on hot summer days.

331 Elderberry Flat

Location: About 35 miles northeast of Grants Pass

Season: Apr–Oct

Sites: 11 basic sites; no hookups

Maximum length: 30 feet

Facilities: Tables, grills, nonflush toilets; no drinking water
Fee per night: None
Management: Medford District Bureau of Land Management
Contact: (541) 618-2200; www.blm.gov/or/
Finding the campground: From the city of Rogue River, go north on East Evans Creek Road for 18 miles. Turn left onto West Fork Evans Creek Road; continue 9 miles to the campground.
GPS coordinates: N42 39.698' / W123 05.867'
About the campground: This out-of-the-way campground serves motorcycle and off-highway-vehicle enthusiasts, so you can expect it to be loud and dusty. A forest of firs and hemlocks shades the sites.

332 Grayback

Location: About 11 miles east of Cave Junction
Season: Mid-May–Sept, weather permitting
Sites: 39 basic sites; no hookups
Maximum length: 35 feet
Facilities: Tables, barbecues, nonflush toilets, drinking water
Fee per night: $$
Management: Siskiyou National Forest
Contact: (541) 592-4000; www.fs.usda.gov/recmain/rogue-siskiyou/recreation
Finding the campground: From the junction of US 199 and OR 46 at Cave Junction, go east on OR 46/FR 46 for 11.1 miles. The campground entrance is on the right. (No trailers may proceed past Grayback Campground.)
GPS coordinates: N42 08.546' / W123 27.682'
About the campground: This campground occupies a mixed, multistoried forest of firs, dogwoods, madrones, filberts, and yews. It is contained within a bend of Sucker Creek at its confluence with Grayback Creek. The barrier-free Grayback Interpretive Trail offers views of Sucker Creek and leads to a falls-viewing platform. The campground lies en route to Oregon Caves National Monument and is within an easy drive of a couple of Illinois Valley wineries.

333 Griffin County Park

Location: About 7 miles west of Grants Pass
Season: Apr–late Oct
Sites: 15 hookup sites, 4 tent sites, 1 yurt; water, electric, and sewer hookups
Maximum length: 40 feet
Facilities: Tables, grills, flush toilets, drinking water, showers, dump station, playground, boat ramp
Fee per night: $$–$$$
Management: Josephine County
Contact: (541) 474-5285; (800) 452-5687 for reservations; www.co.josephine.or.us

Finding the campground: From the intersection of US 199 and Riverbanks Road, south of Grants Pass, go northwest on Riverbanks Road for 6 miles. Turn right at the sign for Griffin Park and drive 1 mile to the park entrance on the left.

GPS coordinates: N42 27.778' / W123 29.300'

About the campground: You will find this lovely tree-shaded campground on a gentle slope along the south bank of the Rogue River. Lower sites overlook a broad gravel bar to the acclaimed scenic and recreational waterway; fishing, rafting, and swimming are among the enticements. Ospreys nest on the far shore, and swallows circle overhead and dart after flies rising from the water's surface.

334 Indian Mary County Park

Location: About 15 miles northwest of Grants Pass

Season: Year-round, with reduced winter services

Sites: 58 hookup sites, 34 basic sites, 2 yurts; water, electric, and sewer hookups

Maximum length: 40 feet

Facilities: Tables, grills, flush toilets, drinking water, showers, dump station, playground, horseshoe pits, volleyball, disc golf, boat ramp

Fee per night: $$–$$$

Management: Josephine County

Contact: (541) 474-5285; (800) 452-5687 for reservations; www.co.josephine.or.us

Finding the campground: From I-5 north of Grants Pass, take exit 61 and go 3.6 miles northwest to Merlin. From there proceed west 6.7 miles on Merlin–Galice Road; the campground is on the right.

GPS coordinates: N42 33.124' / W123 32.484'

About the campground: This showplace campground on the Rogue River offers sweeping, tidy grounds and great river access. Its three camping areas are spread across a tree-shaded grassy flat. The tall native pines, oaks, and maples, along with the various planted trees, make reclining at camp inviting, but a full range of river recreation and family activities are right at your elbow. You can be as lazy or as active as you wish.

335 Lake Selmac County Park: Eagle Loop

Location: About 23 miles southwest of Grants Pass, on Lake Selmac

Season: Mid-May–Sept

Sites: 14 tent sites; no hookups

Maximum length: Suitable for tents only

Facilities: Tables, grills, nonflush toilets, drinking water

Fee per night: $$

Management: Josephine County

Contact: (541) 474-5285; (800) 452-5687 for reservations; www.co.josephine.or.us

Finding the campground: From US 199, 20 miles south of Grants Pass and 7 miles north of Cave Junction, turn east onto Lakeshore Drive and go 2 miles. Bear left to stay on Lakeshore Drive for another 0.6 mile. Turn right onto McMullin Creek Road, and then take a quick right turn off it. At the junction just ahead, turn right for Eagle Loop.

GPS coordinates: N42 15.652' / W123 34.264'

About the campground: One of five campground loops on 160-acre Lake Selmac, this tent-camping area occupies a wooded plateau above the lake. A steep 50-foot slope separates the lakeshore from the camp, but a couple of sites overlook the water. There is nearby access for boating (5 miles per hour maximum) and swimming. Bass, crappie, and trout may tug at your fishing lines.

336 Lake Selmac County Park: Heron and Teal Loops

Location: On Lake Selmac, about 23 miles southwest of Grants Pass
Season: Mid-May–Sept
Sites: 5 tent sites at Heron, 14 tent sites at Teal; no hookups
Maximum length: Suitable for tents only
Facilities: Tables, grills, nonflush toilets, drinking water (both loops); boat launch, dock, fish-cleaning station (Teal Loop)
Fee per night: $$
Management: Josephine County
Contact: (541) 474-5285; (800) 452-5687 for reservations; www.co.josephine.or.us
Finding the campgrounds: From US 199, 20 miles south of Grants Pass and 7 miles north of Cave Junction, turn east onto Lakeshore Drive. Go 2 miles and bear right onto Reeves Creek Road. Go 0.8 mile and bear left onto South Shore Road. Proceed 0.2 mile to Heron Loop or 0.4 mile to Teal Loop.
GPS coordinates: N42 15.532' / W123 34.769'
About the campgrounds: Among the campground loops on Lake Selmac, these two tent areas occupy a plateau of firs, pines, and madrones. Some sites offer parking above the lake with a table right on shore. You can see rolling, wooded hills across the lake. Fishing, boating, swimming, and hiking occupy campers. Watch for ospreys, swans, and coots. A grassy spit at each of the camps gives shore anglers a casting edge.

337 Lake Selmac County Park: Mallard Loop

Location: On Lake Selmac, about 23 miles southwest of Grants Pass
Season: Mid-May–mid-Oct
Sites: 15 hookup sites, 10 basic sites, 6 horse sites, 1 yurt; water, electric, and sewer hookups
Maximum length: 40 feet
Facilities: Tables, grills, flush toilets, drinking water, showers, playground, ball field, boat launch, corrals at horse sites
Fee per night: $$-$$$
Management: Josephine County
Contact: (541) 474-5285; (800) 452-5687 for reservations; www.co.josephine.or.us

Finding the campground: From US 199, 20 miles south of Grants Pass and 7 miles north of Cave Junction, turn east onto Lakeshore Drive and go 2 miles. Bear left to stay on Lakeshore Drive for another 0.6 mile. Turn right onto McMullin Creek Road and take a quick right turn off it. At the next junction proceed straight 0.5 mile to Mallard.

GPS coordinates: N42 15.317' / W123 34.315'

About the campground: One of five campground loops on 160-acre Lake Selmac, this loop offers a choice of grassy or wooded sites set back from the lake. You will find a horse staging area and trails leaving camp, as well as the various lake recreations: boating (5 miles per hour maximum); fishing for bass, crappie, and trout; and swimming. Lake Selmac sits in a pretty wooded basin.

338 Lake Selmac County Park: Osprey Loop

Location: About 23 miles southwest of Grants Pass
Season: Year-round; dry camping in winter
Sites: 21 hookup sites, 14 basic sites, 4 yurts; water, electric, and sewer hookups
Maximum length: 40 feet
Facilities: Tables, grills, flush toilets (nonflush toilet in winter), drinking water, showers, dump station, playground, boat launch, fishing dock
Fee per night: $$–$$$
Management: Josephine County
Contact: (541) 474-5285; (800) 452-5687 for reservations; www.co.josephine.or.us
Finding the campground: From US 199, 20 miles south of Grants Pass and 7 miles north of Cave Junction, turn east onto Lakeshore Drive and go 2 miles. Bear right onto Reeves Creek Road; continue 0.5 mile to reach Osprey Loop on the right.
GPS coordinates: N42 15.707' / W123 35.152'
About the campground: Occupying a gentle, wooded slope, this campground is separated from Lake Selmac by Reeves Creek Road. The glimmer of the lake is nonetheless a vital part of the camp ambience, and guests may boat, fish, or swim. Ospreys sometimes circle over Lake Selmac, giving credence to the loop's name. The shady setting of camp provides a welcome retreat from the fun in the sun.

339 Sam Brown

Location: About 30 miles west of Grants Pass
Season: May–Oct
Sites: 19 basic sites; no hookups
Maximum length: 24 feet
Facilities: Tables, grills, nonflush toilets; drinking water across road at Sam Brown Horse Camp, picnic shelters
Fee per night: $
Management: Siskiyou National Forest
Contact: (541) 471-6500; www.fs.usda.gov/recmain/rogue-siskiyou/recreation

Finding the campground: From I-5 north of Grants Pass, take exit 61 and go 3.6 miles northwest to Merlin. From there proceed west 8.6 miles on Merlin–Galice Road. Turn left (south) onto FR 25 toward Big Pine and Briggs Valley; continue 12.8 miles. Turn right onto FR 2512 and go 0.3 mile; the campground is on the left.

GPS coordinates: N42 26.493' / W123 41.192'

About the campground: The campsites are arranged in two loops at the perimeter of a fenced meadow: Loop A is forested; Loop B is sunnier, occupying the lower meadow toward the creek. The sites have gravel parking and are well spaced for privacy and comfort. The trails that follow Briggs, Taylor, and Dutchy Creeks can all be accessed at or near camp.

340 Sam Brown Horse Camp

Location: About 30 miles west of Grants Pass
Season: May–Oct
Sites: 7 basic sites; no hookups
Maximum length: 24 feet
Facilities: Tables, grills, nonflush toilets, drinking water, corral at each site
Fee per night: $
Management: Siskiyou National Forest
Contact: (541) 471-6500; www.fs.usda.gov/recmain/rogue-siskiyou/recreation
Finding the campground: From I-5 north of Grants Pass, take exit 61 and go 3.6 miles northwest to Merlin. From there proceed west 8.6 miles on Merlin–Galice Road. Turn left (south) onto FR 25 toward Big Pine and Briggs Valley and continue 12.8 miles. Turn right onto FR 2512; go 0.1 mile and again turn right to reach the horse camp in 0.2 mile.
GPS coordinates: N42 26.669' / W123 41.037'
About the campground: This accommodating horse camp occupies a semi-open forest flat, giving campers and their animals plenty of space and convenient access to the area's multiple-use trails. Taylor, Dutchy, and Briggs Creeks all have companion trails to explore. The rustic corrals blend with the setting.

341 Schroeder County Park

Location: On the western outskirts of Grants Pass
Season: Year-round; only a few sites open in winter
Sites: 29 hookup sites, 20 basic sites, 2 yurts; water, electric, and sewer hookups
Maximum length: 40 feet
Facilities: Tables, grills, flush and nonflush toilets, drinking water, showers, playground, ball fields and courts, boat launch
Fee per night: $$–$$$
Management: Josephine County
Contact: (541) 474-5285; (800) 452-5687 for reservations; www.co.josephine.or.us

Finding the campground: From the junction of US 199 and OR 99 in southern Grants Pass, go 0.9 mile south on US 199. Turn right (west) onto Redwood Avenue and follow it 1.4 miles. Turn right onto Willow Lane (signed for the park); continue 0.8 mile to the park.
GPS coordinates: N42 26.089' / W123 22.516'
About the campground: This pleasant campground sits on a tree-shaded flat above a day-use area that actually fronts the Rogue River. The camp offers paved sites, tall oaks, groomed lawns, some privacy hedges, and mature cottonwoods along the river. Ducks and squirrels sometimes enliven the camp. Fishing, swimming, and boating are the primary onsite activities, but the park sits within easy reach of the attractions of Grants Pass.

342 Secret Creek

Location: About 33 miles west of Grants Pass
Season: Spring–fall
Sites: 4 tent sites; no hookups.
Maximum length: Suitable for tents only
Facilities: Tables and fire rings, nonflush toilet; no drinking water
Fee per night: None
Management: Siskiyou National Forest
Contact: (541) 471-6500; www.fs.usda.gov/recmain/rogue-siskiyou/recreation
Finding the campground: From I-5 north of Grants Pass, take exit 61 and go 3.6 miles northwest to Merlin. From there proceed west 8.6 miles on Merlin–Galice Road. Turn left (south) onto FR 25 toward Big Pine and Briggs Valley and go 15.3 miles. Make a left turn followed by a quick right into the campground.
GPS coordinates: N42 25.329' / W123 41.354'
About the campground: This tiny, forested campground is tucked along pretty Secret Creek. Because the sites are closely spaced, the parking is sharply angled, and there are no turnarounds, this camp is strictly for tent camping. The trails along Taylor and Briggs Creeks might bring on the urge to explore; the Secret Way Trail begins near camp.

343 Skull Creek

Location: About 11 miles northwest of Glendale
Season: Year-round
Sites: 5 basic sites; no hookups
Maximum length: 30 feet
Facilities: Tables, fire rings, nonflush toilet; no drinking water
Fee per night: None
Management: Medford District Bureau of Land Management
Contact: (541) 618-2200; www.blm.gov/or/
Finding the campground: Coming from the north on I-5, take exit 103 and head west 2.5 miles toward Riddle. Take the bypass around town to follow Cow Creek BLM Backcountry Byway in

another 3 miles. Once on the byway, travel 29.5 miles southwest along Cow Creek to find the marked turn for this recreation site. The camp is just up the slope to the right.

Coming from the south on I-5, take exit 80. Proceed into Glendale and take Brown Road to Reuben CR, heading west. This road eventually becomes the byway. The marked campground turn-off (a left) is 13.5 miles from the exit.

GPS coordinates: N42 46.329' / W123 34.340'

About the campground: Along Cow Creek Backcountry Byway, these five campsites dot a rise above and across the road from Cow Creek. The sites have level gravel parking pads, and views sweep the neighboring ridges and their mosaics of mixed-age trees. The camp is popular with hunters, and the surrounding countryside has a rich mining legacy. At the Cow Creek Gold Panning Area, reached by going northwest on the byway from camp, you can swill your pan for color.

344 Valley of the Rogue State Park

Location: About 10 miles southeast of Grants Pass

Season: Year-round

Sites: 147 full or partial hookup sites, 21 basic sites, 6 yurts; water and electric hookups

Maximum length: 75 feet

Facilities: Tables, grills, flush toilets, drinking water, showers, dump station, playground, horseshoe pits, boat launch, meeting hall

Fee per night: $$–$$$

Management: Oregon State Parks and Recreation Department

Contact: (541) 582-1118; (800) 452-5687 for reservations; www.oregon.gov/OPRD/PARKS/camping.shtml

Finding the campground: From I-5, south of the city of Rogue River, take exit 45. The state park is north of the rest area here.

GPS coordinates: N42 24.602' / W123 08.957'

About the campground: Although you may hear the drone of freeway traffic, this long, sprawling, attractive campground borders a scenic mile on the Rogue River. Altogether, the state park claims a 3-mile stretch of river and offers ample recreational access. The campsites are spacious with paved parking. Native pines, oaks, and cedars, along with a variety of landscape trees, contribute to the shade and beauty of camp. You can fish, boat, or walk the River Edge Trail. You can even arrange for a shuttle pickup at the park for a jet boat tour.

345 Whitehorse County Park

Location: About 7 miles west of Grants Pass

Season: Apr–late Oct

Sites: 8 hookup sites, 34 basic sites, 1 yurt; water and electric hookups

Maximum length: 40 feet

Facilities: Tables, some barbecues and grills, flush toilets, drinking water, showers, playground, horseshoe pits, volleyball, paved boat ramp

Fee per night: $$–$$$
Management: Josephine County
Contact: (541) 474-5285; (800) 452-5687 for reservations; www.co.josephine.or.us
Finding the campground: From Sixth Street in Grants Pass, go west on G Street, which later becomes Upper River Road and then Lower River Road. Enter the park in 7.3 miles.
GPS coordinates: N42 26.273' / W123 27.521'
About the campground: This fine campground sits on a gentle, wooded hillside above the north bank of the Rogue River. A day-use area claims the lower portion of the park, closer to the river. Attractive lawn and ponderosa pines and oaks lend character to the camp; cottonwoods grow toward the river. Since the park is also a bird sanctuary, naturalists will enjoy the companionship of herons, geese, ospreys, wood ducks, and songbirds. Fishing, rafting, swimming, and riverside nature walks keep visitors delightfully busy.

346 Wolf Creek County Park

Location: In the community of Wolf Creek, about 20 miles north of Grants Pass
Season: Apr–late Oct
Sites: 17 hookup sites, 15 basic sites; water and electric hookups (2 with sewer)
Maximum length: 30 feet
Facilities: Tables, grills, nonflush toilets, drinking water, dump station, playground, disc golf, baseball field, horseshoe pits
Fee per night: $$–$$$
Management: Josephine County
Contact: (541) 474-5285; (800) 452-5687 for reservations; www.co.josephine.or.us
Finding the campground: From I-5 take exit 76 and head west into the town of Wolf Creek. From there follow the signs for the park, which lies at the end of Main Street, 0.3 mile past the historic Wolf Creek Tavern (or Wolf Creek Inn).
GPS coordinates: N42 41.645' / W123 24.231'
About the campground: This quiet, wooded campground sits just outside the small town of Wolf Creek. The town's historic inn, a state heritage site, was a stagecoach stop on the Oregon–California line. The campsites are snuggled among the tall firs, pines, and madrones and have earthen parking. A full green understory helps ensure privacy. Only an intermittent train whistle or a big game at the ball field disturbs the quiet. A foot trail leads from camp to a viewpoint and the summit of London Peak.

Medford Area

	Hookup Sites	Total Sites	Max. RV Length	Hookups	Toilets	Showers	Drinking Water	Dump Station	Recreation	Fee	Can Reserve
347 Applegate Lake Recreation Areas		38	40		F, NF		X		HSFBL	$-$$	X
348 Cantrall-Buckley County Park		30	25		NF	X	X		SF	$$	
349 Doe Point		30	32		F		X		HSFB	$$	
350 Fish Lake		19	40		F		X		HSFBL	$$	
351 Fourbit Ford		7	16		NF		X		F	$$	
352 Jackson		12	T		F		X		SF	$$	
353 Joseph Stewart State Park	151	201	80	WE	F	X	X	X	HSFBLC	$$-$$$	
354 Rogue Elk County Park	16	38	35	WE	F, NF	X	X	X	SFBL	$$-$$$	X
355 Whiskey Spring		34	30		NF		X		H	$$	
356 Willow Lake Recreation Area	31	63	25	WES	F, NF	X	X	X	SFBL	$$-$$$	·
357 Willow Prairie Horse Camp		10	40		NF		X		HR	$$	X

347 Applegate Lake Recreation Areas

Location: On Applegate Reservoir, about 30 miles southwest of Medford
Season: Mid-May–Oct
Sites: 8 RV spaces at Hart-tish; 30 total walk-in tent sites at Hart-tish, Carberry, and Watkins; no hookups
Maximum length: 40 feet
Facilities: Tables, grills, flush toilets (Hart-tish), nonflush toilets (walk-in camps), drinking water (Hart-tish only), boat launch (Hart-tish)
Fee per night: $-$$
Management: Rogue River National Forest
Contact: (541) 899-3800; (800) 452-5687 for reservations; www.fs.usda.gov/recmain/rogue-siskiyou/recreation
Finding the campgrounds: From Jacksonville take OR 238 west toward Grants Pass, going 7.4 miles to Ruch. Turn south onto Applegate Road toward Applegate Dam and Star Ranger Station. Go 14.5 miles to the reservoir: Hart-tish, Watkins, and Carberry Recreation Areas dot the west shore; French Gulch is across Applegate Dam on FR 1075.
GPS coordinates: N42 03.112' / W123 07.630'
About the campgrounds: These camps serve visitors to Applegate Reservoir and the surrounding mountains. Fishing and boating (10 miles per hour maximum) are popular draws, especially

when the reservoir is high. But the area also boasts superb hiking trails. The Collings Mountain Trail offers a challenging skyline hike and passes a trap built for Bigfoot. Other trails wander the reservoir shore or introduce the region's mining past. For each camp, parking is in an open lot, with tables and amenities just strides away.

348 Cantrall-Buckley County Park

Location: About 18 miles southwest of Medford
Season: May–mid-Sept
Sites: 30 basic sites; no hookups
Maximum length: 25 feet
Facilities: Tables, barbecues, nonflush toilets, drinking water, coin-operated showers, playground, volleyball, horseshoe pits
Fee per night: $$
Management: Jackson County
Contact: (541) 774-8183; www.co.jackson.or.us
Finding the campground: From OR 238, 25 miles east of Grants Pass and 8.5 miles west of Jacksonville, turn south onto Hamilton Road. Continue 1 mile to the campground on the right.
GPS coordinates: N42 13.288' / W123 03.974'
About the campground: In an 89-acre woodland of pines, oaks, madrones, and firs sits this county park complex (campground and day-use area) with 1.75 miles of Applegate River frontage. Deer are common here, and birding is popular. Trout fishing and swimming will keep you entertained, or you may want to head east into historic Jacksonville. This town traces its origins to the placer gold discoveries of 1851–52. It retains its old-town charm, and its museums and shops welcome strolling.

349 Doe Point

Location: On Fish Lake, about 38 miles east of Medford
Season: Late May–Sept
Sites: 25 basic sites, 5 walk-in tent sites; no hookups
Maximum length: 32 feet
Facilities: Tables, grills, flush toilets, drinking water
Fee per night: $$
Management: Rogue River National Forest
Contact: (541) 552-2900; www.fs.usda.gov/recmain/rogue-siskiyou/recreation
Finding the campground: From OR 140, 37.5 miles east of Medford and 6.5 miles west of Lake of the Woods, turn south at the sign for Doe Point Campground onto FR 810. Continue 0.5 mile to enter the campground.
GPS coordinates: N42 23.578' / W122 19.433'
About the campground: This attractive campground fronts the north shore of Fish Lake, a big, sparkling mountain lake enlarged by a dam on the North Fork Little Butte Creek. The sites are well spaced and shaded by firs. Across the lake rises Brown Mountain (elevation 7,311 feet). This

shield volcano and the lava flow it produced are among the most recent in the Cascades. Brown Mountain Lava Field covers 13 square miles and measures 250 feet thick. If you hike the Fish Lake Trail to the Pacific Crest Trail (PCT) and walk south along the PCT, you can visit the outskirts of the lava field or traverse it. Fishing and swimming keep most guests at the lake.

350 Fish Lake

Location: On Fish Lake, about 39 miles east of Medford
Season: Late May–Sept
Sites: 19 basic sites; no hookups
Maximum length: 40 feet
Facilities: Tables, grills, flush toilets, drinking water, boat launch, dock, fish-cleaning building
Fee per night: $$
Management: Rogue River National Forest
Contact: (541) 552-2900; www.fs.usda.gov/recmain/rogue-siskiyou/recreation
Finding the campground: From OR 140, 38 miles east of Medford and 6 miles west of Lake of the Woods, turn south toward Fish Lake. Continue 0.6 mile; bear right to enter the campground.
GPS coordinates: N42 23.675' / W122 19.090'
About the campground: This comfortable campground is on the north shore of Fish Lake, a scenic mountain lake enlarged by a dam. The natural lake was only a third this size. Across the lake you can view volcanic Brown Mountain. Fish Lake is open to fishing, swimming, and boating (10 miles per hour maximum or self-propelled). Along its shore is the Fish Lake Trail, which ultimately connects with the Pacific Crest Trail for longer hikes. Sites have paved or earthen parking and double-wide spaces for trailers. Ospreys and eagles commonly soar overhead.

351 Fourbit Ford

Location: About 34 miles northeast of Medford
Season: Late June–Sept
Sites: 7 basic sites; no hookups
Maximum length: 16 feet
Facilities: Tables, grills, nonflush toilets, drinking water
Fee per night: $$
Management: Rogue River National Forest
Contact: (541) 865-2700; www.fs.usda.gov/recmain/rogue-siskiyou/recreation
Finding the campground: From OR 140, 26 miles east of Medford, go 6 miles north on CR 821 to FR 3065. (From Butte Falls, travel 10 miles south on CR 821 to FR 3065.) Turn east and follow FR 3065 for 1.4 miles. The campground is on the left. (The final 1.1 miles are on gravel.)
GPS coordinates: N42 30.088' / W122 24.244'
About the campground: This pleasant campground overlooks Fourbit Creek. Pines and firs shade the camp, which sits in a meadow. The campsites are well spaced but have relatively

short parking spurs. You can fish in the creek, but this is mainly a spot to retreat from daily concerns and enjoy the surroundings.

352 Jackson

Location: About 25 miles southwest of Medford
Season: Year-round; dry camp in winter
Sites: 12 tent sites; no hookups
Maximum length: Suitable for tents only
Facilities: Tables, barbecues, flush toilets, drinking water
Fee per night: $$
Management: Rogue River National Forest
Contact: (541) 899-3800; www.fs.usda.gov/recmain/rogue-siskiyou/recreation
Finding the campground: From Jacksonville take OR 238 west toward Grants Pass. Go 7.4 miles to Ruch; turn south onto Applegate Road toward Applegate Dam and Star Ranger Station. Continue 9.5 miles and turn right to enter the campground.
GPS coordinates: N42 06.772' / W123 05.274'
About the campground: Primarily for tent campers, this campground offers a central parking area and walk-to sites along the Applegate River. Pines, cedars, and madrones lend shade. Swimming is at your own risk. Hiking and the recreational opportunities created by Applegate Reservoir are close by. Nearby McKee Covered Bridge makes a nice photo opportunity.

353 Joseph Stewart State Park

Location: On Lost Creek Reservoir, about 35 miles northeast of Medford
Season: Mar–Oct
Sites: 151 hookup sites, 50 basic sites; water and electric hookups
Maximum length: 80 feet
Facilities: Tables, grills, flush toilets, drinking water, showers, dump station, playground, store, marina, boat rental, boat launch, dock
Fee per night: $$-$$$
Management: Oregon State Parks and Recreation Department
Contact: (541) 560-3334; www.oregon.gov/OPRD/PARKS/camping.shtml
Finding the campground: The campground is north off OR 62, 10 miles southwest of Prospect and about 35 miles northeast of Medford.
GPS coordinates: N42 40.968' / W122 37.095'
About the campground: In Rogue River Country, along the southeast shore of Lost Creek Reservoir stretches this attractive, developed park, with a sweeping groomed lawn, young pines, and some leafy shade trees. Lost Creek Reservoir captures the Rogue, creating a wonderful playground for swimming, fishing, boating, and sailing. Where the river flows free, rafting extends the to-do list. Hiking the area trails or cycling a 6-mile bike path provides a different lake perspective. Cole M. Rivers Fish Hatchery, near the Lost Creek dam, is the largest hatchery in the state and is open for touring.

354 Rogue Elk County Park

Location: About 25 miles northeast of Medford
Season: Mid-Apr–Oct
Sites: 16 hookup sites, 22 basic sites; water and electric hookups
Maximum length: 35 feet
Facilities: Tables, barbecues, flush and nonflush toilets, drinking water, showers, dump station, playground, boat launch
Fee per night: $$-$$$
Management: Jackson County
Contact: (541) 774-8183, reservations accepted; www.co.jackson.or.us
Finding the campground: The campground is south off OR 62, 4.8 miles northeast of Shady Cove.
GPS coordinates: N42 39.745' / W122 45.193'
About the campground: This shaded and landscaped camp fronts the Rogue River downstream from Lost Creek Reservoir. The overflow tent area occupies a more natural forest setting. The Rogue entertains and enchants with fishing, boating, and swimming.

355 Whiskey Spring

Location: About 32 miles east of Medford
Season: Late June–Sept
Sites: 34 basic sites; no hookups
Maximum length: 30 feet
Facilities: Tables, grills, nonflush toilets, drinking water
Fee per night: $$
Management: Rogue River National Forest
Contact: (541) 865-2700; www.fs.usda.gov/recmain/rogue-siskiyou/recreation
Finding the campground: From OR 140, 26 miles east of Medford, go 6 miles north on CR 821 to FR 3065. (From Butte Falls travel 10 miles south on CR 821 to FR 3065.) Turn east and follow FR 3065 for 0.3 mile to the campground on the left.
GPS coordinates: N42 29.807' / W122 25.175'
About the campground: This campground occupies a large flat of pine trees, with a few cedars and firs sprinkled through the ranks. RVers will find several long gravel parking pads, as well as some pull-through sites. Adjacent to camp is a spring-fed beaver pond and Whiskey Creek, a trout stream. In season, spring peepers enliven the night forest; other times it is an owl sounding. Squirrels, deer, beavers, woodpeckers, and wood ducks can be spied. A 1-mile barrier-free trail with cinder surface skirts the beaver pond, Whiskey Creek, and Whiskey Spring while touring rich woodland seasonally decorated with colorful wildflowers.

356 Willow Lake Recreation Area

Location: On Willow Lake, about 35 miles east of Medford
Season: May–mid-Oct, dependent on conditions
Sites: 31 full or partial hookup sites, 32 basic sites, 4 cabins, 2 yurts; water, electric, and sewer hookups
Maximum length: 25 feet
Facilities: Tables, grills, flush and nonflush toilets, drinking water, showers, dump station, boat rentals, launch, dock, fish-cleaning station, store, restaurant
Fee per night: $$–$$$
Management: Jackson County
Contact: (541) 774-8183; www.co.jackson.or.us
Finding the campground: From OR 140, 26 miles east of Medford, go 8 miles north on CR 821 to Willow Lake Road. (From the town of Butte Falls, go 8 miles south on CR 821 to Willow Lake Road.) Turn west and follow Willow Lake Road 0.4 mile to the recreation area.
GPS coordinates: N42 28.317' / W122 27.457'
About the campground: This campground-resort complex occupies more than 900 acres on the west shore of Willow Lake, a large reservoir rimmed by forest. Cross-lake views include Mount McLoughlin. This is a busy place: Swimming, fishing, and canoeing are popular, and a section of the lake is set aside for waterskiing. The RV area features sites with gravel or earthen parking. The tent area claims a mildly rolling, pine-clad slope, with some sites overlooking the water.

357 Willow Prairie Horse Camp

Location: About 29 miles east of Medford
Season: Maintained from mid-May–Sept
Sites: 10 basic sites; no hookups
Maximum length: 40 feet
Facilities: Tables, grills, nonflush toilets, drinking water, corrals
Fee per night: $$
Management: Rogue River National Forest
Contact: (541) 865-2700; (877) 444-6777 for reservations; www.fs.usda.gov/recmain/rogue-siskiyou/recreation
Finding the campground: From OR 140, 26 miles east of Medford and 8 miles west of Lake of the Woods, turn north onto CR 821, heading for Butte Falls. Go 1.6 miles and turn left onto FR 3738. Continue 1.2 miles and bear left on FR 3735. The campground is on the right in 0.2 mile.
GPS coordinates: N42 24.367' / W122 23.455'
About the campground: This fine horse camp sits next to a prairie meadow threaded by the West Branch Willow Creek. Douglas and grand firs supply shade to the well-spaced sites, which are both accommodating and comfortable. Horse trails allow you to explore from camp. The meadow, a reclaimed beaver pond, now has a new population of beavers, which are again raising the water level. Buttercup, lupine, and false hellebore add a touch of color to the soggy area. Overlooking the lea is the restored Willow Prairie Cabin, which is on the National Register of Historic Places; an antler door handle provides admittance.

Ashland Area

	Hookup Sites	Total Sites	Max. RV Length	Hookups	Toilets	Showers	Drinking Water	Dump Station	Recreation	Fee	Can Reserve
358 Emigrant Lake Recreation Area: The Point RV Park and Oaks Slope Campground	32	74	50	WES	F	X	X	X	SFBL	$$–$$$	X
359 Grizzly County Park		21	23		NF		X		HSFBL	$$	
360 Howard Prairie Resort	144	236	40	WES	F	X	X	X	SFBL	$$–$$$	X
361 Hyatt Lake Recreation Site		54	35		F	X	X	X	HFBL	$$	
362 Klum Landing		30	25		F	X	X		SFBL	$$	
363 Lily Glen Horse Camp		12	30		NF		X		FR	$$	
364 Mount Ashland		9	T		NF				H	None	
365 Wildcat and Wildcat Horse Camp		17	20		NF				FBL	$	
366 Willow Point		41	35		NF		X		HSFBL	$$	X

358 Emigrant Lake Recreation Area: The Point RV Park and Oaks Slope Campground

Location: On Emigrant Lake, about 4 miles southeast of Ashland
Season: Mid-Mar–Oct; Oaks Slope Campground: Mid-Apr–mid-Oct
Sites: 32 hookup sites, 42 basic sites; water, electric, and sewer hookups
Maximum length: 50 feet
Facilities: Tables, grills, flush toilets, drinking water, showers, dump station, playground, ball field, horseshoe pits, waterslide, boat rental, 2 boat ramps, food concession
Fee per night: $$–$$$
Management: Jackson County
Contact: (541) 774-8183, reservations recommended; www.co.jackson.or.us
Finding the campground: From I-5 in Ashland, take exit 14 and go southeast on OR 66 for 3.2 miles. Turn left at the sign for Emigrant Lake Recreation Area; continue about 1 mile to the campground on the left.
GPS coordinates: N42 09.532' / W122 37.177'
About the campground: This campground with paved site parking occupies an oak-studded, grassy hillside above popular Emigrant Lake—a large, horseshoe-shaped reservoir hugged by arid valley foothills. Recreational opportunities center on the lake, where you can swim, boat, fish, sail,

water-ski, and sailboard. A waterslide (fee) is open weekends from Memorial Day through Labor Day, with additional days during warm, fair weather.

359 Grizzly County Park

Location: On Howard Prairie Lake, about 21 miles east of Ashland
Season: Mid-Apr–mid-Sept
Sites: 21 basic sites; no hookups
Maximum length: 23 feet
Facilities: Tables, grills, nonflush toilets, drinking water, boat ramp
Fee per night: $$
Management: Jackson County Parks
Contact: (541) 774-8183; www.co.jackson.or.us
Finding the campground: From Ashland drive 19 miles east on Dead Indian Memorial Road. Turn right (south) onto Hyatt Prairie Road; continue 1.9 miles to the campground on the left.
GPS coordinates: N42 15.458' / W122 25.616'
About the campground: This quiet conifer-forested campground offers its guests a mile of lake frontage on this popular boating, fishing, and swimming lake, as well as views of Mount McLoughlin and the forested lake rim. As with the other campgrounds in the area, hiking vies for campers' time. Bass and trout are the catches. Because of the trees, several sites have a tight turning radius.

360 Howard Prairie Resort

Location: On Howard Prairie Lake, about 22 miles east of Ashland
Season: Mid-Apr–Oct
Sites: 144 RV hookup sites, 92 basic sites, RV rentals; water, electric, and sewer hookups
Maximum length: 40 feet
Facilities: Tables, flush toilets, drinking water, showers, laundry, dump station, marina, boat rental, fish-cleaning station, camp store, restaurant
Fee per night: $$–$$$
Management: Jackson County (operated by concessionaire)
Contact: (541) 774-8183; (541) 482-1979 or www.hplake.com for information and reservations; www.co.jackson.or.us
Finding the campground: From Ashland go 19 miles east on Dead Indian Memorial Road toward Lake of the Woods. Turn south onto Hyatt Prairie Road; proceed 3.2 miles to the resort on left.
GPS coordinates: N42 14.631' / W122 24.811'
About the campground: The camping areas surround the large, bustling, full-service resort/marina complex. An attractive shoreline forest contains the camp, successfully keeping the woodland mystique while providing comfort and convenience. Rainbow trout fishing, hiking, and sailing are popular pastimes.

361 Hyatt Lake Recreation Site

Location: On Hyatt Lake, about 20 miles east of Ashland
Season: Late Apr–Sept
Sites: 30 basic sites in the main overnight area, 17 drive-in tent sites, 7 walk-in tent sites; no hookups
Maximum length: 35 feet
Facilities: Tables, grills and barbecues, flush toilets, drinking water, showers, dump station, playground, volleyball, horseshoe pits, 2 boat launches, dock, fish-cleaning station, boat trailer parking
Fee per night: $$
Management: Bureau of Land Management–Medford District
Contact: (541) 618-2200; www.blm.gov/or/
Finding the campground: From OR 66, 17 miles east of Ashland and 44 miles west of Klamath Falls, turn north onto East Hyatt Road at the sign for the reservoir. Go 3 miles and proceed straight for the recreation site as the main road curves left and becomes Hyatt Prairie Road. In 0.1 mile turn left for Hyatt Lake Recreation Site.
GPS coordinates: N42 10.185' / W122 27.856'
About the campground: This star in the portfolio of BLM campgrounds occupies a gentle, forested slope above Hyatt Lake, a popular boating and fishing reservoir. Mount McLoughlin looms to the north. Ospreys sometimes can be seen diving for fish. The sites are mostly shaded by Douglas and grand firs. The Pacific Crest Trail passes through the area not far from camp.

362 Klum Landing

Location: On Howard Prairie Lake, about 27 miles east of Ashland
Season: Mid-Apr–mid-Sept
Sites: 30 basic sites; no hookups
Maximum length: 25 feet
Facilities: Tables, grills, flush toilets, drinking water, showers, boat launch, playground
Fee per night: $$
Management: Jackson County
Contact: (541) 774-8183; www.co.jackson.or.us
Finding the campground: From Ashland drive 19 miles east on Dead Indian Memorial Road. Turn right (south) onto Hyatt Prairie Road and go 4.6 miles. Turn left onto Howard Prairie Dam Road; drive 3 miles farther to the campground on the left.
GPS coordinates: N42 12.470' / W122 22.651'
About the campground: This campground spreads across 156 acres of a pine-and-fir-forested slope at the southern end of Howard Prairie Lake—a big, elongated reservoir that offers swimming, fishing, and boating. The campsites are well shaded, a welcome change from the sun-drenched lake. Because all sites are back-ins and some have difficult approaches, this campground is inappropriate for large RV units. The Pacific Crest Trail offers hiking.

363 Lily Glen Horse Camp

Location: On Howard Prairie Lake, about 20 miles east of Ashland
Season: Mid-Apr–mid-Oct
Sites: 12 basic sites; no hookups
Maximum length: 30 feet
Facilities: Tables, grills, nonflush toilets, drinking water, corrals
Fee per night: $$
Management: Jackson County
Contact: (541) 774-8183; www.co.jackson.or.us
Finding the campground: From Ashland drive 20 miles east on Dead Indian Memorial Road. Turn right (south) to enter the campground. (The turn is 1 mile east of Hyatt Prairie Road.)
GPS coordinates: N42 16.346' / W122 25.827'
About the campground: This campground occupies a flat shaded by ponderosa pines along the shallow north end of Howard Prairie Reservoir. While boating is popular on much of the lake, there is no launch here. Because of that, this camp affords a quieter stay. You can access horse trails nearby; fishing is also popular.

364 Mount Ashland

Location: About 20 miles south of Ashland
Season: Late June–Sept
Sites: 9 basic sites; no hookups
Maximum length: Best suited for tents
Facilities: Tables, barbecues, nonflush toilets; no drinking water
Fee per night: None
Management: Klamath National Forest (California)
Contact: (530) 493-2243; www.fs.usda.gov/recarea/klamath
Finding the campground: From I-5 south of Ashland, take exit 6 and head west for 0.7 mile, following the signs to Mount Ashland. Turn right onto Mount Ashland Road/FR 20 and follow it for 9.3 miles to reach the campground. The final 0.4 mile is on gravel; the campground is 0.7 mile past the ski area.
GPS coordinates: N42 04.523' / W122 42.789'
About the campground: The campsites—primarily walk-in sites—radiate from both sides of FR 20. Campers enjoy the spectacular high-elevation tapestry of the south flank of Mount Ashland: clusters of big-diameter firs, alpine meadows, grassland, and rocky jumbles. Views from the camp are of the rocky crest of Mount Ashland to the north and the snowy crown of 14,000-foot Mount Shasta (in California) to the south. You may spy grouse, juncos, and jays. This camp is close to the Pacific Crest National Scenic Trail, which follows the crest of the Siskiyou Mountains here.

365 Wildcat and Wildcat Horse Camp

Location: On Hyatt Lake, about 22 miles east of Ashland
Season: Late Apr–Oct
Sites: 12 basic sites, 5 horse sites with corrals; no hookups
Maximum length: 20 feet
Facilities: Tables, grills, nonflush toilets, horseshoe pits, boat launch; no drinking water
Fee per night: $
Management: Bureau of Land Management—Medford District
Contact: (541) 618-2200; (541) 482-2031 or (541) 618-2306 for horse camp reservations; www.blm.gov/or/
Finding the campground: From OR 66, 17 miles east of Ashland and 44 miles west of Klamath Falls, turn north onto East Hyatt Road at the sign for the reservoir. Go 3 miles and proceed straight on East Hyatt Road as the main road curves left and becomes Hyatt Prairie Road. Continue 2 miles to Wildcat.
GPS coordinates: N42 10.957' / W122 26.883'
About the campground: Campers will enjoy ample shoreline at this small campground that sits on a forested peninsula stretching into Hyatt Lake. The horse camp occupies a separate area on the shared cove. Ponderosa pines rise among the mixed firs, creating partial to full shade. The roads and site parking are gravel. Fishing, boating, hiking, and relaxing are the main diversions. Horse users find links to the Pacific Crest Trail.

366 Willow Point

Location: On Howard Prairie Lake, about 24 miles east of Ashland
Season: Mid-Apr–mid-Oct
Sites: 41 basic sites; no hookups
Maximum length: 35 feet
Facilities: Tables, grills, nonflush toilets, drinking water, boat launch, fish-cleaning station
Fee per night: $$
Management: Jackson County
Contact: (541) 774-8183, reservations accepted; www.co.jackson.or.us
Finding the campground: From Ashland head east 19 miles on Dead Indian Memorial Road. Turn right (south) onto Hyatt Prairie Road and go 4.6 miles. Turn left onto Howard Prairie Dam Road and continue 0.5 mile to the campground entrance on the left.
GPS coordinates: N42 12.922' / W122 24.093'
About the campground: Situated on 59 acres along Willow Creek and the southwest shore of Howard Prairie Lake, this forested campground affords views of Mount McLoughlin. Fishing, boating, swimming, and sailing are the primary draws of the area, but the Pacific Crest National Scenic Trail passes at the south end of the reservoir for anyone interested in hiking.

Klamath Falls–Klamath Basin Area

	Hookup Sites	Total Sites	Max. RV Length	Hookups	Toilets	Showers	Drinking Water	Dump Station	Recreation	Fee	Can Reserve
367 Aspen Point		60	40		F		X	X	HSFBL	$$	
368 Collier Memorial State Park	50	68	60	WES	F	X	X	X	HF	$$–$$$	
369 Corral Springs Forest Camp		6	40		NF					None	
370 Digit Point		64	30		F, NF		X		HSFBL	$$	
371 Eagle Ridge Park		6	30		NF		X		FBL	None	
372 Fourmile Lake		25	22		NF		X		HSFBL	$$	
373 Gerber Reservoir: North		30	35		NF		X		SFBL	$	
374 Gerber Reservoir: South		25	40		NF		X		SFBL	$	
375 Hagelstein Park		10	30		F		X		FBL	None	
376 Head of the River Forest Camp		5	40		NF				F	None	
377 Jackson Creek Forest Camp		12	25		NF				F	None	
378 Jackson F. Kimball State Recreation Site		10	45		NF				F	$–$$	
379 Keno Recreation Area		25	35		F	X	X	X	SFBL	$$	
380 Klamath County Fairgrounds	12	12	40	WES	F	X	X			$$	
381 Odessa		6	20		NF				FBL	None	
382 Scott Creek Forest Camp		6	20		NF					None	
383 Sunset		64	40		F		X		HSFBL	$$	
384 Surveyor Recreation Site		5	25		NF					None	
385 Topsy Recreation Site		15	40		NF		X		FBL	$	
386 Williamson River		10	30		NF		X		F	$$	

367 Aspen Point

Location: On Lake of the Woods, about 35 miles northwest of Klamath Falls
Season: Late May–mid-Sept
Sites: 60 basic sites; no hookups
Maximum length: 40 feet
Facilities: Tables, grills, flush toilets, drinking water, dump station, boat launch, boat rentals nearby
Fee per night: $$
Management: Winema National Forest
Contact: (541) 883-6714; www.fs.usda.gov/recmain/fremont-winema/recreation

Finding the campground: From OR 140, 34 miles west of Klamath Falls and 44 miles east of Medford, turn south onto FR 3704 and go 0.7 mile. Turn right for the campground.
GPS coordinates: N42 23.042' / W122 12.832'
About the campground: This forested campground occupies the northeast shore of Lake of the Woods, a lovely mountain lake that invites swimming, casting a fishing line, trolling along shore, or sailing the lake's length. Brown Mountain and Mount McLoughlin punctuate the skyline. Trails in the area follow the shoreline, lead to neighboring lakes, and meet up with the Pacific Crest Trail.

368 Collier Memorial State Park

Location: 5 miles north of Chiloquin
Season: Apr–Oct
Sites: 50 hookup sites, 18 basic sites, horse camp across road from main campground; water, electric, and sewer hookups
Maximum length: 60 feet
Facilities: Tables, grills, flush toilets, drinking water, showers, dump station, logging museum, pioneer village, gift shop, 4-corral primitive horse camp
Fee per night: $$–$$$
Management: Oregon State Parks and Recreation Department
Contact: (541) 783-2471; www.oregon.gov/OPRD/PARKS/camping.shtml
Finding the campground: The campground is east off US 97, 5 miles north of Chiloquin and 30 miles north of Klamath Falls.
GPS coordinates: N42 38.485' / W121 52.450'
About the campground: An open-air logging museum and the Spring Creek–Williamson River confluence are the headline attractions at this park in the Klamath Basin. The closely spaced sites are nestled in a second-growth forest of ponderosa and lodgepole pines; bitterbrush and currant bushes dot the needle-strewn forest floor. The camp is located above the Williamson River, across US 97 from Spring Creek and the logging museum. A pedestrian underpass allows for safe passage between the camp and the day-use area. Fishing, hiking the short trails along Spring Creek, and wandering the red cinder paths among the museum exhibits are activities to pursue in the park. Not far from here, Agency and Upper Klamath Lakes beckon with boating, canoeing, fishing, and birding.

369 Corral Springs Forest Camp

Location: About 5 miles north of Chemult
Season: June–mid-Oct
Sites: 6 basic sites; no hookups
Maximum length: 40 feet
Facilities: Tables, grills, nonflush toilets; no drinking water
Fee per night: None
Management: Winema National Forest

Contact: (541) 365-7001; www.fs.usda.gov/recmain/fremont-winema/recreation
Finding the campground: From US 97, 2.8 miles north of Chemult and 5.3 miles south of the junction of US 97 and OR 58, turn west onto gravel FR 9774. Proceed 2 miles to the campground on the right.
GPS coordinates: N43 15.115' / W121 49.312'
About the campground: This improved campground has gravel roads and long, gravel parking spaces. It is set in a lodgepole pine forest with small meadow clearings. It offers a quiet retreat or a traveler's stop and lies along the historic Old Klamath Trail, which was used by Native Americans and early explorers. Early in the year, come prepared for mosquitoes.

370 Digit Point

Location: On Miller Lake, about 13 miles west of Chemult
Season: June–Sept
Sites: 64 basic sites; no hookups
Maximum length: 30 feet
Facilities: Tables, grills, flush and nonflush toilets, drinking water, boat ramp
Fee per night: $$
Management: Winema National Forest
Contact: (541) 365-7001; www.fs.usda.gov/recmain/fremont-winema/recreation
Finding the campground: From US 97, 1 mile north of Chemult, turn west onto gravel FR 9772. Proceed 12 miles to enter the campground on the right.
GPS coordinates: N43 13.654' / W121 57.971'
About the campground: More than 1 mile above sea level, this campground claims a broad peninsula on the southwest shore of Miller Lake—an attractive natural lake on the eastern side of the Cascade Crest. Mixed conifers frame the sites and provide shade. A fine 4-mile trail rings the lake, offering a chance to view wildlife. Boating, fishing, and swimming are popular. From the west end of the Miller Lakeshore Trail, hikers can take a spur to the Pacific Crest National Scenic Trail or cross over the crest to Maidu Lake. The latter is the head of the North Umpqua Wild and Scenic River and marks the start of the North Umpqua National Recreation Trail. Come prepared for mosquitoes at these high lakes.

371 Eagle Ridge Park

Location: About 22 miles northwest of Klamath Falls
Season: Year-round
Sites: 6 basic sites; no hookups
Maximum length: 30 feet
Facilities: Tables, fire rings, nonflush toilets, drinking water, boat launch, dock
Fee per night: None
Management: Klamath County
Contact: (541) 883-5121; www.klamathcounty.org/depts/cdd

Finding the campground: From the junction of US 97 and OR 140 at Klamath Falls, head west on OR 140 for 17.2 miles. Turn right (east) for the park. Follow the park and wildlife viewing signs along a gravel route for 4.4 miles to reach the campground. No trailers are allowed past the boat launch.

GPS coordinates: N42 24.241' / W121 57.156'

About the campground: On Shoalwater Bay on Upper Klamath Lake, this campground occupies a small, open flat at the western foot of pine-and-juniper-clad Eagle Ridge. The sites have basic amenities and gravel parking, but bring your own shade source. At night the lapping of the lake against the shore enables a tranquil sleep. By day the lake invites fishing, boating, and birding for eagles, grebes, cormorants, and geese. Although the road beyond the camp is unsuitable for trailers and passenger vehicles, you can hike or mountain bike along it for 2 miles to the tip of the peninsula, where you will find additional birding and fishing, as well as views of the lake, Pelican Butte, and Mountain Lakes Wilderness.

372 Fourmile Lake

Location: On Fourmile Lake, about 40 miles northwest of Klamath Falls
Season: June–Sept
Sites: 25 basic sites; no hookups
Maximum length: 22 feet
Facilities: Tables, grills, nonflush toilets, drinking water, boat ramp
Fee per night: $$
Management: Winema National Forest
Contact: (541) 883-6714; www.fs.usda.gov/recmain/fremont-winema/recreation
Finding the campground: From OR 140, 34.6 miles west of Klamath Falls, turn north onto gravel FR 3661. Follow it 5.5 miles to Fourmile Lake and the campground.
GPS coordinates: N42 27.276' / W122 14.844'
About the campground: The sites are distributed among the lodgepole pines on the shore of Fourmile Lake, which has been enlarged by a small dam. A few sites overlook the water and the attractive lake basin. This area is a gateway to the Sky Lakes Wilderness; a single trailhead serves as the jumping-off point. Trout fishing, swimming, and boating engage guests at camp.

373 Gerber Reservoir: North

Location: On Gerber Reservoir, about 45 miles east of Klamath Falls
Season: Mid-May–mid-Sept
Sites: 25 basic sites, 5 horse sites (in separate area); no hookups
Maximum length: 35 feet
Facilities: Tables, grills, nonflush toilets, drinking water, boat launch, dock, fish-cleaning station
Fee per night: $
Management: Bureau of Land Management—Lakeview District, Klamath Falls Office
Contact: (541) 883-6916 or (541) 947-2177; www.blm.gov/or/

Finding the campground: From Klamath Falls go 18 miles east on OR 140 to Dairy. Turn right onto OR 70 and go 7 miles southeast to Bonanza. Bear right onto East Langell Valley Road and go another 10.5 miles. Turn left onto Gerber Road and proceed 8.5 miles. Turn right toward Gerber Reservoir Recreation Site and reach a junction in 0.6 mile. Keep left; continue 0.6 mile to the campground, or follow signs to the horse camp.

GPS coordinates (North Campground): N42 13.127' / W121 08.101'

About the campground: Tucked among the ponderosa pines and scraggly junipers is this popular BLM campground on the western shore of Gerber Reservoir, which was created to provide irrigation. Sites near the water are more closely spaced. You may see waterfowl, bald eagles, and ospreys. The potholes northwest of the reservoir attract other birds, including sandhill cranes. Bass, crappie, catfish, and perch are among the game fish here, and the lake is popular with boaters. During World War II, the US military used an island in this reservoir for bombing practice. Today ospreys and pelicans are the only bombers of Gerber Reservoir. Gerber Potholes Trail is a 12-mile hiker/horse loop.

374 Gerber Reservoir: South

Location: On Gerber Reservoir, about 45 miles east of Klamath Falls
Season: Mid-May–mid-Sept
Sites: 25 basic sites; no hookups
Maximum length: 40 feet
Facilities: Tables, grills, nonflush toilets, drinking water, boat launch, fish-cleaning station
Fee per night: $
Management: Bureau of Land Management—Lakeview District, Klamath Falls Office
Contact: (541) 883-6916 or (541) 947-2177; www.blm.gov/or/
Finding the campground: From Klamath Falls go 18 miles east on OR 140 to Dairy. Turn right onto OR 70 and go 7 miles southeast to Bonanza. Bear right onto East Langell Valley Road and go another 10.5 miles. Turn left onto Gerber Road and proceed 8.5 miles. Turn right toward Gerber Reservoir Recreation Site and reach a junction in 0.6 mile. Turn right; continue 0.4 mile to the campground.

GPS coordinates: N42 12.253' / W121 07.794'

About the campground: Gerber Reservoir is a 3,830-acre playground for water-loving campers. Fishing, swimming, boating, and birding are all popular. Near the dam, this camp is generally quieter and has roomier sites set farther back from shore than its northern counterpart. Ponderosa pines supply the shade; a basalt-studded sage prairie fans out from camp. Watch the skies for bald eagles, which nest at the north end of the lake.

375 Hagelstein Park

Location: About 10 miles north of Klamath Falls
Season: Apr–Sept
Sites: 10 basic sites; no hookups
Maximum length: 30 feet
Facilities: Tables, grills, flush toilets, drinking water, boat launch, dock
Fee per night: None
Management: Klamath County
Contact: (541) 883-5121; www.klamathcounty.org/depts/cdd
Finding the campground: The campground is east off US 97, 10 miles north of the junction of US 97 and OR 39 at the north end of Klamath Falls, 15 miles south of Chiloquin. After you turn east off US 97, head north at the T-junction to enter camp on the left.
GPS coordinates: N42 22.974' / W121 48.775'
About the campground: This campground sits beside a small, spring-fed pond and inlet of Upper Klamath Lake. Above camp, yellow wildflowers emblazon the juniper-and-basalt slope of Naylox Mountain. The camp layout includes groomed lawns and natural trees and shrubs for partial shade; parking is on the gravel road shoulder. The attractive base provides boating access to Upper Klamath Lake, where anglers can cast for prized rainbow trout.

376 Head of the River Forest Camp

Location: About 30 miles northeast of Chiloquin
Season: Maintained late May–early Sept
Sites: 5 basic sites; no hookups
Maximum length: 40 feet
Facilities: Tables, grills, nonflush toilets; no drinking water
Fee per night: None
Management: Winema National Forest
Contact: (541) 783-4001; www.fs.usda.gov/recmain/fremont-winema/recreation
Finding the campground: From Chiloquin head northeast on Sprague River Highway for 5.4 miles. Turn left onto paved Williamson River Road and follow it for 7.6 miles. Turn left to remain on Williamson River Road for another 16.8 miles. Turn left onto dirt FR 4648 and continue 0.4 mile; turn left to enter the camp.
GPS coordinates: N42 43.898' / W121 25.243'
About the campground: This small campground is tucked away in a lodgepole pine forest beside the spring at the head of the Williamson River, an acclaimed crystalline water with a prized trout fishery downstream. Pole fencing defines the road and campsites; egresses in the fence provide access to the headwater and its river. Ponderosa pines cluster at the river's head, while clumps of aquatic plants dress the spring in striking contrast to the dried grasses of the forest floor. The camp provides a quiet retreat, putting you in the company of deer, mergansers, kingfishers, and songbirds. In fall the camp serves as a hunter's base.

377 Jackson Creek Forest Camp

Location: About 48 miles northeast of Chiloquin
Season: Maintained June–early Sept
Sites: 12 basic sites; no hookups
Maximum length: 25 feet
Facilities: Tables, fire rings or grills, nonflush toilets; no drinking water
Fee per night: None
Management: Winema National Forest
Contact: (541) 365-7001; www.fs.usda.gov/recmain/fremont-winema/recreation
Finding the campground: From US 97, 24 miles south of Chemult and 21 miles north of Chiloquin, turn east onto Silver Lake Road (CR 676) and go 22 miles. Turn right onto cinder FR 49 at the sign for the campground. Continue 4.6 miles; turn left onto FR 4900.740 to enter the campground in 0.3 mile.
GPS coordinates: N42 59.015' / W121 27.403'
About the campground: This primitive, out-of-the-way campground is housed among ponderosa pines on a flat beside alder-lined Jackson Creek. You'll find spacious sites in this elongated camp. A few old-growth pines tower above the dense stand of young trees. Wildflowers sprinkle the creekside meadows. Hunting, fishing, relaxing, and watching for deer and antelope can entertain camp guests. Because this campground borders private land, confine your rambles to camp. No trespassing.

378 Jackson F. Kimball State Recreation Site

Location: About 18 miles northwest of Chiloquin
Season: Mid-Apr–late Oct
Sites: 10 basic sites; no hookups
Maximum length: 45 feet
Facilities: Tables, grills, nonflush toilets; no drinking water
Fee per night: $–$$
Management: Oregon State Parks and Recreation Department
Contact: (541) 783-2471; www.oregon.gov/OPRD/PARKS/camping.shtml
Finding the campground: From the junction of US 97 and OR 62, about 3 miles south of Chiloquin, go west on OR 62 for 12.5 miles. Turn right onto Sun Mountain Road; proceed 3 miles to the park entrance on the left.
GPS coordinates: N42 44.238' / W121 58.776'
About the campground: This primitive campground occupies a wooded flat at the headwater of Wood River, a spellbinding spring-launched river with water so turquoise that the Crayola company would kill for the color. Aspens and a few ponderosa pines intersperse the firs and lodgepole pines of camp. Because parking is on the gravel road shoulder, with site tables and grills a few strides away, the camp is better suited for tenting. You may spy a beaver lodge on the riverbank. Seasonally you should come prepared for mosquitoes. From camp you can venture out to Fort Klamath Museum, Crater Lake National Park, or the Pacific Crest Trail.

Birding from trail in autumn, Wood River Wetland

379 Keno Recreation Area

Location: In Keno, about 11 miles southwest of Klamath Falls
Season: Memorial Day–mid-Sept
Sites: 25 basic sites; no hookups
Maximum length: 35 feet
Facilities: Tables, grills, flush toilets, drinking water, showers, dump station, playground, horseshoe pits, boat launch, dock
Fee per night: $$
Management: PacifiCorp
Contact: (888) 221-7070; www.pacificorp.com/about/or.html
Finding the campground: From the junction of US 97 and OR 66 in southwest Klamath Falls, go west on OR 66 for 9.8 miles. Turn right at the sign for Keno Recreation Area at the west end of Keno. Continue 0.7 mile on gravel road to enter the campground.
GPS coordinates: N42 08.062' / W121 56.714'

About the campground: This campground rests on a low, broad knoll above a Klamath River reservoir in a pleasant setting of pine, juniper, sage, bitterbrush, and bunchgrass. Beyond camp stretches an arid prairie inhabited by quail and jackrabbits. You may fish, boat, water-ski, bird-watch, and swim at a designated site. Near the dam, cormorants commonly line up on the boom. Elsewhere, white pelicans, great blue herons, egrets, night herons, ospreys, swallows, and ducks bid you to raise your binoculars.

380 Klamath County Fairgrounds

Location: In Klamath Falls
Season: Year-round; dry camping in winter
Sites: 12 hookup sites; water, electric, and sewer hookups
Maximum length: 40 feet
Facilities: Flush toilets, drinking water, showers, playground (across street)
Fee per night: $$
Management: Klamath County
Contact: (541) 883-3796; www.kcfairgrounds.org
Finding the campground: The campground is east off Sixth Street, at the corner of Altamont Drive and South Sixth Street in Klamath Falls. Arrange your stay at the fairgrounds office.
GPS coordinates: N42 12.461' / W121 44.607'
About the campground: In an open field at the north end of the fairgrounds is this designated overnight area for RVs, where you simply back up against a fence to the hookup post. Although not fancy or aesthetic, the sites serve visitors on the go, whether they are involved with fair events or taking in the museums, country music, and natural and historical attractions of Klamath Falls. No dogs are allowed July 10–30. During events, participants have priority access to the campsites.

381 Odessa

Location: About 23 miles northwest of Klamath Falls
Season: Maintained Memorial Day weekend–Labor Day
Sites: 6 basic sites; no hookups
Maximum length: 20 feet
Facilities: Tables, grills, nonflush toilets, primitive boat launch; no drinking water
Fee per night: None
Management: Winema National Forest
Contact: (541) 883-6714; www.fs.usda.gov/recmain/fremont-winema/recreation
Finding the campground: From the junction of US 97 and OR 140 in Klamath Falls, go west on OR 140 for 21.8 miles. Turn right (northeast) onto FR 3639 and drive another 0.8 mile into the campground.
GPS coordinates: N42 25.731' / W122 03.615'
About the campground: Where Odessa Creek empties into Upper Klamath Lake, you will find this small, primitive campground among the ponderosa pines and thick understory of aspen, dogwood,

wild rose, cherry, and other flowering shrubs. The sites have earthen parking and provide a front-row seat to the marshy channels and areas of open water for birding, fishing, canoeing, and boating. You may spot bald eagles, beavers, kingfishers, grebes, frogs, deer, and water snakes. The trout fishing is renowned, with five- and six-pounders not uncommon.

382 Scott Creek Forest Camp

Location: About 25 miles south of Chemult
Season: Maintained June–early Sept
Sites: 6 basic sites; no hookups
Maximum length: 20 feet
Facilities: Tables, grills, nonflush toilets; no drinking water
Fee per night: None
Management: Winema National Forest
Contact: (541) 365-7001; www.fs.usda.gov/recmain/fremont-winema/recreation
Finding the campground: From US 97, about 25 miles south of Chemult and 20 miles north of Chiloquin, head west on gravel West Boundary Road (FR 66) for 3 miles. Turn right onto Sun Mountain Road and go 0.6 mile. Turn left onto FR 2310 and proceed 2.1 miles to FR 060. Turn left and continue 0.2 mile to the campground.
GPS coordinates: N42 53.136' / W121 55.413'
About the campground: Pretty Scott Creek flows alongside this rustic campground set among ponderosa pines and white firs. This is a campground for lounging and catching up with your reading.

383 Sunset

Location: On Lake of the Woods, about 35 miles northwest of Klamath Falls
Season: Late May–late Sept
Sites: 64 basic sites; no hookups
Maximum length: 40 feet
Facilities: Tables, grills, flush toilets, drinking water, boat launch, docks, boat rental nearby
Fee per night: $$
Management: Winema National Forest
Contact: (541) 883-6714; www.fs.usda.gov/recmain/fremont-winema/recreation
Finding the campground: From OR 140, 33 miles west of Klamath Falls and 45 miles east of Medford, turn south onto Dead Indian Memorial Highway. Go 2.5 miles; turn right to enter the campground.
GPS coordinates: N42 22.217' / W122 12.323'
About the campground: This popular campground on the east side of Lake of the Woods allows you to escape to the cool shade of the firs and pines when you are not out on the lake fishing, swimming, and boating. Mount McLoughlin can be seen from shore. The 1-mile Sunset Trail links the camp and Rainbow Bay. Longer trails in the vicinity lead to Fourmile Lake and its entourage of smaller lakes. Hard-core hikers can journey into wilderness.

384 Surveyor Recreation Site

Location: About 30 miles west of Klamath Falls
Season: Year-round; maintained June–Oct
Sites: 5 basic sites; no hookups
Maximum length: 25 feet
Facilities: Tables, grills, nonflush toilets; no drinking water
Fee per night: None
Management: Bureau of Land Management—Lakeview District, Klamath Falls Office
Contact: (541) 883-6916; www.blm.gov/or/
Finding the campground: From the junction of US 97 and OR 66 in southwest Klamath Falls, go west on OR 66 for 15.7 miles. Turn right onto the paved Keno Access Road (BLM 39-7E-31) for Buck Lake and Spencer Creek. Go 14.1 miles and turn left for the campground.

From Dead Indian Memorial Road, 0.5 mile east of Howard Prairie Lake, turn south onto Keno Access Road. Continue 13 miles before turning right into the campground.
GPS coordinates: N42 15.030' / W122 13.684'
About the campground: Tucked in an old-growth fir setting, this primitive camp is an ideal place for quiet reflection. Logs are scattered across the forest floor, which is covered by ferns and the delicate blossoms of prince's pine, starflower, and trillium. The camp has dirt roads and parking and gets light use.

385 Topsy Recreation Site

Location: About 16 miles southwest of Klamath Falls
Season: Mid-May–mid-Sept
Sites: 15 basic sites; no hookups
Maximum length: 40 feet
Facilities: Tables, grills, nonflush toilets, drinking water, boat launch, barrier-free dock and fishing pier
Fee per night: $
Management: Bureau of Land Management—Lakeview District, Klamath Falls Office
Contact: (541) 883-6916; www.blm.gov/or/
Finding the campground: From the junction of US 97 and OR 66 in southwest Klamath Falls, go west on OR 66 for 15.3 miles. Turn left onto gravel Topsy Road as you reach John C. Boyle Reservoir. Follow the signs about 1 mile to the campground entrance on the right.
GPS coordinates: N42 07.525' / W122 02.496'
About the campground: This terraced camp is both pretty and functional, blending into its natural pine setting above John C. Boyle Reservoir. All sites have level gravel parking pads, but some also offer tent platforms. From almost anywhere in camp, you can admire the sparkling water. You can watch birds and wildlife right from your lawn chair; an osprey nest overlooks shore. Crappie, bass, catfish, and panfish tug at the lines of anglers, and the reservoir is open to boating.

386 Williamson River

Location: About 7 miles north of Chiloquin
Season: Memorial Day weekend–Labor Day
Sites: 7 basic sites, 3 tent sites; no hookups
Maximum length: 30 feet
Facilities: Tables, grills, nonflush toilets, drinking water
Fee per night: $$
Management: Winema National Forest
Contact: (541) 783-4001; www.fs.usda.gov/recmain/fremont-winema/recreation
Finding the campground: From Chiloquin go about 5 miles north on US 97. Turn right (east) onto FR 9730 for the Collier and Williamson River Campgrounds. Keep left at the Collier Campground turnoff, going 1.3 miles on FR 9730, a wide, improved-surface road. Turn right and continue another 0.4 mile to the camp.
GPS coordinates: N42 39.490' / W121 51.266'
About the campground: At a distance from US 97, this quiet campground occupies a bench above the Williamson River. Ponderosa and lodgepole pines surround the sites, and dry-land shrubs dot the forest floor. Here the river is shallow, flowing over waving mats of algae. Willows and grass claim the bank below the camp; sage is dominant on the opposite shore. This campground offers convenient access to neighboring Collier Memorial State Park, as well as to the sights, sounds, and stops of the Klamath Basin–Upper Klamath Lake Area.

Central Oregon

Central Oregon includes the eastern slopes of the Central Cascades and the High Lava Plains, which spread out from Bend. The east-central Cascades serve up such outstanding features as the Metolius Wild and Scenic River, the Three Sisters, Mount Bachelor, Tam McArthur Rim, and the Cascade Lakes Area.

Within the High Lava Plains, you will find the Deschutes Wild and Scenic River, Newberry National Volcanic Monument, and Crooked River National Grassland. You can visit ghost towns, rock climb at Smith Rock State Park, hunt for thunder eggs in Ochoco National Forest, go speedboating at Cove Palisades, fish at area reservoirs, and stargaze at Pine Mountain Observatory.

The tourist-oriented communities of Bend and Sisters, along with several ranching towns and the river-floating mecca of Maupin, serve travelers.

The Cascade Range, that snowcapped chain of volcanoes that partitions the state and dominates the skyline in much of Central Oregon, was named by noted botanist David Douglas. Two stages of volcanic activity shaped these mountains. The younger volcanoes occur in the eastern part of the range. Their dry slopes support ponderosa and lodgepole pines and western larches.

The High Lava Plains feature a textured mosaic of sagebrush and native

Ponderosa pine (Pinus ponderosa) trunk, Metolius Wild and Scenic River, Deschutes National Forest

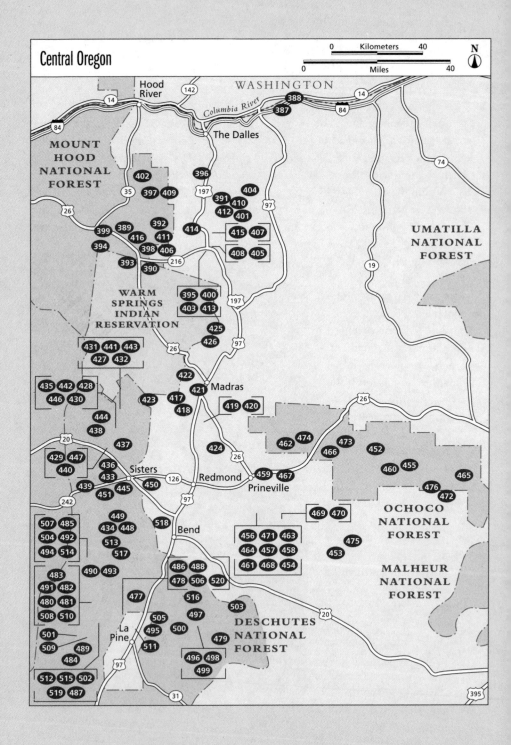

bunchgrass, juniper and pine forests, lava flows and lava-tube caves, obsidian ridges, cinder cones, and caldera lakes. Newberry Volcano, a shield volcano in the center of the state, covers a larger area than any other volcano in Oregon.

Golden and bald eagles, peregrine falcons, ospreys, and nighthawks favor these rugged plains, as do bluebirds and western tanagers. The larcenous gray jay is often a companion in the Cascades.

Given the diversity of the region, you should expect a variety of weather. The Cascades host downhill and cross-country skiing in winter and offer partially shaded trails and cool mountain lakes in summer. Do not be deceived by the dusty lodgepole pine forests; snowmelt can create ponds that breed mosquitoes, sometimes in hordes. Be sure to keep a supply of insect repellent handy.

Weather on the arid plains varies from crisp, chilly days in winter to baking temperatures in summer. Outdoor activities are generally possible year-round, with caving, rock climbing, hiking, mountain biking, and horseback riding among the more popular pursuits. Snowmobiling and ice fishing fill out the winter calendar at Newberry National Volcanic Monument. Throughout Central Oregon, both in the mountains and on the high plains, summertime visitors should be prepared for afternoon thunderstorms.

Rufus Area

	Hookup Sites	Total Sites	Max. RV Length	Hookups	Toilets	Showers	Drinking Water	Dump Station	Recreation	Fee	Can Reserve
387 Giles French Park		Open	40		F		X		FBL	None	
388 Le Page Park	22	42	40	E	F	X	X	X	SFBL	$$-$$$	X

387 Giles French Park

Location: Just northeast of Rufus
Season: Year-round
Sites: Open camping; no hookups
Maximum length: 40 feet
Facilities: Flush toilets, drinking water, boat launch
Fee per night: None
Management: US Army Corps of Engineers
Contact: (541) 506-7819; www.nwp.usace.army.mil
Finding the campground: From I-84, about 25 miles east of The Dalles, take exit 109 for Rufus. Follow the frontage road on the north side of the freeway east for 0.5 mile to the campground.
GPS coordinates: N45 42.367' / W120 42.470'
About the campground: This combination campground and day-use area stretches for 1.7 miles along the Columbia River between the boat launch and John Day Dam. A steep slope plunges from the camp to the rocky riverbank. Overnight parking is allowed on the large gravel- or asphalt-surfaced lots, while tent camping is allowed on the grass. Shade trees are a few steps away, and wind is common in the gorge. Shad and sturgeon fishing, boating, and visiting John Day Dam and its fish-viewing windows keep campers on the go.

388 Le Page Park

Location: About 5 miles northeast of Rufus
Season: Apr–Oct
Sites: 22 hookup sites, 20 walk-in tent sites; electric hookups
Maximum length: 40 feet
Facilities: Flush toilets, drinking water, showers, dump station, boat launch, docks
Fee per night: $$–$$$
Management: US Army Corps of Engineers
Contact: (541) 506-7819 or (541) 739-2713; (877) 444-6777 for reservations; www.nwp.usace.army.mil
Finding the campground: The campground is off I-84 at exit 114.
GPS coordinates: N45 43.681' / W120 39.047'
About the campground: This landscaped park overlooks the John Day River just as it meets the harnessed Columbia River above John Day Dam. The camp provides boaters and anglers with convenient access to the water. Three miles up the John Day River, an 8-site boat-to camp is available for overnight stays. Black locust trees give some shade to the RV spaces that overlook the water. A beach area serves swimmers.

Dufur-Maupin Area

	Hookup Sites	Total Sites	Max. RV Length	Hookups	Toilets	Showers	Drinking Water	Dump Station	Recreation	Fee	Can Reserve
389 Barlow Crossing		6	Small		NF				F	$$	
390 Bear Springs		21	32		NF		X			$$	
391 Beavertail Recreation Site		15	40		NF		X		FBL	$-$$	
392 Bonney Crossing		8	16		NF				HF	$$	
393 Clear Creek Crossing		7	16		NF				HO	$$	
394 Clear Lake		28	32		NF		X		FBL	$$	X
395 Devil's Canyon Recreation Site		4	T		NF				FB	$-$$	
396 Dufur City Park	14	14	40	WES	F	X	X	X	F	$$-$$$	
397 Eightmile		21	30		NF				HC	$$	
398 Forest Creek		8	16		NF				F	$$	
399 Frog Lake		33	22		NF		X		HFBL	$$	X
400 Harpham Flat Recreation Site		9	25		NF				FBL	$-$$	
401 Jones Canyon Recreation Site		8	40		NF				FB	$-$$	
402 Knebal Springs Horse Camp		8	22		NF				HR	$$	
403 Long Bend Recreation Site		4	25		NF				FB	$-$$	
404 Macks Canyon Recreation Site		17	40		NF				HFBLC	$-$$	
405 Maupin City Park	25	47	40	WES	F	X	X		FBL	$$$	
406 McCubbins Gulch		19	25		NF				O	$$	
407 Oak Springs Recreation Site		6	40		NF				FB	$-$$	
408 Oasis Recreation Site		10	40		NF				FB	$-$$	
409 Pebble Ford		3	16		NF				H	$$	
410 Rattlesnake Canyon Recreation Site		8	40		NF				FB	$-$$	
411 Rock Creek Reservoir		33	35		NF		X		HSFBL	$$	X
412 Twin Springs Recreation Site		7	40		NF				FB	$-$$	
413 Wapinitia Recreation Site		6	25		NF				FBL	$-$$	
414 Wasco County Fairgrounds: Hunt RV Park	120	120	60	WE	F	X	X	X		$$-$$$	X
415 White River Recreation Site		3	40		NF				FB	$-$$	
416 White River Station		5	Small		NF				F	$$	

389 Barlow Crossing

Location: About 17 miles southeast of Government Camp
Season: June–Sept
Sites: 6 basic sites; no hookups
Maximum length: Small units only due to road conditions
Facilities: Tables, grills, nonflush toilets; no drinking water
Fee per night: $$
Management: Mount Hood National Forest
Contact: (541) 352-6002; www.fs.usda.gov/recmain/mthood/recreation
Finding the campground: From OR 35 at the White River crossing, 2 miles south of the Mount Hood Meadows ski area and 5 miles north of the junction of US 26 and OR 35, follow FR 48 southeast for 8.8 miles. Turn right (west) onto FR 43 and go 0.6 mile. Turn right onto narrow, dirt Old Barlow Road/FR 3530 to reach the campground in 0.2 mile. Turn right, followed by a second right to locate the sites. (Old Barlow Road is closed from December 15 to April 1 and requires four-wheel-drive beyond the camp turnoff.)
GPS coordinates: N45 13.009' / W121 36.800'
About the campground: In fall, hunters use this quiet, rustic camp, which is situated in a forest of firs and lodgepole pines above 10-foot-wide Barlow Creek, just upstream from its confluence with the White River. The sites have pretty log tables, but the parking is undefined; one site sits at creek level. Nearby interpretive signs tell the story of Barlow Road, an overland segment of the Oregon Trail that linked the Columbia River Gorge to the Willamette Valley. This difficult route allowed pioneers to avoid a treacherous voyage down the Columbia River. Early pioneers cached supplies near here in 1845.

390 Bear Springs

Location: About 24 miles southwest of Maupin
Season: Late May–Sept
Sites: 21 basic sites; no hookups
Maximum length: 32 feet
Facilities: Tables, grills, nonflush toilets, drinking water
Fee per night: $$
Management: Mount Hood National Forest
Contact: (541) 467-2291; www.fs.usda.gov/recmain/mthood/recreation
Finding the campground: From OR 216, 4 miles east of its junction with US 26 and 24 miles west of Maupin, turn south at the sign for the campground. Continue 0.1 mile to the campground entrance on the right.
GPS coordinates: N45 07.036' / W121 31.917'
About the campground: Above the headwaters of Indian Creek, you will find this pleasant forest campground, which has a paved road and gravel parking. Many of the sites are better suited for tents or small RV units because of the spur size and parking access; there is one pull-through site. Grand firs, Douglas firs, and ponderosa pines shade this compact camp. Bring a good book, and settle in.

391 Beavertail Recreation Site

Location: About 21 miles north of Maupin
Season: Year-round
Sites: 15 basic sites; no hookups
Maximum length: 40 feet
Facilities: Tables, nonflush toilets, drinking water, drift boat/raft launch
Fee per night: $-$$
Management: Bureau of Land Management—Prineville District
Contact: (541) 416-6700; www.blm.gov/or/
Finding the campground: From the junction of US 197 and OR 216 East at Tygh Valley (7 miles north of Maupin), go east on OR 216, crossing the Deschutes River at Sherars Bridge in 7 miles. Proceed another 1.1 miles east and turn left (north) onto gravel Deschutes River Access Road, a BLM Backcountry Byway. Go 9.6 miles to the campground on the left.
GPS coordinates: N45 20.165' / W120 56.875'
About the campground: This campground rests on a grassy bench at a bend in the Deschutes River. It offers campers convenient access to superb fishing and river floating (a boater's pass is required for the river). A few trees provide spotty shade. Across the river you can see a steep canyon wall. In this fragile, arid canyon, fires and smoking are prohibited from June 1 to October 15.

392 Bonney Crossing

Location: About 17 miles west of Tygh Valley
Season: Mid-May–Sept
Sites: 8 basic sites; no hookups
Maximum length: 16 feet
Facilities: Tables, grills, nonflush toilets; no drinking water
Fee per night: $$
Management: Mount Hood National Forest
Contact: (541) 467-2291; www.fs.usda.gov/recmain/mthood/recreation
Finding the campground: From the junction of US 197 and OR 216 East at Tygh Valley (7 miles north of Maupin), go west 6 miles on Tygh Valley and Wamic Market Roads to Wamic. Continue west for 6 miles on Rock Creek Dam Road/FR 48. Turn right (north) onto FR 4810 and go 2 miles. Turn right again onto FR 4811 and go 1.2 miles. Turn right onto dirt FR 2710 and go 1.7 miles to the campground.
GPS coordinates: N45 15.388' / W121 23.500'
About the campground: This small campground rests in a transition forest along Badger Creek as it drains out of Badger Creek Wilderness. Douglas firs, oaks, and ponderosa pines contribute to the aesthetics of camp. The creek is captivating and clear. On the north bank look for the Badger Creek Trail, which follows the scenic waterway upstream into the wilderness for prized solitude. You may spot wild turkeys in the grasslands.

393 Clear Creek Crossing

Location: About 29 miles west of Maupin
Season: Mid-May–Sept
Sites: 7 basic sites; no hookups
Maximum length: 16 feet
Facilities: Tables, grills, nonflush toilets; no drinking water
Fee per night: $$
Management: Mount Hood National Forest
Contact: (541) 467-2291; www.fs.usda.gov/recmain/mthood/recreation
Finding the campground: From OR 216, 2 miles east of its junction with US 26 and 26 miles west of Maupin, turn north onto FR 2130 at the sign for the campground. Go 3 miles and turn right to enter the camp. Watch out for free-ranging cattle.
GPS coordinates: N45 08.716' / W121 34.793'
About the campground: This campground is located on Clear Creek within McCubbins Gulch Off-Highway-Vehicle Area, downstream from the McCubbins Gulch diversion. The campsites occupy a mild slope in a setting of mature firs; logs outline the roadway and sites. Clear Creek is aptly named. The log footbridge that spans the creek leads to Clear Creek Trail, a 5-mile-long link between this camp and the rustic Keeps Mill Campground. OHV trails can be accessed off FR 2130; look for them while en route to camp.

394 Clear Lake

Location: About 11 miles southeast of Government Camp
Season: Late May–early Sept
Sites: 28 basic sites, overflow camp; no hookups
Maximum length: 32 feet
Facilities: Tables, grills, nonflush toilets, drinking water, boat launch
Fee per night: $$
Management: Mount Hood National Forest
Contact: (541) 352-6002; (877) 444-6777 for reservations; www.fs.usda.gov/recmain/mthood/recreation
Finding the campground: From Government Camp go southeast on US 26 for 9.5 miles. Turn right onto FR 2630 and continue 1.1 miles to the camp entrance.
GPS coordinates: N45 10.862' / W121 41.874'
About the campground: Located on a slope above Clear Lake and shaded by firs and mountain hemlocks, this campground can fill up on summer weekends. All sites have gravel parking; some have pull-throughs, and some have tree-filtered lake views. Chinquapins, kinnikinnick, and rhododendrons grow in the sunny forest openings. Boating (10 miles per hour maximum) and fishing fill out campers' days. There are opportunities to hike beyond the camp.

395 Devil's Canyon Recreation Site

Location: About 5 miles south of Maupin
Season: Year-round
Sites: 4 tent sites; no hookups
Maximum length: Suitable for tents only
Facilities: Tables, nonflush toilets; no drinking water
Fee per night: $-$$
Management: Bureau of Land Management—Prineville District
Contact: (541) 416-6700; www.blm.gov/or/
Finding the campground: From the Deschutes River bridge on US 197 in Maupin, go south on US 197 for 0.2 mile. Turn right at the BLM sign for Upper River Access and continue 5 miles. The campground is on the right.
GPS coordinates: N45 07.033' / W121 07.802'
About the campground: This primitive campground occupies a sagebrush flat and offers views of a scenic bend in the Deschutes River and a butte rising across the river. Red-winged blackbirds, orioles, mergansers, ducks, swallows, and geese visit the area. Fishing and boating are popular. You will find a launch at Wapinitia Recreation Site, 2 miles downstream. Fires and smoking are prohibited from June 1 to October 15.

396 Dufur City Park

Location: In Dufur
Season: Year-round
Sites: 14 hookup sites, some tent camping; water, electric, and sewer hookups
Maximum length: 40 feet
Facilities: Flush toilets, drinking water, showers, dump station, playground, volleyball, horseshoe pits, ball field, swimming pool
Fee per night: $$-$$$
Management: City of Dufur
Contact: (541) 467-2356
Finding the campground: The campground is at the south end of the city of Dufur; follow signs for the park.
GPS coordinates: N45 27.033' / W121 07.615'
About the campground: At this pleasant city park, camping is available at the edge of the playing fields. The camp rests along Fifteenmile Creek, which offers fishing and nurtures the fully-grown trees that provide shade. The camp is a convenient base from which to explore historic Dufur, a quaint farming and ranching community. The Columbia River Gorge is only minutes away.

397 Eightmile

Location: About 17 miles west of Dufur
Season: June–mid-Oct
Sites: 21 basic sites; no hookups
Maximum length: 30 feet
Facilities: Tables, grills, nonflush toilets; no drinking water
Fee per night: $$
Management: Mount Hood National Forest
Contact: (541) 467-2291; www.fs.usda.gov/recmain/mthood/recreation
Finding the campground: From US 197 take the exit for Dufur. At the south end of town, head west on Dufur Valley Road/FR 44 for 17 miles. Turn right (north) onto FR 4430 to enter the campground on the right in 0.3 mile.

From Oregon 35, 16 miles northeast of Government Camp and 26 miles south of Hood River, turn east onto FR 44. Go 9.8 miles to reach FR 4430; proceed north to the camp.
GPS coordinates: N45 24.391' / W121 27.398'
About the campground: You will find this quiet camp in a mixed-age conifer forest along the upper reaches of Eightmile Creek. The sites are comfortably spaced and fully or partially shaded. At the camp is a trailhead for the 6.2-mile, hike or bike Eightmile Loop Trail. A 0.5-mile barrier-free trail pursues Eightmile Creek downstream to Lower Eightmile Forest Camp. As an alternative place to stay, Lower Eightmile Forest Camp (also called Lower Crossing Campground) has three closely spaced sites (16-foot maximum length) with fee and similar facilities. You can reach it by going 0.5 mile east on FR 44 from its junction with FR 4430 and then 1 mile north on FR 4440.

398 Forest Creek

Location: About 25 miles west of Tygh Valley
Season: Late May–early Oct
Sites: 8 basic sites; no hookups
Maximum length: 16 feet
Facilities: Tables, grills, nonflush toilets; no drinking water
Fee per night: $$
Management: Mount Hood National Forest
Contact: (541) 467-2291; www.fs.usda.gov/recmain/mthood/recreation
Finding the campground: From the junction of OR 216 East and US 197 at Tygh Valley, head west on Tygh Valley and Wamic Market Roads for 6 miles to Wamic. Continue west on Rock Creek Dam Road/FR 48 for 18 miles. Turn left (south) onto gravel FR 4885 and go 1 mile. Turn left onto FR 3530 to enter the campground in 0.2 mile. (The road beyond the camp is not maintained for passenger cars.)
GPS coordinates: N45 10.733' / W121 31.474'
About the campground: Historically a wayside stop for pioneers, this small, quiet campground sits among ponderosa pines, hemlocks, cedars, spruce, and firs. It rests along Forest Creek on Old Barlow Road, part of the Oregon Trail. Barlow was an overland toll road that allowed pioneers to bypass the treacherous voyage on the Columbia River to reach the Willamette Valley's fertile farmland.

399 Frog Lake

Location: About 8 miles southeast of Government Camp
Season: June–mid-Sept
Sites: 33 basic sites; no hookups
Maximum length: 22 feet
Facilities: Tables, grills, nonflush toilets, drinking water, boat launch
Fee per night: $$
Management: Mount Hood National Forest
Contact: (541) 352-6002; (877) 444-6777 for reservations; www.fs.usda.gov/recmain/mthood/recreation
Finding the campground: From Government Camp go southeast on US 26 for 7 miles. Turn left onto FR 2610 to enter the campground in 0.5 mile.
GPS coordinates: N45 13.337' / W121 41.625'
About the campground: This popular campground occupies a forest of hemlocks and firs along the shore of quiet Frog Lake. You can see Mount Hood peeking over the trees, especially from the south end of the day-use area. The camp is a fine base for outdoor recreation: You can fish or take your nonmotorized boat out on the lake or hike nearby trails to Frog Lake Buttes and Twin Lakes. You also have easy access to the Pacific Crest National Scenic Trail.

400 Harpham Flat Recreation Site

Location: About 4 miles south of Maupin
Season: Year-round
Sites: 9 basic sites; no hookups
Maximum length: 25 feet
Facilities: Tables, nonflush toilets, boat launch; no drinking water
Fee per night: $–$$
Management: Bureau of Land Management—Prineville District
Contact: (541) 416-6700; www.blm.gov/or/
Finding the campground: From the Deschutes River bridge on US 197 in Maupin, go south on US 197 for 0.2 mile. Turn right at the BLM sign for Upper River Access. Drive 3.5 miles to reach the campground entrance on the right.
GPS coordinates: N45 08.170' / W121 07.267'
About the campground: Adjacent to a popular raft put-in, this campground bustles with activity. It occupies a broad, sunny flat where the river canyon broadens; campers should bring a good shade source and ample water. Fishing, boating, rafting, and sightseeing keep Deschutes River campers returning again and again. Fires and smoking are prohibited from June 1 to October 15.

401 Jones Canyon Recreation Site

Location: About 19 miles north of Maupin
Season: Year-round
Sites: 8 basic sites; no hookups
Maximum length: 40 feet
Facilities: Tables, nonflush toilets, boat launch (downstream at Beavertail); no drinking water
Fee per night: $-$$
Management: Bureau of Land Management—Prineville District
Contact: (541) 416-6700; www.blm.gov/or/
Finding the campground: From the junction of US 197 and OR 216 East at Tygh Valley (7 miles north of Maupin), go east on OR 216, crossing the Deschutes River at Sherars Bridge in 7 miles. Continue east 1.1 miles. Turn left (north) onto gravel Deschutes River Access Road, a BLM Back-country Byway, and go 7.7 miles; the campground is on the left.
GPS coordinates: N45 18.467' / W120 57.477'
About the campground: Tall clumps of sagebrush isolate the sites of this treeless camp above the Deschutes River, just downstream from Jones Canyon. The camp has fine river canyon views, world-class fishing, and nearby access for boating and rafting. The Deschutes is a prized Wild and Scenic River. Boaters must secure permits and should find out where and when motorized boats are permissible. River otters can sometimes be spied. Fires and smoking are prohibited from June 1 to October 15.

402 Knebal Springs Horse Camp

Location: About 25 miles west of Dufur
Season: May–Sept
Sites: 8 basic sites; no hookups
Maximum length: 22 feet
Facilities: Tables, fire rings, nonflush toilets, horse-loading ramp, hitching rail, corrals, trough; no drinking water
Fee per night: $$
Management: Mount Hood National Forest
Contact: (541) 467-2291; www.fs.usda.gov/recmain/mthood/recreation
Finding the campground: From FR 44, 21.7 miles west of Dufur (at the south end of town) and 5.1 miles east of OR 35, turn north onto the paved FR 17 and go 0.5 mile. Bear right onto FR 1720; continue 2.6 miles to enter the campground via gravel FR 150 on the right. Be alert for the turnoff.
GPS coordinates: N45 26.050' / W121 28.794'
About the campground: This serviceable, comfortable campground is intended for equestrian campers only. The campsites are partially shaded by firs, pines, and larches. Trail 474, the Knebal Springs Trail, passes the camp and connects with other horse trails in the area. The springs at camp are fenced.

403 Long Bend Recreation Site

Location: About 5 miles south of Maupin
Season: Year-round
Sites: 4 basic sites; no hookups
Maximum length: 25 feet
Facilities: Tables, nonflush toilets; no drinking water
Fee per night: $–$$
Management: Bureau of Land Management—Prineville District
Contact: (541) 416-6700; www.blm.gov/or/
Finding the campground: From the Deschutes River bridge on US 197 in Maupin, go south on US 197 for 0.2 mile; turn right at the BLM sign for Upper River Access. Drive another 4.4 miles to reach the campground entrance on the right.
GPS coordinates: N45 07.604' / W121 07.757'
About the campground: This linear camp claims a narrow strip of shoreline along the Deschutes River. White alders line the riverbank, and hackberry grows at the upper edge of the camp. Across the river you can see cliffs, rims, and an active rail line. The Deschutes River provides fishing and boating, but strong undercurrents make swimming dangerous. Fires and smoking are prohibited from June 1 to October 15.

404 Macks Canyon Recreation Site

Location: About 29 miles north of Maupin
Season: Year-round
Sites: 17 basic sites; no hookups
Maximum length: 40 feet
Facilities: Tables, nonflush toilets, boat launch; no drinking water
Fee per night: $–$$
Management: Bureau of Land Management—Prineville District
Contact: (541) 416-6700; www.blm.gov/or/
Finding the campground: From the junction of US 197 and OR 216 East at Tygh Valley (7 miles north of Maupin), go east on OR 216, crossing the Deschutes River at Sherars Bridge in 7 miles. Continue 1.1 miles east and turn left (north) onto gravel Deschutes River Access Road, a BLM Backcountry Byway. Go 17 miles to reach the campground.
GPS coordinates: N45 23.461' / W120 52.694'
About the campground: This campground occupies a site where prehistoric Indian tribes wintered in pit houses more than 2,000 years ago. Present-day campers are similarly attracted to the mostly open river flat because of its convenient access to the Deschutes River and superb fishing and boating. The abandoned railroad grade on this side of the canyon serves hikers and bicyclists. It extends from the north end of the camp downstream to Deschutes River State Recreation Area. The trail offers fine river views and occasional river access, but beware of rattlesnakes in the rocky reaches and off-trail. Fires and smoking are prohibited June 1 to October 15; boaters should familiarize themselves with river rules.

405 Maupin City Park

Location: In Maupin
Season: Year-round
Sites: 25 hookup sites, 22 tent sites; water, electric, and sewer hookups
Maximum length: 40 feet
Facilities: Tables, flush toilets, drinking water, showers, free wireless, docking and launch (fee), community building with kitchen for rent; no campfires
Fee per night: $$$
Management: City of Maupin
Contact: (541) 395-2252; www.cityofmaupin.com
Finding the campground: The park is off Bakeoven Road in Maupin, on the east shore of the Deschutes River.
GPS coordinates: N45 10.449' / W121 04.396'
About the campground: Across the bridge from Maupin, this city park provides a lovely overnight camping facility. The hookup sites have concrete two-tracks on which to park, the shade of locust trees, and superb river views. The open-lawn tent area is reached across a footbridge over Bakeoven Creek. A grain elevator on Bakeoven Road adds to the rural atmosphere. This is a fine place to relax, watch the rafters float by, join in a river trip, or fish, boat, or sightsee.

406 McCubbins Gulch

Location: About 24 miles southwest of Maupin
Season: Mid-May–Sept
Sites: 15 basic sites, 4 overflow sites; no hookups
Maximum length: 25 feet
Facilities: Tables, grills, nonflush toilets; no drinking water
Fee per night: $$
Management: Mount Hood National Forest
Contact: (541) 467-2291; www.fs.usda.gov/recmain/mthood/recreation
Finding the campground: From OR 216, 5 miles east of its junction with US 26 and 23 miles west of Maupin, turn north onto FR 2110 at the sign for the campground. Go 1.1 miles and turn right onto gravel FR 230. Continue another 0.3 mile to the campground entrance on the right.
GPS coordinates: N45 06.901' / W121 28.973'
About the campground: This off-highway-vehicle (OHV) campground claims a mild slope and flat along McCubbins Gulch, a diversion of Clear Creek. The silt-bottomed stream flows along the lower edge of camp. A bridge across it leads to one of the OHV trails in the area; others start near the camp entrance. The camp floor is somewhat rolling, rutted, and barren, but the tall firs and pines are pleasant. Dust and noise are part of the deal, so if you are not an OHV enthusiast, avoid this camp. *NOTE:* Avoid trespassing onto tribal lands, which are private.

407 Oak Springs Recreation Site

Location: About 4 miles north of Maupin
Season: Year-round
Sites: 6 basic sites; no hookups
Maximum length: 40 feet
Facilities: Tables, nonflush toilets; no drinking water
Fee per night: $–$$
Management: Bureau of Land Management—Prineville District
Contact: (541) 416-6700; www.blm.gov/or/
Finding the campground: From US 197 in Maupin, go east on Bakeoven Road to Deschutes River Access Road. Turn left (north) and proceed downstream 4 miles to the campground on the left.
GPS coordinates: N45 13.135' / W121 04.484'
About the campground: This camp on the Deschutes River has a central, gravel parking area with tables set up around it. At the south end of camp, a basalt outcrop grades to the river. A few residences dot the opposite arid slope, while Oak Springs provide a splash of uncharacteristic green. Fishing, boating, rafting, and relaxing are the pursuits of campers. Undercurrents in the river make swimming dangerous. Fires and smoking are prohibited from June 1 to October 15.

408 Oasis Recreation Site

Location: About 1 mile north of Maupin
Season: Year-round
Sites: 10 basic sites; no hookups
Maximum length: 40 feet
Facilities: Tables, nonflush toilets; no drinking water
Management: Bureau of Land Management—Prineville District
Fee per night: $–$$
Contact: (541) 416-6700; www.blm.gov/or/
Finding the campground: From US 197 in Maupin, go east on Bakeoven Road to Deschutes River Access Road. Turn left (north) and proceed 1.2 miles downstream to the campground entrance on the left.
GPS coordinates: N45 10.954' / W121 04.978'
About the campground: One of the larger BLM camps along the Lower Deschutes River, Oasis occupies a long stretch of shore. Native grasses grow in the camp, while sagebrush grows at the periphery and willows and alders along the bank. Here the canyon lacks the wild and rocky disposition it reveals farther downstream, but the river still hosts boating and fishing and captivates onlookers. For whitewater excitement, schedule a float trip with one of the outfitters in Maupin. Fires and smoking are prohibited from June 1 to October 15.

Whitewater rafting, Deschutes Wild and Scenic River, Lower Deschutes National Backcountry Byway

409 Pebble Ford

Location: About 18 miles west of Dufur
Season: Mid-May–Sept
Sites: 3 basic sites; no hookups
Maximum length: 16 feet
Facilities: Tables, grills, nonflush toilets; no drinking water
Fee per night: $$
Management: Mount Hood National Forest
Contact: (541) 467-2291; www.fs.usda.gov/recmain/mthood/recreation
Finding the campground: From FR 44, 17.5 miles west of Dufur (at the south end of town) and 9.3 miles east of OR 35, turn south on the gravel road indicated for the campground. Continue 0.1 mile to the entrance.
GPS coordinates: N45 24.015' / W121 27.801'
About the campground: In a setting of firs, cedars, and ponderosa pines, this small campground straddles a tributary; a footbridge links the camp halves. Sites have gravel parking, and most have tables and grills. Trails explore the surrounding forest.

410 Rattlesnake Canyon Recreation Site

Location: About 23 miles north of Maupin
Season: Year-round
Sites: 8 basic sites; no hookups
Maximum length: 40 feet
Facilities: Tables, nonflush toilets, boat launch (upstream at Beavertail); no drinking water
Fee per night: $-$$
Management: Bureau of Land Management—Prineville District
Contact: (541) 416-6700; www.blm.gov/or/
Finding the campground: From the junction of US 197 and OR 216 East at Tygh Valley (7 miles north of Maupin), go east on OR 216, crossing the Deschutes River at Sherars Bridge in 7 miles. Continue east another 1.1 miles and turn left (north) onto gravel Deschutes River Access Road, a BLM Backcountry Byway. Continue 10.5 miles to the campground on the left.
GPS coordinates: N45 20.182' / W120 55.886'
About the campground: This camp occupies a mild bench above the Deschutes Wild and Scenic River. Its sites blend into the expanse of sagebrush and rabbitbrush. Trees grow closer to the river, a cliff overlooks camp, and a tableland sits across the river. Fishing, boating, and rafting are the primary diversions. The river canyon funnels various birds past camp; bats may be active at dusk. Undercurrents make swimming dangerous. Boaters should familiarize themselves with river rules. Fires and smoking are prohibited June 1 to October 15.

411 Rock Creek Reservoir

Location: On Rock Creek Reservoir, about 13 miles west of Tygh Valley
Season: Mid-May–Sept
Sites: 33 basic sites; no hookups
Maximum length: 35 feet
Facilities: Tables, grills, nonflush toilets, drinking water, boat ramp (nonmotorized boats or electric trolling only)
Fee per night: $$
Management: Mount Hood National Forest
Contact: (541) 467-2291; (877) 444-6777 for reservations; www.fs.usda.gov/recmain/mthood/recreation
Finding the campground: From the junction of OR 216 East and US 197 at Tygh Valley, head west on Tygh Valley and Wamic Market Roads for 6 miles to Wamic. Continue west on Rock Creek Dam Road/FR 48 for 6.5 miles. Turn right (west) onto FR 4820 and go 0.2 mile. Turn right onto FR 120 and continue 0.2 mile to the campground.
GPS coordinates: N43 23.898' / W122 55.648'
About the campground: This campground is located on the south side of the dam that captures Rock Creek and creates the reservoir. A picnic area is on the north side. Oaks and small ponderosa pines grow in the basin. The lake offers trout fishing, swimming, and silent (motorless) boating.

412 Twin Springs Recreation Site

Location: About 16 miles north of Maupin
Season: Year-round
Sites: 7 basic sites; no hookups
Maximum length: 40 feet
Facilities: Tables, nonflush toilets; no drinking water
Fee per night: $–$$
Management: Bureau of Land Management—Prineville District
Contact: (541) 416-6700; www.blm.gov/or/
Finding the campground: From the junction of US 197 and OR 216 East at Tygh Valley (7 miles north of Maupin), go east on OR 216, crossing the Deschutes River at Sherars Bridge in 7 miles. Continue east 1.1 miles and turn left (north) onto gravel Deschutes River Access Road, a BLM Backcountry Byway. Go 4 miles to the campground on the left.
GPS coordinates: N45 18.560' / W121 00.357'
About the campground: This shadeless campground occupies a low, sagebrush-covered plateau above the Deschutes River. Basalt cliffs rise across the river. The railroad track that traverses the opposite shore represents the victor in a battle to see which railroad would serve the canyon. The abandoned grade on the campground side is used now by hikers and bicyclists; you can access the grade at Macks Canyon, at the north end of Deschutes River Access Road. Fishing, boating, and rafting are the river pursuits, but undercurrents make swimming dangerous. Fires and smoking are prohibited from June 1 to October 15.

413 Wapinitia Recreation Site

Location: About 3 miles south of Maupin
Season: Year-round
Sites: 6 basic sites; no hookups
Maximum length: 25 feet
Facilities: Tables, nonflush toilets, boat launch; no drinking water
Fee per night: $–$$
Management: Bureau of Land Management—Prineville District
Contact: (541) 416-6700; www.blm.gov/or/
Finding the campground: From the Deschutes River bridge on US 197 in Maupin, go south on US 197 for 0.2 mile. Turn right at the BLM sign for Upper River Access; drive 3 miles to the campground entrance on the right.
GPS coordinates: N45 08.645' / W121 07.533'
About the campground: This campground fronts the Deschutes River where bald, rounded ridges shape the canyon. Junipers dot the opposite slope, and white alders edge the river. Fishing, boating, rafting, and enjoying the remote canyon quiet are reasons to visit. Fires and smoking are prohibited from June 1 to October 15.

414 Wasco County Fairgrounds: Hunt RV Park

Location: In Tygh Valley
Season: May–Nov
Sites: 120 hookup sites, multiple tent camping locations; water and electric hookups
Maximum length: 60 feet
Facilities: Flush toilets, drinking water, showers, dump station, horse stalls for rent
Fee per night: $$–$$$
Management: Wasco County
Contact: (541) 483-2288, reservations accepted
Finding the campground: From the junction of US 197 and OR 216 East at Tygh Valley (7 miles north of Maupin), go west on Tygh Valley Road for 0.3 mile. Turn right onto Main Street; follow it for 0.1 mile. Turn right onto Fairgrounds Road; continue 1.8 miles to the fairgrounds and Hunt RV Park.
GPS coordinates: N45 15.167' / W121 12.399'
About the campground: You will find this pleasant wayside on a flat surrounded by the bald, rolling hills of the Plateau Country. Mature trees shade the camp's groomed lawns. When events are not taking place at the fairgrounds, the camp can be quite restful. Otherwise you will find a bustling mini-village of RVs and tents.

415 White River Recreation Site

Location: About 5 miles north of Maupin
Season: Year-round
Sites: 3 basic sites; no hookups
Maximum length: 40 feet
Facilities: Tables, nonflush toilets; no drinking water
Fee per night: $–$$
Management: Bureau of Land Management—Prineville District
Contact: (541) 416-6700; www.blm.gov/or/
Finding the campground: From US 197 in Maupin, head east on Bakeoven Road to Deschutes River Access Road. Turn left (north) and proceed 5.2 miles downriver to the campground entrance on the left.
GPS coordinates: N45 13.951' / W121 04.065'
About the campground: This camp has a gravel parking area partitioned into marked spaces; tables paired with the sites occupy the lot's perimeter. Sagebrush and a few riverside alders are the only vegetation on this otherwise open flat. Like the other camps of the Deschutes River corridor, this one serves up breathtaking river and canyon views and great fishing. The White River confluence is across the Deschutes River from camp. Maupin is the base for several river-running outfitters, should you seek a livelier look at the Deschutes. Fires and smoking are prohibited from June 1 to October 15.

416 White River Station

Location: About 18 miles southeast of Government Camp
Season: Mid-May–Sept
Sites: 5 basic sites; no hookups
Maximum length: Small units only due to narrow, bumpy entry road
Facilities: Tables, grills, nonflush toilets; no drinking water
Fee per night: $$
Management: Mount Hood National Forest
Contact: (541) 467-2291; www.fs.usda.gov/recmain/mthood/recreation
Finding the campground: From OR 35 at the White River crossing, 2 miles south of the Mount Hood Meadows ski area and 5 miles north of the junction of US 26 and OR 35, follow FR 48 southeast for 8.8 miles. Turn right (west) onto FR 43 and go 0.6 mile. Turn left onto narrow, dirt Old Barlow Road/FR 3530 to reach the campground on the left in 1.2 miles. *NOTE:* Old Barlow Road is closed Dec 15–Apr 1.
GPS coordinates: N45 11.892' / W121 36.062'
About the campground: First used by pioneers on the Oregon Trail, this quiet camp occupies a semi-open flat along the White River. A few big firs rise among the lodgepole pines, while alders and cottonwoods grow beside the river. The roomy and widely spaced sites have log tables and undefined parking. Interpretive signs introduce the history of the area. The White River originates from glaciers on Mount Hood and rolls turbulent, cloudy, and fast past the camp.

Madras-Redmond Area

	Hookup Sites	Total Sites	Max. RV Length	Hookups	Toilets	Showers	Drinking Water	Dump Station	Recreation	Fee	Can Reserve
417 The Cove Palisades State Park: Crooked River	91	91	60	WE	F	X	X	X	SFBL	$$$	X
418 The Cove Palisades State Park: Deschutes River	82	174	60	WES	F	X	X		HSFBL	$$$	X
419 Haystack		24	32		NF		X		FBL	$$	
420 Haystack Reservoir: West Shore		14	32		NF				FBL	$$	
421 Jefferson County Fairgrounds RV Park	63	63	60	WES	F	X	X	X		$$	X
422 Pelton Park	33	52	40	E	F	X	X		SFBL	$$-$$$	X
423 Perry South		64	40		NF		X		SFBL	$$	X
424 Skull Hollow		28	25		NF					$	
425 South Junction Recreation Site		11	T		NF				F	$-$$	
426 Trout Creek Recreation Site		21	25		NF				HFBLC	$-$$	

417 The Cove Palisades State Park: Crooked River

Location: About 10 miles southwest of Madras, about 25 miles northwest of Redmond
Season: Year-round
Sites: 91 hookup sites, 3 deluxe cabins nearby; water and electric hookups
Maximum length: 60 feet
Facilities: Tables, grills, flush toilets, drinking water, showers, dump station, boat launch (at day-use area)
Fee per night: $$$
Management: Oregon State Parks and Recreation Department
Contact: (541) 546-3412; (800) 452-5687 for reservations; www.oregon.gov/OPRD/PARKS/camping.shtml
Finding the campground: From US 97/26 in Madras, take Culver Highway southwest at the sign for Cove Palisades and go 7.1 miles. Turn right (west) onto Gem Lane; follow the signs for the state park through a series of turns to reach the campground on the left in 2.5 miles.

From Redmond go north on US 97 for 16 miles. Turn left (west) at the sign for the park; continue to follow the park signs another 8.5 miles to the campground on the left.
GPS coordinates: N44 32.384' / W121 15.319'
About the campground: This campground claims a high plateau above the Crooked River Arm of Lake Billy Chinook. Although it lacks a lake overlook, the campground provides views of Mount Jefferson and Three Fingered Jack. The flat is landscaped with lawn and trees for some shade, and the sites have paved parking. For lake recreation, just take the short drive downhill into the core

of the park. The turnoff for the marina and restaurant is a mile from the camp. The day-use boat launch, picnic area, and swimming area are 1.1 miles away.

418 The Cove Palisades State Park: Deschutes River

Location: About 14 miles southwest of Madras and 29 miles northwest of Redmond
Season: May–mid-Sept
Sites: 82 hookup sites, 92 basic sites; water, electric, and sewer hookups
Maximum length: 60 feet
Facilities: Tables, grills, flush toilets, drinking water, showers, store, playground, boat launch (at day-use area), fish-cleaning station
Fee per night: $$$
Management: Oregon State Parks and Recreation Department
Contact: (541) 546-3412; (800) 452-5687 for reservations; www.oregon.gov/OPRD/PARKS/camping.shtml
Finding the campground: From US 97/26 in Madras, take Culver Highway southwest at the sign for Cove Palisades and go 7.1 miles. Turn right (west) onto Gem Lane; follow the signs for the state park through a series of turns to reach the campground on the left in 7 miles.

From Redmond go north on US 97 for 16 miles. Turn left (west) at the sign for the park; continue to follow the signs another 13 miles to the campground.
GPS coordinates: N44 32.305' / W121 16.638'
About the campground: This campground occupies a canyon near the Deschutes River Arm of Lake Billy Chinook. Native junipers, along with locusts, cottonwoods, and willows, shade the developed camp. Nature trails lead to Ship Rock and to the day-use swimming area. A longer hiking trail climbs to and then traverses the summit plateau of The Peninsula, which overlooks the camp. This landmark, shaped by the Deschutes and Crooked River Arms of Lake Billy Chinook, dishes up fine views of the lake and another area landmark, The Island. You can access the lake at the park's day-use areas on either side of the camp. Billy Chinook is one of the state's premier recreational waters for boating, fishing, swimming, and waterskiing.

419 Haystack

Location: On Haystack Reservoir, about 12 miles south of Madras and 22 miles north of Redmond
Season: Mid-May–Sept
Sites: 24 basic sites; no hookups
Maximum length: 32 feet
Facilities: Tables, grills, nonflush toilets, drinking water, boat launch, covered picnic tables (at Haystack Reservoir)
Fee per night: $$
Management: Crooked River National Grassland
Contact: (541) 475-9272; www.fs.usda.gov/recmain/centraloregon/recreation

Finding the campground: From US 97, 8 miles south of Madras and 18 miles north of Redmond, turn east onto Jericho Lane. Go 1.2 miles and turn right onto Haystack Road. Continue 2.1 miles to the campground entrance road; follow it left for 0.5 mile to the campground.

GPS coordinates: N44 29.608' / W121 08.470'

About the campground: This campground is on a juniper-and-sagebrush-covered slope above the east shore of Haystack Reservoir. It has paved roads and parking and presents views of Haystack and Juniper Buttes, Mount Jefferson, and the surrounding high desert and distant Cascades. Because of the wind and sun, keep the sunscreen handy. The lake is regularly stocked with fish. Sailboards, boats, and geese ply the sun-spangled water.

420 Haystack Reservoir: West Shore

Location: On Haystack Reservoir, about 10 miles south of Madras and 20 miles north of Redmond

Season: Year-round

Sites: 14 RV sites; no hookups

Maximum length: 32 feet

Facilities: Tables, grills, nonflush toilets, paved boat launch; no drinking water

Fee per night: $$

Management: Crooked River National Grassland

Contact: (541) 475-9272; (541) 416-6640; www.fs.usda.gov/recmain/centraloregon/recreation

Finding the campground: From US 97, 8 miles south of Madras and 18 miles north of Redmond, turn east onto Jericho Lane and go 1.2 miles. Turn right onto Haystack Road; continue 0.6 mile to the campground on the left.

GPS coordinates: N44 29.596' / W121 09.556'

About the campground: This camp claims a narrow strip of shoreline on the west side of Haystack Reservoir. Views from the camp include the arid, juniper-dotted hills; the open expanse of the Crooked River National Grassland; and Haystack and Juniper Buttes. Although basically a camping-dedicated parking lot, the campground makes up for it with lake access for boating, fishing, and sailboarding.

421 Jefferson County Fairgrounds RV Park

Location: In Madras

Season: Year-round

Sites: 63 hookup sites, some tent camping; water, electric, and sewer hookups

Maximum length: 60 feet

Facilities: Tables, flush toilets, drinking water, showers, dump station

Fee per night: $$

Management: Jefferson County

Contact: (541) 475-6288 or (541) 325-5050, reservations accepted; http://cowdeo.com

Finding the campground: From US 97/26 at the south end of Madras, turn west onto Fairgrounds Road. Go 0.1 mile and turn right toward the RV camp entrance.

GPS coordinates: N44 37.238' / W121 08.212'

About the campground: This RV camp occupies an open, gravel flat at the eastern edge of the Jefferson County Fairgrounds. It offers a clean, orderly layout, has a table at each site, and is highly convenient for event participants or attendees. Make reservations well in advance. The open lawn adjacent to the RV spaces welcomes repose.

422 Pelton Park

Location: On Lake Simtustus, about 13 miles northwest of Madras
Season: Late Apr–Sept
Sites: 33 hookup sites, 19 basic sites, 13 yomes; electric hookups
Maximum length: 40 feet
Facilities: Tables, fire rings, flush toilets, drinking water, showers, camp store/cafe, volleyball, horseshoe pits, swimming area, marina boat rental and moorage, launch, fish-cleaning station
Fee per night: $$–$$$
Management: Portland General Electric
Contact: (541) 325-5292 (park and reservations); (541) 475-0516 (independently operated store and marina); www.portlandgeneral.com/community_environment/
Finding the campground: From the junction of US 97 and US 26 West in Madras, go north on US 26W for 9.4 miles. Turn left at Pelton Junction onto Pelton Dam Road. Continue 3.3 miles to enter the park on the right.
GPS coordinates: N44 41.097' / W121 14.282'
About the campground: This campground and its accompanying day-use area occupy 0.5 mile of the Lake Simtustus shore for a full lineup of wet fun. The canyon junipers provide welcome shade. The camp has paved parking, dry lawns, picturesque junipers, and a few natural boulders and outcrops. Some sites overlook the lake. Much of Lake Simtustus has a maximum boat speed of 10 miles per hour, but there is an area designated for speed craft. Kokanee, steelhead, rainbow and brown trout, and smallmouth bass make for excellent fishing and, later, dining. You will need both a valid state fishing license and a Warm Springs Indian Reservation license; you can buy both at the camp store. Pelton Wildlife Overlook, just north of the park, is a popular spot to visit.

423 Perry South

Location: On Lake Billy Chinook, about 30 miles southwest of Madras
Season: Late May–mid-Sept
Sites: 55 basic sites, 9 tent sites; no hookups
Maximum length: 50 feet
Facilities: Tables, grills, nonflush toilets, drinking water, boat launch, dock, fish-cleaning station
Fee per night: $$
Management: Deschutes National Forest
Contact: (541) 549-7700; (877) 444-6777 for reservations; www.fs.usda.gov/recmain/centraloregon/recreation

Finding the campground: From US 97/26 in Madras, take Culver Highway southwest at the sign for Cove Palisades and go 7.1 miles. Turn right (west) onto Gem Lane; follow the signs for the state park through a series of turns, remaining on the main road to and through the park. Eventually the route becomes FR 64. After going 20.3 miles from the Culver Highway turnoff, you will come to the junction of FR 64 and FR 1170. Stay on FR 64 and drive another 2.5 miles to reach the campground. (Carrying a Deschutes National Forest map can help you track your progress.)

GPS coordinates: N44 35.041' / W121 27.061'

About the campground: This popular camp straddles FR 64 in a narrow draw above the Metolius River Arm of Lake Billy Chinook. A dry forest houses the camp; at the lower camp you will find some big pines and a spring. The lower camp also sits closer to the lake, but the upper camp is the quieter retreat. Boating, swimming, fishing, and waterskiing entertain guests. You must have both a state license and a Warm Springs tribal license to fish the Metolius River Arm of Lake Billy Chinook. Nesting bald eagles are treated to a mandated quiet on this part of the lake until April 15 each year. By the time the campground opens, the success of their nests is secured.

424 Skull Hollow

Location: About 13 miles northeast of Redmond
Season: Year-round
Sites: 28 basic sites; no hookups
Maximum length: 25 feet
Facilities: Tables, grills, nonflush toilets; no drinking water
Fee per night: $
Management: Crooked River National Grassland
Contact: (541) 475-9272; www.fs.usda.gov/recmain/centraloregon/recreation
Finding the campground: From Redmond drive 3 miles north on US 97. Turn right (east) at the sign for O'Neil and Lone Pine and follow O'Neil Road for 4.8 miles. Turn left onto Lone Pine Road and continue 5.3 miles. Turn left onto FR 5710 and go 0.1 mile; turn left to enter the campground.
GPS coordinates: N44 24.848' / W121 02.315'
About the campground: This amazing campground, seemingly in the middle of nowhere and modest in offering, blossoms into a tent city on weekends. The reason is Smith Rock State Park to the southwest, a world-renowned rock-climbing area on the Crooked River. The camp also lies within easy reach of the Gray Butte Trail for hiking and mountain biking, the Endurance Trail for horseback riding, and the wide-open spaces of the Crooked River National Grassland. The camp occupies a juniper-dotted sage-grassland. In this fragile, dry landscape, pay heed to fire restrictions, and use common sense when parking.

425 South Junction Recreation Site

Location: About 36 miles north of Madras
Season: Year-round
Sites: 11 tent sites; no hookups

Maximum length: Suitable for tents only
Facilities: Tables, nonflush toilets; no drinking water
Fee per night: $-$$
Management: Bureau of Land Management—Prineville District
Contact: (541) 416-6700; www.blm.gov/or/
Finding the campground: From the junction of US 197 and US 97 at Shaniko Junction (21 miles south of Maupin and 26 miles north of Madras), go west on South Junction Road, which begins paved and becomes gravel. Follow it 9.2 miles to a fork; bear right and go another 0.4 mile to enter the camp via a narrow dirt road.
GPS coordinates: N44 51.429' / W121 03.668'
About the campground: Located on the east shore of the Deschutes River, across from Warm Springs Indian Reservation and the Warm Springs River confluence, these campsites are well spaced among the juniper and sagebrush of the grassland slope. Each site features a shade tree or two. The river, a strong enticement to anglers and daydreamers, is 0.1 mile from camp, across a BLM fence and a railroad track. A stile allows for an easy passage over the fence; be alert when crossing the tracks. Fires and smoking are prohibited from June 1 to October 15.

426 Trout Creek Recreation Site

Location: About 16 miles north of Madras
Season: Year-round
Sites: 21 basic sites; no hookups
Maximum length: 25 feet
Facilities: Tables, nonflush toilets, boat launch; no drinking water
Fee per night: $-$$
Management: Bureau of Land Management—Prineville District
Contact: (541) 416-6700; www.blm.gov/or/
Finding the campground: From Madras go 3 miles north on US 97. Turn left onto Cora Lane and then immediately left again onto Clark Drive. Proceed 8 miles to Gateway (the road name changes en route). In Gateway turn right onto Clemmens Drive toward Trout Creek. Drive 4.3 miles, passing through a narrow tunnel with 14-foot clearance and down a steep gravel road to the base of the canyon. Turn left and continue 0.3 mile to the recreation site. (The road is not recommended for trailers.)
GPS coordinates: N44 48.968' / W121 05.624'
About the campground: This recreation site occupies a pretty canyon along the Deschutes River. Sites claim a broad flat of native grasses, sagebrush, and rabbitbrush, with a light sprinkling of junipers. In this sun-drenched canyon, the juniper-shaded sites are quickly snapped up. Just downstream looms an impressive butte. An abandoned railroad grade, now a multiple-use trail, journeys upstream to Mecca Flat, offering views of, and occasional access to, the river. Fishing and boating are popular. Fires and smoking are prohibited from June 1 to October 15.

Sisters Area

	Hookup Sites	Total Sites	Max. RV Length	Hookups	Toilets	Showers	Drinking Water	Dump Station	Recreation	Fee	Can Reserve
427 Allen Springs		16	30		NF				HF	$$	
428 Allingham		10	50		NF		X	X	HF	$$	
429 Blue Bay		25	50		NF		X		HFBL	$$	X
430 Camp Sherman		15	50		NF		X		HF	$$	X
431 Candle Creek		10	20		NF				HF	$$	
432 Canyon Creek		7	20		NF				HF	$$	
433 Cold Spring		23	50		NF		X		H	$$	
434 Driftwood		18	T		NF				HSFB	$$	
435 Gorge		18	50		NF				HF	$$	
436 Graham Corral Horse Camp		13	30		NF		X		HR	$$	
437 Indian Ford		25	50		NF					$$	
438 Jack Creek		19	50		NF				HR	$$	
439 Lava Camp Lake		12	20		NF				HF	None	
440 Link Creek		33	50		NF		X		HSFBL	$$-$$$	X
441 Lower Bridge		12	40		NF		X		HF	$$	
442 Pine Rest		7	T		NF				HF	$$	
443 Pioneer Ford		18	50		NF		X		HF	$$	
444 Sheep Springs Horse Camp		11	40		NF		X		HR	$$	X
445 Sisters Cow Camp Horse Camp		5	40		NF				HR	None	
446 Smiling River		36	50		NF		X		HF	$$	X
447 South Shore		38	50		NF		X		HSFBL	$$	X
448 Three Creek Lake		11	20		NF				HSFB	$$	
449 Three Creek Meadow		20	40		NF				HFR	$$	
450 Three Sisters Overnight Park	25	60	40	WE	F		X	X		$$-$$$	
451 Whispering Pines Horse Camp		9	40		NF				HR	$$	

427 Allen Springs

Location: About 20 miles northwest of Sisters
Season: Year-round, access dependent on snow
Sites: 7 basic sites, 9 tent sites; no hookups
Maximum length: 30 feet
Facilities: Tables, grills, nonflush toilets; no drinking water
Fee per night: $$
Management: Deschutes National Forest
Contact: (541) 549-7700; www.fs.usda.gov/recmain/centraloregon/recreation
Finding the campground: From Sisters go west on US 20 for 9.3 miles. Turn right (north) onto paved FR 14; follow it for 11.1 miles to the campground entrance on the left.
GPS coordinates: N44 31.669' / W121 37.712'
About the campground: One of a string of choice family campgrounds along the Metolius Wild and Scenic River, this camp occupies a bend of the river. Sites typically rest among the fir, cedar, and ponderosa pine trees, except the walk-in sites, which occupy a meadow at the downstream end of the camp. Because river trails trace both banks, you can fashion a 6-mile loop hike between Lower Bridge (downstream) and the bridge at Wizard Falls Fish Hatchery (upstream). Fly-fishing lines often dance over the stunning water, while geese dwell in the quiet afforded by the river bend.

428 Allingham

Location: About 16 miles northwest of Sisters
Season: Mid-May–mid-Sept
Sites: 10 basic sites; no hookups
Maximum length: 50 feet
Facilities: Tables, grills, nonflush toilets, drinking water, dump station
Fee per night: $$
Management: Deschutes National Forest
Contact: (541) 549-7700; www.fs.usda.gov/recmain/centraloregon/recreation
Finding the campground: From Sisters go west on US 20 for 9.3 miles. Turn right (north) onto paved FR 14 and follow it for 6 miles. Turn left onto FR 1419 at the sign that reads To CAMP SHERMAN. Go 0.2 mile and turn right onto paved FR 900 (signed for campgrounds). Go 0.7 mile to reach the campground on the left.
GPS coordinates: N44 28.337' / W121 38.269'
About the campground: This Metolius River campground has several pull-through sites and is well suited for RVs and large trailers. Ponderosa pines and bitterbrush set the stage for your stay. Views are of the glassy river, its green banks, and the cabins on the opposite shore. Fly fishing, hiking the trails, and visiting Wizard Falls Fish Hatchery are area pursuits.

429 Blue Bay

Location: On Suttle Lake, about 14 miles northwest of Sisters
Season: Mid-May–mid-Sept
Sites: 25 basic sites; no hookups
Maximum length: 50 feet
Facilities: Tables, grills, nonflush toilets, drinking water, boat launch, fish-cleaning station
Fee per night: $$
Management: Deschutes National Forest
Contact: (541) 549-7700; (877) 444-6777 for reservations; www.fs.usda.gov/recmain/centraloregon/recreation
Finding the campground: From US 20, 13 miles west of Sisters and 6.5 miles east of Santiam Pass, turn south onto paved FR 2070 toward Suttle and Blue Lakes (the east access road). Go 1 mile to the campground entrance on the right.
GPS coordinates: N44 25.235' / W121 43.915'
About the campground: In a select-cut forest of firs and ponderosa pines, this campground offers semi-sunny sites along the south shore of Suttle Lake, a big, natural lake that boasts a full range of lake recreation. Vine maples claim the lower story. The campground has paved roads and gravel parking pads, some of which are pull-throughs. Entertainment here includes boating, fishing, waterskiing, and hiking the 3.25-mile Shoreline Trail. Elsewhere on the lake you will find suitable swimming areas. Most days, boaters and anglers must contend with a strong afternoon wind.

430 Camp Sherman

Location: About 16 miles northwest of Sisters
Season: Year-round, access dependent on snow
Sites: 15 basic sites; no hookups
Maximum length: 50 feet
Facilities: Tables, grills, nonflush toilets, drinking water (seasonally), picnic shelter
Fee per night: $$
Management: Deschutes National Forest
Contact: (541) 549-7700; (877) 444-6777 for reservations; www.fs.usda.gov/recmain/centraloregon/recreation
Finding the campground: From Sisters go west on US 20 for 9.3 miles. Turn right (north) onto paved FR 14 and follow it for 6 miles. Turn left onto FR 1419 at the sign that reads To Camp Sherman. Go 0.2 mile and turn right onto paved FR 900 (signed for campgrounds). Continue 0.2 mile to reach the campground on the left.
GPS coordinates: N44 27.821' / W121 38.368'
About the campground: This campground occupies a flat of mixed-age ponderosa pines; the mature pines parade reddish yellow trunks. A grassy meadow extends to the river, while bitterbrush claims the roadside. Wildflower-decorated islands and banks contribute to the charm of the river. Relaxing, birding, hiking, fly fishing, and sightseeing are among the pastimes here.

431 Candle Creek

Location: About 16 miles northwest of Sisters
Season: Mid-May–mid-Sept
Sites: 10 basic sites; no hookups
Maximum length: 20 feet
Facilities: Tables, grills, nonflush toilets; no drinking water
Fee per night: $$
Management: Deschutes National Forest
Contact: (541) 549-7700; www.fs.usda.gov/recmain/centraloregon/recreation
Finding the campground: From Sisters go west on US 20 for 9.3 miles. Turn right (north) onto paved FR 14 and follow it for 13.6 miles to Lower Bridge, where the road name changes to FR 12 upon crossing. (The road begins paved but changes to gravel.) Go 1 mile on FR 12 and turn right onto FR 980. Proceed 1.5 miles to the campground.
GPS coordinates: N44 34.505' / W121 37.163'
About the campground: This peaceful campground sits on a forested bluff above the Metolius River at the Candle Creek confluence. Alders and vine maples grow along the swift waterway, which is open to catch-and-release fishing. You can access the West Metolius Trail from camp; it leads along the river.

432 Canyon Creek

Location: About 18 miles northwest of Sisters
Season: Mid-May–mid-Sept
Sites: 7 basic sites; no hookups
Maximum length: 20 feet
Facilities: Tables, grills, nonflush toilets; no drinking water
Fee per night: $$
Management: Deschutes National Forest
Contact: (541) 549-7700; www.fs.usda.gov/recmain/centraloregon/recreation
Finding the campground: From Sisters go west on US 20 for 9.3 miles. Turn right (north) onto paved FR 14 and follow it for 2.6 miles. Turn left onto FR 1419 at the sign for Camp Sherman and go 2.2 miles. Proceed straight onto FR 1420, following the signs for Sheep Springs Horse Camp, for 3.4 miles. Turn right onto gravel FR 1420.400; continue 0.7 mile to the campground.
GPS coordinates: N44 30.085' / W121 38.495'
About the campground: At the convergence of Canyon Creek and the Metolius River, you will find this small, pleasant campground in a setting of ponderosa pines, bitterbrush, and bunchgrass. The West Metolius Trail departs from camp on a 9-mile journey down the river to Candle Creek. The hike serves up spectacular scenes of sun-gilded riffles, channels, and deep pools; grassy islands showy with wildflowers; families of geese and mergansers; and the dancing lines of the fly fishers. River color ranges from icy blue to satiny black.

433 Cold Spring

Location: 4 miles west of Sisters
Season: Mid-May–mid-Oct
Sites: 23 basic sites; no hookups
Maximum length: 50 feet
Facilities: Tables, grills, nonflush toilets, drinking water
Fee per night: $$
Management: Deschutes National Forest
Contact: (541) 549-7700; www.fs.usda.gov/recmain/centraloregon/recreation
Finding the campground: From the junction of US 20 and OR 242 at the west end of Sisters, go west on OR 242 for 4 miles to the campground.
GPS coordinates: N44 18.637' / W121 37.799'
About the campground: Lovely ponderosa pines and an aspen grove create a soothing setting for your stay. There are both pull-through and back-in gravel parking spurs. Spring Trail begins near the campground entrance and leads 0.25 mile through mixed woods and across a spring to a lava outcrop. You can scramble to the top of the outcrop for a new perspective on the area or follow an old jeep trail away from the site to extend your journey. The area is particularly appealing in early October, when the aspens turn yellow and jet-black ravens pass between the trees. Birding is popular here.

434 Driftwood

Location: On Three Creek Lake, about 16 miles southwest of Sisters
Season: June–mid-Oct, dependent on snow
Sites: 18 basic sites; no hookups
Maximum length: Generally not recommended for RVs because of the short site spurs
Facilities: Tables, grills, nonflush toilets, primitive boat ramp (no motors); no drinking water
Fee per night: $$
Management: Deschutes National Forest
Contact: (541) 549-7700; www.fs.usda.gov/recmain/centraloregon/recreation
Finding the campground: From US 20 in Sisters, turn south at the sign for Three Creek Lake onto South Elm, which later becomes FR 16. Go 15.7 miles to the campground entrance on the right. (The final 1.6 miles are on gravel.)
GPS coordinates: N44 06.188' / W121 37.470'
About the campground: On the north shore of Three Creek Lake, you will find this lakeside campground tucked among the lodgepole and whitebark pines and true firs. Only half the sites have parking spurs; otherwise parking is along the widened road shoulder. This shimmering man-made lake sits at the foot of Tam McArthur Rim. Drift logs ring the lake, hinting at the camp's name. The sites receive only partial shade, and you should come prepared for mosquitoes. Fishing, nonmotorized boating, and hiking the trails to Tam McArthur Rim and Little Three Creek Lake engage guests.

435 Gorge

Location: About 17 miles northwest of Sisters
Season: Mid-May–mid-Sept
Sites: 18 basic sites; no hookups
Maximum length: 50 feet
Facilities: Tables, grills, nonflush toilets; no drinking water
Fee per night: $$
Management: Deschutes National Forest
Contact: (541) 549-7700; www.fs.usda.gov/recmain/centraloregon/recreation
Finding the campground: From Sisters go west on US 20 for 9.3 miles. Turn right (north) onto paved FR 14 and follow it for 6 miles. Turn left onto FR 1419 at the sign pointing to Camp Sherman and go 0.2 mile. Turn right onto paved FR 900 (signed for campgrounds). Continue 1.8 miles to the campground on the left.
GPS coordinates: N44 29.117' / W121 38.354'
About the campground: This Metolius River campground occupies a ponderosa pine flat, with bitterbrush growing in the understory. Sites are partially sunny, and a number of them offer pull-through parking, which will appeal to visitors with larger rigs. The banks of the Metolius here are grassy, and fly fishing is the order of the day.

436 Graham Corral Horse Camp

Location: About 7 miles northwest of Sisters
Season: Mid-May–mid-Oct
Sites: 13 basic sites; no hookups
Maximum length: 30 feet
Facilities: Tables, grills, nonflush toilets, drinking water, central partitioned corral, horse-loading chute, corrals at 4 sites, hitching rails, livestock water
Fee per night: $$
Management: Deschutes National Forest
Contact: (541) 549-7700; www.fs.usda.gov/recmain/centraloregon/recreation
Finding the campground: From the junction of US 20 and OR 242 at the west end of Sisters, go 4 miles west on US 20. Turn left onto gravel FR 1012 toward the Cold Springs Cutoff and Graham Corral and go 1 mile. Turn right onto FR 1012.300 and go another mile. Turn right onto FR 340 and continue 0.6 mile to the campground.
GPS coordinates: N44 20.687' / W121 38.604'
About the campground: Along the lengthy Metolius-Windigo National Recreation Trail, this horse camp occupies the site where numerous roundups were held from the late 1800s to the early 1900s. Here sheep and cows that ranged the Cache Mountain–Metolius River area were gathered and counted. The central corral seen and used today re-creates the historic scene. Present-day campers enjoy a spacious facility in a beautiful setting of ponderosa pines and bitterbrush. To the north above the treetops, you may glimpse Black Butte.

437 Indian Ford

Location: About 6 miles northwest of Sisters
Season: Mid-May–mid-Sept
Sites: 25 basic sites; no hookups
Maximum length: 50 feet
Facilities: Tables, grills, nonflush toilets; no drinking water
Fee per night: $$
Management: Deschutes National Forest
Contact: (541) 549-7700; www.fs.usda.gov/recmain/centraloregon/recreation
Finding the campground: From Sisters go 5.6 miles west on US 20. Turn right onto FR 11 and immediately make a right turn into the campground.
GPS coordinates: N44 21.481' / W121 36.632'
About the campground: This camp sits beside a narrow creek in a tranquil setting of big ponderosa pines, aspens, bunchgrass, and sagebrush. The ford at this location was mentioned in the journals of nineteenth-century explorer John C. Fremont. The camp is convenient for through-travelers on US 20. You can watch birds right from your site, but there is traffic noise. With this campground as a base, you can hike to the top of Black Butte or fly-fish the Metolius Wild and Scenic River. The frontier village of Sisters holds a different appeal, with its galleries and boutiques.

438 Jack Creek

Location: About 17 miles northwest of Sisters
Season: Mid-May–mid-Oct
Sites: 19 basic sites; no hookups
Maximum length: 50 feet
Facilities: Tables, grills and fire rings, nonflush toilets; no drinking water
Fee per night: $$
Management: Deschutes National Forest
Contact: (541) 549-7700; www.fs.usda.gov/recmain/centraloregon/recreation
Finding the campground: From Sisters go west on US 20 for 12 miles. Turn right (north) onto paved FR 12 and follow it for 4.4 miles. Turn left onto FR 1230 and go 0.6 mile. Cross a bridge and turn left onto FR 1232. Continue 0.2 mile to the campground entrance on the left.
GPS coordinates: N44 29.027' / W121 42.098'
About the campground: Big, impressive pines rise above this casual camp, but the primary attraction is Jack Creek, one of the prettiest creeks in the country. Cold and crystalline, Jack Creek originates from a spring and wends its way around islands and under logs dressed in mosaics of fern, giant lupine, grass, and young trees. A trail leads upstream from the camp to the source spring, Head of Jack Creek. Near the FR 1230 bridge, you can access the long-distance Metolius-Windigo Trail. Jack Creek is closed to angling.

439 Lava Camp Lake

Location: About 14 miles southwest of Sisters
Season: Mid-June–Oct, dependent on snow
Sites: 12 basic sites; no hookups
Maximum length: 20 feet
Facilities: Tables, grills, nonflush toilets; no drinking water
Fee per night: None
Management: Deschutes National Forest
Contact: (541) 549-7700; www.fs.usda.gov/recmain/centraloregon/recreation
Finding the campground: From the junction of US 20 and OR 242 at the west end of Sisters, go west on OR 242 for 14 miles. Turn left onto red-cinder FR 900. Go 0.4 mile to the camp, bypassing a parking lot for the Pacific Crest Trail.
GPS coordinates: N44 15.643' / W121 47.050'
About the campground: You will find this rustic camp just off McKenzie Pass Scenic Highway (OR 242) next to tiny, mud-bottomed Lava Camp Lake. The sites rest on a terrace above the lake and along the shoreline in a mixed forest of lodgepole pines, mountain hemlocks, and firs. Half a mile west on OR 242, Dee Wright Observatory serves up fine views of the Three Sisters and Mount Washington Wilderness Areas, the Cascade volcanoes, and the mosaic of forest and lava flow. The fortresslike observatory, constructed of volcanic rock, sits atop the flow. The arrangement of its open-air windows pinpoints landmarks. The twisting scenic highway presents additional wilderness views, as well as access to the Pacific Crest and other trails. In fall the red blush of vine maples suggests a drive.

440 Link Creek

Location: On Suttle Lake, about 15 miles northwest of Sisters
Season: Late Apr–late Nov
Sites: 33 basic sites, 3 yurts (available year-round); no hookups
Maximum length: 50 feet
Facilities: Tables, grills, nonflush toilets, drinking water (in summer), boat dock, launch, fish-cleaning station
Fee per night: $$–$$$
Management: Deschutes National Forest
Contact: (541) 549-7700; (877) 444-6777 for reservations; www.fs.usda.gov/recmain/centraloregon/recreation
Finding the campground: From US 20, 13 miles west of Sisters and 6.5 miles east of Santiam Pass, turn south onto paved FR 2070 toward Suttle and Blue Lakes (the east access road). Go 2.3 miles to the campground entrance on the right.
GPS coordinates: N44 25.042' / W121 45.318'
About the campground: This campground sits next to Link Creek on the southwest shore of Suttle Lake. Mixed pines and firs tower above the camp, while sticky laurel bushes grow in the more open areas. The campground has paved roads, and the sites feature either gravel or paved parking pads, some of them pull-throughs. Several sites overlook the huge natural lake. Boating, fishing,

waterskiing, swimming, and hiking the 3.25-mile Shoreline Trail keep campers entertained. After-noon winds commonly wash over the lake. In fall look for kokanee spawning in Link Creek.

441 Lower Bridge

Location: About 23 miles northwest of Sisters
Season: Mid-May–mid-Oct
Sites: 12 basic sites; no hookups
Maximum length: 40 feet
Facilities: Tables, grills, nonflush toilets, drinking water
Fee per night: $$
Management: Deschutes National Forest
Contact: (541) 549-7700; www.fs.usda.gov/recmain/centraloregon/recreation
Finding the campground: From Sisters go west on US 20 for 9.3 miles. Turn right (north) onto paved FR 14 and follow it 13.5 miles to the campground. The entrance is on the right as you arrive at Lower Bridge.
GPS coordinates: N44 33.449' / W121 37.212'
About the campground: This pleasant, shady camp sits downstream from Lower Bridge (Bridge 99), on the stretch of water where fishing with flies and barbless lures is allowed. Fishing on the Metolius Wild and Scenic River is catch-and-release only to protect wild fish. The sites occupy a terraced forest slope above the river. Western tanagers sometimes decorate the tree branches. Foot trails trace the riverbanks in both directions. Upstream, a 6-mile loop hike is possible by crossing the river on the bridge at Wizard Falls Fish Hatchery.

442 Pine Rest

Location: About 17 miles northwest of Sisters
Season: Year-round, dependent on snow
Sites: 7 tent sites; no hookups
Maximum length: Suitable for tents only
Facilities: Tables, grills, nonflush toilets, picnic shelter; no drinking water
Fee per night: $$
Management: Deschutes National Forest
Contact: (541) 549-7700; www.fs.usda.gov/recmain/centraloregon/recreation
Finding the campground: From Sisters go west on US 20 for 9.3 miles. Turn right (north) onto paved FR 14 and follow it for 6 miles. Turn left onto FR 1419 at the sign for Camp Sherman and go 0.2 mile. Turn right onto paved FR 900 (signed for campgrounds); continue 1.5 miles to the campground on the left.
GPS coordinates: N44 28.904' / W121 38.290'
About the campground: For tent campers, this area extends a pleasant stay along the Meto-lius River. Sites are spread across a shrub and meadow flat beneath ponderosa pines, firs, and larches. On the opposite shore, a few cabins overlook the river. The rustic stone and log picnic shelter is an attractive camp structure. You may well want to try your hand at fly fishing.

443 Pioneer Ford

Location: About 22 miles northwest of Sisters
Season: Mid-May–mid-Sept
Sites: 18 basic sites; no hookups
Maximum length: 50 feet
Facilities: Tables, grills, nonflush toilets, drinking water, picnic shelter
Fee per night: $$
Management: Deschutes National Forest
Contact: (541) 549-7700; www.fs.usda.gov/recmain/centraloregon/recreation
Finding the campground: From Sisters go west on US 20 for 9.3 miles. Turn right (north) onto paved FR 14 and follow it for 12.6 miles to the campground on the left.
GPS coordinates: N44 33.127' / W121 37.343'
About the campground: Part of the Metolius River lineup of popular family campgrounds, Pioneer Ford provides convenient access to fly fishing, riverside trails, the Wizard Falls Fish Hatchery, and the Head of the Metolius (the originating spring for this spectacular river). The sites occupy an attractive flat of cedars, firs, and pines.

444 Sheep Springs Horse Camp

Location: About 22 miles northwest of Sisters
Season: May–Oct
Sites: 11 basic sites; no hookups
Maximum length: 40 feet
Facilities: Tables, grills, nonflush toilets, drinking water (creek for livestock), 4-place box stall at each site
Fee per night: $$
Management: Deschutes National Forest
Contact: (541) 549-7700; (877) 444-6777 for reservations (required); www.fs.usda.gov/recmain/centraloregon/recreation
Finding the campground: From US 20, 12 miles west of Sisters and 7.5 miles east of Santiam Pass, turn north onto FR 12 and follow it for 7.9 miles. (FR 12 begins paved but becomes gravel.) Turn left onto FR 1260 and go 1.1 miles. Turn right onto FR 1260.200 and go another 1.3 miles. The campground entrance is on the right.
GPS coordinates: N44 31.367' / W121 41.987'
About the campground: Set aside for the exclusive use of people camping with horses, this campground extends a pleasant, quiet stay in a forest of ponderosa pines and mixed firs. A pole fence separates the camp from Sheep Springs Meadow. Across the road from the camp is the Metolius-Windigo Trail, on which long-distance rides are possible. Deer seeking stray wisps of hay sometimes venture into camp.

445 Sisters Cow Camp Horse Camp

Location: About 4 miles southwest of Sisters
Season: Apr–Oct
Sites: 5 basic sites; no hookups
Maximum length: 40 feet
Facilities: Tables, grills, nonflush toilets, springwater for horses only, large central corral, loading ramp; no drinking water
Fee per night: None
Management: Deschutes National Forest
Contact: (541) 549-7700; www.fs.usda.gov/recmain/centraloregon/recreation
Finding the campground: From Sisters go west on OR 242 for 1.3 miles. Turn left (southwest) onto FR 15, a paved and gravel route, and follow it for 2.4 miles. Turn left to enter the camp in 0.2 mile.
GPS coordinates: N44 16.455' / W121 36.906'
About the campground: Located on a broad, grassy flat with mature ponderosa pines, the sites of this horse camp encircle a large, partitioned corral. In the 1920s this camp was a cattle roundup and shipping site; hence the awkward name. The long-distance Metolius-Windigo Trail passes camp.

446 Smiling River

Location: About 17 miles northwest of Sisters
Season: May–Oct
Sites: 36 basic sites; no hookups
Maximum length: 50 feet
Facilities: Tables, grills, nonflush toilets, drinking water
Fee per night: $$
Management: Deschutes National Forest
Contact: (541) 549-7700; (877) 444-6777 for reservations; www.fs.usda.gov/recmain/centraloregon/recreation
Finding the campground: From Sisters go west on US 20 for 9.3 miles. Turn right (north) onto paved FR 14 and follow it for 6 miles. Turn left onto FR 1419 at the sign for Camp Sherman and go 0.2 mile. Turn right onto paved FR 900 (signed for campgrounds); continue 1 mile to the campground on the left.
GPS coordinates: N44 28.505' / W121 38.200'
About the campground: Of the string of Metolius River camps, this one is well suited for large RVs and trailers. It has many pull-through sites and offers attractive riverside stays beneath some lovely ponderosa pines. Across the river are some privately owned cabins and a beautiful meadow. Standing hip-deep in the river, fly fishers tempt wild fish with their dancing lines and arsenal of flies.

447 South Shore

Location: On Suttle Lake, about 14 miles northwest of Sisters
Season: May–Sept
Sites: 38 basic sites; no hookups
Maximum length: 50 feet
Facilities: Tables, grills, nonflush toilets, drinking water, boat dock, launch, fish-cleaning station
Fee per night: $$
Management: Deschutes National Forest
Contact: (541) 549-7700; (877) 444-6777 for reservations; www.fs.usda.gov/recmain/centraloregon/recreation
Finding the campground: From US 20, 13 miles west of Sisters and 6.5 miles east of Santiam Pass, head south on paved FR 2070 toward Suttle and Blue Lakes (the east access road). Go 1.1 miles to the campground on the right.
GPS coordinates: N44 25.059' / W121 44.565'
About the campground: On the south shore of Suttle Lake—a huge natural lake in a scenic, tree-lined basin—this campground offers the full gamut of water fun. The midday sun can pierce through the canopy of tall firs and big ponderosa pines, but generally campsites enjoy good shade throughout the day. There are paved roads through the camp and gravel or paved parking pads. Lakeside sites are snapped up quickly. Boating, fishing, waterskiing, and swimming, as well as hiking the 3.25-mile Shoreline Trail and just relaxing at camp, should keep everyone in the family happy. To avoid having to battle the afternoon winds, shore anglers will want to rise early.

448 Three Creek Lake

Location: On Three Creek Lake, 16 miles southwest of Sisters
Season: July–Oct
Sites: 11 basic sites; no hookups
Maximum length: 20 feet
Facilities: Tables, grills, nonflush toilets; no drinking water
Fee per night: $$
Management: Deschutes National Forest
Contact: (541) 549-7700; www.fs.usda.gov/recmain/centraloregon/recreation
Finding the campground: From US 20 in Sisters, go south at the sign for Three Creek Lake on South Elm, which later becomes FR 16. Go 16 miles to the campground. (The final 1.9 miles are on gravel.)
GPS coordinates: N44 05.716' / W121 37.425'
About the campground: Sandwiched between Three Creek Lake and Tam McArthur Rim, this campground sits in the shadow of the towering rim in a setting of firs, mountain hemlocks, and lodgepole pines. Clark's nutcrackers may visit the treetops. Wildflowers speckle the grassy lakeshore. This popular camp offers quiet lake recreation and superb hiking to the top of Tam McArthur Rim, from which there are dizzying views and access to Broken Top. Mosquitoes can be annoying. A tiny, rustic store near the camp entrance sells tackle and bait and rents rowboats.

449 Three Creek Meadow

Location: About 15 miles southwest of Sisters
Season: June–mid-Oct, dependent on snow
Sites: 11 basic sites, adjacent horse camp with 9 sites; no hookups
Maximum length: 40 feet
Facilities: Tables, grills, nonflush toilets, corrals at horse camp; no drinking water
Fee per night: $$
Management: Deschutes National Forest
Contact: (541) 549-7700; www.fs.usda.gov/recmain/centraloregon/recreation
Finding the campground: From US 20 in Sisters, head south at the sign for Three Creek Lake on South Elm, which later becomes FR 16. Go 14.7 miles to enter the family campground, 14.9 miles to enter the horse camp. (The final mile is not paved.)
GPS coordinates: N44 06.742' / W121 37.531'
About the campground: This campground duo sits among the lodgepole pines on the fringe of sensitive Three Creek Meadow. Wildflowers often dress the meadow, and deep, sparkling streams thread through it. Tam McArthur Rim looms to the south, retaining its snow for much of the year. It makes for a striking view, at times with a halo of clouds. At the camp, shade is limited, and mosquitoes can be a bother. An open flat serves large camping rigs. Hiking, horseback riding, and fishing engage visitors. The shops, galleries, and eateries of Sisters may lure you back to town.

450 Three Sisters Overnight Park

Location: In Sisters
Season: Mid-Apr–Oct
Sites: 25 full hookup sites, 35 basic sites, some hike/bike-in sites; water and electric hookups
Maximum length: 40 feet
Facilities: Tables, fire pits, flush toilets, drinking water, dump station
Fee per night: $$–$$$
Management: City of Sisters
Contact: (541) 323-5220 or (541) 549-6022; www.ci.sisters.or.us/parks.html
Finding the campground: The campground is on the south side of US 20 at the east end of Sisters, just west of the junction of US 20 and OR 126 East.
GPS coordinates: N44 17.244' / W121 32.519'
About the campground: This campground occupies a scenic pine flat on the east shore of Whychus Creek; a day-use area claims the west shore. Beneath the big pines you will find lawn or natural vegetation. The park is convenient for travelers and a fine base from which to explore Sisters, a picturesque frontier-character village that is perfect for strolling; galleries, shops, and eateries invite you inside. Sisters is at the heart of a prized recreational area. From camp you can easily get to Bend, Smith Rock State Park, Tam McArthur Rim, the Metolius River, the McKenzie River, McKenzie Pass, and the Three Sisters and Mount Washington Wilderness Areas.

451 Whispering Pines Horse Camp

Location: About 10 miles southwest of Sisters
Season: May–Oct
Sites: 9 basic sites; no hookups
Maximum length: 40 feet
Facilities: Tables, grills, nonflush toilets, 4-horse corrals; no drinking water
Fee per night: $$
Management: Deschutes National Forest
Contact: (541) 549-7700; www.fs.usda.gov/recmain/centraloregon/recreation
Finding the campground: From Sisters go west on OR 242 for 5.7 miles. Turn left (south) onto gravel FR 1018 toward Whispering Pines; continue 4.3 miles. Turn left onto FR 1520 and drive another 0.2 mile to the campground entrance on the left.
GPS coordinates: N44 15.182' / W121 41.440'
About the campground: This equestrian camp has a meadow floor with an open stand of mature ponderosa pines and a punctuation of clustered firs. The sites are large, comfortable, and functional. Trout Creek flows past the camp. Contact the Sisters Ranger District about horse trails in the area.

Prineville Area

	Hookup Sites	Total Sites	Max. RV Length	Hookups	Toilets	Showers	Drinking Water	Dump Station	Recreation	Fee	Can Reserve
452 Allen Creek Horse Camp		11	24		NF				FR	None	
453 Antelope Flat Reservoir		24	30		NF		X		FBL	$	
454 Big Bend Recreation Site		15	25		NF				FBL	$-$$	
455 Big Spring		6	20		NF					None	
456 Castle Rock Recreation Site		6	35		NF				F	$	
457 Chimney Rock Recreation Site		16	24		NF		X		HF	$	
458 Cobble Rock Recreation Site		15	25		NF				F	$	
459 Crook County RV Park	81	90	70	WESC	F	X	X	X	F	$$-$$$	X
460 Deep Creek		6	24		NF		X		F	$	
461 Devil's Post Pile Recreation Site		7	25		NF				F	$	
462 Dry Creek Horse Camp		5	20		NF				HR	None	
463 Lone Pine Recreation Site		8	25		NF				F	$-$$	
464 Lower Palisades Recreation Site		15	35		NF				F	$	
465 Mud Spring Horse Camp		11	20		NF				HR	None	
466 Ochoco Forest Camp		5	24		NF		X		HF	$$	
467 Ochoco Lake Crook County Park		26	35		F	X	X		FBL	$$	
468 Poison Butte Recreation Site		5	T Small		NF				F	$	
469 Prineville Reservoir State Park (Main Campground)	44	67	54	WES	F	X	X		SFBL	$$-$$$	X
470 Prineville Reservoir State Park: Jasper Point	30	30	30	WE	F	X	X	X	SFBL	$$$	X
471 Stillwater Recreation Site		10	35		NF				F	$	
472 Sugar Creek		17	24		NF		X			$	
473 Walton Lake		30	30		NF		X		HSFBL	$$	
474 Wildcat		17	30		NF		X		HF	$	
475 Wiley Flat		5	24		NF					None	
476 Wolf Creek		16	20		NF					$	

452 Allen Creek Horse Camp

Location: About 44 miles east of Prineville
Season: May–Sept
Sites: 11 basic sites; no hookups
Maximum length: 24 feet
Facilities: Some tables and grills, nonflush toilet, 16 stalls, water for livestock; no drinking water
Fee per night: None
Management: Ochoco National Forest
Contact: (541) 416-6500; www.fs.usda.gov/recmain/centraloregon/recreation
Finding the campground: From Prineville go east on US 26 about 17 miles. Bear right (northeast) onto Ochoco Creek Road/FR 22. Follow it 27 miles to the campground on the right.
GPS coordinates: N44 23.892' / W120 10.298'
About the campground: This campground has a casual setup and serves people camping with horses. It claims an attractive ponderosa pine flat along picturesque Allen Creek. Old roads leading from the camp invite exploration. Water is available for your stock, but you will need to bring water for your own drinking and cooking.

453 Antelope Flat Reservoir

Location: On Antelope Flat Reservoir, about 44 miles southeast of Prineville
Season: May–Sept
Sites: 24 basic sites; no hookups
Maximum length: 30 feet
Facilities: Tables, grills, nonflush toilets, boat launch, drinking water
Fee per night: $
Management: Ochoco National Forest
Contact: (541) 416-6500; www.fs.usda.gov/recmain/centraloregon/recreation
Finding the campground: From the junction of Main Street and US 26 in Prineville, go east on US 26 for 1 mile. Turn right (south) toward Paulina on North Combs Flat Road (Paulina Highway) and go 30.2 miles. Turn right onto gravel FR 17. After 10.1 miles FR 17 turns left onto FR 16, only to quickly veer right away from it. The campground is 2.8 miles farther on FR 17.
GPS coordinates: N44 00.088' / W120 23.539'
About the campground: This campground occupies a dry forest setting of ponderosa pines, junipers, and bunchgrass above Antelope Flat Reservoir. Canoes and fishing boats ply the lake, which is rimmed by low dusky hills clad in pine and sage. Sites have defined parking, and paths from camp lead to shore and a boat ramp. The camp is generally relaxing, unless it is a bad mosquito season.

454 Big Bend Recreation Site

Location: 19 miles south of Prineville
Season: Year-round
Sites: 15 basic sites; no hookups
Maximum length: 25 feet
Facilities: Tables, fire rings, nonflush toilets, nearby boat launch (at Prineville Reservoir); no drinking water
Fee per night: $-$$
Management: Prineville District Bureau of Land Management
Contact: (541) 416-6700; www.blm.gov/or/
Finding the campground: From US 26 in Prineville, head south on Main Street/OR 27, the Lower Crooked River BLM Backcountry Byway. Proceed 19 miles to the turnoff for the camp.
GPS coordinates: N44 06.757' / W120 47.660'
About the campground: At this Crooked River recreation site below Prineville Reservoir, the camping spots sit among the junipers. Visitors have easy access to the river for fishing and to the reservoir (1.2 miles upstream) for both fishing and boating. The reservoir looks its best when it is full, blue, and reflecting its arid surroundings. Fires and smoking are prohibited from June 1 to October 15.

455 Big Spring

Location: About 55 miles east of Prineville
Season: May–Oct
Sites: 6 basic sites; no hookups
Maximum length: 20 feet
Facilities: A few tables and crude fire rings, nonflush toilets; no drinking water
Fee per night: None
Management: Ochoco National Forest
Contact: (541) 477-6900; www.fs.usda.gov/recmain/centraloregon/recreation
Finding the campground: From Prineville go east on US 26 about 17 miles. Bear right (northeast) onto Ochoco Creek Road/FR 22; follow it 8 miles to the Ochoco Ranger Station. From there go east on FR 42 for 28 miles. Turn left onto FR 4270 and go 1.5 miles more. Turn left onto FR 100 to reach the campground in another 0.1 mile.
GPS coordinates: N44 19.921' / W119 59.473'
About the campground: At this primitive camp you can recline in a mixed setting of pine forest and meadow and enjoy nature's peace. Wildflowers decorate the meadow, but there are very few parking options for large units when the meadow periphery is wet. The campground's remote locale serves hunters well.

Crooked Wild and Scenic River, Lower Crooked River National Backcountry Byway

456 Castle Rock Recreation Site

Location: About 12 miles south of Prineville
Season: Year-round
Sites: 6 basic sites; no hookups
Maximum length: 35 feet
Facilities: Tables, grills, nonflush toilets; no drinking water
Fee per night: $
Management: Bureau of Land Management—Prineville District
Contact: (541) 416-6700; www.blm.gov/or/
Finding the campground: From US 26 in Prineville, head south on Main Street/OR 27, the Lower Crooked River BLM Backcountry Byway, for 12.3 miles to the campground.
GPS coordinates: N44 09.449' / W120 50.098'
About the campground: Where the Crooked River Canyon broadens, you will find this camp, which is a little drier and sunnier than its upstream counterparts. Here the west canyon wall is arid with a ragged rim; the east canyon wall parades exciting rock features. A single pull-through site accommodates large units. Fishing is popular. Fires and smoking are prohibited from June 1 to October 15.

457 Chimney Rock Recreation Site

Location: 16 miles south of Prineville
Season: Year-round
Sites: 16 basic sites; no hookups
Maximum length: 24 feet
Facilities: Tables, nonflush toilets, drinking water, fishing dock for individuals with disabilities
Fee per night: $
Management: Bureau of Land Management—Prineville District
Contact: (541) 416-6700; www.blm.gov/or/
Finding the campground: From US 26 in Prineville, head south on Main Street/OR 27, the Lower Crooked River BLM Backcountry Byway. Proceed 16 miles to the campground on the right.
GPS coordinates: N44 08.112' / W120 48.844'
About the campground: A fishing dock is center stage at this campground on the Crooked Wild and Scenic River. RVers typically prefer the upstream end of the camp, which has a broad gravel lot for easy parking. The sites downstream tend to be fairly short, although a few near the turn-around loop are fine for RVs. Swallows nest in the cliffs across the river, and Chimney Rock looms above the camp. You may choose to lace on your hiking boots for a closer look at the camp's namesake; the trailhead sits across the road from camp. The Rim Trail travels 1.4 miles and gains 500 feet in elevation to reach the saddle of Chimney Rock. From this lofty vantage you can admire the Central Cascades, as well as the Crooked River and its canyon. Fires and smoking are prohibited from June 1 to October 15.

458 Cobble Rock Recreation Site

Location: 17 miles south of Prineville
Season: Year-round
Sites: 15 basic sites; no hookups
Maximum length: 25 feet
Facilities: Tables, grills, nonflush toilets; no drinking water
Fee per night: $
Management: Bureau of Land Management—Prineville District
Contact: (541) 416-6700; www.blm.gov/or/
Finding the campground: From US 26 in Prineville, head south on Main Street/OR 27, the Lower Crooked River BLM Backcountry Byway. Proceed 17 miles to the campground.
GPS coordinates: N44 07.693' / W120 48.592'
About the campground: This campground on the Crooked River has gravel roads and defined road shoulder or pullout parking. Although fire rings are provided, a strict ban on fires and smoking is in effect from June 1 to October 15 to protect this fragile, dry canyon. The camp has a dotting of junipers, and a few ponderosa pines grow near the river. Views include nearby Chimney Rock, columnar buttes and crests, and a palisades just across the river from the campground. When the fish are not biting, you can hike the Rim Trail to Chimney Rock. The trailhead is 1 mile north, across OR 27 from Chimney Rock Recreation Site.

459 Crook County RV Park

Location: In Prineville
Season: Year-round
Sites: 81 hookup sites, 9 tent sites, 2 cabins; water, electric, sewer, and cable hookups
Maximum length: 70 feet
Facilities: Flush toilets, drinking water, showers, dump station, Internet access, playground at nearby Crooked River Park
Fee per night: $$–$$$
Management: Crook County
Contact: (541) 447-2599; (800) 609-2599 for reservations; www.ccprd.org/RVPark.php
Finding the campground: From US 26 in Prineville, head south on Main Street/OR 27 at the sign for the fairgrounds. Go 0.5 mile and turn left to enter the RV park.
GPS coordinates: N44 17.614' / W120 50.649'
About the campground: This comfortable RV park is ideal for campers attending fairground events or sightseeing in Prineville. It has formal tent pads and long, paved parking spaces. The young trees in camp have yet to provide much shade, but there are some big cottonwoods and weeping willows in the neighborhood. OR 27 is a Bureau of Land Management Backcountry Byway, serving up a scenic drive along the Lower Crooked River. Crooked River Park, across the road from the camp, has a playground and offers fishing.

460 Deep Creek

Location: About 50 miles east of Prineville
Season: May–Sept
Sites: 6 basic sites; no hookups
Maximum length: 24 feet
Facilities: Tables, grills, nonflush toilet, drinking water
Fee per night: $
Management: Ochoco National Forest
Contact: (541) 416-6500; www.fs.usda.gov/recmain/centraloregon/recreation
Finding the campground: From Prineville go east on US 26 about 17 miles. Bear right (northeast) onto Ochoco Creek Road/FR 22 and follow it 8 miles to the Ochoco Ranger Station. From there go east on FR 42 for 24 miles; turn right into the campground.
GPS coordinates: N44 19.684' / W120 04.567'
About the campground: Located along the North Fork Crooked River near its confluence with Deep Creek, this rustic camp boasts many big yellow-bellied pines. Sites offer a mix of sun and shade, and most have tables and grills. The river calls to anglers, while the casual rock collector can usually discover an agate or two among the cobbles on shore.

461 Devil's Post Pile Recreation Site

Location: About 18 miles south of Prineville
Season: Year-round
Sites: 7 basic sites; no hookups
Maximum length: 25 feet
Facilities: Tables, grills, nonflush toilets; no drinking water
Fee per night: $
Management: Bureau of Land Management—Prineville District
Contact: (541) 416-6700; www.blm.gov/or/
Finding the campground: From US 26 in Prineville, head south on Main Street/OR 27, the Lower Crooked River BLM Backcountry Byway. Proceed 17.5 miles to the campground.
GPS coordinates: N44 07.717' / W120 48.036'
About the campground: This camp sits among junipers at a bend in the Crooked River. It has back-in and pull-through sites. Camp guests while away their time fishing, relaxing, and admiring the canyon setting. Fires and smoking are prohibited from June 1 to October 15.

462 Dry Creek Horse Camp

Location: About 17 miles northeast of Prineville
Season: Apr–Oct
Sites: 5 basic sites; no hookups
Maximum length: 20 feet
Facilities: Tables, grills, nonflush toilet, corrals; no drinking water
Fee per night: None
Management: Ochoco National Forest
Contact: (541) 416-6500; www.fs.usda.gov/recmain/centraloregon/recreation
Finding the campground: From Prineville go east on US 26 for 9 miles. Turn left onto Mill Creek Road/FR 33 and go 5 miles. Turn left onto FR 3370 and continue another 2.4 miles. Turn left onto FR 200 and go 0.1 mile to the campground. (The road into the camp is not suitable for large RVs.)
GPS coordinates: N44 25.250' / W120 40.226'
About the campground: Established for the equestrian camper, this facility offers convenient, serviceable sites in a forest of pines and firs near Brennan Palisades. There are rustic pole corrals and split-rail fences. Dry Creek is across the road, as is the Giddy-Up-Go Trail, a 12-mile loop ride.

463 Lone Pine Recreation Site

Location: About 14 miles south of Prineville
Season: Year-round
Sites: 8 basic sites; no hookups
Maximum length: 25 feet
Facilities: Tables, grills, nonflush toilets; no drinking water
Fee per night: $–$$
Management: Bureau of Land Management—Prineville District
Contact: (541) 416-6700; www.blm.gov/or/
Finding the campground: From US 26 in Prineville, head south on Main Street/OR 27, the Lower Crooked River BLM Backcountry Byway. Proceed 14.3 miles to the campground.
GPS coordinates: N44 07.791' / W120 50.278'
About the campground: This is one of several BLM campgrounds on the east bank of the Crooked River. Lone Pine primarily has a juniper setting, but a ponderosa pine here and there lends credence to the camp's name. The canyon crest shapes a lovely skyline. The sites have defined parking, and there is direct fishing access from camp. Fires and smoking are prohibited from June 1 to October 15.

464 Lower Palisades Recreation Site

Location: About 15 miles south of Prineville
Season: Year-round
Sites: 15 basic sites; no hookups
Maximum length: 35 feet
Facilities: Tables, fireplaces, nonflush toilets, 2 small fishing docks for individuals with disabilities; no drinking water
Fee per night: $
Management: Bureau of Land Management—Prineville District
Contact: (541) 416-6700; www.blm.gov/or/
Finding the campground: From US 26 in Prineville, head south on Main Street/OR 27, the Lower Crooked River BLM Backcountry Byway. Proceed 15.3 miles to this riverside campground.
GPS coordinates: N44 07.874' / W120 49.438'
About the campground: This is one of the more developed campgrounds along the Crooked Wild and Scenic River and the byway. The sites are well spaced and have good river access, and the junipers create at least some shade at each site. Across the river from the camp rise bulging, cobbled palisade cliffs. A barrier-free trail accesses the fishing docks. Along the river corridor, a ban on smoking and fires is in effect from June 1 to October 15.

465 Mud Spring Horse Camp

Location: About 87 miles east of Prineville
Season: June–Oct
Sites: 11 horse campsites; no hookups
Maximum length: 20 feet
Facilities: Tables, nonflush toilets, metal horse corrals; no drinking water
Fee per night: None
Management: Ochoco National Forest
Contact: (541) 477-6900; www.fs.usda.gov/recmain/centraloregon/recreation
Finding the campground: From Paulina (56 miles southeast of Prineville), go east on CR 112 (the Paulina Highway toward Suplee) for 4.2 miles. Turn left onto gravel CR 113, which becomes FR 58 and later changes to gravel; travel 20 miles. Turn left onto FR 5840 and go another 6 miles. Turn right onto FR 5840.400 and proceed 0.7 mile to the campground.
GPS coordinates: N44 18.115' / W119 39.836'
About the campground: This serene but primitive campground on the southeast flank of Wolf Mountain will appeal to the escapist. It enjoys a setting of big meadows and big pines and allows campers to spread out. False hellebore, widow grass, buttercup, wyethia, violet, and larkspur color the meadow. Trail 821, the South Prong Trail, provides hiker/horse access to Black Canyon Wilderness. Hunters use this camp in the fall.

466 Ochoco Forest Camp

Location: About 25 miles northeast of Prineville
Season: Mid-May–Sept
Sites: 5 basic sites; no hookups
Maximum length: 24 feet
Facilities: Tables, grills, nonflush toilet, drinking water, log picnic shelter
Fee per night: $$
Management: Ochoco National Forest
Contact: (541) 416-6500; www.fs.usda.gov/recmain/centraloregon/recreation
Finding the campground: From Prineville go east on US 26 about 17 miles. Bear right onto paved Ochoco Creek Road/FR 22; proceed 8 miles to the campground, which is adjacent to the Ochoco Ranger Station.
GPS coordinates: N44 23.771' / W120 25.350'
About the campground: This quiet little camp sits beside pretty Ochoco Creek, which cuts a deep groove through a brushy meadow as it meanders past camp. Ponderosa pines and alders frame the sites and are interspersed with native grasses and shrubs. Across the road from the camp starts the Lookout Mountain Trail, which leads past magnificent old-growth ponderosa pines and through grasslands decorated with springtime irises to attain a superb Ochoco Forest vantage.

467 Ochoco Lake Crook County Park

Location: 7 miles east of Prineville
Season: Apr–Oct
Sites: 22 basic sites, 4 hike/bike sites; no hookups
Maximum length: 35 feet
Facilities: Tables, grills, flush toilets, drinking water, showers, boat launch, fish-cleaning station
Fee per night: $$
Management: Crook County
Contact: (541) 447-1209; www.ccprd.org/OchocoLake.php
Finding the campground: From Prineville go east on US 26 for 7 miles to the park on the right.
GPS coordinates: N44 18.329' / W120 42.051'
About the campground: This park features groomed lawns shaded by junipers on a slope above Ochoco Reservoir, which is open for recreation. Fishing and boating are the chief attractions. Arid, juniper-dotted tablelands and hills shape the basin and view. Blacktop trails allow short strolls along the lake.

468 Poison Butte Recreation Site

Location: About 18 miles south of Prineville
Season: Year-round
Sites: 5 tent sites; no hookups
Maximum length: Small rigs only
Facilities: Tables, fire rings, nonflush toilets; no drinking water
Fee per night: $
Management: Bureau of Land Management—Prineville District
Contact: (541) 416-6700; www.blm.gov/or/
Finding the campground: From US 26 in Prineville, head south on Main Street/OR 27, the Lower Crooked River BLM Backcountry Byway. Proceed 18.2 miles to the campground.
GPS coordinates: N44 07.257' / W120 47.934'
About the campground: This is one of the smaller camps along the Crooked River. Like the others, it is set in a juniper forest, but some big ponderosa pines loom across the river. The river here slows, broadens, and grows shallow enough that anglers can often wade across it. White rocks and grassy banks complement the green water, and geese and herons may favor the site with a visit. Fires and smoking are prohibited from June 1 to October 15.

469 Prineville Reservoir State Park (Main Campground)

Location: On Prineville Reservoir, about 16 miles southeast of Prineville
Season: Year-round
Sites: 44 full or partial hookup sites, 23 basic sites, 5 cabins; water, electric, and sewer hookups
Maximum length: 54 feet
Facilities: Tables, grills, flush toilets, drinking water, showers, boat launch, docks, fish-cleaning station
Fee per night: $$-$$$
Management: Oregon State Parks and Recreation Department
Contact: (541) 447-4363; (800) 452-5687 for reservations; www.oregon.gov/OPRD/PARKS/camping.shtml
Finding the campground: From the junction of Main Street and US 26 in Prineville, go east on US 26 for 1 mile. Turn right (south) onto North Combs Flat Road and follow it 1.2 miles. Turn right onto Juniper Canyon Road and continue 13 miles to a junction. Head right and drive 0.7 mile more to the main campground.
GPS coordinates: N44 07.775' / W120 43.317'
About the campground: This developed camp is located on a juniper canyon slope above Prineville Reservoir. Some sites overlook the water, and most receive a mix of sun and shade. Noise from the speedboats and personal watercraft carries across the water, but these recreational activities are among the reasons folks come to the park. Fishing and swimming are two of the quieter pursuits. Big Island adds to views of this vast, sparkling lake.

470 Prineville Reservoir State Park: Jasper Point

Location: On Prineville Reservoir, about 18 miles southeast of Prineville
Season: May–Sept
Sites: 30 partial hookup sites; water and electric hookups
Maximum length: 30 feet
Facilities: Tables, grills, flush toilets, drinking water, showers, dump station, boat launch
Fee per night: $$$
Management: Oregon State Parks and Recreation Department
Contact: (541) 447-4363; (800) 452-5687 for reservations; www.oregon.gov/OPRD/PARKS/camping.shtml
Finding the campground: From the junction of Main Street and US 26 in Prineville, go east on US 26 for 1 mile. Turn right (south) onto North Combs Flat Road and follow it 1.2 miles. Turn right onto Juniper Canyon Road; continue 13 miles to a junction. Bear left and go another 2.5 miles to Jasper Point.
GPS coordinates: N44 08.144' / W120 41.710'
About the campground: Linked by a 1.75-mile lakeside trail to the primary state park campground, this camp claims another sun-basked, juniper-studded slope above Prineville Reservoir. It offers direct access to the lake for fishing, boating, waterskiing, and riding personal watercraft. The lake boasts excellent fishing, and in this hot climate, swimming is popular.

471 Stillwater Recreation Site

Location: About 13 miles south of Prineville
Season: Year-round
Sites: 10 basic sites; no hookups
Maximum length: 35 feet
Facilities: Tables, grills, nonflush toilets; no drinking water
Fee per night: $
Management: Bureau of Land Management—Prineville District
Contact: (541) 416-6700; www.blm.gov/or/
Finding the campground: From US 26 in Prineville, head south on Main Street/OR 27, the Lower Crooked River BLM Backcountry Byway. Proceed 13.2 miles to the camp.
GPS coordinates: N44 08.710' / W120 49.756'
About the campground: Along the scenic byway and a slow stretch of the Crooked River, you will find this camp cradled between canyon walls of differing character: one rock, the other juniper-grassland. Fishing is the primary recreation, although relaxing is a close second. To protect the arid canyon habitat, a ban on fires and smoking is in effect from June 1 to October 15.

472 Sugar Creek

Location: About 70 miles east of Prineville
Season: May–Oct
Sites: 17 basic sites; no hookups
Maximum length: 24 feet
Facilities: Tables, grills, nonflush toilets, drinking water, barrier-free trail to creek
Fee per night: $
Management: Ochoco National Forest
Contact: (541) 477-6900; www.fs.usda.gov/recmain/centraloregon/recreation
Finding the campground: From Paulina (56 miles southeast of Prineville), go east on CR 112 (the Paulina Highway) toward Suplee. Go 4.2 miles and turn left onto gravel CR 113/FR 58. Continue 8.5 miles to the campground entrance on the right.
GPS coordinates: N44 14.030' / W119 48.313'
About the campground: You will find this relaxing campground in an attractive forest of ponderosa pines on the banks of Sugar Creek. The warbling of songbirds and the telegraphic knocking of woodpeckers are likely to accompany your stay here. Bald eagles have a winter roost nearby. Split-rail fences add charm to the scene, and a barrier-free trail allows for creek viewing.

473 Walton Lake

Location: On Walton Lake, about 32 miles northeast of Prineville
Season: Late May–late Sept
Sites: 30 basic sites; no hookups
Maximum length: 30 feet
Facilities: Tables, grills, nonflush toilet, drinking water, boat ramp (electric motors only), swimming area, barrier-free fishing pier
Fee per night: $$
Management: Ochoco National Forest
Contact: (541) 416-6500; www.fs.usda.gov/recmain/centraloregon/recreation
Finding the campground: From Prineville go east on US 26 about 17 miles. Bear right onto paved Ochoco Creek Road/FR 22. Proceed another 15 miles, following the signs to the campground.
GPS coordinates: N44 26.018' / W120 20.167'
About the campground: This popular campground is located along the shore of Walton Lake, a former mountain meadow that was transformed into a quiet mountain lake by a small earthen dam. Campsites dot the ponderosa pine forest on the north and south shores; site parking is either on the roadside or on spurs. The lake is stocked with trout three times each summer, so the fishing is usually pretty good. Quiet boating, swimming, hiking the lakeside trail, watching the antics of otters or muskrats, and just relaxing in camp are other potential activities. The campground also has a trailhead for Round Mountain National Recreation Trail, a more challenging hike.

474 Wildcat

Location: About 19 miles northeast of Prineville
Season: May–Sept
Sites: 17 basic sites; no hookups
Maximum length: 30 feet
Facilities: Tables, grills, nonflush toilets, drinking water
Fee per night: $
Management: Ochoco National Forest
Contact: (541) 416-6500; www.fs.usda.gov/recmain/centraloregon/recreation
Finding the campground: From Prineville go east on US 26 for 9 miles. Turn left (north) onto Mill Creek Road/FR 33; drive another 10.4 miles to the campground entrance on the right. (Part of the route is on gravel.)
GPS coordinates: N44 26.396' / W120 34.727'
About the campground: Firs and ponderosa pines shade this East Fork Mill Creek campground, which is a gateway to Mill Creek Wilderness. The East Fork is your guide upstream into the wilderness—a wildflower showcase with areas of recovered burn, thriving forest, and the intriguing forked monolith of Twin Pillars. Another fine rock destination is Steins Pillar. To reach its trailhead, go 4 miles south from camp on FR 33, turn east onto FR 500, and continue 2 miles. Steins Pillar is a 350-foot-tall, freestanding column of pinkish stone streaked with black.

475 Wiley Flat

Location: About 44 miles southeast of Prineville
Season: May–Sept
Sites: 5 basic sites; no hookups
Maximum length: 24 feet
Facilities: Tables, some grills, nonflush toilets; no drinking water
Fee per night: None
Management: Ochoco National Forest
Contact: (541) 416-6500; www.fs.usda.gov/recmain/centraloregon/recreation
Finding the campground: From the Paulina Highway, 33 miles east of Prineville and 23 miles west of Paulina, turn south onto gravel Drake Creek Road/FR 16 and go 10.4 miles. Turn right onto FR 400; follow the rough road 0.8 mile into the campground.
GPS coordinates: N44 02.540' / W120 17.832'
About the campground: Although this out-of-the-way campground can accommodate large vehicles, the rocky access road promises a rattling ride, and the dirt roads within the camp are impassable in wet weather. The headwater spring of Wiley Creek sends a silver thread through this quiet meadow dotted with mixed age pines. Arnica, wild strawberry, wild geranium, violet, and cinquefoil are among the meadow wildflowers. Birds, filtered sunlight, and the rich vanilla scent of pines can contribute to the relaxing atmosphere. Hunters frequent this area in fall.

476 Wolf Creek

Location: About 70 miles east of Prineville
Season: May–Sept
Sites: 16 basic sites; no hookups
Maximum length: 20 feet
Facilities: Tables, grills, nonflush toilets; no drinking water
Fee per night: $
Management: Ochoco National Forest
Contact: (541) 477-6900; www.fs.usda.gov/recmain/centraloregon/recreation
Finding the campground: From Paulina (56 miles southeast of Prineville), go east on CR 112 (the Paulina Highway) toward Suplee for 4.2 miles. Turn left onto gravel CR 113/FR 58 and continue 7.2 miles to the junction of FR 58 and FR 42. Turn left onto FR 42 and go 1.7 miles. Sites are on both sides of FR 42.
GPS coordinates: N44 15.161' / W119 49.572'
About the campground: A rustic, zigzagging rail fence wraps around this campground, which sits beside Wolf Creek in a meadow dotted with ponderosa pines. The murmur of the small, attractive creek is soothing. This camp now incorporates Wolf Creek Industrial Camp, across the road.

Bend Area

	Hookup Sites	Total Sites	Max. RV Length	Hookups	Toilets	Showers	Drinking Water	Dump Station	Recreation	Fee	Can Reserve
477 Big River		10	26		NF				FBL	$$	X
478 Bull Bend		12	30		NF				SFBL	$$	
479 China Hat		13	30		NF					None	
480 Cow Meadow		18	26		NF				FBL	$$	
481 Crane Prairie		146	30		NF		X		FBL	$$	X
482 Cultus Corral Horse Camp		10	30		NF				R	$$	
483 Cultus Lake		55	30		NF		X		HSFBL	$$	
484 East Davis		17	50		NF		X		FB	$$	
485 Elk Lake		26	25		NF		X		HSFBL	$$	
486 Fall River		10	30		NF				F	$$	
487 Gull Point		79	30		F, NF		X	X	FBL	$$	X
488 La Pine State Recreation Area	128	128	85	WES	F	X	X	X	HSFBL	$$-$$$	X
489 Lava Flow		6	25		NF				FBL	None	
490 Lava Lake		43	30		NF		X		HFBL	$$	
491 Little Cultus		31	30		NF		X		HFBL	$$	
492 Little Fawn		20	30		NF		X		HFBL	$$	X
493 Little Lava Lake		13	30		NF		X		FBL	$$	X
494 Mallard Marsh		15	25		NF				FBL	$$	
495 McKay Crossing		16	26		NF				HF	$$	
496 Newberry National Volcanic Monument: Chief Paulina Horse Camp		14	26		NF				HFBR	$$	X
497 Newberry National Volcanic Monument: Cinder Hill		108	30		NF		X		HFBL	$$	X
498 Newberry National Volcanic Monument: East Lake		29	26		F		X		HSFBL	$$	
499 Newberry National Volcanic Monument: Little Crater		49	30		NF		X		HFBL	$$	
500 Newberry National Volcanic Monument: Paulina Lake		69	30		F		X	X	HFBL	$$	X
501 North Davis Creek		14	25		NF		X		FBL	$$	
502 North Twin		20	30		NF				HSFBL	$$	
503 Pine Mountain		6	30		NF					None	
504 Point		9	25		NF				HSFBL	$$	
505 Prairie		17	30		NF		X		HF	$$	

	Hookup Sites	Total Sites	Max. RV Length	Hookups	Toilets	Showers	Drinking Water	Dump Station	Recreation	Fee	Can Reserve
506 Pringle Falls		7	25		NF				FB	$$	
507 Quinn Meadow Horse Camp		26	30		NF		X		HR	$$	
508 Quinn River		41	30		NF		X		HFBL	$$	X
509 Reservoir		24	30		NF				FBL	$$	
510 Rock Creek		30	30		NF		X		FBL	$$	
511 Rosland	1	11	40	WE	NF		X		F	$$	
512 Sheep Bridge		20	30		NF		X		FBL	$$	
513 Soda Creek		10	25		NF				F	$$	
514 South		23	26		NF				FBL	$$	
515 South Twin		21	26		NF		X		HSFBL	$$	
516 Swamp Wells Horse Camp		5	30		NF				HOR	None	
517 Todd Creek Horse Camp		7	30		NF				R	NWF Pass	
518 Tumalo State Park	23	77	44	WES	F	X	X		SF	$$-$$$	X
519 West South Twin		24	30		F		X		HSFBL	$$	
520 Wyeth		5	25		NF				FB	$$	

477 Big River

Location: About 22 miles southwest of Bend
Season: May–Oct
Sites: 10 basic sites; no hookups
Maximum length: 26 feet
Facilities: Tables, grills, nonflush toilet, boat launch (nonmotorized boats); no drinking water
Fee per night: $$
Management: Deschutes National Forest
Contact: (541) 383-4000; (877) 444-6777 for reservations; www.fs.usda.gov/recmain/centraloregon/recreation
Finding the campground: From US 97, 17.5 miles south of Bend and 4.9 miles north of the turnoff for La Pine State Recreation Area, turn west for Fall River on FR 42 (labeled Vandevert Road and then South Century Drive). Proceed 4.6 miles to the camp.
GPS coordinates: N43 49.012' / W121 29.841'
About the campground: Shaded by lodgepole and small ponderosa pines, this campground overlooks a slow stretch of the Deschutes River. A few shrubs intersperse the grasses and needle mat of the forest floor. The dirt access road can be rutted, so take it easy when entering camp. Fishing is the main attraction here. The boat ramp is on the opposite side of FR 42.

478 Bull Bend

Location: About 37 miles southwest of Bend
Season: May–mid-Oct
Sites: 12 basic sites; no hookups
Maximum length: 30 feet
Facilities: Tables, grills, nonflush toilets, boat launch (nonmotorized boats); no drinking water
Fee per night: $$
Management: Deschutes National Forest
Contact: (541) 383-4000; www.fs.usda.gov/recmain/centraloregon/recreation
Finding the campground: From US 97 at Wickiup Junction, 27 miles south of Bend, go west on CR 43 for 8 miles. Turn left (south) onto gravel FR 4370; continue 1.5 miles to the campground.
GPS coordinates: N43 43.517' / W121 37.708'
About the campground: This camp occupies a piney peninsula in a horseshoe bend of the Deschutes River. Bitterbrush and currant grow beneath the trees. Fishing, swimming, canoeing, and rafting are popular pursuits. You can fashion a short float trip around the camp peninsula by putting in at the upstream end of the river bend and taking out downstream.

479 China Hat

Location: About 65 miles southeast of Bend
Season: Apr–Oct
Sites: 13 basic sites; no hookups
Maximum length: 30 feet
Facilities: Tables, grills, nonflush toilets; no drinking water
Fee per night: None
Management: Deschutes National Forest/Central Oregon Combined Off Highway Vehicle Operations
Contact: (541) 383-4000; www.fs.usda.gov/recmain/centraloregon/recreation
Finding the campground: From US 97 at La Pine (about 30 miles south of Bend), head east on FR 22 and go 26.4 miles. Turn left (north) onto FR 18 and continue 5.9 miles to the camp entry road on the left.
GPS coordinates: N43 39.457' / W121 02.248'
About the campground: This primitive campground sits south of its namesake peak in a forest that has been greatly thinned to eliminate an insect infestation. It serves off-highway-vehicle (OHV) enthusiasts, and state OHV permits are required. Campers have access to the East Fort Rock OHV Trail System.

480 Cow Meadow

Location: On Crane Prairie Reservoir, about 47 miles southwest of Bend
Season: May–mid-Sept
Sites: 18 basic sites; no hookups
Maximum length: 26 feet
Facilities: Tables, grills, nonflush toilets, boat launch; no drinking water
Fee per night: $$
Management: Deschutes National Forest
Contact: (541) 383-4000; www.fs.usda.gov/recmain/centraloregon/recreation
Finding the campground: From Bend head southwest on Cascade Lakes Highway, which is variously labeled Century Drive, CR 46, or FR 46. Go 45 miles and turn left onto FR 40. Go 0.4 mile and then turn right onto gravel FR 970. Continue 2 miles on FR 970 and FR 620. The campground entrance is on the right off FR 620 just after you cross the bridge over the Deschutes River.
GPS coordinates: N43 48.769' / W121 46.559'
About the campground: Along the Deschutes River where it feeds into Crane Prairie Reservoir, you will find this quiet camp in the lodgepole pines. The sites are rustic and open. Boaters are restricted to a speed of 10 miles per hour, and anglers have a choice of dipping their line in the river or the reservoir. Ospreys commonly patrol over the water.

481 Crane Prairie

Location: On Crane Prairie Reservoir, about 48 miles southwest of Bend
Season: Late Apr–mid-Oct
Sites: 140 basic sites, 6 tent sites; no hookups
Maximum length: 30 feet
Facilities: Tables, grills, nonflush toilets, drinking water, 2 boat launches, dock, fish-cleaning station
Fee per night: $$
Management: Deschutes National Forest
Contact: (541) 383-4000; (877) 444-6777 for reservations; www.fs.usda.gov/recmain/centraloregon/recreation
Finding the campground: From US 97 at Wickiup Junction, 27 miles south of Bend, head west on CR 43 and then FR 42, traveling a total of 16.5 miles. Turn right (north) onto FR 4270 and proceed 4.2 miles to this campground on the left.
GPS coordinates: N43 47.868' / W121 45.563'
About the campground: The comfortably arranged sites are distributed across a gentle slope of lodgepole pines above and along Crane Prairie Reservoir, which is noted for its nesting ospreys. Views are of the reservoir, its sculpted shore, Mount Bachelor, South Sister, and Broken Top. Fishing, boating, birding, and relaxing will fill your days.

482 Cultus Corral Horse Camp

Location: About 45 miles southwest of Bend
Season: Late May–late Sept
Sites: 10 basic sites; no hookups
Maximum length: 30 feet
Facilities: Tables, grills, nonflush toilets, 4-horse corral at each site; no drinking water
Fee per night: $$
Management: Deschutes National Forest
Contact: (541) 383-4000; www.fs.usda.gov/recmain/centraloregon/recreation
Finding the campground: From Bend head southwest on Cascade Lakes Highway, which is variously labeled Century Drive, CR 46, or FR 46. Go 45 miles and turn right onto gravel FR 4630. Proceed 0.4 mile and turn left to enter the campground.
GPS coordinates: N43 49.438' / W121 48.053'
About the campground: This quiet horse camp rests in a cutover forest of lodgepole pines near the Cultus River. The facility is one of a growing number in the state catering to equestrians. There is a trailhead in the camp and other horse trails a short drive away. Check with the Bend Ranger District about specific rides. This particular camp is sunny and dry, so you might want to bring a shade source.

483 Cultus Lake

Location: On Cultus Lake, about 48 miles southwest of Bend
Season: Late May–late Sept
Sites: 55 basic sites; no hookups
Maximum length: 30 feet
Facilities: Tables, grills, nonflush toilets, drinking water, boat launch
Fee per night: $$
Management: Deschutes National Forest
Contact: (541) 383-4000; www.fs.usda.gov/recmain/centraloregon/recreation
Finding the campground: From Bend head southwest on Cascade Lakes Highway, which is variously labeled Century Drive, CR 46, or FR 46. Go 46 miles; turn right onto FR 4635 and go 2 miles to enter the campground.
GPS coordinates: N43 50.144' / W121 50.048'
About the campground: This campground offers pleasant, forested sites just above Cultus Lake, a large natural lake open to boating, fishing, swimming, waterskiing, sailing, and sailboarding. During the day the area resounds with the roar of boat motors, laughing voices, and general bustle; by night it quiets down. The camp offers direct access to the Winopee Trail, which leads into Three Sisters Wilderness and visits a series of tranquil high-mountain lakes. Other trails lead from Cultus Lake to Deer and Little Cultus Lakes.

484 East Davis

Location: On Davis Lake, about 65 miles southwest of Bend
Season: Apr–late Sept
Sites: 17 basic sites; no hookups
Maximum length: 50 feet
Facilities: Tables, grills, nonflush toilets, drinking water
Fee per night: $$
Management: Deschutes National Forest
Contact: (541) 433-3200; www.fs.usda.gov/recmain/centraloregon/recreation
Finding the campground: From OR 58, 3.4 miles east of Crescent Lake, turn northeast onto Crescent Cutoff Road and go 3.2 miles. Turn left onto FR 46. (From US 97 at Crescent, you would go about 9 miles west on CR 61, the Crescent Cutoff Road, to FR 46 and turn right.) Follow FR 46 north 7.8 miles and turn left onto FR 850. You will come to a T-junction in 0.2 mile. Go left on FR 855 and drive 1.9 miles to the camp entrance on the right.
GPS coordinates: N43 35.332' / W121 51.149'
About the campground: This campground sits alongside Odell Creek on the south shore of Davis Lake; some sites overlook the lakeshore. Views include Maiden Peak, South Sister, Broken Top, and Mount Bachelor. The sites are still mostly shadeless after a fire in 2003. A lava flow, which dammed the creek, formed this natural lake. The lake level fluctuates from year to year, dependent on snowfall. Because the nutrient-rich lake provides a good food source for birds, naturalists will want to keep their binoculars handy. Only fly fishing is allowed.

485 Elk Lake

Location: On Elk Lake, about 31 miles southwest of Bend
Season: May–late Sept
Sites: 22 basic sites, 4 tent sites; no hookups
Maximum length: 25 feet
Facilities: Tables, grills, nonflush toilets, drinking water, boat launch
Fee per night: $$
Management: Deschutes National Forest
Contact: (541) 383-4000; www.fs.usda.gov/recmain/centraloregon/recreation
Finding the campground: From Bend head southwest on Cascade Lakes Highway, which is variously labeled Century Drive, CR 46, or FR 46. Go 31 miles and turn left into the campground.
GPS coordinates: N43 58.842' / W121 48.446'
About the campground: Lodgepole pines enfold this campground on the north shore of Elk Lake. While the camp has a couple of pull-through sites, many of the sites offer uneven or otherwise difficult parking, so RVers will need to search for the ideal site. Elk Lake is a 390-acre natural lake that hosts boating (10 miles per hour limit), fishing, and sailboarding. A lakeside resort rents boats. Hiking is also popular. Across the lake you can see Mount Bachelor peeking over a ridge.

Fly fishing at Fall River Falls, La Pine State Park

486 Fall River

Location: About 30 miles southwest of Bend
Season: May–Oct
Sites: 10 basic sites; no hookups
Maximum length: 30 feet
Facilities: Tables, grills, nonflush toilet; no drinking water
Fee per night: $$
Management: Deschutes National Forest
Contact: (541) 383-4000; www.fs.usda.gov/recmain/centraloregon/recreation
Finding the campground: From US 97, 17.5 miles south of Bend and 4.9 miles north of the turnoff for La Pine State Recreation Area, turn west onto FR 42 (labeled Vandevert Road and then South Century Drive). Proceed 12.2 miles to the campground.
GPS coordinates: N43 46.361' / W121 37.264'
About the campground: This camp, which rests in a thinned stand of lodgepole and small ponderosa pines, receives only patchy shade. A sparkling, shallow stretch of spring-fed Fall River flows below the camp. It is open to fly fishing only. Fall River Fish Hatchery is 3.2 miles northeast of the camp on FR 42.

487 Gull Point

Location: On Wickiup Reservoir, about 46 miles southwest of Bend
Season: Late Apr–mid-Oct
Sites: 79 basic sites; no hookups
Maximum length: 30 feet
Facilities: Tables, grills, flush and nonflush toilets, drinking water, dump station, boat launch, fish-cleaning station
Fee per night: $$
Management: Deschutes National Forest
Contact: (541) 383-4000; (877) 444-6777 for reservations; www.fs.usda.gov/recmain/centraloregon/recreation
Finding the campground: From US 97 at Wickiup Junction, 27 miles south of Bend, go west on CR 43 and FR 42 for 15.6 miles. Turn left onto FR 4260 and go 3 miles to the campground entrance on the right.
GPS coordinates: N43 42.332' / W121 45.671'
About the campground: This large camp occupies a peninsula where the Deschutes River Channel meets the main body of Wickiup Reservoir. Davis Mountain and Maiden Peak can be admired from the campground shore. The sites have a nice complement of natural vegetation, and a few big ponderosa pines draw the eyes skyward. Gulls and ospreys fish the reservoir. At the main reservoir activities range from fishing and boating to waterskiing, yet the area is wild enough that deer and elk may be seen in the vicinity of the campground. As the water level is drawn down in late summer, marshy areas commingle with the open water.

488 La Pine State Recreation Area

Location: About 27 miles southwest of Bend
Season: Year-round
Sites: 128 full or partial hookup sites, 10 cabins; water, electric, and sewer hookups
Maximum length: 85 feet
Facilities: Tables, flush toilets, drinking water, showers, dump station, meeting hall
Fee per night: $$–$$$
Management: Oregon State Parks and Recreation Department
Contact: (541) 536-2071; (800) 452-5687 for reservations; www.oregon.gov/OPRD/PARKS/camping.shtml
Finding the campground: From US 97, about 22 miles south of Bend, take the marked turn for the state recreation area and head west. You will reach the campground in just over 5 miles.
GPS coordinates: N43 46.094' / W121 32.422'
About the campground: Site of Oregon's largest ponderosa pine, this state park offers a pleasant campground and day-use area along the Deschutes River and within easy access of the sights and activities of Newberry National Volcanic Monument. Above the river the camp offers developed, easy-to-access sites in an open stand of lodgepole and ponderosa pines. The sites with sewers are more closely spaced. Near camp, a trail travels along the rim overlooking the river. A small,

gravelly beach at the day-use area is available for unguarded swimming. Because the park terrain does not lend itself to easy river access, anglers may need to do some scouting. A 1,000-foot, paved path descends to Big Tree, the 500-year-old ponderosa pine with a diameter of 8.6 feet.

489 Lava Flow

Location: On Davis Lake, 65 miles southwest of Bend
Season: Apr–Oct, dependent on snow
Sites: 6 basic sites; no hookups
Maximum length: 25 feet; better suited for tents and small units
Facilities: Tables, fire rings, nonflush toilets, rustic boat put-in; no drinking water
Fee per night: None
Management: Deschutes National Forest
Contact: (541) 433-3200; www.fs.usda.gov/recmain/centraloregon/recreation
Finding the campground: From OR 58, 3.4 miles east of Crescent Lake, turn northeast onto Crescent Cutoff Road and go 3.2 miles. Turn left onto FR 46. (From US 97 at Crescent, you would go about 9 miles west on CR 61, the Crescent Cut-off Road, to FR 46 and turn right.) Follow FR 46 north for 10.7 miles and turn left onto gravel FR 850 at the sign for the campground. Travel 0.8 mile on FR 850 to enter the campground on the right.
GPS coordinates: N43 37.420' / W121 49.233'
About the campground: This family campground rests in a mixed forest punctuated by big trees alongside a lava flow at Davis Lake, a large natural lake. From camp you can see where fire has silvered parts of the lake basin. The camp's southern extent adds dispersed sites, expanding the camping opportunity after September. Until then, nesting bald eagles have the sole occupancy of this gated reach. Davis Lake is open to fly fishing only. Because the shallow lake provides essential habitat for wildlife, small, quiet boats are in order.

490 Lava Lake

Location: On Lava Lake, about 39 miles southwest of Bend
Season: Mid-May–mid-Oct
Sites: 38 basic sites, 5 tent sites; no hookups
Maximum length: 30 feet
Facilities: Tables, grills, nonflush toilets, drinking water, boat launch
Fee per night: $$
Management: Deschutes National Forest
Contact: (541) 383-4000; www.fs.usda.gov/recmain/centraloregon/recreation
Finding the campground: From Bend head southwest on Cascade Lakes Highway, which is variously labeled Century Drive, CR 46, or FR 46. Go about 38 miles and turn left (east) onto FR 4600.500. Proceed 1 mile to the camp.
GPS coordinates: N43 54.807' / W121 46.012'

About the campground: Here on scenic Lava Lake, the campground and day-use area sit next door to rustic Lava Lake Resort. The campsites occupy a thinned stand of lodgepole pines; the day-use tables overlook an attractive, multihued wetland. The scalloped shore of Lava Lake is well suited for canoeing. In keeping with the tranquil mood of the lake, the boat speed is limited to 10 miles per hour. Near the boat ramp is Lava Lake Trailhead, a gateway to other area lakes and Edison Ice Cave. Views from the shore include South Sister, Broken Top, and Mount Bachelor.

491 Little Cultus

Location: On Little Cultus Lake, about 50 miles southwest of Bend
Season: Late May–late Sept
Sites: 31 basic sites; no hookups
Maximum length: 30 feet
Facilities: Tables, grills, nonflush toilets, drinking water, boat launch
Fee per night: $$
Management: Deschutes National Forest
Contact: (541) 383-4000; www.fs.usda.gov/recmain/centraloregon/recreation
Finding the campground: From Bend head southwest on Cascade Lakes Highway, which is variously labeled Century Drive, CR 46, or FR 46. Go 46 miles, turn right (west) onto FR 4635, and follow it 0.8 mile. Turn left onto gravel FR 4630 and stay on it for 1.7 miles. Proceed straight onto FR 4636. Continue 1 mile, staying on FR 4636 to the campground.
GPS coordinates: N43 48.012' / W121 51.967'
About the campground: This appealing campground rests among lodgepole pines on the shore of Little Cultus Lake. Its trio of camp clusters stretch along 1 mile of shore. Logs frame the camp roads and sites, and in places the lupine is quite lovely. This lake offers a quieter recreational experience than its larger companion, Cultus Lake, where waterskiing is allowed. At Little Cultus the pace is typically slower and the crowd more sedate. Boats are restricted to a speed of 10 miles per hour. As you troll the waters, you can lean back and enjoy views of Cultus Butte and the distant High Cascades. Area trails lead to Cultus Lake and to mountain lakes in the Three Sisters Wilderness Area.

492 Little Fawn

Location: On Elk Lake, about 37 miles southwest of Bend
Season: Late May–mid-Sept
Sites: 20 basic sites; no hookups
Maximum length: 30 feet
Facilities: Tables, grills, nonflush toilets, drinking water, boat launch
Fee per night: $$
Management: Deschutes National Forest
Contact: (541) 383-4000; (877) 444-6777 for reservations; www.fs.usda.gov/recmain/centraloregon/recreation

Finding the campground: From Bend head southwest on Cascade Lakes Highway, which is variously labeled Century Drive, CR 46, or FR 46. Go 35.5 miles and turn left (east) onto FR 4625, a paved and gravel route, to reach the campground entrance in 1.7 miles.

GPS coordinates: N43 57.813' / W121 47.803'

About the campground: This campground claims a slope on the southeast shore of Elk Lake. A few firs help fill out the lodgepole pine forest. Although some sites are right along shore, all are within easy access of this large natural lake. Among the recreational opportunities are boating (10 miles per hour limit), fishing, sailboarding, and hiking the Elk Lake Trail, which links the lake recreation sites and delivers new perspectives on the area.

493 Little Lava Lake

Location: On Little Lava Lake, about 40 miles southwest of Bend
Season: May–mid-Oct
Sites: 13 basic sites; no hookups
Maximum length: 30 feet
Facilities: Tables, grills, nonflush toilets, drinking water, boat launch
Fee per night: $$
Management: Deschutes National Forest
Contact: (541) 383-4000; (877) 444-6777 for reservations; www.fs.usda.gov/recmain/centraloregon/recreation
Finding the campground: From Bend head southwest on Cascade Lakes Highway, which is variously labeled Century Drive, CR 46, or FR 46. After about 38 miles turn left (east) onto FR 4600.500 and go 0.7 mile. Turn right onto FR 4600.520 and drive another 0.4 mile to the camp.
GPS coordinates: N43 54.605' / W121 45.715'
About the campground: Despite its name, Little Lava Lake is good size but smaller than neighboring Lava Lake. It appeals to canoeists because of its beautiful wetland shore and views of Broken Top and Mount Bachelor. The campsites are well spaced in a lodgepole pine forest above the shore. If you enjoy birding, you may spot swallows, ospreys, gulls, ducks, and cormorants at the lake and nuthatches and other woodland varieties in the forest.

494 Mallard Marsh

Location: On Hosmer Lake, about 37 miles southwest of Bend
Season: Late May–late Sept
Sites: 15 basic sites; no hookups
Maximum length: 25 feet
Facilities: Tables, grills, nonflush toilets, canoe launch; no drinking water
Fee per night: $$
Management: Deschutes National Forest
Contact: (541) 383-4000; www.fs.usda.gov/recmain/centraloregon/recreation

Finding the campground: From Bend head southwest on Cascade Lakes Highway, which is variously labeled Century Drive, CR 46, or FR 46. Go 35.5 miles and turn left (east) onto FR 4625. Follow it for 1.2 miles and turn right into the campground.

GPS coordinates: N43 57.787' / W121 47.071'

About the campground: A combination of wetland and open water, Hosmer Lake is a picturesque place to canoe. Birders and naturalists also are drawn here. The lake is stocked with trout and Atlantic salmon for catch-and-release fly fishing only. The upper segment of the lake is three to four times bigger than the lower lake; the open water reflects Mount Bachelor and Red Crater. The camp is in a tranquil forest of lodgepole pines and firs, and Elk Lake is close by (only about 5 miles to the north) for swimming, sailboarding, or watching the sun set from its Sunset View Picnic Area.

495 McKay Crossing

Location: About 29 miles south of Bend
Season: May–late Sept
Sites: 16 basic sites; no hookups
Maximum length: 26 feet
Facilities: Tables, grills, nonflush toilets; no drinking water
Fee per night: $$
Management: Deschutes National Forest
Contact: (541) 383-4000; www.fs.usda.gov/recmain/centraloregon/recreation
Finding the campground: From US 97, 23.5 miles south of Bend, turn east onto FR 21 and continue 3.2 miles. Turn left onto FR 2120 and go another 2.2 miles to reach the campground.
GPS coordinates: N43 43.021' / W121 22.657'
About the campground: This Paulina Creek campground offers quiet, fairly private sites in a setting of lodgepole and small ponderosa pines. From camp you can access the Peter Skene Ogden National Recreation Trail, which travels upstream 6 miles to Paulina Lake and caters to multiple use: It is open to foot, horse, and mountain bike travel. Lower Paulina Falls, a picturesque 25-foot falls on the main creek, is only 500 feet from camp. The many attractions of Newberry National Volcanic Monument are within easy reach by vehicle.

496 Newberry National Volcanic Monument: Chief Paulina Horse Camp

Location: About 37 miles south of Bend
Season: June–late Sept
Sites: 14 basic sites; no hookups
Maximum length: 26 feet
Facilities: Tables, grills, nonflush toilets, 2- and 4-horse stalls, water for horses; no drinking water
Fee per night: $$
Management: Deschutes National Forest

Contact: (541) 383-4000; (877) 444-6777 for reservations; www.fs.usda.gov/recmain/centraloregon/recreation

Finding the campground: From US 97, 23.5 miles south of Bend, head east on FR 21 for 13.9 miles; the campground is on the right.

GPS coordinates: N43 42.168' / W121 15.285'

About the campground: Situated across FR 21 from Paulina Lake, this equestrian camp puts you right in the heart of Newberry Volcano and gives you easy access to the scenic and recreational opportunities of the area. The camp is in a pleasant, dry forest setting. Area trail rides include tours of the Newberry Crater, Paulina Peak, and Peter Skene Ogden Trails. The Newberry Crater Trail passes through the camp. You can expect dusty trail conditions. Besides riding, you can also fish and boat at Paulina Lake or its twin, East Lake.

497 Newberry National Volcanic Monument: Cinder Hill

Location: On East Lake, about 42 miles south of Bend

Season: June–late Sept

Sites: 108 basic sites; no hookups

Maximum length: 30 feet

Facilities: Tables, grills, nonflush toilets, drinking water, boat launch

Fee per night: $$

Management: Deschutes National Forest

Contact: (541) 383-4000; (877) 444-6777 for reservations; www.fs.usda.gov/recmain/centraloregon/recreation

Finding the campground: From US 97, 23.5 miles south of Bend, head east on FR 21 for 17.6 miles. Turn left (north) onto FR 2100.700 and go 0.5 mile to the campground.

GPS coordinates: N43 44.106' / W121 11.747'

About the campground: This camp stretches for 0.7 mile through lodgepole pine forest on the east shore of East Lake. The twin caldera lakes of Newberry Volcano—East and Paulina—were formed in much the same manner as Crater Lake, and they are equally blue and clear. Grassy spits at camp extend into the lake, shaping quiet coves that attract ducks. East Lake is a favorite with boaters and anglers, and a rustic resort nearby rents boats. Newberry National Volcanic Monument boasts a superb trail system for hiking, mountain biking, and horseback riding; birding and sightseeing also engage guests. Pumice and ash domes, obsidian slopes, stone pillars, and waterfalls are among the area sights.

498 Newberry National Volcanic Monument: East Lake

Location: On East Lake, about 40 miles southeast of Bend

Season: June–mid-Oct

Sites: 29 basic sites; no hookups

Maximum length: 26 feet

Facilities: Tables, grills, flush toilets, drinking water, boat launch

East Lake Campground, Newberry National Volcanic Monument

Fee per night: $$
Management: Deschutes National Forest
Contact: (541) 383-4000; www.fs.usda.gov/recmain/centraloregon/recreation
Finding the campground: From US 97, 23.5 miles south of Bend, turn east onto FR 21. Continue 16.6 miles to the campground entrance on the left.
GPS coordinates: N43 43.059' / W121 12.694'
About the campground: On the south shore of 1,000-acre East Lake, these campsites sit close together in a stand of lodgepole pines. East Lake is one of a pair of deepwater lakes contained in the collapsed bowl of Newberry Volcano. The lake is popular with boaters and with anglers, who vie for rainbow and German brown trout and kokanee, as well. A sandy beach is found at the boat launch, and fine trails explore the geologic wonderland of Newberry National Volcanic Monument.

499 Newberry National Volcanic Monument: Little Crater

Location: On Paulina Lake, about 39 miles south of Bend
Season: June–mid-Oct
Sites: 49 basic sites; no hookups
Maximum length: 30 feet
Facilities: Tables, grills, nonflush toilets, drinking water, boat launch
Fee per night: $$

Management: Deschutes National Forest
Contact: (541) 383-4000; www.fs.usda.gov/recmain/centraloregon/recreation
Finding the campground: From US 97, 23.5 miles south of Bend, turn east onto FR 21 and go 14.5 miles. Turn left (north) onto FR 2100.570 and proceed 0.5 mile to the campground.
GPS coordinates: N43 42.772' / W121 14.605'
About the campground: This camp stretches for 0.5 mile through lodgepole pines along the east shore of Paulina Lake, one of two big, clear, azure-blue lakes cradled in Newberry Crater; East Lake is the other. A shoreline trail rings Paulina Lake, traversing forest, obsidian flow, and slopes dotted with junipers and manzanitas. In addition to lake views, the trail serves up fine looks at craggy Paulina Peak on the southern skyline. The Peter Skene Ogden and Paulina Falls Trails explore the banks of the outlet. Boating (10 miles per hour speed limit), fishing, birding, mountain biking, horseback riding, and sightseeing are other potential pastimes. The winding, sometimes rough drive to the top of Paulina Peak delivers a jaw-dropping vista of the Cascade volcanoes, the caldera lakes, Paulina Pinnacles, and Fort Rock.

500 Newberry National Volcanic Monument: Paulina Lake

Location: On Paulina Lake, about 36 miles south of Bend
Season: Late May–late Sept
Sites: 69 basic sites; no hookups
Maximum length: 30 feet
Facilities: Tables, grills, flush toilets, drinking water, dump station, boat launch
Fee per night: $$
Management: Deschutes National Forest
Contact: (541) 383-4000; (877) 444-6777 for reservations; www.fs.usda.gov/recmain/centraloregon/recreation
Finding the campground: From US 97, 23.5 miles south of Bend, turn east onto FR 21. Go 12.9 miles and turn left into the campground.
GPS coordinates: N43 42.728' / W121 16.427'
About the campground: Below Paulina Peak, on the south shore of picture-pretty Paulina Lake, you will find these closely spaced campsites among the lodgepole pines. This is one of two azure-blue lakes cradled in Newberry Crater; East Lake is the other. From camp you will find easy access to the Paulina Lake, Peter Skene Ogden, and Paulina Falls Trails, as well as to fishing, sailing, and boating (10 miles per hour limit) on Paulina Lake. Sightseeing stops and short hikes unravel the geological story of Newberry Volcano.

501 North Davis Creek

Location: On Wickiup Reservoir, 56 miles southwest of Bend
Season: Apr–Sept
Sites: 14 basic sites; no hookups
Maximum length: 25 feet

Facilities: Tables, grills, nonflush toilets, drinking water, boat launch
Fee per night: $$
Management: Deschutes National Forest
Contact: (541) 383-4000; www.fs.usda.gov/recmain/centraloregon/recreation
Finding the campground: From Bend head southwest on Cascade Lakes Highway, which is variously labeled Century Drive, CR 46, or FR 46. Go 56 miles and turn left to enter the campground.
GPS coordinates: N43 40.543' / W121 49.447'
About the campground: This campground occupies a stand of young lodgepole pines on a long inlet arm of Wickiup Reservoir. In the late 1980s the site was logged because of a pine beetle infestation. Sparkling North Davis Creek merges with the reservoir here. The inlet bay is clear and quickly grows deep, but the sandy shore broadens as the water level drops later in the year. Although a poor shade source, the tight array of trees contributes a bit of privacy to sites. Besides fishing and boating, you can lace on the hiking boots and head for Moore Creek Trailhead. Hike destinations include Davis, Bobby, and Charlton Lakes; Gerdine Butte; and The Twins. You can reach the trailhead by taking the signed road across the highway from the camp.

502 North Twin

Location: On North Twin Lake, about 43 miles southwest of Bend
Season: Apr-mid-Oct
Sites: 20 basic sites; no hookups
Maximum length: 30 feet
Facilities: Tables, grills, nonflush toilets, boat launch; no drinking water
Fee per night: $$
Management: Deschutes National Forest
Contact: (541) 383-4000; www.fs.usda.gov/recmain/centraloregon/recreation
Finding the campground: From the Wickiup Junction on US 97, 27 miles south of Bend, turn west onto CR 43 and go 11 miles. Continue west on FR 42 for another 4.6 miles. Turn left onto FR 4260, go 0.2 mile, and turn left into the campground.
GPS coordinates: N43 43.874' / W121 45.638'
About the campground: This campground in the pines sits on the shore of perfectly round North Twin Lake. The sites have gravel parking and not much privacy, given the open spacing of the trees and the lack of ground vegetation. The postcard-pretty lake edged with grasses and snags invites quiet boating (no motors allowed), swimming, and fishing. A trail leads 1 mile from the camp to the lake's mirror image, South Twin Lake, where there is a rustic resort.

503 Pine Mountain

Location: About 33 miles southeast of Bend
Season: May–Sept
Sites: 6 basic sites; no hookups
Maximum length: 30 feet
Facilities: Tables, nonflush toilets; no drinking water
Fee per night: None
Management: Deschutes National Forest
Contact: (541) 383-4000; www.fs.usda.gov/recmain/centraloregon/recreation
Finding the campground: From Bend go east on US 20 for 25 miles to Millican. Turn south onto Pine Mountain Road/FR 2017, leaving the pavement. Continue 7.7 miles toward Pine Mountain Observatory to reach the campground. Much of the winding route is on washboard.
GPS coordinates: N43 47.464' / W120 56.594'
About the campground: Near the University of Oregon Pine Mountain Observatory, you will find this campground among the pines at an elevation of 6,250 feet. Lupine and bunchgrass pierce the needle mat. The observatory operates three telescopes and is typically open to the public on Friday and Saturday evenings from Memorial Day weekend through the last weekend in September. A donation is suggested, and "dark moons" are the best times to visit. Amateur astronomers bring their own telescopes to the lofty locale. Although stargazing is the chief activity, birders enjoy the spot too. The open sage summit also supplies panoramic views of the encompassing forest, the Cascade volcanoes, and the high desert. There are no open fires during summer and fall because of fire danger, but the restriction also preserves the viewing darkness. Keep the noise down during the day so as not to disturb the astronomers' sleep.

504 Point

Location: On Elk Lake, 34 miles southwest of Bend
Season: Late May–late Sept
Sites: 9 basic sites; no hookups
Maximum length: 25 feet
Facilities: Tables, grills, nonflush toilets, boat launch; no drinking water
Fee per night: $$
Management: Deschutes National Forest
Contact: (541) 383-4000; www.fs.usda.gov/recmain/centraloregon/recreation
Finding the campground: From Bend head southwest on Cascade Lakes Highway, which is variously labeled Century Drive, CR 46, or FR 46. Go 34 miles and turn left into the campground.
GPS coordinates: N43 57.997' / W121 48.491'
About the campground: This campground claims the forested southwest corner of Elk Lake, a large natural lake from which you can see Mount Bachelor, Broken Top, and South Sister. The lake welcomes fishing, swimming, and boating (10 miles per hour maximum). Next door to the camp is Beach Picnic Area, which offers a broad sandy beach, a nice sandy lake bottom for wading, but no lifeguard. At the picnic area you can access the Elk Lake Trail.

505 Prairie

Location: About 27 miles south of Bend
Season: Mid-May–late Sept
Sites: 17 basic sites; no hookups
Maximum length: 30 feet
Facilities: Tables, grills, nonflush toilets, drinking water
Fee per night: $$
Management: Deschutes National Forest
Contact: (541) 383-4000; www.fs.usda.gov/recmain/centraloregon/recreation
Finding the campground: From US 97, 23.5 miles south of Bend, turn east onto FR 21. Go 3.1 miles and turn right into the campground.
GPS coordinates: N43 43.528' / W121 25.418'
About the campground: Situated in a mixed-pine forest, this campground offers nice, big sites overlooking Paulina Prairie and Creek. It is a picturesque place to kick back and relax, but it also offers a base from which to explore Newberry National Volcanic Monument, the Deschutes River, Wickiup Reservoir, and the Bend area.

506 Pringle Falls

Location: About 35 miles southwest of Bend
Season: May–Oct
Sites: 7 basic sites; no hookups
Maximum length: 25 feet
Facilities: Tables, grills, nonflush toilet; no drinking water
Fee per night: $$
Management: Deschutes National Forest
Contact: (541) 383-4000; www.fs.usda.gov/recmain/centraloregon/recreation
Finding the campground: From US 97 at the Wickiup Junction, 27 miles south of Bend, go west on CR 43 for 7.4 miles. Turn right (north) onto gravel FR 4330.500 and go 0.2 mile. Turn left at the camp turnoff and continue about 0.5 mile to the campground.
GPS coordinates: N43 44.863' / W121 36.127'
About the campground: You will find this pine-shaded campground on the Deschutes River, near the parklike stands of ponderosa pines in Pringle Falls Experimental Forest. The channel-like river next to camp is deep and swift. Fishing, rafting, and canoeing are popular; you can put in right at camp. According to a sign at the turn onto FR 4330.500, Tetherow Boat Launch is 3 miles downstream.

507 Quinn Meadow Horse Camp

Location: About 32 miles southwest of Bend
Season: June–late Sept
Sites: 26 basic sites; no hookups
Maximum length: 30 feet
Facilities: Tables, grills, nonflush toilets, drinking water, tie stalls and 2- and 4-horse corrals, community shelter, manure dump
Fee per night: $$
Management: Deschutes National Forest
Contact: (541) 383-4000; www.fs.usda.gov/recmain/centraloregon/recreation
Finding the campground: From Bend head southwest on Cascade Lakes Highway, which is variously labeled Century Drive, CR 46, or FR 46. Go 31 miles, turn left (east) onto the camp entrance road, and follow it 0.5 mile into the campground.
GPS coordinates: N43 59.801' / W121 47.192'
About the campground: This beautiful campground caters to equestrians. Sites are dispersed among the lodgepole pines, mountain hemlocks, and firs at the edge of Quinn Meadow, a long, broad sweep of grass threaded by Quinn Creek. The sites are ample and private and encourage reclining at camp. Trails from the camp follow Quinn Creek or lead into the Three Sisters Wilderness and the Horse Lakes Area, giving riders numerous choices.

508 Quinn River

Location: On Crane Prairie Reservoir, about 48 miles southwest of Bend
Season: Apr–mid-Sept
Sites: 41 basic sites; no hookups
Maximum length: 30 feet
Facilities: Tables, grills, nonflush toilets, drinking water, boat launch
Fee per night: $$
Management: Deschutes National Forest
Contact: (541) 383-4000; (877) 444-6777 for reservations; www.fs.usda.gov/recmain/centraloregon/recreation
Finding the campground: From Bend head southwest on Cascade Lakes Highway, which is variously labeled Century Drive, CR 46, or FR 46. After driving about 48 miles, turn left into the campground.
GPS coordinates: N43 47.097' / W121 50.193'
About the campground: This camp occupies a lodgepole pine flat along Quinn River at Crane Prairie Reservoir. The forest is semi-open as a result of a pine beetle infestation and a winter blowdown. The large boat ramp accesses a snag-riddled section of the reservoir where Quinn River empties into it. Boaters are restricted to a speed of 10 miles per hour, and there is no anchoring within 100 feet of any trees that hold osprey nests. Billy Quinn Historical Trail starts at the camp and visits Quinn River Spring (the source of this short river), the Cy Bingham lodgepole pine, and the grave of Billy Quinn, a pioneer sheepman. The trail ends at Osprey Observation Point, which

can also be reached by car, less than 1 mile south on Cascade Lakes Highway. More than half the ospreys in Oregon nest at Crane Prairie Reservoir.

509 Reservoir

Location: On Wickiup Reservoir, about 60 miles southwest of Bend
Season: Apr–Sept
Sites: 24 basic sites; no hookups
Maximum length: 30 feet
Facilities: Tables, grills, nonflush toilets, boat launch; no drinking water
Fee per night: $$
Management: Deschutes National Forest
Contact: (541) 383-4000; www.fs.usda.gov/recmain/centraloregon/recreation
Finding the campground: From Bend head southwest on Cascade Lakes Highway, which is variously labeled Century Drive, CR 46, or FR 46. Go 58 miles, turn left onto FR 44, and proceed 1.7 miles to the campground.
GPS coordinates: N43 40.247' / W121 46.405'
About the campground: This campground sprawls along a lodgepole pine flat on the southwest shore of Wickiup Reservoir. Although the pines are small, they grow densely enough to lend privacy to the campsites. You will need to bring a shade source however. If you get a lakeside site, you can moor your boat on the sandy shore right next to your camp. Boating and fishing are the primary draws at this large reservoir; kokanee is among the catch.

510 Rock Creek

Location: On Crane Prairie Reservoir, about 50 miles southwest of Bend
Season: Apr–late Sept
Sites: 30 basic sites; no hookups
Maximum length: 30 feet
Facilities: Tables, grills, nonflush toilets, drinking water, boat launch, fish-cleaning station
Fee per night: $$
Management: Deschutes National Forest
Contact: (541) 383-4000; www.fs.usda.gov/recmain/centraloregon/recreation
Finding the campground: From Bend head southwest on Cascade Lakes Highway, which is variously labeled Century Drive, CR 46, or FR 46. Go about 50 miles and turn left into the campground.
GPS coordinates: N43 46.088' / W121 50.027'
About the campground: On the west shore of Crane Prairie Reservoir, you will find this camp in a semi-open stand of lodgepole pines and bitterbrush. Cross-reservoir views are of Mount Bachelor and South Sister; Cultus Butte rises to the north. Songbirds animate the trees in the campground, while an osprey's screech may draw your eyes skyward. The camp is just 2.5 miles south of Osprey Observation Point, an interpretive and viewing site. The snags of the reservoir provide nesting sites

for the lake's osprey population. Trout fishing and boating (10 miles per hour maximum) are the primary activities.

511 Rosland

Location: About 28 miles south of Bend
Season: Late May–mid-Oct
Sites: 1 hookup site, 10 basic sites; water and electric hookups
Maximum length: 40 feet
Facilities: Tables, grills, nonflush toilets, drinking water
Fee per night: $$
Management: La Pine Parks and Recreation District
Contact: (541) 536-2223
Finding the campground: From US 97, 2 miles north of La Pine and 27 miles south of Bend, turn west onto Burgess Road toward Wickiup Reservoir. Proceed 1.5 miles to the campground on the left.
GPS coordinates: N43 42.197' / W121 30.233'
About the campground: Along the winding, willow-lined Little Deschutes River, this campground occupies a habitat of lodgepole pines, bitterbrush, and native grasses. Sites have limited shade. Back in the 1820s trappers used this location as a base. Lightly trafficked and peaceful, it's becoming better known. Fishing is the most popular pastime.

512 Sheep Bridge

Location: On Wickiup Reservoir, about 43 miles southwest of Bend
Season: Apr–Oct
Sites: 20 basic sites; no hookups
Maximum length: 30 feet
Facilities: Tables, grills, nonflush toilets, drinking water, boat launch
Fee per night: $$
Management: Deschutes National Forest
Contact: (541) 383-4000; www.fs.usda.gov/recmain/centraloregon/recreation
Finding the campground: From US 97 at Wickiup Junction, 27 miles south of Bend, go west on CR 43 and FR 42 for 15.6 miles. Turn left onto FR 4260, go 0.8 mile, and turn right to reach the campground.
GPS coordinates: N43 43.939' / W121 47.123'
About the campground: You will find this campground in a mixed-age forest of lodgepole pines along the meandering Deschutes River Channel of Wickiup Reservoir. Younger trees shape the outskirts of camp; a few bigger pines within the campground afford at least some shade. Boats are limited to 10 miles per hour on the channel. Fishing is popular.

513 Soda Creek

Location: On Sparks Lake, about 26 miles southwest of Bend
Season: June–Sept
Sites: 10 basic sites; no hookups
Maximum length: 25 feet
Facilities: Tables, grills, nonflush toilets; no drinking water
Fee per night: $$
Management: Deschutes National Forest
Contact: (541) 383-4000; www.fs.usda.gov/recmain/centraloregon/recreation
Finding the campground: From Bend head southwest on Cascade Lakes Highway, which is variously labeled Century Drive, CR 46, or FR 46. Go 26 miles and turn left (east) onto FR 400 at the sign for Sparks Lake. Drive 0.1 mile to the camp area.
GPS coordinates: N44 01.519' / W121 43.676'
About the campground: This campground sits at the northern end of Sparks Lake and Meadow, where Soda Creek feeds into the lake. The sites are situated among the pines and firs at the edge of the meadow, which stretches for more than 1 mile and is almost as wide. The High Cascades contribute to views. The area is noted for its abundance of wildlife; watch for elk, deer, and birds. Canoeing the shallow lake, fly fishing, and hiking into Three Sisters Wilderness are ways to enjoy your stay. Interpretive boards tell the history of Soda Creek. A short drive following the signs to the trailheads on FR 400 leads to the Ray Atkeson Nature Trail. The trail honors the Oregon photographer laureate by showcasing one of his favorite subjects—Sparks Lake with South Sister.

514 South

Location: On Hosmer Lake, about 37 miles southwest of Bend
Season: Mid-May–late Sept
Sites: 23 basic sites; no hookups
Maximum length: 26 feet
Facilities: Tables, grills, nonflush toilets, boat launch; no drinking water
Fee per night: $$
Management: Deschutes National Forest
Contact: (541) 383-4000; www.fs.usda.gov/recmain/centraloregon/recreation
Finding the campground: From Bend head southwest on Cascade Lakes Highway, which is variously labeled Century Drive, CR 46, or FR 46. Go 35.5 miles and turn left (east) onto FR 4625. Follow it for 1.2 miles and turn right into the campground.
GPS coordinates: N43 57.640' / W121 47.314'
About the campground: Together with Mallard Marsh Campground, this camp provides access to Hosmer Lake, a scenic wetland and open water that is stocked with trout and Atlantic salmon for catch-and-release fly fishing only. The large lake is ideal for canoeing. You can paddle through open water and reeds, grasses, and water lilies; watch for wildlife; and enjoy the watery reflections of Mount Bachelor and Red Crater. Like Mallard Marsh, this campground is situated among the lodgepole pines and firs. Because its road is often rutted, the camp is unsuitable for big RVs.

515 South Twin

Location: On South Twin Lake at Wickiup Reservoir, about 45 miles southwest of Bend
Season: Apr–mid-Oct
Sites: 21 basic sites; no hookups
Maximum length: 26 feet
Facilities: Tables, grills, nonflush toilets, drinking water, boat launches
Fee per night: $$
Management: Deschutes National Forest
Contact: (541) 383-4000; www.fs.usda.gov/recmain/centraloregon/recreation
Finding the campground: From US 97 at the Wickiup Junction, 27 miles south of Bend, go west on CR 43 and FR 42 for 15.6 miles. Turn left onto FR 4260, go 2 miles, and turn left into the campground.
GPS coordinates: N43 43.030' / W121 46.211'
About the campground: This camp is housed in a mature forest of lodgepole and ponderosa pines along South Twin Lake, a picturesque circular body of water cupped by forest. Its fortress-like ring of trees differentiates it from North Twin Lake, where a grassy shore holds back the trees. A mile-long trail links the two lakes. Activities at South Twin include fishing, nonmotorized boating, and swimming. For additional fishing and boating, across FR 4260 from the camp is a boat launch on the Deschutes River Channel (10 miles per hour maximum). A neighboring resort puts a cup of espresso just strides from the camp.

516 Swamp Wells Horse Camp

Location: About 18 miles southeast of Bend
Season: Apr–Oct
Sites: 5 basic sites; no hookups
Maximum length: 30 feet
Facilities: Tables, grills, nonflush toilets, watering troughs; no drinking water
Fee per night: None
Management: Deschutes National Forest
Contact: (541) 383-4000; www.fs.usda.gov/recmain/centraloregon/recreation
Finding the campground: From US 97, 4 miles south of Bend, turn east onto FR 18 and go 5.4 miles. Turn right (south) onto FR 1810 and continue 5.8 miles. Turn left (east) onto FR 1816 and drive another 3 miles to the campground.
GPS coordinates: N43 51.203' / W121 13.012'
About the campground: This camp occupies a cutover stand of pines and offers access to area trails and jeep tracks for horseback riding, hiking, and all-terrain-vehicle travel. Although the terrain appears relatively flat, the camp occupies the skirt of Newberry Volcano, which shows a steady, gradual incline to the caldera rim. Swamp Wells Trail travels 9 miles south to the crater; the trail's northern destination is Horse Butte.

517 Todd Creek Horse Camp

Location: About 25 miles southwest of Bend
Season: June–Oct, dependent on snow
Sites: 7 basic sites; no hookups
Maximum length: 30 feet
Facilities: Tables, grills, nonflush toilet, corrals; no drinking water
Fee per night: Northwest Forest Pass required
Management: Deschutes National Forest
Contact: (541) 383-4000; www.fs.usda.gov/recmain/centraloregon/recreation
Finding the campground: From Bend head southwest on Cascade Lakes Highway, which is variously labeled Century Drive, CR 46, or FR 46. Go 24 miles and turn left on FR 4600.390. Proceed 0.6 mile to the horse camp.
GPS coordinates: N44 00.986' / W121 41.804'
About the campground: Below Mount Bachelor, this equestrian campground is located in the lodgepole pines at Todd Creek, but bring your own shade source. Riders find access to the long-distance Metolius-Windigo National Recreation Trail, which is being set up with a series of horse camps a day's ride apart. When not on the trail, you can check out the sights and activities afforded along the scenic highway.

518 Tumalo State Park

Location: About 5 miles northwest of Bend
Season: Year-round
Sites: 23 hookup sites, 54 basic sites, 7 yurts, some hike/bike sites; water, electric, and sewer hookups
Maximum length: 44 feet
Facilities: Tables, grills, flush toilets, drinking water, showers, playground
Fee per night: $$–$$$
Management: Oregon State Parks and Recreation Department
Contact: (541) 382-3586; (800) 452-5687 for reservations; www.oregon.gov/OPRD/PARKS/camping.shtml
Finding the campground: From the junction of US 20 and US 97 at the north end of Bend, go west on US 20 for 3.7 miles. Turn south at the sign for the park onto the Old McKenzie–Bend Highway and proceed 1.1 miles to the campground entrance on the left. A day-use area is on the right.
GPS coordinates: N44 07.725' / W121 19.835'
About the campground: This campground rests along the Deschutes River, where the water has been drawn down for irrigation. Picturesque rocks and yellow irises may complement the water. The sites have paved parking, but some of the basic sites will require more RV leveling than others. The camp is set in a juniper forest, with a few aspen trees and grassy plots tucked between the sites. Most sites have partial shade. A designated swimming area in the day-use area is popular in summer. The attractions of Bend may call you away from the camp.

519 West South Twin

Location: On Wickiup Reservoir, about 45 miles southwest of Bend
Season: Apr–late Sept
Sites: 24 basic sites; no hookups
Maximum length: 30 feet
Facilities: Tables, grills, flush toilets, drinking water, boat launches
Fee per night: $$
Management: Deschutes National Forest
Contact: (541) 383-4000; www.fs.usda.gov/recmain/centraloregon/recreation
Finding the campground: From US 97 at Wickiup Junction, 27 miles south of Bend, go west on CR 43 and FR 42 for 15.6 miles. Turn left onto FR 4260, go 2 miles, and turn right into the campground.
GPS coordinates: N43 42.950' / W121 46.388'
About the campground: Located along the Deschutes River Channel of Wickiup Reservoir, this structured campground retains its native ground vegetation, which contributes to the privacy of the sites and the attractiveness of the camp. Lodgepole and ponderosa pines make up the surrounding forest. From camp you have direct access to the river channel for boating (10 miles per hour maximum) and fishing. Just across FR 4260 is South Twin Lake, where you can engage in nonmotorized boating or hike the 1-mile trail to North Twin Lake.

520 Wyeth

Location: 8 miles west of La Pine
Season: Late Apr–mid-Oct
Sites: 5 basic sites; no hookups
Maximum length: 25 feet
Facilities: Tables, grills, nonflush toilets, boat takeout; no drinking water
Fee per night: $$
Management: Deschutes National Forest
Contact: (541) 383-4000; www.fs.usda.gov/recmain/centraloregon/recreation
Finding the campground: From US 97, 2 miles north of La Pine and 27 miles south of Bend, head west on Burgess Road (CR 43) toward Wickiup Reservoir. Go 7.9 miles and turn left onto gravel FR 4370 at the sign for the campground. Go 0.2 and turn left into the campground.
GPS coordinates: N43 44.320' / W121 36.842'
About the campground: This rustic campground with its partly shaded sites sits beside the Deschutes River in a ponderosa pine forest punctuated by a few big yellow bellies (old-growth pines). Anglers find easy fishing access to the smooth, fast stretch of river. Birdsongs and fish splashes add to the peace found at camp.

Eastern Oregon

Eastern Oregon rolls out an exciting canvas for discovery. It unites John Day Fossil Beds; Steens Mountain; the history, beauty, and wildlife of the Blue Mountains; and the chiseled, icy grandeur of the Elkhorn and Wallowa Mountains. It also cradles the harsh beauty of Hells Canyon, unbroken desert expanses, enormous desert lakes, hot springs, and the weathered orange canyonlands at the southeast corner of the state. Yes, Eastern Oregon rolls out wide-open spaces and extends a lifetime ticket to adventure. It is a land that supports black bears, coyotes, deer, antelope, elk, bighorn sheep, mountain goats, wild horses, golden and bald eagles, and sturgeon. The land wears the tracks of the Oregon Trail and the telltale signs of dashed mining hopes. Topping it all is the glittery vault of the midnight sky.

Settlement in the eastern part of the state is light and generally widely scattered. I-84 strings together the larger communities at the northeast corner of the state: Pendleton, La Grande, Baker City, and Ontario. Lakeview and Burns are the "big cities" of the southern extreme. Because of this light development, travelers need to be more self-sufficient and better prepared for the unexpected. Filling gas tanks; having a reliable spare tire, some tools, electrical tape, and other items for emergency repairs; carrying extra water and blankets; and checking on road and weather conditions are all cornerstones to safety.

This region typically experiences four seasons (although some are rushed), with extremes of heat and cold often registered. The extent of snow depends largely on elevation and your location with regard to the storm track. Chilly dry realms or snowy wonderlands can be found in winter. Summer bakes the desert reaches, making the mountain cool all the more desirable.

Hiking, fishing, birding, horseback riding, hunting, whitewater rafting, rock collecting, boating, skiing, snowmobiling, and snowshoeing are among the active pursuits. Museums, rodeos, county fairs, and historic sites expand the region's appeal.

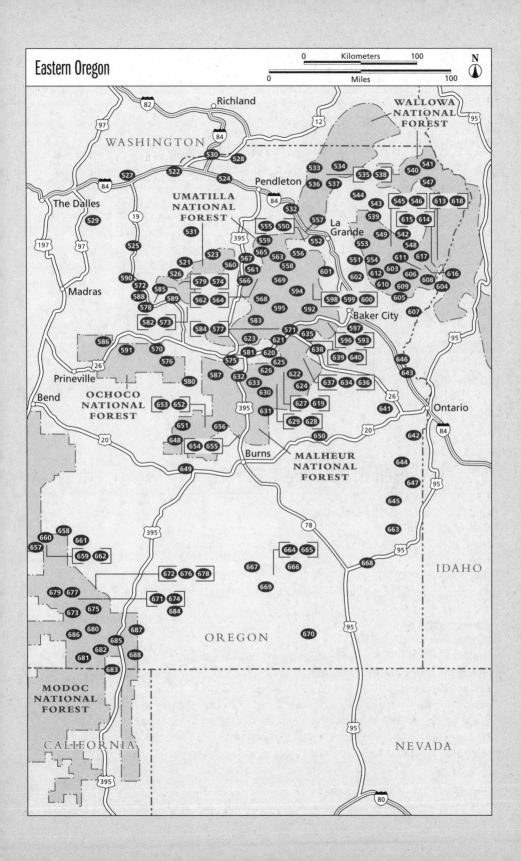

Columbia Plateau Area

	Hookup Sites	Total Sites	Max. RV Length	Hookups	Toilets	Showers	Drinking Water	Dump Station	Recreation	Fee	Can Reserve
521 Anson Wright Memorial Park	24	49	35	WES	F	X	X		HF	$$-$$$	X
522 Boardman Marina Park	63	67	80	WES	F	X	X	X	SFBL	$$-$$$	X
523 Cutsforth County Park	36	52	35	WES	F,NF	X	X		HF	$$	X
524 Fort Henrietta RV Park	8	8	40	WESC	F	X	X	X		$$-$$$	X
525 J. B. Burns Park	17	17	40	WES	F	X	X	X		$$	X
526 Morrow County Off-Highway-Vehicle Park	4	66	60	WES	F,NF	X	X		O	$$-$$$	
527 Port of Arlington Marina and RV Park	11	31	40	WES	F		X		FBL	$-$$$	
528 Sand Station Recreation Area		15	40		NF				SFB	None	
529 Sherman County RV Park	33	33	40	WES	F	X	X	X		$-$$	X
530 Umatilla Marina and RV Park	26	35	60	WES	F	X	X	X	SFBL	$$-$$$	X
531 Willow Creek	23	23	40	WES	F	X	X	X	FBL	$$	X

521 Anson Wright Memorial Park

Location: 25 miles south of Heppner
Season: Late May–Oct
Sites: 24 full or partial hookup sites, 25 basic/tent sites, 1 cabin; water, electric, and sewer hookups
Maximum length: 35 feet
Facilities: Tables, fire rings, flush toilets, drinking water, showers, playground, fishing pond and creek
Fee per night: $$-$$$
Management: Morrow County
Contact: (541) 989-9500, reservations accepted; www.morrowcountyparks.org/
Finding the campground: The campground is west off OR 207, 25 miles south of Heppner.
GPS coordinates: N45 06.399' / W119 37.504'
About the campground: Ponderosa pines and Douglas firs shade this quiet campground at the foot of the western slope of Rock Creek Canyon. The cool nights sometimes catch campers off guard, so keep the blankets handy. Campers will find routes to walk, and anglers can try their luck in the pond or Rock Creek. Swimming, rock hunting, and simply relaxing complete a stay.

522 Boardman Marina Park

Location: On Lake Umatilla, in Boardman
Season: Year-round
Sites: 63 hookup sites, 4 tent sites (open Friday and Saturday nights only); water, electric, and sewer hookups
Maximum length: 80 feet
Facilities: Tables, flush toilets, drinking water, showers, laundry facility, dump station, free wireless, playground, recreation hall, sports field, horseshoe pits, marina, launch, moorage, docks
Fee per night: $$–$$$
Management: Boardman Parks
Contact: (541) 481-7217; (888) 481-7217 for reservations; www.boardmanmarinapark.com/
Finding the campground: Take exit 164 off I-84 at Boardman and head north to reach the park in less than 1 mile.
GPS coordinates: N45 50.728' / W119 42.318'
About the campground: This campground rests on a grassy Columbia River flat, with leafy shade trees and wind fences at the more-open sites. There are both back-in and pull-through spaces; all are paved. Lake Umatilla (the harnessed Columbia River) invites recreation with a designated swimming area and fishing and boating. Stiff winds common to the gorge may fill the sails of sailboats and sailboards. At the day-use area, look for petroglyphs, rescued when the dam was built. Binoculars come in handy, as McNary and Irrigon Wildlife Areas and Umatilla National Wildlife Refuge are all in the vicinity.

523 Cutsforth County Park

Location: 20 miles southeast of Heppner
Season: Late May–mid-Nov
Sites: 36 full or partial hookup sites, 14 basic sites, 2 tent, 2 cabins; water, electric, and sewer hookups
Maximum length: 35 feet
Facilities: Tables, grills, flush and nonflush toilets, drinking water, showers, playground, fishing pond, horse pens, sale of ice and ice cream
Fee per night: $$
Management: Morrow County
Contact: (541) 989-9500, reservations accepted; www.morrowcountyparks.org/
Finding the campground: From OR 207 at the south end of Heppner, turn east onto Willow Creek Road (Blue Mountain Scenic Byway) and go 20 miles. The park is on the right.
GPS coordinates: N45 11.341' / W119 19.375'
About the campground: The primary campground occupies the eastern half of this park. The sites are dispersed through a mixed forest of pine, spruce, fir, and larch. The pond and a day-use area, as well as the dry camp, claim the park's more open western half. The pond is stocked with pan-size trout and is fun for the whole family. In this natural setting, deer, bears, coyotes, muskrats, and raccoons have been spied. Campers should cover and safely store food at night to prevent raccoon raids.

524 Fort Henrietta RV Park

Location: In Echo, about 10 miles southeast of Hermiston
Season: Year-round
Sites: 8 full or partial hookup sites, limited tent camping (check on availability); water, electric, sewer, and cable hookups
Maximum length: 40 feet
Facilities: Some tables, flush toilets, drinking water, showers, dump station, Oregon Trail interpretive panel
Fee per night: $$–$$$
Management: City of Echo
Contact: (541) 376-8411 (city); (541) 571-3597 (onsite camp hosts) for information and reservations; www.echo-oregon.com/fort.html
Finding the campground: Take exit 188 off I-84 and go south on Old Pendleton River Road toward Echo. In 1.1 mile bear right per the trailer emblem, and in another 0.3 mile turn right onto West Main in Echo. Go 0.2 mile to reach the park on the left, before the Umatilla River bridge.
GPS coordinates: N45 44.525' / W119 11.867'
About the campground: Along the Umatilla River at the western edge of Echo, you will find this small, attractive city park and overnight wayside. The park recalls Oregon's past: Pioneers on the Oregon Trail camped and crossed the river here, and this was the site of the frontier post Fort Henrietta. The park's replica blockhouse recalls the old fort.

525 J. B. Burns Park

Location: In Condon
Season: Apr–Oct
Sites: 17 hookup sites, tent camping on grass; water, electric, and sewer hookups
Maximum length: 40 feet
Facilities: Some tables, flush toilets, drinking water, showers, dump station, picnic pavilion, horseshoe pits
Fee per night: $$
Management: Gilliam County
Contact: (541) 384-5395, reservations accepted
Finding the campground: The campground is at Gilliam County Fairgrounds, off OR 19 at the north end of Condon.
GPS coordinates: N45 14.552' / W120 10.856'
About the campground: This campground serves participants and attendees of Gilliam County Fairground events, as well as through-travelers when events are not ongoing. Hookup sites have gravel parking and are typically shadeless, but a few sites edge a grassy area where conifers grow. Tent camping is allowed on a designated lawn. The park is near the Gilliam County Historical Society Museum, which features a restored 1884 log cabin and a complex of early 1900s buildings.

526 Morrow County Off-Highway-Vehicle Park

Location: About 30 miles south of Heppner
Season: Late May–mid-Nov
Sites: 4 full hookup sites, 51 basic sites with water, 6 dry sites, 5 tent sites, 9 cabins, group site areas; water, electric, and sewer hookups
Maximum length: 60 feet or more
Facilities: Tables, fire rings, flush and nonflush toilets, drinking water, showers, cabins, restaurant, trout ponds, helmet rentals
Fee per night: $$–$$$
Management: Morrow County
Contact: (541) 989-9500; www.morrowcountyparks.org
Finding the campground: From Heppner go south on OR 207 about 30 miles. Turn left (east) onto FR 21 at the marked turnoff for the park. The entrance is on the right in about 500 yards.
GPS coordinates: N45 01.461' / W119 40.592'
About the campground: Adjacent to OR 207, this campground is the product of off-highway-vehicle (OHV) fees and the cooperative efforts of Morrow County and the Oregon Department of Parks and Recreation. At a 4,300-foot elevation, the park consists of rolling pine-clad hills covering 9,000 acres and webbed by 320 miles of trail. Ask at the welcome/registration center about purchasing a trail map. The park's track system allows you to match your skill level with the selected route. Quads, dirt bikes, and 4×4s are all welcome. The good-size campsites are arranged in camp clusters radiating from the welcome center. Pines and open grass characterize the camps, with the group sites in an open gravel lot. OHV stickers are required on all off-highway vehicles. No campfires are permitted in the dry season.

527 Port of Arlington Marina and RV Park

Location: In Arlington
Season: Year-round
Sites: 11 RV hookup sites, 20 RV dry sites, tent sites (inquire first to avoid sprinklers); water, electric, and sewer hookups
Maximum length: 40 feet
Facilities: Some aluminum tables, flush toilets, drinking water, boat launch, transient mooring slips, free wireless
Fee per night: $–$$$
Management: Port of Arlington
Contact: (541) 454-2868
Finding the campground: Take exit 137 off I-84; continue north to the waterfront in Arlington.
GPS coordinates: N45 43.376' / W120 12.335'
About the campground: This overnight facility is located on a strip of land between the port channel and the main Columbia River. In addition to the assigned hookup sites, dry camping is allowed at the paved parking lot that overlooks the port channel. The area serves as a convenient, although sometimes noisy, overnight stop and puts boaters and anglers smack in the middle of the Columbia River action.

528 Sand Station Recreation Area

Location: About 12 miles east of Umatilla
Season: Year-round
Sites: 5 basic sites, 10 walk-in tent sites; no hookups
Maximum length: 40 feet
Facilities: Covered tables at basic sites, tables and barbecues at tent sites, nonflush toilets; no drinking water
Fee per night: None
Management: US Army Corps of Engineers
Contact: (541) 922-2268; www.nww.usace.army.mil/
Finding the campground: From the intersection of I-82 and US 730 in Umatilla, go east on US 730 for 11.5 miles. The campground is on the left.
GPS coordinates: N45 55.320' / W119 07.173'
About the campground: This small, dry camp sits on the shore of Lake Wallula. A few black locust trees provide modest but treasured shade on this otherwise sun-drenched flat. Cross-lake views are of the steppes and tablelands of Washington State. A designated swimming area and fishing keep camp guests entertained. Truck travel on US 730 can break the calm at night.

529 Sherman County RV Park

Location: In Moro
Season: Year-round
Sites: 33 hookup sites, tent camping area; water, electric, and sewer hookups
Maximum length: 40 feet
Facilities: Tables, barbecues, flush toilets, drinking water, showers, laundry, dump station, playground, horse stalls
Fee per night: $-$$
Management: Sherman County
Contact: (541) 565-3127 for information and reservations; www.sherman-county.com/
Finding the campground: From US 97 in Moro, turn east onto First Street. Continue 0.8 mile to this RV park at the Sherman County Fairgrounds.
GPS coordinates: N45 28.698' / W120 43.054'
About the campground: This campground occupies an open plateau next to the Sherman County Fairgrounds and serves fairground participants and through-travelers. Wheat fields spread in all directions; views feature Mounts Hood and Adams. Sites have grassy divides with young planted trees but no shade yet. Wind, a signature of the Columbia Plateau, is common here, so hold onto your paper plates. The county historical museum in town (open May through October) may invite a look.

530 Umatilla Marina and RV Park

Location: On Lake Umatilla, in Umatilla
Season: Year-round
Sites: 26 hookup sites, 9 tent sites; water, electric, and sewer hookups
Maximum length: 60 feet
Facilities: Tables, flush toilets, drinking water, showers, dump station, covered shelters, boat launch
Fee per night: $$–$$$
Management: Umatilla Marina
Contact: (541) 922-3939; www.umatillarvpark.com
Finding the campground: From the intersection of I-82 and US 730, go west on US 730 for less than 0.1 mile. Turn right onto Brownell Boulevard and go 0.3 mile. Turn left onto Third Street; continue 0.3 mile before turning right onto Quincy Avenue to enter the park.
GPS coordinates: N45 55.458' / W119 19.920'
About the campground: This is a split-level facility, with the marina and day-use area fronting the river and the campground on the upper plateau. The campground is landscaped, with lawn and planted shade trees that are starting to fill out. Sites have gravel parking and a nice spacing. Superb fishing and boating on the Columbia River (here, Lake Umatilla) attract park guests. In the day-use area, you will find a designated swimming area; elsewhere trails lead to McNary Nature Trail and McNary National Wildlife Refuge.

531 Willow Creek

Location: About 1 mile southeast of Heppner
Season: Mar–Oct
Sites: 9 full and 14 partial hookup sites (manager will try to accommodate tent campers); water, electric, and sewer hookups
Maximum length: 40 feet
Facilities: Some tables, flush toilets, drinking water, showers, dump station, boat launch
Fee per night: $$
Management: City of Heppner
Contact: (541) 676-5576, reservations accepted; www.heppner.net/wcpd
Finding the campground: From OR 207 at the south end of Heppner, turn east onto Willow Creek Road (Blue Mountain Scenic Byway). Go 0.6 mile to this park on the left.
GPS coordinates: N45 20.648' / W119 33.001'
About the campground: Near the dam, this campground terraces an open, grassy slope above Willow Creek Lake. The facility has paved roads and site parking and small, planted trees. Awnings make for more comfortable stays. The openness allows for views of the lake and its rimming grassland hills and folded terrain. The lake supports trout, crappie, and bass. Besides anglers in fishing boats, you may see water-skiers on the reservoir.

	Hookup Sites	Total Sites	Max. RV Length	Hookups	Toilets	Showers	Drinking Water	Dump Station	Recreation	Fee	Can Reserve
532 Emigrant Springs State Park	20	58	60	WES	F	X	X		HR	$$-$$$	X
533 Harris Memorial Park: Gene Palmer	26	31	40	WE	F		X		HFO	$$-$$$	X
534 Jubilee Lake		53	40		F, NF		X		HFBL	$$	
535 Target Meadows		18	20		NF		X		H	$$	
536 Umatilla Forks		12	30		NF		X		HF	$$	
537 Woodland		6	30		NF					$	
538 Woodward		15	20		NF		X			$$	

532 Emigrant Springs State Park

Location: About 26 miles southeast of Pendleton
Season: Apr–late Oct (water generally available mid-Apr–mid-Oct)
Sites: 20 hookup sites, 32 basic sites, 6 horse campsites, 8 cabins; water, electric, and sewer hookups
Maximum length: 60 feet
Facilities: Tables, grills, flush toilets, drinking water, showers, community building, corrals at horse sites, Oregon Trail exhibit
Fee per night: $$–$$$
Management: Oregon State Parks and Recreation Department
Contact: (541) 983-2277; (800) 452-5687 for reservations; www.oregon.gov/OPRD/PARKS/camping.shtml
Finding the campground: From I-84, 25 miles southeast of Pendleton, take exit 234 for the state park. Follow the signs to the park, on the west side of the freeway in less than 1 mile.
GPS coordinates: N45 32.420' / W118 27.698'
About the campground: This campground rests in a deep woods setting of fir and spruce just off the interstate and along the historic Oregon Trail. On a wooded rise at the north end of the park, the horse camp is isolated from both the family campground and the day-use area. Horse trails and nature trails invite exploration. Historically, travelers on the Oregon Trail camped here, filling their barrels at a spring. South of the park, at the Spring Creek exit, you will find another Oregon Trail site, the forest service's Blue Mountain Crossing interpretive site and trail, where you can see actual ruts left by the pioneer wagons.

533 Harris Memorial Park: Gene Palmer

Location: About 13 miles southeast of Milton-Freewater
Season: Mar–Nov, dependent on weather
Sites: 26 hookup sites, 5 tent sites; water and electric hookups
Maximum length: 40 feet
Facilities: Tables, grills, flush toilets, drinking water; picnic shelter, playground, and horseshoe pits at day-use area
Fee per night: $$–$$$
Management: Umatilla County
Contact: (541) 938-5330, reservations accepted; www.co.umatilla.or.us/harris_park.htm
Finding the campground: At the south end of Milton-Freewater, turn east off OR 11 (South Main Street) onto 14th Street, signed for Harris County Park and Upper Walla Walla River. Signs will then point you through a couple of quick turns before the road becomes Walla Walla River Road, leaving town. After 5 miles bear right onto South Fork Walla Walla River Road and proceed 7.3 miles more to the park. The final 2 miles are on gravel.
GPS coordinates: N45 50.153' / W118 10.875'
About the campground: This comfortable county campground with two camping areas sits along the South Fork Walla Walla River below a basalt-tiered, arid grassland hill. You may choose between the side-by-side hookup sites along a neatly trimmed lawn or the individual hookup sites (with paved spurs) in the pine-scrub outskirts. Driving 0.4 mile past the camp, you will reach a trailhead for the South Fork Walla Walla River Trail, which dishes up a splendid river canyon tour. This trail is open to both nonmotorized and motorcycle travel.

534 Jubilee Lake

Location: About 11 miles north of Tollgate
Season: Early July–early Sept
Sites: 48 basic sites, 5 tent sites; no hookups
Maximum length: 40 feet
Facilities: Tables, grills, flush and nonflush toilets, drinking water, boat launch
Fee per night: $$
Management: Umatilla National Forest—Walla Walla Ranger District
Contact: (509) 522-6290; www.fs.usda.gov/recmain/umatilla/recreation
Finding the campground: In Tollgate (20.2 miles east of Weston and 21.8 miles west of Elgin), turn north off OR 204 onto gravel FR 64, signed for Target Meadows Campground and Jubilee Lake. Go 11 miles and turn right on FR 250 to enter the campground.
GPS coordinates: N45 49.819' / W117 58.002'
About the campground: Man-made Jubilee Lake sits in a beautiful mountain setting. It welcomes boating (self-propelled or electric motor) and is stocked with trout. Sites claim the high-elevation forest above the lake; some are better suited for RVs than others. Most enjoy good privacy. A 2.5-mile trail, partially paved, encircles the lake, allowing for new perspectives and access for shore fishing. For more-avid hikers, the Wenaha-Tucannon Wilderness lies to the lake's northeast.

535 Target Meadows

Location: About 3 miles north of Tollgate
Season: Early July–early Sept
Sites: 16 basic sites, 2 tent sites; no hookups
Maximum length: 20 feet
Facilities: Tables, grills, nonflush toilets, drinking water
Fee per night: $$
Management: Umatilla National Forest—Walla Walla Ranger District
Contact: (509) 522-6290; www.fs.usda.gov/recmain/umatilla/recreation
Finding the campground: In Tollgate (20.2 miles east of Weston and 21.8 miles west of Elgin), turn north off OR 204 onto gravel FR 64, signed for Target Meadows Campground and Jubilee Lake. Go 0.3 mile and turn left onto FR 6401. Continue 1.5 miles; turn right onto FR 050 to enter campground in 0.5 mile.
GPS coordinates: N45 48.343' / W118 04.629'
About the campground: This quiet campground occupies the spruce and true fir perimeter of Target Meadows, a moist, textured meadow expanse that is especially pretty when the stalks of false hellebore sport creamy floral crowns. Burnt Cabin Trailhead is found at the end of FR 050; the trail from there leads to the South Fork Walla Walla River. From the 1800s to 1906, Target Meadows was used as a US Army firing range; mounds in the area still hold cavalry bullets.

536 Umatilla Forks

Location: About 35 miles east of Pendleton
Season: Mid-May–mid-Oct
Sites: 6 basic sites, 6 tent sites; no hookups
Maximum length: 30 feet
Facilities: Tables, grills, nonflush toilets, drinking water
Fee per night: $$
Management: Umatilla National Forest—Walla Walla Ranger District
Contact: (509) 522-6290; www.fs.usda.gov/recmain/umatilla/recreation
Finding the campground: From Mission Junction, 2 miles north of I-84 at exit 216, east of Pendleton, head east on Mission Road. At the intersections, follow the route signed for Gibbon, continuing northeast along the Umatilla River for 27 miles to reach the Umatilla Forks Campground on FR 32.
GPS coordinates: N45 43.596' / W118 11.180'
About the campground: Along the South Fork Umatilla River above the North Fork confluence, this linear campground, with a separate tent area, stretches below bald hills and long grassy ridges. A few pines and firs shade the sites, while cottonwoods and alders favor the riverbank. The camp offers quiet and access to trails for hiking and horseback riding; several enter the North Fork Umatilla Wilderness. Wildflowers abound, and wildlife sightings are common. Hunting, fishing, and trail bike riding (on trails outside the wilderness) are other area pursuits.

537 Woodland

Location: About 5 miles southeast of Tollgate, 17 miles northwest of Elgin
Season: Early July–early Sept
Sites: 6 basic sites; no hookups
Maximum length: 30 feet
Facilities: Tables, grills, nonflush toilets; no drinking water
Fee per night: $
Management: Umatilla National Forest–Walla Walla Ranger District
Contact: (509) 522-6290; www.fs.usda.gov/recmain/umatilla/recreation
Finding the campground: The campground is east off OR 204, 16.5 miles northwest of Elgin and 5.2 miles southeast of Tollgate.
GPS coordinates: N45 43.994' / W118 01.795'
About the campground: With a single pull-through site for larger RVs, this small campground occupies a ridge forest of spruce, lodgepole pine, and western larch. Campers may choose between deep shade and partially sunny sites. The camp is convenient for travelers, relatively quiet, and serves as a base for hunters. Umatilla Breaks Viewpoint is not far from the camp.

538 Woodward

Location: West end of Tollgate
Season: Early July–early Sept
Sites: 15 basic sites; no hookups
Maximum length: 20 feet
Facilities: Tables, grills, nonflush toilets, drinking water, picnic shelter
Fee per night: $$
Management: Umatilla National Forest–Walla Walla Ranger District
Contact: (509) 522-6290; www.fs.usda.gov/recmain/umatilla/recreation
Finding the campground: On the west side of Tollgate, this campground is south off OR 204 on FR 020. Find the turn 20 miles east of Weston, 22 miles west of Elgin.
GPS coordinates: N45 46.675' / W118 05.941'
About the campground: This forested campground sits on the west shore of marshy ringed Langdon Lake, which is private. Although the lake can be admired from camp, there is no access. Camasses favor the moist shore, and grasses grade to the open water. Lichens drape the true firs and spruce.

Enterprise Area

	Hookup Sites	Total Sites	Max. RV Length	Hookups	Toilets	Showers	Drinking Water	Dump Station	Recreation	Fee	Can Reserve
539 Boundary		8	T		NF				HF	None	
540 Coyote		29	20		NF					None	
541 Dougherty		8	T		NF					None	
542 Hurricane Creek		13	T		NF				HF	$	
543 The Lions Park		Open	40		NF		X	X		Donation	
544 Minam State Park		12	70		NF		X		FBL	$	
545 Shady		12	25		NF				HF	$	
546 Two Pan		10	T		NF				HFR	$	
547 Vigne		6	18		NF					$	
548 Wallowa Lake State Recreation Area	121	210	90	WES	F	X	X	X	HSFBLR	$$–$$$	X
549 Williamson		9	40		NF				HF	$	

539 Boundary

Location: About 8 miles south of Wallowa
Season: June–Oct
Sites: 8 tent sites; no hookups
Maximum length: Suitable for tents only
Facilities: Tables, grills, nonflush toilets; no drinking water
Fee per night: None
Management: Wallowa-Whitman National Forest
Contact: (541) 426-4978; www.fs.usda.gov/recmain/wallowa-whitman/recreation
Finding the campground: From OR 82 in Wallowa, head southwest for 0.3 mile on West First Street. Turn left at Bear Creek Road/FR 8250, which begins paved and changes to gravel, following it for 7.1 miles. Bear right onto FR 8250.040 to pass through the campground in 0.7 mile.
GPS coordinates: N45 28.367' / W117 33.488'
About the campground: This rustic campground straddles the end of FR 8250.040, just before the Bear Creek Trailhead. Many of the sites line the shore of Bear Creek; most are fully shaded by the mature fir-spruce forest. While there are gravel parking pads, the narrowness of the road and the restricted mobility in the canyon make these sites better suited for tents. Bear Creek courses beautiful and clear; its parallel trail offers a fine introduction to Wallowa-Whitman National Forest and the Eagle Cap Wilderness.

Deer, Wallowa County

540 Coyote

Location: About 41 miles northeast of Enterprise
Season: June–Oct
Sites: 8 basic sites, 21 tent sites; no hookups
Maximum length: 20 feet
Facilities: Most sites with tables and grills, nonflush toilets; no drinking water
Fee per night: None
Management: Wallowa-Whitman National Forest
Contact: (541) 426-4978; www.fs.usda.gov/recmain/wallowa-whitman/recreation
Finding the campground: From Enterprise take OR 3 (Northwest First Street in town) north at the sign for Flora and Lewiston. Go 14.7 miles and turn right onto FR 46/Wellamotkin Drive, which begins paved and becomes gravel. A sign at the turn indicates Starvation and Davis Creeks. Continue 26.3 miles and turn left onto FR 4650 at a sign for the campground. Sites are on the right, 0.1 mile ahead. *NOTE:* Be alert for free-ranging cattle along FR 46.
GPS coordinates: N45 50.543' / W117 06.788'
About the campground: This campground in the "boonies" has a blended habitat of open grassland and conifer groves; the sites are well scattered for privacy. Generally, though, your camp companions tend to be wildlife, not humans. Bring water for drinking and cooking. Red Hill Lookout, passed en route to camp, offers vistas out to the Peavine and Joseph Creek drainages. Fall hunting season brings more faces to camp.

541 Dougherty

Location: About 47 miles northeast of Enterprise
Season: June–Oct
Sites: 8 tent sites; no hookups
Maximum length: Small units; best suited for tents
Facilities: Some tables and fire rings, nonflush toilets; no drinking water
Fee per night: None
Management: Wallowa-Whitman National Forest
Contact: (541) 426-4978; www.fs.usda.gov/recmain/wallowa-whitman/recreation
Finding the campground: From Enterprise take OR 3 (Northwest First Street in town) north at the sign for Flora and Lewiston. Go 14.7 miles and turn right on FR 46/Wellamotkin Drive, which begins paved and becomes gravel. A sign at the turn indicates Starvation and Davis Creeks. Continue 32.3 miles to enter this campground on the left. *NOTE:* Be alert for free-ranging cattle along FR 46.
GPS coordinates: N45 51.147' / W117 01.900'
About the campground: Near Dougherty Spring, this primitive outpost is a great place for solitude, reflection, and nature study. In fall it attracts hunting parties. The undeveloped sites dot a broad plateau of open meadow and clustered conifers. Wildflowers sprinkle color through the meadow.

542 Hurricane Creek

Location: About 6 miles south of Enterprise, 4 miles southwest of Joseph
Season: June–Oct
Sites: 8 basic, 5 tent sites; no hookups
Maximum length: Best suited for tents
Facilities: Some tables, grills or fire rings, nonflush toilets; no drinking water
Fee per night: $
Management: Wallowa-Whitman National Forest
Contact: (541) 426-4978; www.fs.usda.gov/recmain/wallowa-whitman/recreation
Finding the campground: From Joseph turn west off OR 82 onto West Wallowa Avenue at the sign for the airport and Hurricane Creek; this road later becomes Airport Lane. Go 2.1 miles, meeting Hurricane Creek Road at the curve. Turn left onto Hurricane Creek Road and go 1.8 miles to reach the campground. (Bearing right on Hurricane Creek Road leads to Enterprise.)
GPS coordinates: N45 19.997' / W117 17.893'
About the campground: This camp overlooks the impressive waters of Hurricane Creek, a racing Wallowa Mountain waterway. The sites are fully forested, snuggled among the Douglas and true firs, maples, and shrubs. The limited turnaround and narrow, rock-studded road through camp better serve campers with tents or small units with good clearance. Upstream on Hurricane Creek Road/FR 8250, you will find the trailhead for Hurricane Creek Trail and Eagle Cap Wilderness.

543 The Lions Park

Location: In the city of Wallowa
Season: May–Oct
Sites: Open camping area; no hookups
Maximum length: 40 feet
Facilities: Few tables and grills, nonflush toilets, drinking water, dump station
Fee per night: Donation
Management: The Lions Club
Contact: (541) 886-3027
Finding the campground: From OR 82 at the west end of Wallowa, turn north onto the Truck Route; proceed 0.1 mile to this park on the left.
GPS coordinates: N45 34.628' / W117 32.142'
About the campground: An open lawn and a few dotting pines shape the scene at this convenient travelers' wayside. Willows and cottonwoods edge the camp. The Wallowa County Museum may suggest an outing; among its collection are Nez Perce artifacts. The Wallowa Mountains region is noted for its outdoor recreation.

544 Minam State Park

Location: At Minam, about 13 miles west of Wallowa
Season: Apr–early Oct
Sites: 12 basic sites; no hookups
Maximum length: 70 feet
Facilities: Tables, grills, nonflush toilets, drinking water, raft put-in (below the bridge)
Fee per night: $
Management: Oregon State Parks and Recreation Department
Contact: (800) 551-6949; www.oregon.gov/OPRD/PARKS/camping.shtml
Finding the campground: From OR 82, 15 miles east of Elgin and 13.4 miles west of Wallowa, turn north at the sign for the state park. Follow the gravel road downstream 1.6 miles to the campground.
GPS coordinates: N45 38.244' / W117 43.719'
About the campground: This canyon campground occupies a flat above the Wallowa River, downstream from the Minam-Wallowa confluence. It offers groomed lawns, with paved roads and parking. Big ponderosa pines and smaller firs spot shade across the park grounds. A fuller wooded slope rises at the back of the camp, while cross-river views feature a steep canyon wall topped by a basalt crest. A foot trail and abandoned jeep trail downstream from the camp provide fishing access. Rafting and spring and fall steelhead fishing are popular.

545 Shady

Location: About 17 miles south of Lostine
Season: June–Oct
Sites: 12 basic sites; no hookups
Maximum length: 25 feet
Facilities: Tables, grills, nonflush toilets; no drinking water
Fee per night: $
Management: Wallowa-Whitman National Forest
Contact: (541) 426-4978; www.fs.usda.gov/recmain/wallowa-whitman/recreation
Finding the campground: From OR 82 at Lostine, go south on Lostine River Road/FR 8210 toward the Lostine River Campgrounds. The road begins paved and becomes gravel, with areas of heavy washboard. The campground is on the right in 16.6 miles.
GPS coordinates: N45 15.481' / W117 22.993'
About the campground: This campground pairs up with the sparkling beauty of the Lostine Wild and Scenic River and trails leading into the Eagle Cap Wilderness. Outfitters operate along FR 8210 for anyone wanting to get well into the Wallowa Mountains backcountry. Lakes, meadows, pristine streams, alpine forests, and wildlife await. If relaxing at camp is more to your liking, this campground merits a look with its song of the river and conifer shade.

546 Two Pan

Location: About 17 miles south of Lostine
Season: June–Oct
Sites: 5 horse campsites, 5 walk-in tent sites; no hookups
Maximum length: Small units; best suited for tents
Facilities: Tables, grills, nonflush toilets, stock loading ramp, stock watering trough, hitching rails; no drinking water
Fee per night: $
Management: Wallowa-Whitman National Forest
Contact: (541) 426-4978; www.fs.usda.gov/recmain/wallowa-whitman/recreation
Finding the campground: From OR 82 at Lostine, go south on Lostine River Road/FR 8210 toward the Lostine River Campgrounds. The road begins paved and becomes gravel, with sometimes heavy washboard. Reach the Two Pan campgrounds and trailhead at road's end in 17.3 miles.
GPS coordinates: N45 15.038' / W117 22.610'
About the campground: This small, rustic campground in fir-spruce forest offers tent camping in the periphery of the trailhead parking lot and has a separate horse camping area on the left as you arrive at this popular gateway to Eagle Cap Wilderness. Trails from camp follow the east and west forks of the Lostine River upstream into the high-mountain splendor, with Minam Lake, the Wallowa Lakes Basin, and the Minam River as possible destinations. Besides hiking, fishing is popular.

547 Vigne

Location: About 40 miles northeast of Enterprise
Season: June–Oct
Sites: 6 basic sites; no hookups
Maximum length: 18 feet
Facilities: Tables, grills, nonflush toilets; no drinking water
Fee per night: $
Management: Wallowa-Whitman National Forest
Contact: (541) 426-4978; www.fs.usda.gov/recmain/wallowa-whitman/recreation
Finding the campground: From Enterprise take OR 3 (Northwest First Street in town) north at the sign for Flora and Lewiston. Go 14.7 miles and turn right onto FR 46/Wellamotkin Drive, which begins paved and becomes gravel. Continue 13.7 miles; turn right onto narrow, paved, sometimes rough FR 4625 and proceed 11.3 miles to enter the campground on the right. The final 1.5 miles is on gravel. *NOTE:* Entry to the campground requires a difficult right-hook turn.
GPS coordinates: N45 44.742' / W117 01.318'
About the campground: This lightly used rustic campground occupies a corridor of pine, fir, and shrubs along Chesnimnus Creek, a small, shallow creek threading through a pretty canyon. Sites have dirt parking, and the road through camp is dirt. A turnaround loop helps ease access to and from the sites.

548 Wallowa Lake State Recreation Area

Location: On Wallowa Lake, about 6 miles south of Joseph
Season: Mid-Apr–late Oct; 10 sites (no water) and yurts open year-round
Sites: 121 hookup sites, 89 basic sites, 2 yurts; water, electric, and sewer hookups
Maximum length: 90 feet
Facilities: Tables, flush toilets, drinking water, showers, dump station, marina, launch, moorage, picnic shelters
Fee per night: $$–$$$
Management: Oregon State Parks and Recreation Department
Contact: (541) 432-4185; (800) 452-5687 for reservations; www.oregon.gov/OPRD/PARKS/camping.shtml
Finding the campground: From Joseph drive 6 miles south on OR 82. Bear right at the fork to reach the state park campground.
GPS coordinates: N45 16.813' / W117 12.770'
About the campground: This popular campground sits on the south shore of Wallowa Lake, a large glacial moraine lake watched over by snowy peaks. In a lawn-and-forest setting, the camp offers comfortable, developed sites within footsteps of the oval lake, its recreation, and prized trails into the Eagle Cap Wilderness. Nearby attractions include Chief Joseph's grave, the steepest vertical-lift gondola in North America (Wallowa Lake Tramway), horse concessions for trail rides, and Wallowa Loop Scenic Drive.

549 Williamson

Location: About 11 miles south of Lostine
Season: June–Oct
Sites: 9 basic sites; no hookups
Maximum length: 40 feet
Facilities: Tables, grills, nonflush toilets; no drinking water
Fee per night: $
Management: Wallowa-Whitman National Forest
Contact: (541) 426-4978; www.fs.usda.gov/recmain/wallowa-whitman/recreation
Finding the campground: From OR 82 at Lostine, go south on Lostine River Road/FR 8210 toward the Lostine River Campgrounds. The road begins paved and becomes gravel, with areas of heavy washboard. The campground is on the right in 10.8 miles.
GPS coordinates: N45 20.587' / W117 24.796'
About the campground: This campground occupies a wooded slope above the Lostine Wild and Scenic River, one of the prized waterways of the region and the state. Lodgepole pine, fir, and larch create partial shade; the parking spaces are leveled and graveled. Fishing and hiking amuse visitors, with area packers offering an easier way into the wilderness. Dispersed sites and forest camps can be found along FR 8210 for additional camping options.

La Grande Area

	Hookup Sites	Total Sites	Max. RV Length	Hookups	Toilets	Showers	Drinking Water	Dump Station	Recreation	Fee	Can Reserve
550 Birdtrack Springs		22	40		NF				F	$	
551 Catherine Creek State Park		20	50		F	X			F	$	
552 Hilgard Junction State Park		17	30		F	X			FBL	$	
553 Moss Springs		8	25		NF				HR	$	
554 North Fork Catherine Creek		7	Small		NF				HFR	None	
555 Red Bridge State Park		20	40		F	X			F	$	
556 Spool Cart		12	40		NF				F	$	
557 Spring Creek		4	35		NF					None	
558 Umapine		8	None		NF				0	None	

550 Birdtrack Springs

Location: About 15 miles west of La Grande, 42 miles east of Ukiah

Season: May–mid-Nov, dependent on weather

Sites: 22 basic sites; no hookups

Maximum length: 40 feet

Facilities: Tables, grills, nonflush toilets; no drinking water

Fee per night: $

Management: Wallowa-Whitman National Forest

Contact: (541) 963-7186; www.fs.usda.gov/recmain/wallowa-whitman/recreation

Finding the campground: From I-84 north of La Grande, take exit 252 and go 5.4 miles west on OR 244. The campground is on the left.

GPS coordinates: N45 17.983' / W118 18.416'

About the campground: This campground enjoys a peaceful setting of tall ponderosa pines, firs, and larches. Wild rose, grass, and currant contribute to the forest carpet. The sites are well spaced, with gravel parking. Songbirds complement a stay. At the camp's western edge, a rail fence surrounds the namesake natural spring. Although it can supply water when it tests pure, play it safe and bring what you will need. Across OR 244, visitors can access the Grande Ronde River for fishing.

551 Catherine Creek State Park

Location: 8 miles southeast of Union
Season: Mid-Apr–mid-Oct
Sites: 20 basic sites; no hookups
Maximum length: 50 feet
Facilities: Tables, grills, flush toilets, drinking water
Fee per night: $
Management: Oregon Department of Parks and Recreation
Contact: (800) 551-6949; www.oregon.gov/OPRD/PARKS/camping.shtml
Finding the campground: From Union go 8 miles southeast on OR 203 to this state park on the right.
GPS coordinates: N45 09.147' / W117 44.461'
About the campground: This state park picnic area and campground sit along a 0.5-mile stretch of broad, smooth-flowing Catherine Creek. Planted deciduous and native ponderosa pine trees shade the lawns, while cottonwoods tower above the creek. Despite its proximity to OR 203, the location exudes tranquility. Visitors can fish, cool their ankles, or seek out area trails into Wallowa-Whitman National Forest and the Eagle Cap Wilderness.

552 Hilgard Junction State Park

Location: About 10 miles west of La Grande
Season: Mid-Apr–mid-Oct
Sites: 17 basic sites; no hookups
Maximum length: 30 feet
Facilities: Tables, grills, flush toilets, drinking water, horseshoe pits, rafting access
Fee per night: $
Management: Oregon State Parks and Recreation Department
Contact: (800) 551-6949; www.oregon.gov/OPRD/PARKS/camping.shtml
Finding the campground: From I-84 north of La Grande, take exit 252 and follow the signs to the park. It is on the west side of the freeway off OR 244.
GPS coordinates: N45 20.455' / W118 14.061'
About the campground: This campground occupies a narrow strip between I-84 and the Grande Ronde River. It is a pretty spot but can be noisy when large trucks tackle the interstate grade. Usually, though, the river wins out. Cottonwoods shade the dandelion-sprinkled lawn, and a forested slope rises across from camp. This is an Oregon Trail site, and to its northwest off I-84 is Blue Mountain Crossing, a forest service interpretive site and trail, where historic wagon ruts can be seen. Fishing and rafting are popular river activities.

553 Moss Springs

Location: About 8 miles east of Cove
Season: June–Oct
Sites: 8 basic sites; no hookups
Maximum length: 25 feet
Facilities: Tables, grills, nonflush toilets, corrals, horse-loading ramp; no drinking water
Fee per night: $
Management: Wallowa-Whitman National Forest
Contact: (541) 963-7186; www.fs.usda.gov/recmain/wallowa-whitman/recreation
Finding the campground: From OR 237 in Cove, turn east onto French Street (opposite the high school) toward Moss Springs Campground. French Street then bends into Mill Creek Lane, which later becomes FR 6220. Follow these paved and gravel routes for 8.4 miles to the campground. FR 6220 can be steep and narrow.
GPS coordinates: N45 16.511' / W117 40.750'
About the campground: This campground occupies a forested rim at a popular hiker and equestrian gateway to the Eagle Cap Wilderness. The sites are well spaced, comfortable, and well used, especially during hunting season. Horse Ranch Trail descends from this Wallowa Mountain plateau, passing through a historic horse ranch at the bottom of the canyon, to meet the pristine Minam River and its trail to discovery. If you visit the ranch area, travel lightly, and pitch backpack and horse camps well away from this fragile historical resource. The terrain resembles Hells Canyon as much as the Wallowa high country: View basalt-tiered grassland rims and rocky summits.

554 North Fork Catherine Creek

Location: About 17 miles southeast of Union
Season: June–Oct
Sites: 7 basic sites; no hookups
Maximum length: Best suited for tents or pickup campers
Facilities: Tables, fire rings, nonflush toilets, horse-loading ramp; no drinking water
Fee per night: None
Management: Wallowa-Whitman National Forest
Contact: (541) 963-7186; www.fs.usda.gov/recmain/wallowa-whitman/recreation
Finding the campground: From Union go 11 miles southeast on OR 203. Turn left (east) onto Catherine Creek Lane/FR 7785, a single-lane road. The trailhead and its parking are at road's end in 5.7 miles. The campsites dot the sides of FR 7785 for 1 mile, leading up to the trailhead.
GPS coordinates: N45 09.179' / W117 36.993'
About the campground: The sites extend a quiet, no-frills getaway and offer access to Eagle Cap Wilderness. Mature conifers lend shade, while wildflowers decorate the grasses. North Fork Catherine Creek races black and satiny between shrub-lined banks. From the trailhead the North Fork Catherine Creek Trail heads across a creek bridge and upcanyon to visit engaging high meadows and enter the wilderness.

555 Red Bridge State Park

Location: About 16 miles west of La Grande
Season: Mid-Apr–mid-Oct
Sites: 10 basic sites, 10 walk-in tent sites; no hookups
Maximum length: 40 feet
Facilities: Tables, grills, flush toilets, drinking water, horseshoe pits
Fee per night: $
Management: Oregon State Parks and Recreation Department
Contact: (800) 551-6949; www.oregon.gov/OPRD/PARKS/camping.shtml
Finding the campground: From I-84 north of La Grande, take exit 252 and go 7.3 miles west on OR 244. The park is on the left. There's a fee station at the parking area.
GPS coordinates: N45 17.452' / W118 19.925'
About the campground: At this Grande Ronde River park, RVers can dry-camp in the designated spaces. Tent campers are welcome to walk in and pitch their tents along the grassy, pine-clad river bench at the park's east end. Ponderosa pines create a scenic, shady rest, while red osier dogwoods grow toward shore. Fishing is the pastime.

556 Spool Cart

Location: About 25 miles southwest of La Grande
Season: May–mid-Nov, dependent on weather
Sites: 12 basic sites; no hookups
Maximum length: 40 feet
Facilities: Tables, grills, nonflush toilets; no drinking water
Fee per night: $
Management: Wallowa-Whitman National Forest
Contact: (541) 963-7186; www.fs.usda.gov/recmain/wallowa-whitman/recreation
Finding the campground: From I-84 north of La Grande, take exit 252 and go 11.7 miles west on OR 244. (If following OR 244 from Ukiah, go 35 miles east.) Turn south onto Grande Ronde Road/FR 51, crossing the bridge over the river, and go 4.5 miles. The campground is on the right.
GPS coordinates: N45 12.150' / W118 23.684'
About the campground: At this Grande Ronde River campground, large, extra-wide paved parking spaces help get you settled. The camp claims a relaxing spot on the river for reverie or fishing. The sites are fully or partially shaded by a forest of ponderosa pine, fir, larch, and spruce.

557 Spring Creek

Location: About 14 miles northwest of La Grande
Season: May–mid-Nov, dependent on weather
Sites: 4 basic sites; no hookups
Maximum length: 35 feet
Facilities: Tables, grills, nonflush toilets; no drinking water
Fee per night: None
Management: Wallowa-Whitman National Forest
Contact: (541) 963-7186; www.fs.usda.gov/recmain/wallowa-whitman/recreation
Finding the campground: From I-84, 13 miles north of La Grande, take exit 248 for Spring Creek Road/FR 21. Continue west 1.4 miles to the campground on the right.
GPS coordinates: N45 21.549' / W118 18.678'
About the campground: Conveniently located off I-84 near an Oregon Trail interpretive site, this campground occupies an attractive meadow-and-forest setting. Sites are relatively level and radiate off the campground loop road. The surrounding area is a winter range for elk (December–April), as well as a woodpecker nesting area; keep an eye on the ponderosa pines for clues. Bats too can be seen. The Oregon Trail site is reached by heading 3 miles north from the exit, following signs. A lovely carved entrance sign welcomes you.

558 Umapine

Location: About 39 miles southwest of La Grande
Season: May–Oct
Sites: 5 basic sites, 3 group sites; no hookups
Maximum length: None
Facilities: Tables, grills, nonflush toilets; no drinking water
Fee per night: None
Management: Wallowa-Whitman National Forest
Contact: (541) 963-7186; www.fs.usda.gov/recmain/wallowa-whitman/recreation
Finding the campground: From I-84 at Hilgard Junction, 9 miles west of La Grande, head west on OR 244 for about 22 miles. Turn south onto gravel FR 5160, following it 8 miles to the marked campground turnoff.
GPS coordinates: N45 06.927' / W118 33.734'
About the campground: This camp caters to the needs of off-highway-vehicle and dirt bike enthusiasts, with trails knitted through the surrounding Winom-Frazier area. The camp is mostly open, with a few small western larch trees. A shade source will make your time in camp more comfortable.

Ukiah Area

	Hookup Sites	Total Sites	Max. RV Length	Hookups	Toilets	Showers	Drinking Water	Dump Station	Recreation	Fee	Can Reserve
559 Bear Wallow		8	20		NF				H	$	
560 Divide Well		11	40		NF					None	
561 Drift Fence		6	40		NF					None	
562 Driftwood		6	Small		NF				FB	None	
563 Frazier		20	40		NF				O	$$	
564 Gold Dredge		7	20		NF				F	None	
565 Lane Creek		7	40		NF				F	$	
566 Tollbridge		5	25		NF				F	$	
567 Ukiah–Dale Forest State Scenic Corridor		27	40		F		X		F	$	
568 Welch Creek		6	30		NF				F	$	
569 Winom Creek (Off-Highway-Vehicle) Campground		9	40		NF				FO	$	

559 Bear Wallow

Location: 11 miles east of Ukiah
Season: Late May–mid-Nov
Sites: 8 basic sites; no hookups
Maximum length: 20 feet
Facilities: Tables, grills, nonflush toilets; no drinking water
Fee per night: $
Management: Umatilla National Forest
Contact: (541) 427-3231; www.fs.usda.gov/recmain/umatilla/recreation
Finding the campground: From Ukiah go east on OR 244 for 11 miles; turn north to enter the campground.
GPS coordinates: N45 15.784' / W118 45.223'
About the campground: This campground rests at the foot of a slope of ponderosa pines where Bear Wallow Creek supplies a pleasant backdrop murmur. The slope holds many of the big red-trunked pines, with a few right in camp. The barrier-free Bear Wallow Creek Interpretive Trail leads you through the streamside habitat, where interpretive panels describe how the creek is managed for steelhead. Big larches, false hellebore bogs, and wildflowers add to the trail's discovery.

560 Divide Well

Location: About 24 miles west of Ukiah
Season: Late May–mid-Nov
Sites: 11 basic sites; no hookups
Maximum length: 40 feet
Facilities: Tables, crude fire rings, nonflush toilets; no drinking water
Fee per night: None
Management: Umatilla National Forest
Contact: (541) 427-3231; www.fs.usda.gov/recmain/umatilla/recreation
Finding the campground: From US 395 near Ukiah, go west on FR 53 for about 14 miles to Four Corners. Turn left onto FR 5327; continue southeast about 9 miles to the campground. Expect some heavy washboard.
GPS coordinates: N45 06.185' / W119 08.569'
About the campground: This rustic camp offers a peaceful retreat among the pines and firs, while the large flat gives horse trailers maneuvering room. Generally the camp is lightly trafficked, serving hunters in the fall. Mule deer and Rocky Mountain elk dwell in the area of the camp, and 11 miles south via FR 5316 (not suitable for RVs) is Potamus Point, which delivers an overlook of the John Day River drainage and interesting rock formations.

561 Drift Fence

Location: About 8 miles southeast of Ukiah, 45 miles northwest of Granite
Season: Late May–mid-Nov
Sites: 6 basic sites; no hookups
Maximum length: 40 feet
Facilities: Tables, nonflush toilet; no drinking water
Fee per night: None
Management: Umatilla National Forest
Contact: (541) 427-3231; www.fs.usda.gov/recmain/umatilla/recreation
Finding the campground: From FR 52 (Blue Mountain Scenic Byway), 7.5 miles southeast of Ukiah and 44.5 miles northwest of Granite, turn south to enter campground. The roads through camp can be rutted and rolling.
GPS coordinates: N45 04.294' / W118 52.499'
About the campground: At this traditional hunter's camp on Blue Mountain Scenic Byway, the sites occupy a full, mature forest of ponderosa pine and western larch at the edge of a wildflower meadow. Bridge Creek Interpretive Trail, located 2.4 miles northwest of the camp (toward Ukiah), offers a 0.5-mile walk on a gravel-surfaced trail to an overlook of the Bridge Creek drainage, where elk and other wildlife can be spied.

562 Driftwood

Location: About 20 miles southeast of Ukiah
Season: Late May–mid-Nov
Sites: 6 basic sites; no hookups
Maximum length: Small units
Facilities: Tables, fire rings, nonflush toilets, raft put-in; no drinking water
Fee per night: None
Management: Umatilla National Forest
Contact: (541) 427-3231; www.fs.usda.gov/recmain/umatilla/recreation
Finding the campground: From US 395, 1 mile north of Dale and 14 miles south of the junction of US 395 and OR 244 near Ukiah, turn east onto gravel Texas Bar Road toward Olive Lake. In 0.6 mile turn left onto FR 55. After another 4.2 miles, turn right to enter the campground.
GPS coordinates: N45 01.118' / W118 51.445'
About the campground: This forest camp on the North Fork John Day Wild and Scenic River affords beautiful views of the river and the basalt rims of the downstream canyon. A small gravel beach allows for easy river access. This waterway hosts the only natural run of chinook salmon in the John Day watershed; special fishing regulations apply. The river also invites rafting and tube floating. Ponderosa pines shade the camp.

563 Frazier

Location: About 18 miles east of Ukiah
Season: Late May–mid-Nov
Sites: 20 basic sites; no hookups
Maximum length: 40 feet
Facilities: Tables, grills, nonflush toilets, off-highway-vehicle (OHV) loading ramp, covered picnic area; no drinking water
Fee per night: $$
Management: Umatilla National Forest
Contact: (541) 427-3231; www.fs.usda.gov/recmain/umatilla/recreation
Finding the campground: From Ukiah go east on OR 244 for 17 miles. Turn south onto gravel FR 5226 to enter the campground on the left in 0.5 mile.
GPS coordinates: N45 09.593' / W118 38.370'
About the campground: Pine and larch trees partially shade these well-spaced sites along Frazier Creek, at the northern gateway to Winom-Frazier OHV Complex. A legend at the entry kiosk shows an entire network of possible trail rides. Oddly enough, wildflowers thrive in this area too.

564 Gold Dredge

Location: About 22 miles southeast of Ukiah
Season: Late May–mid-Nov
Sites: 7 basic sites; no hookups
Maximum length: 20 feet
Facilities: Tables, grills, nonflush toilets; no drinking water
Fee per night: None
Management: Umatilla National Forest
Contact: (541) 427-3231; www.fs.usda.gov/recmain/umatilla/recreation
Finding the campground: From US 395, 1 mile north of Dale and 14 miles south of the junction of US 395 and OR 244 near Ukiah, turn east onto gravel Texas Bar Road toward Olive Lake. At 0.6 mile go left onto FR 55 and continue 4.8 miles. Now proceed straight on FR 5506 for 1.9 miles to reach the campground off FR 030.
GPS coordinates: N45 00.103' / W118 49.006'
About the campground: Although sites can accommodate larger units, with the difficult turn into and out of camp, individuals driving larger units may choose to bypass this facility. The shady retreat along the North Fork John Day River has site parking on the grassy river bench. False hellebore adorns the moist meadow reaches. Special fishing regulations apply to protect the anadromous fishery of this watershed. The campground's name reflects the gold mining that took place along the river in the early 1900s.

565 Lane Creek

Location: 10 miles east of Ukiah
Season: Late May–mid-Nov
Sites: 7 basic sites; no hookups
Maximum length: 40 feet
Facilities: Tables, grills, nonflush toilets; no drinking water
Fee per night: $
Management: Umatilla National Forest
Contact: (541) 427-3231; www.fs.usda.gov/recmain/umatilla/recreation
Finding the campground: From Ukiah go east on OR 244 for 10 miles. Turn north to enter the campground.
GPS coordinates: N45 11.378' / W118 45.974'
About the campground: Tiny Lane Creek flows at the eastern edge of this rustic campground, where towering ponderosa pines and western larches thread through the forest. Sites are bathed in a mix of sun and shadow. Fishing on Camas Creek (along OR 244) may divert campers from their leisure; otherwise this is an eat, sleep, yawn, and stretch destination.

566 Tollbridge

Location: About 16 miles south of Ukiah
Season: Late May–mid-Nov
Sites: 5 basic sites; no hookups
Maximum length: 25 feet
Facilities: Tables, fire rings, nonflush toilets; no drinking water
Fee per night: $
Management: Umatilla National Forest
Contact: (541) 427-3231; www.fs.usda.gov/recmain/umatilla/recreation
Finding the campground: From US 395, 1 mile north of Dale and 14 miles south of the junction of US 395 and OR 244 near Ukiah, turn east onto gravel Texas Bar Road toward Olive Lake and FR 10. In 0.6 mile bear right onto FR 10; in another 0.1 mile turn right to enter the campground.
GPS coordinates: N44 59.819' / W118 56.092'
About the campground: Below FR 10, this camp claims the narrow meadow shore of Desolation Creek just upstream from its confluence with the North Fork John Day River. Hawthorn, box elder, a conifer or two, and a lilac bush dot the camp flat. High canyon rims overlook the setting. The camp is a favorite of hunters and fishermen; be sure to check the sportfishing regulations for special rules.

567 Ukiah–Dale Forest State Scenic Corridor

Location: About 2 miles south of Ukiah
Season: Mid-Apr–mid-Oct
Sites: 27 basic sites; no hookups
Maximum length: 40 feet
Facilities: Tables, grills, flush toilets, drinking water
Fee per night: $
Management: Oregon State Parks and Recreation Department
Contact: (800) 551-6949; www.oregon.gov/OPRD/PARKS/camping.shtml
Finding the campground: The campground is east off US 395, 1.4 miles south of the junction of US 395 and OR 244 near Ukiah, 14 miles north of Dale.
GPS coordinates: N45 07.502' / W118 58.328'
About the campground: This attractive wayside sits within a scenic corridor embracing a 14-mile stretch of Camas Creek, a beautiful, alternately glassy and riffling waterway contained by meadow and shrub shores. The creek appeals to anglers, kayakers, and rafters. Ponderosa pines shade this comfortable campground. Cross-creek views are of a rock-and-forest slope. All sites have paved parking; some directly overlook the creek. The camp water source is an artesian well.

568 Welch Creek

Location: About 30 miles southeast of Ukiah
Season: Late May–mid-Nov
Sites: 6 basic sites; no hookups
Maximum length: 30 feet
Facilities: Tables, fire rings, nonflush toilets; no drinking water
Fee per night: $
Management: Umatilla National Forest
Contact: (541) 427-3231; www.fs.usda.gov/recmain/umatilla/recreation
Finding the campground: From US 395, 1 mile north of Dale and 14 miles south of the junction of US 395 and OR 244 near Ukiah, turn east onto gravel Texas Bar Road toward Olive Lake and FR 10. After 0.6 mile bear right onto FR 10; continue 14 miles and turn right to enter the campground.
GPS coordinates: N44 52.619' / W118 46.700'
About the campground: This primitive camp occupies an open meadow flat along Desolation Creek, which is large and swift flowing. Pine and larch trees rim the camp, while the slope across the creek holds a congestion of lodgepole pines and a maze of interlocking logs. The camp is well used by hunters in fall, and an off-highway-vehicle trail starts to the camp's east, off FR 10. Birding and fishing (special regulations apply) are other diversions.

569 Winom Creek (Off-Highway-Vehicle) Campground

Location: About 25 miles southeast of Ukiah, 29 miles northwest of Granite
Season: Late May–mid-Nov
Sites: 7 basic sites, 2 group sites; no hookups
Maximum length: 40 feet
Facilities: Tables, grills, nonflush toilets, group picnic shelters, off-highway-vehicle (OHV) loading ramp; no drinking water
Fee per night: $
Management: Umatilla National Forest
Contact: (541) 427-3231; www.fs.usda.gov/recmain/umatilla/recreation
Finding the campground: From FR 52, 24 miles southeast of Ukiah and 28 miles northwest of Granite, turn south. Follow the winding, coarse-grade gravel road 0.7 mile to the OHV camp.
GPS coordinates: N45 00.684' / W118 38.402'
About the campground: At the outskirts of the Tower Fire zone, this basic forest camp is tucked away in the Winom Creek valley in a setting of tall, thin lodgepole pines punctuated by big larch trees. The Tower Fire had a hit-or-miss pattern, sparing the camp but altering its views. This campground is a gateway to the North Fork John Day Wilderness, which is open only to foot and horse travel, and is an OHV staging area for the Winom-Frazier OHV Trail System.

John Day Country

	Hookup Sites	Total Sites	Max. RV Length	Hookups	Toilets	Showers	Drinking Water	Dump Station	Recreation	Fee	Can Reserve
570 Barnhouse		6	20		NF					None	
571 Bates State Park		34	60		NF		X		HC	$-$$	
572 Bear Hollow County Park		20	25		NF		X			$$	
573 Big Bend Recreation Site		4	40		NF				FS	$	
574 Bull Prairie Lake		28	40		NF		X	X	HFBL	$$	
575 Clyde Holliday State Recreation Site	31	31	60	WE	F	X	X	X	FB	$$-$$$	
576 Cottonwood		6	20		NF					None	
577 Deerhorn Camp		5	25		NF				F	$	
578 Donnelly-Service Creek River Access		6	40		NF				SFBL	$	
579 Fairview		5	20		NF					None	
580 Frazier		10	20		NF					None	
581 Grant County Fairgrounds	24	24	70	WES	F	X	X	X		$$-$$$	
582 Lone Pine Recreation Site		5	40		NF				F	$	
583 Lower Camp Creek		6	40		NF					$	
584 Middle Fork		10	30		NF				F	$	
585 Muleshoe Recreation Site		9	35		NF				SFBL	$	
586 Ochoco Divide		28	32		NF					$$	
587 Oregon Mine		5	40		NF					None	
588 Shelton Wayside State Park		40	35		NF		X		H	$$	
589 Spray Riverfront Park		8	40		NF		X		FBL	$$	
590 Wheeler County RV Park	12	12	40	WESC	F	X	X	X		$$	
591 Wildwood		5	T		NF					None	

570 Barnhouse

Location: About 18 miles southeast of Mitchell
Season: May–Oct
Sites: 6 basic sites; no hookups
Maximum length: 20 feet
Facilities: Tables, a few fire rings, nonflush toilets; no drinking water
Fee per night: None
Management: Ochoco National Forest
Contact: (541) 477-6900; www.fs.usda.gov/recmain/centraloregon/recreation
Finding the campground: From US 26, 13 miles east of Mitchell, turn south onto FR 12. Go 5 miles, ascending to the campground turnoff on the right.
GPS coordinates: N44 28.379' / W119 56.163'
About the campground: In a full forest of fir, pine, and larch, you will find these primitive campsites. Most have tables; a few have a grill or fire ring. Parking is what you make of it. The buzzing of insects or the knocking of a woodpecker only magnifies the quiet. Hiking and hunting can be done nearby.

571 Bates State Park

Location: About 30 miles northeast of John Day
Season: Mid-May–Oct, dependent on snow
Sites: 28 basic sites, 6 hiker/biker tent sites; no hookups
Maximum length: 60 feet
Facilities: Tables, grills, nonflush toilets, drinking water
Fee per night: $–$$
Management: Oregon State Parks and Recreation Department
Contact: (541) 932-4453; www.oregon.gov/OPRD/PARKS/camping.shtml
Finding the campground: From the junction of US 26 and OR 7 (Austin Junction), go north on OR 7 for 1 mile. Turn west onto Middle Fork Lane/CR 20 to enter the state park and campground on the left in 0.4 mile.
GPS coordinates: N44 35.528' / W118 30.746'
About the campground: This camp unveiled in 2012 smacks of both newness and history. It lacks the shade and comfort of long-established campgrounds, but it tells a story. It occupies the site of a one-time lumber mill company town (1917 through the 1960s). Today only the millpond and a lilac bush speak to the former population of 400 and the mill that supported them. Situated along the Middle Fork John Day River and its side creeks, the camp serves both as a John Day Country travel base and a jump-off to the outdoor recreation that once entertained the townspeople. The park has 3 miles of hiking trail, and OR 7 is on the TransAmerica Bicycle Trail and the Journey Through Time National Scenic Byway.

Byway sign, Journey Through Time National Scenic Byway

572 Bear Hollow County Park

Location: About 7 miles southeast of Fossil
Season: Year-round
Sites: 20 basic sites; no hookups
Maximum length: 25 feet
Facilities: Tables, grills, nonflush toilets, drinking water
Fee per night: $$
Management: Wheeler County
Contact: (541) 763-2010; www.wheelercounty-oregon.com/parks.html
Finding the campground: The campground is west off OR 19, 6.5 miles south of Fossil and 12.5 miles north of the junction of OR 19 and OR 207 South (near Service Creek).
GPS coordinates: N44 56.247' / W120 07.223'
About the campground: This campground, set in a forest of grand and Douglas firs, has a restful, rustic appeal. Most of the parking spaces require some leveling. This park is popular with hunters in fall and serves John Day Country travelers.

573 Big Bend Recreation Site

Location: 3 miles northeast of Kimberly
Season: Year-round
Sites: 4 basic sites; no hookups
Maximum length: 40 feet
Facilities: Tables, fire rings, nonflush toilets; no drinking water
Fee per night: $
Management: Bureau of Land Management—Prineville District
Contact: (541) 416-6700; www.blm.gov/or/
Finding the campground: The recreation site is south off the Kimberly–Long Creek Highway, 3 miles northeast of Kimberly and 11 miles southwest of Monument.
GPS coordinates: N44 46.839' / W119 36.673'
About the campground: These well-spaced sites claim a broad river bench, where the North Fork John Day River swings a lazy bend. Each site is paired with at least one juniper for shade; parking is on the grassy flat. Across from the camp rises a steep, grassy slope with rimrock tiers and showings of mountain mahogany. You can fish, swim, or explore the John Day Country. Deer sometimes frequent the river. Fires and smoking are prohibited from June to mid-October.

574 Bull Prairie Lake

Location: On Bull Prairie Reservoir, about 20 miles north of Spray
Season: Mid-May–mid-Oct
Sites: 28 basic sites; no hookups
Maximum length: 40 feet
Facilities: Tables, grills, nonflush toilets, drinking water, dump station, boat launch, wheelchair-accessible fishing platform and trail
Fee per night: $$
Management: Umatilla National Forest
Contact: (541) 676-9187; www.fs.usda.gov/recmain/umatilla/recreation
Finding the campground: From OR 207, 17 miles north of Spray and 38 miles south of Heppner, turn east onto FR 2039. Go 3 miles and bear right to enter the campground.
GPS coordinates: N44 58.329' / W119 39.844'
About the campground: At this relaxing family retreat, campsites are tucked throughout the mature, mixed-conifer forest surrounding Bull Prairie Reservoir, a scenic man-made lake ringed by cattails and stocked with trout. In keeping with the quiet of the setting, the lake is open to nonmotorized boating only. The 1.25-mile Lake Shore Trail travels the lake perimeter for a pleasant start or cap to your day.

575 Clyde Holliday State Recreation Site

Location: 8 miles west of John Day
Season: Mar–Nov
Sites: 31 hookup sites, 2 tepees; water and electric hookups
Maximum length: 60 feet
Facilities: Tables, grills, flush toilets, drinking water, showers, dump station, horseshoe pits
Fee per night: $$–$$$
Management: Oregon State Parks and Recreation Department
Contact: (541) 932-4453; www.oregon.gov/OPRD/PARKS/camping.shtml
Finding the campground: The campground is south off US 26, 8 miles west of John Day.
GPS coordinates: N44 25.000' / W119 05.399'
About the campground: In the shadow of the Blue Mountains and in the heart of John Day Country you will find this attractive, landscaped campground on the John Day River. Fishing and sightseeing are popular activities. In John Day be sure to look for the Kam Wah Chung State Heritage Site, a Chinese trading post and apothecary from the mid- to late 1800s. It is shown by guided tour daily, May through October; call (800) 551-6949 for information and hours. Elsewhere, the units of the John Day Fossil Beds National Monument unfold an exciting geologic timeline and spectacular scenery. The John Day River offers rafting opportunities.

576 Cottonwood

Location: About 27 miles southeast of Mitchell
Season: May–Oct
Sites: 6 basic sites; no hookups
Maximum length: 20 feet
Facilities: A few tables and crude fire rings, nonflush toilets; no drinking water
Fee per night: None
Management: Ochoco National Forest
Contact: (541) 477-6900; www.fs.usda.gov/recmain/centraloregon/recreation
Finding the campground: From US 26, 13 miles east of Mitchell, turn south onto FR 12, which begins paved and becomes gravel, for a hefty ascent. Go 13.5 miles and turn left onto FR 200, proceeding 0.3 mile more to the campground.
GPS coordinates: N44 23.270' / W119 51.307'
About the campground: This is a campground for the do-it-yourself camper. Sites are informal, with just a table or a fire ring marking the spot. The location unites a mature pine-fir forest, a false hellebore meadow, and a prairie meadow for a pleasant place to kick back and relax. Hunters often base here in fall.

577 Deerhorn Camp

Location: About 22 miles northeast of Prairie City
Season: Late May–mid-Oct
Sites: 5 basic sites; no hookups
Maximum length: 25 feet
Facilities: Tables, grills, nonflush toilets; no drinking water
Fee per night: $
Management: Malheur National Forest
Contact: (541) 820-3800; www.fs.usda.gov/recmain/malheur/recreation
Finding the campground: From the junction of Main Street and US 26 in Prairie City, go east on US 26 for 15.3 miles. Turn north onto OR 7 toward Sumpter and Baker City, and go 1.1 miles. Turn left onto CR 20 toward Susanville and travel 5.1 miles to the campground on the left.
GPS coordinates: N44 37.340' / W118 34.900'
About the campground: This small campground occupies a transition habitat, where a false hellebore meadow and ponderosa pine forest meet. It rests along the picturesque Middle Fork John Day River and engages guests with fishing, wildlife viewing, and hunting. Most sites have gravel parking.

578 Donnelly-Service Creek River Access

Location: About 13 miles southwest of Spray
Season: Year-round
Sites: 6 walk-in tent sites; no hookups
Maximum length: 40 feet
Facilities: Tables, nonflush toilets, primitive boat launch; no drinking water
Fee per night: $
Management: Bureau of Land Management—Prineville District
Contact: (541) 416-6700; www.blm.gov/or/
Finding the campground: From the junction of OR 19 and OR 207 South, near Service Creek (12.3 miles southwest of Spray), turn south onto OR 207. Proceed 0.3 mile to the recreation site on the left.
GPS coordinates: N45 51.147' / W117 01.900'
About the campground: Primarily a base for rafters, this campground occupies an arid flat on the John Day River. Only a couple of pines and scattered junipers dot the flat; the tables are paired with these trees for a retreat from the sun. The setting is one of basalt-tiered grassland rims, butte-dressed skylines, and river-canyon cliffs. Fishing and swimming are other amusements.

579 Fairview

Location: 39 miles south of Heppner
Season: June–Oct
Sites: 5 basic sites; no hookups
Maximum length: 20 feet
Facilities: Tables, grills, nonflush toilets, drinking water
Fee per night: None
Management: Umatilla National Forest
Contact: (541) 676-9187; www.fs.usda.gov/recmain/umatilla/recreation
Finding the campground: The campground is west off OR 207, 16 miles north of Spray and 39 miles south of Heppner.
GPS coordinates: N44 57.329' / W119 42.572'
About the campground: You will find these five well-spaced campsites in a ponderosa pine stand on a slope below OR 207. Part of the campground looks out at a burn. The camp is convenient for travelers and welcomes lazing about.

580 Frazier

Location: About 28 miles northeast of Paulina
Season: May–Oct
Sites: 10 basic sites; no hookups
Maximum length: 20 feet
Facilities: Tables, crude fire rings, nonflush toilets; no drinking water
Fee per night: None
Management: Ochoco National Forest
Contact: (541) 477-6900; www.fs.usda.gov/recmain/centraloregon/recreation
Finding the campground: From Paulina (56 miles east of Prineville), go east on CR 112, the Paulina Highway, for 4.2 miles. Turn left onto gravel CR 113/FR 58. Stay on FR 58, following this paved and gravel route for 22.2 miles. Turn left onto narrow, sometimes rough FR 5800.500 and proceed 1.6 miles to the camp.
GPS coordinates: N44 13.261' / W119 34.626'
About the campground: This primitive forest campground provides a quiet escape from everyday demands. It has a pine-meadow setting and well-spaced, informal sites for personal privacy. Aspens with dancing leaves shade a headwater spring of Frazier Creek. The campground, a favorite with hunters, is also just a short hop away from the South Fork John Day River via FR 58 eastbound.

581 Grant County Fairgrounds

Location: In the town of John Day
Season: Year-round
Sites: 24 hookup sites, tent camping on grass; water, electric, and sewer hookups
Maximum length: 70 feet
Facilities: Tables, grills, flush toilets, drinking water, showers, dump station
Fee per night: $$–$$$
Management: Grant County
Contact: (541) 575-1900, reservations accepted; www.grantcountyfairgrounds.com/rvpark.php
Finding the campground: From US 26 in John Day, turn north onto Northwest Bridge Street to reach the signed turn for the RV camp on the right at the second fairgrounds entrance.
GPS coordinates: N44 25.270' / W118 57.171'
About the campground: This campground with full-size shade trees and side-by-side paved sites is a perfect base for fair attendees and area sightseers. A river walk, convenient access to the services of town, the acclaimed Kam Wah Chung & Co. Museum, and the historical offerings of town keep you close to base. The famous John Day River and John Day Fossil Beds yell "Road trip!"

582 Lone Pine Recreation Site

Location: About 2 miles northeast of Kimberly
Season: Year-round
Sites: 5 basic sites; no hookups
Maximum length: 40 feet
Facilities: Tables, fire rings, nonflush toilets; no drinking water
Fee per night: $
Management: Bureau of Land Management—Prineville District
Contact: (541) 416-6700; www.blm.gov/or/
Finding the campground: The campground is off the Kimberly–Long Creek Highway, 1.7 miles northeast of Kimberly.
GPS coordinates: N44 46.657' / W119 37.396'
About the campground: This small campground rests on a flat along the North Fork John Day River. A cottonwood grove shades some sites; the others are mostly sunny. Nighttime unites the song of the river and the click of crickets and brings on the erratic flight of bats. Days are filled with fishing, swimming, and exploring John Day Country and the scattered units of John Day Fossil Beds National Monument.

583 Lower Camp Creek

Location: About 50 miles north of John Day
Season: June–Oct
Sites: 6 basic sites; no hookups
Maximum length: 40 feet
Facilities: Tables, grills, nonflush toilets; no drinking water
Fee per night: $
Management: Malheur National Forest
Contact: (541) 820-3800; www.fs.usda.gov/recmain/malheur/recreation
Finding the campground: From the junction of US 26 and OR 7 (Austin Junction), go north on OR 7 for 1 mile. Turn west onto Middle Fork Lane/CR 20. Go 18.7 miles and turn south onto FR 36 to reach the campground on the right in 1.6 miles.
GPS coordinates: N44 40.387' / W118 47.953'
About the campground: This quiet little camp sits in the ponderosa pine forest above Camp Creek. It offers a place to retreat and reflect on warm summer days. Hunters base here in the fall.

584 Middle Fork

Location: About 23 miles northeast of Prairie City
Season: May–mid-Oct
Sites: 10 basic sites; no hookups
Maximum length: 30 feet
Facilities: Tables, grills, nonflush toilets; no drinking water
Fee per night: $
Management: Malheur National Forest
Contact: (541) 820-3800; www.fs.usda.gov/recmain/malheur/recreation
Finding the campground: From the junction of Main Street and US 26 in Prairie City, go east on US 26 for 15.3 miles. Turn north onto OR 7 toward Sumpter and Baker City. Go 1.1 miles and turn left onto CR 20 toward Susanville. Proceed 6.6 miles to the campground on the left.
GPS coordinates: N44 37.801' / W118 36.343'
About the campground: This linear campground stretches alongside the Middle Fork John Day River, with most of its sites overlooking the river; all have gravel parking. The young and middle-aged pines and firs that dress the flat provide at least partial shade for the sites. Alders, a few dogwoods, and meadow vegetation claim the shore. The campground appeals to outdoor interests with fishing and hunting and is near Vinegar Hill–Indian Rock Scenic Area.

585 Muleshoe Recreation Site

Location: About 10 miles west of Spray
Season: Year-round
Sites: 6 basic sites, 3 walk-in tent sites; no hookups
Maximum length: 35 feet
Facilities: Tables, nonflush toilet, primitive boat launch; no drinking water
Fee per night: $
Management: Bureau of Land Management—Prineville District
Contact: (541) 416-6700; www.blm.gov/or/
Finding the campground: From Spray go 10.3 miles west on OR 19 North/OR 207 South; the campground is on the left.
GPS coordinates: N44 48.431' / W119 58.007'
About the campground: This campground rests on a small plateau above the John Day River. The walk-in sites are tucked into a juniper grove; the basic sites have gravel parking spurs and claim an open sagebrush flat that offers unobstructed river views. The folded tableland ridges, cliffs, and rims that shape the canyon contribute to the beauty. Below camp, hackberry and wild rose grow near the popular raft put-in/take-out site. Fishing, rafting, and swimming attract visitors to this region and campground.

586 Ochoco Divide

Location: 18 miles southwest of Mitchell
Season: Late May–Sept
Sites: 28 basic sites, bicycle camp; no hookups
Maximum length: 32 feet
Facilities: Tables, grills, nonflush toilets; no drinking water
Fee per night: $$
Management: Ochoco National Forest
Contact: (541) 416-6500; www.fs.usda.gov/recmain/centraloregon/recreation
Finding the campground: The campground is east off US 26, 30 miles northeast of Prineville and 18 miles southwest of Mitchell.
GPS coordinates: N44 30.004' / W120 23.186'
About the campground: At Ochoco Pass on US 26, you will find this camp among the old-growth ponderosa pines and firs. The camp primarily caters to the passer-through, so individuals who opt to linger generally enjoy quiet days perfect for birding and relaxing. An old road leads away from the campground for an easy leg stretch. The Painted Hills Unit of John Day Fossil Beds National Monument is a half-hour's drive northeast of the camp.

587 Oregon Mine

Location: About 32 miles southwest of John Day
Season: Late May–mid-Oct
Sites: 5 basic sites; no hookups
Maximum length: 40 feet
Facilities: Tables, grills, nonflush toilet, corral; no drinking water
Fee per night: None
Management: Malheur National Forest
Contact: (541) 820-3800; www.fs.usda.gov/recmain/malheur/recreation
Finding the campground: From US 26, 13 miles east of Dayville and 18 miles west of John Day, turn south onto paved Fields Creek Road/FR 21. Follow it 13.4 miles and turn right onto FR 2170. The campground is on the left in 0.5 mile.
GPS coordinates: N44 16.558' / W119 17.854'
About the campground: This small, out-of-the-way, improved rustic campground has great charm with its shrub-and-meadow floor, towering ponderosa pine trees, rustic rail fencing, and shrub-lined Murderers Creek flowing at its back. Deer and, according to the forest service, wild horses sometimes visit the camp. Nearby, the Cedar Grove National Recreation Trail explores a rare Alaskan cedar grove for a 2.2-mile round-trip hike. To reach the trailhead, return to FR 21 and go 3.5 miles north. Turn left (west) onto FR 2150, following it 6 miles to the trailhead.

588 Shelton Wayside State Park

Location: About 10 miles southeast of Fossil
Season: Mid-Apr–Oct
Sites: 40 basic sites; no hookups
Maximum length: 35 feet
Facilities: Tables, grills, nonflush toilets, drinking water
Fee per night: $$
Management: Leased to Wheeler County
Contact: (541) 763-2010
Finding the campground: The campground is west off OR 19, 10.3 miles south of Fossil and 8.7 miles north of the junction of OR 19 and OR 207 South.
GPS coordinates: N44 53.736' / W120 05.750'
About the campground: Service Creek flows through this linear campground, which stretches for 1 mile at the foot of a forested ridge traversed by trail. The camp has a meadow floor, which is partially shaded by the pine-fir complex. Arnica and mock orange lend seasonal color. The wayside offers a base for exploring the scattered units of John Day Fossil Beds National Monument or participating in the John Day River recreation.

589 Spray Riverfront Park

Location: In Spray
Season: Usually Mar–Dec; closed during flood stage
Sites: 8 basic sites; no hookups
Maximum length: 40 feet (Large units may have difficulty taking the turn into the camp.)
Facilities: Tables, grills, nonflush toilets, boat launch/landing (fee), drinking water
Fee per night: $$
Management: City of Spray
Contact: (541) 468-2069
Finding the campground: From OR 19/OR 207 in Spray, turn south onto Main Street and follow it 0.2 mile. Turn left at the river bridge to enter the campground.
GPS coordinates: N44 49.599' / W119 47.636'
About the campground: Located on a grassy flat on a bend in the John Day River, this campground offers anglers, drift boaters, and rafters convenient access. Seasonally, the locust trees and birdhouses are noisy with birds. Desert canyon rims and ridges add to the scenery. The park has gravel parking at the sites and the boat landing. The Spray Pioneer Museum, built in 1912, may suggest a trip into town.

590　Wheeler County RV Park

Location: In the town of Fossil
Season: Year-round
Sites: 12 hookup sites; water, electric, sewer, and cable hookups
Maximum length: 40 feet
Facilities: Tables, barbecue grills, flush toilets, drinking water, showers, dump station
Fee per night: $$
Management: Wheeler County
Contact: (541) 763-4560; www.wheelercounty-oregon.com/fairgrounds.html
Finding the campground: From OR 19 in Fossil, turn north on Main Street toward the fairgrounds. Go 0.2 mile and turn right onto Third Street; the fairgrounds campground is at road's end.
GPS coordinates: N44 59.866' / W120 12.682'
About the campground: This campground claims an open flat at the base of an arid grass hill at the edge of the fairgrounds. The closely spaced sites have gravel parking pads and grassy divides with small planted trees. The camp's location is its primary appeal, serving fair-participants and visitors exploring the surrounding John Day Fossil Country, with its popular river and rich geology. The county fair runs the first week of August.

591　Wildwood

Location: About 34 miles northeast of Prineville
Season: May–Sept
Sites: 5 tent sites; no hookups
Maximum length: Suitable for tents only
Facilities: Tables, grill, nonflush toilets; no drinking water
Fee per night: None
Management: Ochoco National Forest
Contact: (541) 416-6500; www.fs.usda.gov/recmain/centraloregon/recreation
Finding the campground: From US 26, 27 miles northeast of Prineville and 21 miles southwest of Mitchell, turn east onto gravel FR 2630. Go 4 miles; turn left on FR 2210 and proceed 3 miles to the camp.
GPS coordinates: N44 29.024' / W120 20.175'
About the campground: Along the old Prineville–Mitchell Highway, this camp has long been a traveler's wayside, although now it is farther off the beaten track for greater relaxation. Its remoteness appeals to great horned owls. The primitive camp occupies a pine-fir slope with a needle-and-cone-strewn floor. It is another place to commune with nature, read a book, or seek out area trails or hunting opportunities.

Granite-Sumpter Area

	Hookup Sites	Total Sites	Max. RV Length	Hookups	Toilets	Showers	Drinking Water	Dump Station	Recreation	Fee	Can Reserve
592 McCully Forks		7	18		NF				F	$	
593 Millers Lane		8	20		NF				HSFB	$	
594 North Fork John Day		20	40		NF				HFR	$	
595 Olive Lake		28	40		NF				HFBL	$$	
596 Southwest Shore		16	35		NF				HSFBL	$	
597 Union Creek	38	70	40	WES	F	X	X	X	HSFBL	$$-$$$	X

592 McCully Forks

Location: About 3 miles northwest of Sumpter
Season: June–Sept
Sites: 7 basic sites; no hookups
Maximum length: 18 feet
Facilities: Tables, grills, nonflush toilets; no drinking water
Fee per night: $
Management: Wallowa-Whitman National Forest
Contact: (541) 523-4476; www.fs.usda.gov/recmain/wallowa-whitman/recreation
Finding the campground: From Sumpter (about 30 miles west of Baker City via OR 7 and Sumpter Highway), go 2.8 miles north on Sumpter Highway. The campground is on the right.
GPS coordinates: N44 46.009' / W118 14.817'
About the campground: Along Elkhorn Scenic Byway, this small rustic camp straddles McCully Creek. Fir and spruce trees shade the sites. Farther from the creek grow lodgepole pines, and dogwoods are common. Because of the narrowness of the canyon, parking is constrained, but the campground remains popular, filling on summer weekends. The historic Sumpter Valley Railroad or Dredge may suggest a side trip.

593 Millers Lane

Location: On Phillips Lake, about 9 miles southeast of Sumpter
Season: June–Sept
Sites: 4 basic sites, 4 tent sites; no hookups
Maximum length: 20 feet
Facilities: Tables, grills, nonflush toilets, boat ramp (at Southwest Shore Campground); no drinking water
Fee per night: $
Management: Wallowa-Whitman National Forest
Contact: (541) 523-4476; www.fs.usda.gov/recmain/wallowa-whitman/recreation
Finding the campground: From OR 7, 22.2 miles west of Baker City and 3.8 miles east of the Sumpter Junction, turn south onto paved Hudspeth Lane toward Southwest Shore and Millers Lane Campgrounds. Go 1.2 miles and turn left onto gravel FR 2220 to reach this campground on the left in another 1.3 miles.
GPS coordinates: N44 40.361' / W118 04.083'
About the campground: Along the south shore of Phillips Lake, a large, man-made platter that fluctuates, you will find this small campground with exceptional cross-lake viewing of the Elkhorns. Sites occupy a ponderosa pine forest, with a rail fence separating the camp from the shore. Adjacent to camp are dry meadows. Fishing, swimming, and boating make this campground popular on summer weekends. A hiking path follows the lakeshore.

594 North Fork John Day

Location: About 8 miles north of Granite
Season: Late May–early Oct
Sites: 15 basic sites, 5 tent sites; no hookups
Maximum length: 40 feet
Facilities: Tables, grills, nonflush toilets; adjacent horse feeding station, loading ramp, and corrals (horses not allowed in main campground); no drinking water
Fee per night: $
Management: Umatilla National Forest
Contact: (541) 427-3231; www.fs.usda.gov/recmain/umatilla/recreation
Finding the campground: The campground is off FR 52 at its intersection with FR 73, 8.3 miles north of Granite and 39 miles southeast of Ukiah.
GPS coordinates: N44 54.845' / W118 24.126'
About the campground: Along the North Fork John Day Wild and Scenic River at the intersection of the Elkhorn and Blue Mountain Scenic Byways is this pleasant, sunny campground in the lodgepole pines. The North Fork John Day National Recreation Trail leaves one end of the camp and follows the river into the North Fork John Day Wilderness. The trail travels past mounds of tailings, active claims, and decaying cabins, all part of the mining era here. Special fishing regulations protect the anadromous fishery.

595 Olive Lake

Location: 12 miles west of Granite
Season: Late May–mid-Oct
Sites: 23 basic sites, 5 tent sites; no hookups
Maximum length: 40 feet
Facilities: Tables, grills, nonflush toilets, boat dock and launch; no drinking water
Fee per night: $$
Management: Umatilla National Forest
Contact: (541) 427-3231; www.fs.usda.gov/recmain/umatilla/recreation
Finding the campground: From Granite travel 12 miles west on FR 10, a good, wide gravel road, to reach the campground on the left. From US 395 north of Dale, follow FR 55 east 0.6 mile to FR 10. Continue east on FR 10 for another 26.2 miles to reach the campground turnoff.
GPS coordinates: N44 47.080' / W118 35.821'
About the campground: This campground is on the east shore of peaceful Olive Lake. Lodgepole pines, firs, spruces, and larches contribute to the forested basin. Enlarged by an earthen dam, the lake invites fishing and boating. Fremont Powerhouse Historic District (8 miles east of camp) makes an interesting side trip. This restored station powered the gold boom of eastern Oregon. Its wooden pipeline can be seen in several places throughout the area. Near camp, trails venture into North Fork John Day Wilderness and Indian Rock–Vinegar Hill Scenic Area.

596 Southwest Shore

Location: On Phillips Lake, about 9 miles southeast of Sumpter
Season: Early June–Sept
Sites: 16 basic sites; no hookups
Maximum length: 35 feet
Facilities: Tables, grills, nonflush toilets, boat ramp; no drinking water
Fee per night: $
Management: Wallowa-Whitman National Forest
Contact: (541) 523-4476; www.fs.usda.gov/recmain/wallowa-whitman/recreation
Finding the campground: From OR 7, 22.2 miles west of Baker City and 3.8 miles east of the Sumpter Junction, turn south onto paved Hudspeth Lane toward Southwest Shore and Millers Lane Campgrounds. Go 1.2 miles and turn left onto gravel FR 2220; the campground is on the left in another 0.5 mile.
GPS coordinates: N44 40.531' / W118 04.868'
About the campground: On the south shore of Phillips Lake, a large, recreational reservoir in the shadow of the Elkhorn Mountains, sits this popular campground with prized views. Sites receive a mix of sun and shade and are generally well spaced across the ponderosa pine and sagebrush flat. Fishing, boating, swimming, and hiking the south shore trail for photographs and nature study keep guests busy. At the marshy ends of the reservoir are nesting boxes for geese.

597 Union Creek

Location: On Phillips Lake, about 10 miles southeast of Sumpter
Season: May–Sept
Sites: 38 full or partial hookup sites, 32 basic sites; water, electric, and sewer hookups
Maximum length: 40 feet
Facilities: Tables, grills, flush toilets, drinking water, showers, dump station, docks, paved multilane boat ramp, fish-cleaning station
Fee per night: $$–$$$
Management: Wallowa-Whitman National Forest
Contact: (541) 523-4476; (877) 444-6777 for reservations; www.fs.usda.gov/recmain/wallowa-whitman/recreation
Finding the campground: The campground is south off OR 7, 19 miles west of Baker City and 7 miles east of the Sumpter Junction.
GPS coordinates: N44 41.411' / W118 01.784'
About the campground: This fully developed campground sits on the north shore of 5-mile-long, 2,450-acre Phillips Lake. Sites terrace the pine-forested slope of the lake basin, with paths leading to the lakeshore, launch, and picnic area. Visitors can enjoy a full day of fun in the sun on the lake and then retreat to the shade of their camp. The roped-off swimming area suggests a refreshing dip, or you can walk the shoreline trail to explore this vast impoundment on the Powder River. Fresh-caught bass or trout may top the dinner menu. Historic Sumpter and Baker City suggest short road trips.

North Powder–Anthony Lakes Area

	Hookup Sites	Total Sites	Max. RV Length	Hookups	Toilets	Showers	Drinking Water	Dump Station	Recreation	Fee	Can Reserve
598 Anthony Lake		37	22		NF		X		HFBL	$$	X
599 Grande Ronde Lake		8	16		NF		X		HFBL	$-$$	
600 Mud Lake		7	16		NF				HFB	$	
601 Pilcher Creek Reservoir Recreation Site		17	40		NF		X		FBL	None	
602 Thief Valley Recreation Area		10	32		NF		X		FBL	None	

598 Anthony Lake

Location: About 40 miles northwest of Baker City

Season: July–Sept

Sites: 16 basic sites, 21 tent sites; no hookups

Maximum length: 22 feet

Facilities: Tables, grills, nonflush toilets, drinking water, boat ramp

Fee per night: $$

Management: Wallowa-Whitman National Forest

Contact: (541) 523-4476; (877) 444-6777 for reservations; www.fs.usda.gov/recmain/wallowa-whitman/recreation

Finding the campground: From I-84 take exit 285 (the North Powder–Anthony Lakes exit). Go west on North Powder River Lane and FR 73 for 20 miles, following the signs to Anthony Lakes. The campground is on the left off FR 73.

GPS coordinates: N44 57.748' / W118 13.734'

About the campground: This camp occupies a high-elevation forest of small-diameter firs and lodgepole pines along Anthony Lake (elevation 7,100 feet). Campers are treated to a breathtaking setting that pairs the stunning granite peaks of the Elkhorn Crest with the midnight blue of the mountain lake. Anthony Lake welcomes trout fishing, human-powered boating, or a shoreline stroll. Opportunities for more-challenging hikes are boundless, including several high-lakes destinations and the Elkhorn Crest. For vehicle sightseeing, this campground is on the 106-mile Elkhorn Scenic Byway, which makes a loop.

599 Grande Ronde Lake

Location: About 41 miles northwest of Baker City
Season: July–Sept
Sites: 8 basic sites; no hookups
Maximum length: 16 feet
Facilities: Tables, grills, nonflush toilets, drinking water, primitive boat ramp
Fee per night: $–$$
Management: Wallowa-Whitman National Forest
Contact: (541) 523-4476; www.fs.usda.gov/recmain/wallowa-whitman/recreation
Finding the campground: From I-84 take exit 285 (the North Powder–Anthony Lakes exit). Go west on North Powder River Lane and FR 73 for 21 miles, following the signs to Anthony Lakes. Turn right onto FR 43, go 0.2 mile, and bear left to enter the campground.
GPS coordinates: N44 58.543' / W118 14.497'
About the campground: The campsites sit in a high-elevation conifer forest overlooking the broad, wet wildflower meadow that separates this campground from Grande Ronde Lake. The submerged grasses and dotting cow lilies add to the charm of this small, circular mountain lake, where quiet boating is allowed and the trout fishing can be good. This camp puts visitors within easy access of Anthony Lake–Elkhorn Crest recreation, a lineup that includes hiking, sightseeing, photography, and scenic driving.

600 Mud Lake

Location: About 40 miles northwest of Baker City
Season: July–Sept
Sites: 7 basic sites; no hookups
Maximum length: 16 feet
Facilities: Tables, grills, nonflush toilets; no drinking water
Fee per night: $
Management: Wallowa-Whitman National Forest
Contact: (541) 523-4476; www.fs.usda.gov/recmain/wallowa-whitman/recreation
Finding the campground: From I-84 take exit 285 (the North Powder–Anthony Lakes exit). Go west on North Powder River Lane and FR 73 for about 20 miles, following the signs to Anthony Lakes. The campground is on the right.
GPS coordinates: N44 57.857' / W118 13.936'
About the campground: Across the road from Anthony Lake and the Anthony Lakes Ski Area, this camp is set back from Mud Lake, tucked away in lodgepole pines and spruce. Shallow Mud Lake is ringed by a broad meadow expanse. Although the setting is serene, mosquitoes can be bothersome. Visitors enjoy the high-country splendor of the Elkhorn Mountains: chiseled granite peaks, high lakes, lush meadows, elk herds, and wildflower showcases. You may hike, fish, row your boat, and sightsee.

601 Pilcher Creek Reservoir Recreation Site

Location: About 30 miles northwest of Baker City
Season: May–mid-Oct, weather permitting
Sites: 17 basic sites; no hookups
Maximum length: 40 feet
Facilities: Tables, barbecues or fire rings, nonflush toilets, drinking water, primitive boat launch
Fee per night: None
Management: Union County
Contact: (541) 963-1016; www.union-county.org
Finding the campground: From I-84 take exit 285 (the North Powder–Anthony Lakes exit). Go west on North Powder River Lane, proceeding straight at the junction. After 7.6 miles turn right onto gravel Tucker Flat Road. Continue 2 miles and turn right to enter the campground.
GPS coordinates: N45 03.367' / W118 05.026'
About the campground: The centerpiece here is the broad platter of Pilcher Creek Reservoir, cupped by low, rounded meadow-and-forest rises and a scenic aspen-filled dip. Views include the rugged beauty of the Elkhorn Mountains. The camp offerings are primitive, and the primary activities are boating (5 miles per hour) and fishing. With Elkhorn Wildlife Area bordering the recreation site, deer, elk, and other wildlife can be seen at the camp. Balsamroot colors the meadow in spring.

602 Thief Valley Recreation Area

Location: About 15 miles south of Union
Season: Maintained May–mid-Oct, weather permitting
Sites: 10 basic sites; no hookups
Maximum length: 32 feet
Facilities: Tables, barbecues, nonflush toilets, drinking water, boat launch
Fee per night: None
Management: Union County
Contact: (541) 963-1016; www.union-county.org
Finding the campground: From OR 237, 7.8 miles south of Union and 7.3 miles north of I-84 exit 285 (the North Powder–Anthony Lakes exit), turn east onto Telocaset Lane, a good gravel road. After 1.8 miles turn left to remain on Telocaset Lane. Continue 4.2 miles before turning right for the reservoir. Go 1.5 miles to the recreation area.
GPS coordinates: N45 01.508' / W117 47.225'
About the campground: This shadeless flat overlooks the broad, open water of Thief Valley Reservoir, built for irrigation and open to recreation. Low sage-grass ridges shape the basin, while a few willows cluster along the lake rim. The reservoir is open for boating, fishing, swimming, and windsurfing. The jetty offers fishing access for individuals with disabilities. Some big trout are pulled from the reservoir, but by June an algae bloom overtakes the lake, ending the catch. In winter the lake is open for ice fishing.

Richland-Halfway Area

	Hookup Sites	Total Sites	Max. RV Length	Hookups	Toilets	Showers	Drinking Water	Dump Station	Recreation	Fee	Can Reserve
603 Boulder Park		7	Small		NF				HR	None	
604 Copperfield Park	62	72	40	WE	F	X	X	X	SFBL	$-$$	
605 Eagle Forks		7	20		NF		X		HF	$	
606 Fish Lake		15	20		NF		X		HFBL	$	
607 Hewitt/Holcomb County Parks	27	62	30	WE	F	X	X		FBL	$$	X
608 Lake Fork		10	22		NF				HF	$	
609 McBride		6	16		NF					None	
610 Tamarack		12	22		NF		X		F	$	
611 Twin Lakes		8	15		NF				HF	None	
612 Two Color		11	22		NF				F	None	

603 Boulder Park

Location: About 40 miles northeast of Baker City and 52 miles southeast of La Grande

Season: June–Oct

Sites: 7 basic sites; no hookups

Maximum length: Best suited for tents and smaller units

Facilities: Tables, grills, nonflush toilets, stock feeders, holding facilities, trailer parking; no drinking water

Fee per night: None

Management: Wallowa-Whitman National Forest

Contact: (541) 963-7186; www.fs.usda.gov/recmain/wallowa-whitman/recreation

Finding the campground: From OR 203 at Medical Springs, head southeast on Collins Road/ Eagle Creek Drive toward Boulder Park. The road soon widens and becomes gravel. Go 1.6 miles and turn left onto FR 67. Continue 13.5 miles and turn left (west) onto FR 77. Continue 0.7 mile to FR 7755. Turn right onto FR 7755 and proceed about 3.8 miles to the campground. Main Eagle Trailhead is 0.25 mile past the campground at road's end.

GPS coordinates: N45 03.983' / W117 24.590'

About the campground: Tucked among the mixed conifers, Boulder Park sits at the Main Eagle Trailhead and is primarily intended to serve people traveling with stock animals. The Main Eagle Trail is a popular southern approach to Eagle Cap Wilderness, and the nearby Fake Creek Trail offers a chance to vary your travels. Beautiful views of the Wallowa Mountains and Eagle Creek, a Wild and Scenic Waterway, are just strides away, with some views obtained right from camp. Campers without stock will likely prefer the family sites at nearby Two Color Campground.

604 Copperfield Park

Location: On the Snake River, about 17 miles east of Halfway
Season: Year-round
Sites: 62 hookup sites, 10 tent sites; water and electric hookups
Maximum length: 40 feet
Facilities: Tables, barbecues or grills, flush toilets, drinking water, showers, dump station, boat launch (0.6 mile downstream from park)
Fee per night: $-$$
Management: Idaho Power
Contact: (800) 422-3143, no reservations accepted; www.idahopower.com

Finding the campground: From Halfway go east on OR 86 for 16.6 miles to enter this park at the river.

GPS coordinates: N44 58.390' / W116 51.434'

About the campground: On the one-time site of the rough-and-tumble mining city of Copperfield, Oregon, sits this pleasant, groomed, developed park with lots of open lawn and a few big pines. Park offerings include a swimming area on the broad, harnessed Snake River, with boating access nearby. This section of the river, Hells Canyon Reservoir, is popular with fishermen; warmwater fish species are the primary catch. North (downstream) from the camp, Hells Canyon Reservoir Trail offers a wonderful hike, with views of the steep-walled canyon and broad, cloudy river. Trailhead parking is limited, with no developed turnaround.

Motor home at campground, Copperfield Park

605 Eagle Forks

Location: About 10 miles north of Richland
Season: June–Oct
Sites: 7 basic sites; no hookups
Maximum length: 20 feet
Facilities: Tables, grills, nonflush toilets, drinking water
Fee per night: $
Management: Wallowa-Whitman National Forest
Contact: (541) 742-7511; www.fs.usda.gov/recmain/wallowa-whitman/recreation
Finding the campground: At the western edge of Richland, turn north off OR 86 at a sign for Sparta, following Sparta Road 2.3 miles to Newbridge. Continue north on Eagle Creek Road/FR 7735, which changes to dirt. Go another 7.3 miles and turn left for the campground.
GPS coordinates: N44 53.516' / W117 15.679'
About the campground: On a wooded rise, this camp threaded by Little Eagle Creek overlooks main Eagle Creek, a Wild and Scenic Waterway. Pines and firs shade the campground, while alders and willows fan the waters. At the upstream end of the campground, the 7-mile Martin Bridge Trail pursues Eagle Creek upstream for an engaging canyon tour. The trail ends at Martin Bridge, a former stage stop on the Union–Cornucopia Wagon Road that linked the area's historic gold-mining districts to Union and Baker City. The creek is open to fishing.

606 Fish Lake

Location: On Fish Lake, about 20 miles north of Halfway
Season: July–Oct
Sites: 15 basic sites; no hookups
Maximum length: 20 feet; best suited for tents
Facilities: Tables, grills, nonflush toilets, drinking water, boat launch (small boats)
Fee per night: $
Management: Wallowa-Whitman National Forest
Contact: (541) 742-7511; www.fs.usda.gov/recmain/wallowa-whitman/recreation
Finding the campground: From Main Street in Halfway, turn north onto Fish Lake Road at the sign for Fish Lake. Go 3.2 miles and turn left onto gravel Clear Creek Road/FR 66, which is signed for a snow park. In 4 miles turn right onto FR 66; continue 12.5 miles to enter the campground on the left. Much of the way is on narrow, single-lane gravel or dirt road.
GPS coordinates: N45 02.989' / W117 05.821'
About the campground: At an elevation of 6,600 feet, you will find this inviting mountain lake in a basin of spired trees, meadow, and scree. A small earthen dam has enlarged the lake, a couple of islands contribute to its charm, and avalanche lilies decorate its shore as the snow recedes. Come prepared for mosquitoes and cold nights. Fishing is the draw.

607 Hewitt/Holcomb County Parks

Location: About 2 miles east of Richland
Season: Year-round
Sites: 27 hookup sites, 20 basic sites, 15 tent sites; water and electric hookups
Maximum length: 30 feet
Facilities: Tables, barbecues, flush toilets, drinking water, showers, covered gazebos, playground, boating and angling docks, boat launches, fish-cleaning station
Fee per night: $$
Management: Baker County
Contact: (541) 523-8342; (541) 893-6147 for reservations; www.bakercounty.org
Finding the campground: From Richland go east on OR 86 for 0.8 mile. Bear right onto the road signed for Hewitt Park; proceed 1.5 miles to the park campground at road's end.
GPS coordinates: N44 45.405' / W117 07.632'
About the campground: This campground stretches along the Powder River Arm of Brownlee Reservoir. The park's sloping acre of green lawn stands in contrast to the dusky, dry grass canyon. Most visitors come for the boating and fishing, for which the lake is noted. The RV camping area is an extensive paved lot, with numbered sites and accompanying tables and barbecues and planted shade trees at its perimeter. A separate tent camping area on a constructed terrace close to the water provides tenters with a flat spot to camp beneath the trees. All sites are just steps from the water, and trophy catfish can entice anglers out at night.

608 Lake Fork

Location: About 18 miles northeast of Halfway
Season: Late May–Oct
Sites: 10 basic sites; no hookups
Maximum length: 22 feet
Facilities: Tables, grills, nonflush toilets; no drinking water
Fee per night: $
Management: Wallowa-Whitman National Forest
Contact: (541) 426-4978; www.fs.usda.gov/recmain/wallowa-whitman/recreation
Finding the campground: From OR 86, 10 miles east of Halfway, turn north onto FR 39, the Wallowa Mountain Loop Road. Continue 8 miles to reach the campground on the left.
GPS coordinates: N45 00.551' / W116 54.832'
About the campground: This quiet campground along Lake Fork Creek consists of shady, well-spaced sites in a multistory mixed forest of fir, pine, and larch. Just north of the camp, the Lake Fork Trail offers hikes to Big Elk Creek (2 miles) or Fish Lake (11 miles). The campground is conveniently located along Wallowa Mountain Loop Road, which accesses the sights, trails, and attractions of Wallowa-Whitman National Forest and Hells Canyon National Recreation Area.

609 McBride

Location: About 16 miles northwest of Halfway
Season: Mid-May–Oct
Sites: 6 basic sites; no hookups
Maximum length: 16 feet
Facilities: Tables, grills, nonflush toilets; no drinking water
Fee per night: None
Management: Wallowa-Whitman National Forest
Contact: (541) 742-7511; www.fs.usda.gov/recmain/wallowa-whitman/recreation
Finding the campground: From OR 86 just west of the highway summit, 6 miles west of Halfway and 47 miles east of Baker City, turn north onto gravel, washboard FR 77. Follow it for 10.4 miles to the campground on the left.
GPS coordinates: N44 56.082' / W117 13.302'
About the campground: Along Brooks Ditch, this campground extends a quiet forest retreat. In fall, hunters swell the camp population. Opposite the campground turnoff is FR 7715, which travels 4.5 miles to the road's end and Summit Point Trailhead and a vista. Views pan south-southwest. Hiking the Cliff River Trail from here leads past Summit Point Lookout Tower, which is reached via the spur at 0.6 mile. Destinations include Little Eagle Meadows, Nip and Tuck Passes, and some prized high-mountain lakes, if you are a power hiker or backpacker. Bears frequent the Summit Point area.

610 Tamarack

Location: About 36 miles northeast of Baker City
Season: June–Oct
Sites: 12 basic sites; no hookups
Maximum length: 22 feet
Facilities: Tables, grills, nonflush toilets, drinking water
Fee per night: $
Management: Wallowa-Whitman National Forest
Contact: (541) 742-7511; www.fs.usda.gov/recmain/wallowa-whitman/recreation
Finding the campground: From OR 203 at Medical Springs (20 miles northeast of Baker City), turn southeast onto Collins Road/Eagle Creek Drive toward Boulder Park. The road quickly widens and changes to gravel. Go 1.6 miles and turn left onto FR 67. Continue 13.5 miles. Bear right (east) on FR 77 and go 0.6 mile to the campground.
GPS coordinates: N45 01.194' / W117 27.194'
About the campground: This campground occupies a sunny location above Eagle Creek, with log-defined parking, grassy sites, and an open forest of larch, spruce, and fir. The creek adds a scenic ribbon and a restful voice. By taking FR 7750 north off FR 77, 0.3 mile west of camp, you can access the Two Color Trail, which travels to Two Color Lake. But you need not hike far to enjoy the walk and observe the Wallowa Mountains' signature grandeur. In camp, an all-ability trail accesses fishing platforms.

611 Twin Lakes

Location: About 25 miles northeast of Halfway
Season: June–Sept
Sites: 8 basic sites; no hookups
Maximum length: 15 feet; best suited for tents
Facilities: Tables, grills, nonflush toilets; no drinking water
Fee per night: None
Management: Wallowa-Whitman National Forest
Contact: (541) 426-4978; www.fs.usda.gov/recmain/wallowa-whitman/recreation
Finding the campground: From Main Street in Halfway, turn north onto Fish Lake Road for Fish Lake. Go 3.2 miles and turn left onto gravel Clear Creek Road/FR 66, which is signed for a snow park. In 4 miles turn right onto FR 66 and continue 17.6 miles to the campground on the left. Much of the way is on narrow, single-lane gravel or dirt road.
GPS coordinates: N45 04.757' / W117 03.266'
About the campground: Here you'll find meadowy ponds and a quiet split-level campground. Lodgepole pines, firs, and larches dress the camp, and Russel Mountain presides over the area. A fire several years ago left a wake of silver snags and logs that continue to be part of the Twin Lakes mosaic. At the campground a boardwalk ramp spans the meadowy shore to provide fishing access on the open water.

612 Two Color

Location: About 36 miles northeast of Baker City
Season: June–Oct
Sites: 11 basic sites; no hookups
Maximum length: 22 feet
Facilities: Tables, grills, nonflush toilets; no drinking water
Fee per night: None
Management: Wallowa-Whitman National Forest
Contact: (541) 963-7186; www.fs.usda.gov/recmain/wallowa-whitman/recreation
Finding the campground: From OR 203 at Medical Springs (20 miles northeast of Baker City), turn southeast onto Collins Road/Eagle Creek Drive toward Boulder Park. The road soon widens and becomes gravel. Go 1.6 miles and turn left onto FR 67. Continue 13.5 miles and turn left (west) onto FR 77. Continue 0.7 mile and bear right onto FR 7755 to reach the campground in 0.5 mile.
GPS coordinates: N45 02.261' / W117 26.731'
About the campground: In a mixed-conifer stand with a grassy floor, this campground offers both sun and shade. Flowing past camp is Eagle Creek, wide and clear rushing, with richly vegetated banks. Following FR 7755 north to its end, in about 3 miles, will take you to Fake Creek and Main Eagle Trails. They roll out long-distance hikes but also have satisfying scenery and stops for day hikers.

Upper Imnaha River Area

	Hookup Sites	Total Sites	Max. RV Length	Hookups	Toilets	Showers	Drinking Water	Dump Station	Recreation	Fee	Can Reserve
613 Blackhorse		15	25		NF				F	$	
614 Coverdale		11	15		NF				F	$	
615 Hidden		10	25		NF				F	$	
616 Indian Crossing		14	20		NF				HFR	$	
617 Lick Creek		9	40		NF					$	
618 Ollokot		12	30		NF		X		F	$	

613 Blackhorse

Location: About 36 miles southeast of Joseph
Season: June–Oct
Sites: 15 basic sites; no hookups
Maximum length: 25 feet
Facilities: Tables, grills, nonflush toilets; no drinking water
Fee per night: $
Management: Wallowa-Whitman National Forest
Contact: (541) 426-4978; www.fs.usda.gov/recmain/wallowa-whitman/recreation
Finding the campground: From OR 82 in Joseph, turn east onto East Wallowa Avenue at the sign for Imnaha and Halfway; the road later becomes the Imnaha Highway. Go 7.8 miles and turn right (south) onto Wallowa Mountain Loop Road. Continue 28.6 miles to the campground on the left.
GPS coordinates: N45 09.517' / W116 52.422'
About the campground: Along the Imnaha Wild and Scenic River and Wallowa Mountain Loop Road, you will find this camp with well-spaced sites. Meadow openings intersperse the forest of fir, ponderosa pine, and larch, creating a mix of sun and shade. The Imnaha River is captivating in its color, clarity, and overall persona. Besides fishing, camp guests may take a short drive to Hells Canyon Overlook or check out the trails at Indian Crossing (look for the signed turns, south on Wallowa Mountain Loop Road).

614 Coverdale

Location: About 41 miles southeast of Joseph
Season: June–Oct
Sites: 2 basic sites, 9 tent sites; no hookups
Maximum length: 15 feet; primarily a tent area
Facilities: Tables, grills, nonflush toilets; no drinking water
Fee per night: $
Management: Wallowa-Whitman National Forest
Contact: (541) 426-4978; www.fs.usda.gov/recmain/wallowa-whitman/recreation
Finding the campground: From OR 82 in Joseph, turn east onto East Wallowa Avenue at the sign for Imnaha and Halfway; the road later becomes the Imnaha Highway. Go 7.8 miles and turn right (south) onto Wallowa Mountain Loop Road. Continue 29 miles and turn right onto FR 3960. Near milepost 4 on FR 3960, turn left onto FR 100 to enter the campground.
GPS coordinates: N45 06.437' / W116 55.386'
About the campground: This primitive Imnaha River campground sits at the edge of a riparian wildflower meadow in an open flat of mixed-age ponderosa pine. Sites spread across the untamed, natural setting, which can be overgrown in places. Shrubs edge the clear-rushing river. The rustic campground holds great tranquility, but the mosquitoes can be annoying. Fishing, hiking, and horseback riding are area pursuits.

615 Hidden

Location: About 44 miles southeast of Joseph
Season: June–Oct
Sites: 10 basic sites; no hookups
Maximum length: 25 feet
Facilities: Tables, grills, nonflush toilets; no drinking water
Fee per night: $
Management: Wallowa-Whitman National Forest
Contact: (541) 426-4978; www.fs.usda.gov/recmain/wallowa-whitman/recreation
Finding the campground: From OR 82 in Joseph, turn east onto East Wallowa Avenue at the sign for Imnaha and Halfway; the road later becomes the Imnaha Highway. Go 7.8 miles and turn right (south) onto Wallowa Mountain Loop Road. Continue 29 miles and turn right onto FR 3960. Proceed 6.9 miles to enter the campground on the left.
GPS coordinates: N45 06.833' / W116 58.751'
About the campground: This nicely forested campground has bookend outcrops. Footpaths from each site lead to the Imnaha Wild and Scenic River. Sites enjoy partial to full shade beneath a canopy of fir, pine, and larch. Upstream the river is braided by meadow islands; downstream the river is rushing. Campers pass their days fishing, watching wildlife, and exploring area trails. Some campsites have been upgraded for people with disabilities.

616 Indian Crossing

Location: About 46 miles southeast of Joseph
Season: June–Oct
Sites: 8 basic sites, 6 horse sites; no hookups
Maximum length: 20 feet
Facilities: Tables, grills, nonflush toilets, horse hitching rails, troughs, loading ramp; no drinking water
Fee per night: $
Management: Wallowa-Whitman National Forest
Contact: (541) 426-4978; www.fs.usda.gov/recmain/wallowa-whitman/recreation
Finding the campground: From OR 82 in Joseph, turn east onto East Wallowa Avenue at the sign for Imnaha and Halfway; the road later becomes the Imnaha Highway. Go 7.8 miles and turn right (south) onto Wallowa Mountain Loop Road. Continue 29 miles and turn right onto FR 3960. Proceed 8.7 miles to the campground and trailhead at road's end.
GPS coordinates: N45 06.784' / W117 00.810'
About the campground: As a main gateway to the Eagle Cap Wilderness, this open-forest campground is popular with hikers, equestrians, anglers, and hunters. The camp straddles the Imnaha Wild and Scenic River, with the horse camp claiming the north shore and the family sites on the south shore. Nearby trails pursue the river upstream into the wilderness and climb the ridge to Duck Lake. Some campsites have been upgraded for people with disabilities.

617 Lick Creek

Location: About 23 miles southeast of Joseph
Season: June–Oct
Sites: 9 basic sites; no hookups
Maximum length: 40 feet
Facilities: Tables, grills, nonflush toilets; no drinking water
Fee per night: $
Management: Wallowa-Whitman National Forest
Contact: (541) 426-4978; www.fs.usda.gov/recmain/wallowa-whitman/recreation
Finding the campground: From OR 82 in Joseph, turn east onto East Wallowa Avenue at the sign for Imnaha and Halfway; the road later becomes the Imnaha Highway. Go 7.8 miles and turn right (south) onto Wallowa Mountain Loop Road. Continue 15.1 miles to the campground.
GPS coordinates: N45 09.508' / W117 02.075'
About the campground: This fine family campground sits among the scattered firs and lodgepole pines in a meadow setting along Lick Creek. The campground has paved roads and gravel parking. Deer commonly browse in the wildflower meadow. In early August false hellebore, with its showy crown of flowers, gives the meadow dimension and texture. Wallowa Mountain Loop Road is the "yellow brick road" to many trails and sights in Hells Canyon National Recreation Area and the Eagle Cap Wilderness.

618 Ollokot

Location: About 37 miles southeast of Joseph
Season: June–Oct
Sites: 12 basic sites; no hookups
Maximum length: 30 feet
Facilities: Tables, grills, nonflush toilets, drinking water
Fee per night: $
Management: Wallowa-Whitman National Forest
Contact: (541) 426-4978; www.fs.usda.gov/recmain/wallowa-whitman/recreation
Finding the campground: From OR 82 in Joseph, turn east onto East Wallowa Avenue at the sign for Imnaha and Halfway; the road later becomes the Imnaha Highway. Go 7.8 miles and turn right (south) onto Wallowa Mountain Loop Road. Continue 29.1 miles to the campground on the left.
GPS coordinates: N45 09.138' / W116 52.608'
About the campground: On a low plateau above the Imnaha Wild and Scenic River, this campground occupies a ponderosa pine stand, with parklike spacing and a meadow floor. The campsites have gravel parking and are generally sunny. Campers can access the river fairly easily for fishing and admiring. Wallowa Mountain Loop Road is the avenue to outward exploration, hiking, and sightseeing.

Prairie City Area

	Hookup Sites	Total Sites	Max. RV Length	Hookups	Toilets	Showers	Drinking Water	Dump Station	Recreation	Fee	Can Reserve
619 Crescent		4	18		NF				F	None	
620 Depot Park	20	20	40	WES	F	X	X	X		$$	
621 Dixie		10	25		NF		X			$	
622 Elk Creek		5	T		NF					None	
623 Magone Lake		21	16		NF		X		HSFBL	$$	
624 North Fork Malheur		5	T		NF				HF	None	
625 Slide Creek Horse Camp and Campground		6	30		NF				HR	$ horse	
626 Strawberry		10	16		NF		X		H	$	
627 Trout Farm		6	30		NF		X		F	$	

619 Crescent

Location: About 17 miles south of Prairie City
Season: Late May–mid-Oct
Sites: 4 basic sites; no hookups
Maximum length: 18 feet
Facilities: Tables, grills, nonflush toilets; no drinking water
Fee per night: None
Management: Malheur National Forest
Contact: (541) 820-3800; www.fs.usda.gov/recmain/malheur/recreation
Finding the campground: From US 26 in Prairie City, turn south onto Main Street and go 0.3 mile. Turn left onto Bridge Street and continue east from it onto CR 62. After 16.6 miles turn right to enter the campground.
GPS coordinates: N44 16.895' / W118 32.710'
About the campground: This tiny campground sits along the John Day River in a forest of fir, spruce, and lodgepole pine. Sites are partially shaded and have gravel parking. Here the river spans 5 to 7 feet wide and flows clear and fast. The river fishery is acclaimed, but no taking of Dolly Varden (bull) trout is permitted.

620 Depot Park

Location: In Prairie City
Season: May–Oct
Sites: 20 RV hookup sites, open lawn for tent camping; water, electric, and sewer hookups
Maximum length: 40 feet
Facilities: Tables, flush toilets, drinking water, showers, dump station, picnic shelter
Fee per night: $$
Management: Prairie City
Contact: (541) 820-3605; www.prairiecityoregon.com
Finding the campground: From US 26 in Prairie City, turn south onto Main Street and go 0.3 mile. This city park is on the left at the intersection with Bridge Street.
GPS coordinates: N44 27.467' / W118 42.377'
About the campground: This charming city park welcomes weary travelers with its neatly trimmed lawns, shade trees, and babbling Strawberry Creek. Sites are available on a first-come, first-served basis. At the park you'll also find a 1910 historic depot (museum), railroad boxcar, wagon, and rustic statue, as well as a gazebo and picnic shelter. Each RV space has paved parking and a lawn meridian with a table. Tent campers can make use of the picnic shelter when preparing and eating meals. Seasonally open for tours, the museum has ten rooms of pioneer memorabilia.

621 Dixie

Location: About 10 miles east of Prairie City
Season: Late May–mid-Oct
Sites: 10 basic sites; no hookups
Maximum length: 25 feet
Facilities: Tables, grills, nonflush toilets, drinking water
Fee per night: $
Management: Malheur National Forest
Contact: (541) 820-3800; www.fs.usda.gov/recmain/malheur/recreation
Finding the campground: From the intersection of Main Street and US 26 in Prairie City, go east on US 26 for 9.5 miles. Turn left (north) into the campground.
GPS coordinates: N44 32.320' / W118 35.402'
About the campground: At Dixie Summit (elevation 5,000 feet), this terraced campground occupies a lodgepole pine–dominated forest, with larch and fir in the mix. Dwarf and true huckleberry grow beneath the trees. Sites are partially shaded, with gravel parking. Set back from US 26, the campground offers a quiet night's sleep. Hunting and berry picking are among the activities. In winter a snow park attracts visitors to the area.

622 Elk Creek

Location: About 25 miles southeast of Prairie City
Season: Late May–mid-Oct
Sites: 5 basic sites; no hookups
Maximum length: Best suited for tents or pickup campers
Facilities: Tables, grills, nonflush toilets; no drinking water
Fee per night: None
Management: Malheur National Forest
Contact: (541) 820-3800; www.fs.usda.gov/recmain/malheur/recreation
Finding the campground: From US 26 in Prairie City, turn south onto Main Street and go 0.3 mile. Turn left onto Bridge Street and continue east from it on CR 62. After 7.8 miles turn left onto paved FR 13. Continue 16 miles to FR 16. Turn right (south) onto FR 16 to reach the campground in another 1.5 miles.

From US 395 at Seneca, go east on FR 16 for 40 miles to reach the campground.
GPS coordinates: N44 14.766' / W118 23.907'
About the campground: This small campground is sandwiched between FR 16 and Elk Creek. Ponderosa and lodgepole pines dominate the camp, with a few Douglas and grand firs interwoven. Despite its proximity to FR 16, the campground conveys a feeling of isolation. It is not far from the hiking at North Fork Malheur River (southwest of camp, taking FR 1675 off FR 16) and Little Malheur River (northeast of camp off FR 1672).

623 Magone Lake

Location: About 19 miles northwest of Prairie City
Season: Late May–mid-Oct
Sites: 18 basic sites, 3 tent sites; no hookups
Maximum length: 16 feet
Facilities: Tables, grills, nonflush toilets, drinking water, dock, boat launch for human-powered craft
Fee per night: $$
Management: Malheur National Forest
Contact: (541) 820-3800; www.fs.usda.gov/recmain/malheur/recreation
Finding the campground: From Prairie City drive west on US 26 for 3.4 miles. Turn north onto Bear Creek Road/CR 18 and go 13 miles. Turn left onto FR 3620, following it for 1.5 miles. Turn right onto FR 3618 to reach the campground in 1.5 miles. Signs point the way along the paved and gravel route.

An alternative entry is east off US 395, 9 miles north of Mount Vernon. Follow CR 32/FR 36 and FR 3618 for 10 miles to the campground.
GPS coordinates: N44 33.167' / W118 54.685'
About the campground: This popular campground occupies the forested shore of Magone Lake. In the 1800s a natural landslide captured the waters of Lake Creek to form this 50-acre lake, which now offers swimming, fishing, and quiet boating. Muskrats and duck families inhabit the lake. A 1.5-mile trail encircles the water, and the 0.5-mile Magone Slide Trail leaves FR 3618 near the day-use area.

624 North Fork Malheur

Location: About 29 miles southeast of Prairie City
Season: Late May–mid-Oct
Sites: 5 basic sites; no hookups
Maximum length: Best suited for tents or smaller units
Facilities: Tables, grills, nonflush toilets; no drinking water
Fee per night: None
Management: Malheur National Forest
Contact: (541) 820-3800; www.fs.usda.gov/recmain/malheur/recreation
Finding the campground: From US 26 in Prairie City, turn south onto Main Street and go 0.3 mile. Turn left onto Bridge Street and continue east on CR 62. After 7.8 miles turn left onto paved FR 13. Continue 16 miles to paved FR 16. Turn right (south) onto FR 16, reaching the campground turnoff on the left in another 2.2 miles. Now follow dirt FR 1675 for 2.5 miles to enter the campground on the right.

From US 395 at Seneca, go east on FR 16 for 39.3 miles to reach the campground turnoff (FR 1675) on the right.
GPS coordinates: N44 12.534' / W118 22.937'
About the campground: Rimmed by fence, this picturesque camp unites a lovely forest of ponderosa pine and larch, a meadowy shore and islands, and the braided, glimmering water of the North Fork Malheur Wild and Scenic River. Gates at either end of the camp provide access to the river, where angler paths travel along shore. Following FR 1675 past the camp for less than 1 mile takes you to the North Fork Malheur Trailhead. Although there is an ample parking area, the road is narrow and rough in spots. Access is best for high-clearance and smaller units. The trail extends for a dozen miles and offers a wonderful river-forest sojourn.

625 Slide Creek Horse Camp and Campground

Location: About 9 miles south of Prairie City
Season: Mid-May–mid-Nov
Sites: 3 basic sites, 3 horse sites; no hookups
Maximum length: 30 feet
Facilities: Tables, grills, nonflush toilets, corrals at horse camp; no drinking water
Fee per night: None for basic sites; $ for horse sites
Management: Malheur National Forest
Contact: (541) 820-3800; www.fs.usda.gov/recmain/malheur/recreation
Finding the campgrounds: From US 26 in Prairie City, turn south onto Main Street and go 0.3 mile. Turn left and then right on Bridge Street, which becomes CR 60 as it heads south out of town. The route begins paved and becomes gravel and changes to FR 6001 upon entering the national forest. Reach these two camp areas in about 9 miles.
GPS coordinates: N44 20.505' / W118 39.456'
About the campgrounds: These small rustic campgrounds near the confluence of Slide and Strawberry Creeks have grassy floors and an open-forest look. As an entryway to the Strawberry

Mountain Wilderness, the camps are popular with hunters and hikers. Near these camps, the Slide Creek Connector Trail heads east off FR 6001 and links up with the wilderness trail network near Slide Lake. Stock can be watered at Strawberry Creek.

626 Strawberry

Location: About 11 miles south of Prairie City
Season: Maintained mid-June–mid-Oct
Sites: 10 basic sites; no hookups
Maximum length: 16 feet
Facilities: Tables, grills, nonflush toilets, drinking water
Fee per night: $
Management: Malheur National Forest
Contact: (541) 820-3800; www.fs.usda.gov/recmain/malheur/recreation
Finding the campground: From US 26 in Prairie City, turn south onto Main Street and go 0.3 mile. Turn left and then right on Bridge Street, which becomes CR 60 as it heads south out of town. The road begins paved and becomes gravel and changes to FR 6001 upon entering the national forest. Reach the campground in 10.8 miles.
GPS coordinates: N44 19.177' / W118 40.423'
About the campground: At more than a mile high, this popular camp in high-elevation forest is the primary base and access to Strawberry Mountain Wilderness, a prized area of high lakes, snow-patched peaks, tinsel-like streams, waterfalls, and wildflower-spangled meadows and crests. Adjacent to the camp is trailhead parking, and the Strawberry Basin Trail is your pass to the grandeur.

627 Trout Farm

Location: About 15 miles south of Prairie City
Season: Late May–mid-Oct
Sites: 6 basic sites; no hookups
Maximum length: 30 feet
Facilities: Tables, grills, nonflush toilets, drinking water, picnic shelter
Fee per night: $
Management: Malheur National Forest
Contact: (541) 820-3800; www.fs.usda.gov/recmain/malheur/recreation
Finding the campground: From US 26 in Prairie City, turn south onto Main Street and go 0.3 mile. Turn left on Bridge Street and continue east on CR 62. After 14.9 miles turn right for the campground.
GPS coordinates: N44 18.279' / W118 33.117'
About the campground: Along the upper John Day River and a small fishing pond sits this tranquil campground in a full fir forest. Often the pond shows thick vegetation, but small trout and families of ducks still animate the water. A barrier-free trail partially rims the pond, providing fishing access for all.

	Hookup Sites	Total Sites	Max. RV Length	Hookups	Toilets	Showers	Drinking Water	Dump Station	Recreation	Fee	Can Reserve
628 Big Creek		15	25		NF		X		FC	$	
629 Murray		5	25		NF				F	$	
630 Parish Cabin		17	35		NF		X		F	$	
631 Rock Springs		12	25		NF				O	$	
632 Starr		9	30		NF					$	
633 Wickiup		6	22		NF				F	$	

628 Big Creek

Location: About 19 miles northeast of Seneca
Season: Late May–mid-Oct
Sites: 15 basic sites; no hookups
Maximum length: 25 feet
Facilities: Tables, grills, nonflush toilets, drinking water
Fee per night: $
Management: Malheur National Forest
Contact: (541) 820-3800; www.fs.usda.gov/recmain/malheur/recreation
Finding the campground: From US 395 at Seneca, turn east onto paved FR 16 and go 18.7 miles. Turn left onto gravel FR 815 for the campground.
GPS coordinates: N44 11.308' / W118 36.962'
About the campground: This camp with some closely spaced sites occupies a flat of ponderosa and lodgepole pines between Big Creek and Logan Valley, an expansive meadow with a kaleidoscope of wildflowers and abundant wildlife. Sightings of deer, antelope, sandhill crane, and coyote are common. An egress in the camp's rail fence leads to Big Creek, with its alder-lined banks and deep pools. Consult the camp information board for details about the Big Creek Area mountain bike trails, which make use of nearby seldom-used and closed forest roads.

629 Murray

Location: About 20 miles northeast of Seneca
Season: Late May–mid-Oct
Sites: 5 basic sites; no hookups
Maximum length: 25 feet
Facilities: Tables, grills, nonflush toilets; no drinking water
Fee per night: $
Management: Malheur National Forest
Contact: (541) 820-3800; www.fs.usda.gov/recmain/malheur/recreation
Finding the campground: From US 395 at Seneca, turn east onto paved FR 16 and go 17.2 miles. Turn left onto gravel FR 1600.924 and proceed 2.6 miles to the campground. It is on the left before the junction with FR 1648.
GPS coordinates: N44 12.748' / W118 38.344'
About the campground: This campground occupies a semi-open mixed forest along Lake Creek. Within camp reigns a regal old-growth ponderosa pine. Lake Creek is a fast-rushing water, with forested shores. South of camp 0.5 mile, near the Lake Creek Youth Camp, you will find Trail 307, a closed jeep trail to explore.

630 Parish Cabin

Location: 11 miles northeast of Seneca
Season: Late May–mid-Oct
Sites: 17 basic sites; no hookups
Maximum length: 35 feet
Facilities: Tables, grills, nonflush toilets, drinking water
Fee per night: $
Management: Malheur National Forest
Contact: (541) 820-3800; www.fs.usda.gov/recmain/malheur/recreation
Finding the campground: From US 395 at Seneca, turn east onto paved FR 16 and go 11 miles; the campground is on the left.

From US 26 at John Day, go south on US 395 for 10.1 miles. Turn left (east) onto CR 65/FR 15 at the sign for Canyon Meadows and Wickiup Campground. Proceed 13.7 miles and turn right onto FR 16. The campground is on the right in 0.1 mile.
GPS coordinates: N44 10.760' / W118 45.964'
About the campground: This campground occupies a flat of lodgepole pines along picturesque Bear Creek. Lush meadow banks decorated in wildflowers and shrubs contain the meandering stream. The sites have partial shade and gravel parking spaces; a few sites have pull-through parking. Look for indications of beaver along the creek.

631 Rock Springs

Location: About 40 miles northeast of Burns/Hines, 42 miles south of John Day
Season: May–Oct
Sites: 12 basic sites; no hookups
Maximum length: 25 feet
Facilities: Tables, grills, nonflush toilets; no drinking water
Fee per night: $
Management: Malheur National Forest
Contact: (541) 820-3800; www.fs.usda.gov/recmain/malheur/recreation
Finding the campground: From the junction of US 395 and US 20 West in Burns/Hines, follow US 395 north for 35.2 miles. Turn right onto CR 73, which becomes FR 17 as you enter the national forest. Go 4.4 miles and turn right onto gravel FR 1700.054 to reach the campground on the left in 0.8 mile.
GPS coordinates: N44 00.018' / W118 50.388'
About the campground: Sites are dispersed through this open ponderosa pine forest with its meadow floor and small whispering aspens. The camp is mostly used by hunters and off-highway-vehicle users. A pine butterfly hatch defoliated many of the trees in 2011.

632 Starr

Location: About 16 miles south of John Day
Season: Late May–mid-Oct
Sites: 9 basic sites; no hookups
Maximum length: 30 feet
Facilities: Tables, grills, nonflush toilets; no drinking water
Fee per night: $
Management: Malheur National Forest
Contact: (541) 820-3800; www.fs.usda.gov/recmain/malheur/recreation
Finding the campground: From John Day go south on US 395 for 15.5 miles to enter the campground on the right at the highway summit (elevation 5,125 feet).
GPS coordinates: N44 15.552' / W119 01.122'
About the campground: This campground occupies a ponderosa pine forest and shrub-meadow flat. Across the road from the camp is a winter sports area with warming hut and sledding hill. The closed roads that serve cross-country skiers and snowshoers in winter double as hiking trails in summer. The camp is near Fall Mountain Lookout, a 20-foot fire tower built in 1933. Although the public can no longer enter the historic fire tower, they may still choose to visit it. North of the campground take FR 4920 northwest off US 395 to high-clearance FR 4920.607; walk uphill to the lookout.

633 Wickiup

Location: About 23 miles northeast of Seneca
Season: Late May–mid-Oct
Sites: 6 basic sites; no hookups
Maximum length: 22 feet
Facilities: Tables, grills, nonflush toilets; no drinking water
Fee per night: $
Management: Malheur National Forest
Contact: (541) 820-3800; www.fs.usda.gov/recmain/malheur/recreation
Finding the campground: From US 26 at John Day, go south on US 395 for 10.1 miles. Turn left (east) onto paved CR 65/FR 15 at the sign for Canyon Meadows and Wickiup Campground. Proceed 7.7 miles to reach campground on the right off FR 1516, which heads to Dry Soda Lookout.
GPS coordinates: N44 12.997' / W118 51.145'
About the campground: At the foot of a forested slope, this campground occupies a pine-fir flat along Canyon Creek at the Wickiup confluence. The sparkling water courses over a pebble-and-rock bed, creating a restful backdrop rush. Wild roses and dogwoods accent the flat. West of the camp off FR 15 is the trailhead for Table Mountain Loop, and few hikers can resist the call of the nearby Strawberry Mountain Wilderness.

Unity Area

	Hookup Sites	Total Sites	Max. RV Length	Hookups	Toilets	Showers	Drinking Water	Dump Station	Recreation	Fee	Can Reserve
634 Elk Creek		10	25		NF				0	$	
635 Oregon		8	28		NF		X		0	$	
636 South Fork		18	40		NF		X		FO	$	
637 Stevens		7	40		NF				HFO	$	
638 Unity Lake State Park	35	35	40	WE	F	X	X	X	SFBL	$$-$$$	
639 Wetmore		12	18		NF		X		H	$	
640 Yellow Pine		21	30		NF		X		H	$	

634 Elk Creek

Location: About 9 miles southwest of Unity
Season: Mid-May–mid-Oct
Sites: 10 basic sites; no hookups
Maximum length: 25 feet, with a longer wheelchair-accessible site
Facilities: Tables, grills, nonflush toilets; no drinking water
Fee per night: $
Management: Wallowa-Whitman National Forest
Contact: (541) 523-4476; www.fs.usda.gov/recmain/wallowa-whitman/recreation
Finding the campground: From US 26 at Unity, go 8.9 miles southwest on South Fork Road (CR 600/FR 6005) to reach this campground on the left. The final 4.6 miles is on gravel.
GPS coordinates: N44 24.036' / W118 19.728'
About the campground: This camp, with gravel road, occupies a tall pine–dry grass forest alongside sparkling creek-size South Fork Burnt River. Alders grow riverside. Off-highway-vehicle (OHV) users find a central area for trailer parking and OHV trails that link to the Sumpter Area. State OHV rules and licenses required.

635 Oregon

Location: About 13 miles northwest of Unity
Season: Mid-May–mid-Oct
Sites: 8 basic sites; no hookups
Maximum length: 28 feet
Facilities: Tables, grills, nonflush toilets, drinking water
Fee per night: $
Management: Wallowa-Whitman National Forest
Contact: (541) 523-4476; www.fs.usda.gov/recmain/wallowa-whitman/recreation
Finding the campground: The campground is north off US 26, 12.7 miles west of Unity and 23.6 miles east of Prairie City.
GPS coordinates: N44 32.786' / W118 20.480'
About the campground: Ideal for US 26 travelers, this campground provides fully to partially shaded sites in a forest of ponderosa pine and fir. Shrubs and wildflowers decorate the understory. The sites have gravel parking. From the camp an off-highway-vehicle trail heads both north and south. Unity Reservoir, Monument Rock Wilderness, and the historic Sumpter Valley Railroad also suggest outings.

636 South Fork

Location: About 8 miles southwest of Unity
Season: Mid-May–mid-Oct
Sites: 18 basic sites; no hookups
Maximum length: 40 feet
Facilities: Tables, grills, nonflush toilets, drinking water
Fee per night: $
Management: Wallowa-Whitman National Forest
Contact: (541) 523-4476; www.fs.usda.gov/recmain/wallowa-whitman/recreation
Finding the campground: From US 26 at Unity, go 7.5 miles southwest on South Fork Road (CR 600/FR 6005) to reach this campground on the left. The final 3.2 miles is on gravel.
GPS coordinates: N44 24.235' / W118 18.345'
About the campground: This campground hugs the pretty South Fork Burnt River. A meadow floor spills beneath the towering pines, firs, and larches. Several of the sites overlook the sparkling river and its alder banks. If you steal up to the water, fishing is possible. Hikers may choose to investigate nearby Monument Rock Wilderness. An off-highway-vehicle access trail leaves from camp.

637 Stevens

Location: About 9 miles southwest of Unity
Season: Mid-May–mid-Oct
Sites: 7 basic sites; no hookups
Maximum length: 40 feet
Facilities: Tables, grills, nonflush toilets; no drinking water
Fee per night: $
Management: Wallowa-Whitman National Forest
Contact: (541) 523-4476; www.fs.usda.gov/recmain/wallowa-whitman/recreation
Finding the campground: From US 26 at Unity, go 8.5 miles southwest on South Fork Road (CR 600/FR 6005) to reach this campground on the right. The final 4.2 miles is on gravel.
GPS coordinates: N44 24.012' / W118 19.270'
About the campground: Under a mixed pine canopy along the gurgling South Fork Burnt River, this camp serves hikers, fishers, hunters, and off-highway-vehicle users. Some beautiful big old yellow-bellies grace the stand. Monument Rock Wilderness, passed en route to camp, invites hikers to explore.

638 Unity Lake State Park

Location: About 4 miles north of Unity
Season: Apr–Oct
Sites: 35 hookup sites, 2 cabins; water and electric hookups
Maximum length: 40 feet
Facilities: Tables, fire rings, flush toilets, drinking water, showers, dump station, boat launch, dock
Fee per night: $$–$$$
Management: Oregon State Parks and Recreation Department
Contact: (541) 932-4453; www.oregon.gov/OPRD/PARKS/camping.shtml
Finding the campground: From Unity go west on US 26 for 1.7 miles. Turn north onto OR 245 toward Hereford and Baker City and go another 2.5 miles. Turn left at the sign for Unity Lake State Park and proceed into the park.
GPS coordinates: N44 30.009' / W118 11.205'
About the campground: At this landscaped campground, the planted shade trees are still growing, but the adjoining day-use area is well shaded. Unity Lake harnesses the Burnt River and rests in an arid basin in the Blue Mountains. Views are of the surrounding sage-grass hills and their volcanic crests. The blue water is a strong enticement to fish, boat, swim, or windsurf. Best fishing is during spring and fall; the catch is trout, bass, and crappie.

639 Wetmore

Location: About 10 miles northwest of Unity
Season: Mid-May–mid-Oct
Sites: 12 basic sites; no hookups
Maximum length: 18 feet
Facilities: Tables, grills, nonflush toilets, drinking water
Fee per night: $
Management: Wallowa-Whitman National Forest
Contact: (541) 523-4476; www.fs.usda.gov/recmain/wallowa-whitman/recreation
Finding the campground: This campground is north off US 26, 10.2 miles west of Unity and 27.1 miles east of Prairie City.
GPS coordinates: N44 31.478' / W118 18.209'
About the campground: This family campground occupies a rolling terrain of fir, ponderosa pine, and larch. An understory of mixed shrubs and wild roses attracts browsing deer. At the west end of the camp, a 0.5-mile paved, barrier-free trail journeys along a gurgling tributary and past old-growth pines and volcanic outcrops to switchback uphill to neighboring Yellow Pine Campground. Possible car outings include Unity Reservoir or the Sumpter Valley Railroad.

640 Yellow Pine

Location: About 11 miles northwest of Unity
Season: Mid-May–mid-Oct
Sites: 21 basic sites; no hookups
Maximum length: 30 feet
Facilities: Tables, grills, nonflush toilets, drinking water
Fee per night: $
Management: Wallowa-Whitman National Forest
Contact: (541) 523-4476; www.fs.usda.gov/recmain/wallowa-whitman/recreation
Finding the campground: The campground is north off US 26, 10.8 miles west of Unity and 26.5 miles east of Prairie City.
GPS coordinates: N44 31.775' / W118 18.726'
About the campground: This pleasant campground is tucked off US 26 in a gently rolling terrain punctuated with mature yellow-bellied ponderosa pines. Younger pines and firs fill out the forest. From the east end of the campground, a barrier-free nature trail travels 0.5 mile to Wetmore Campground. Deer sometimes visit the camp.

Ontario Area

	Hookup Sites	Total Sites	Max. RV Length	Hookups	Toilets	Showers	Drinking Water	Dump Station	Recreation	Fee	Can Reserve
641 Bully Creek Reservoir County Park	40	40	40	E	F	X	X	X	SFBL	$$	X
642 Cow Hollow County Park	21	21	40	E	F	X				Donation	
643 Farewell Bend State Recreation Area	101	131	56	WE	F	X	X	X	SFBL	$$-$$$	X
644 Lake Owyhee State Park	57	74	55	WE	F	X	X	X	SFBL	$$-$$$	X
645 Leslie Gulch–Slocum Creek		12	20	NF					HSFBL	None	
646 Spring Recreation Site		35	30	NF			X		SFBL	$	
647 Succor Creek State Park		18	Small	NF					H	None	

641 Bully Creek Reservoir County Park

Location: On Bully Creek Reservoir, about 11 miles northwest of Vale
Season: Mid-Apr–mid-Nov
Sites: 40 hookup sites; electric hookups
Maximum length: 40 feet
Facilities: Tables, grills, flush toilets, drinking water, showers, dump station, boat launch, dock
Fee per night: $$
Management: Malheur County
Contact: (541) 473-2969, reservations accepted; www.malheurco.org/parks
Finding the campground: From US 20 at the west end of Vale, go west on Graham Boulevard for 7 miles. Continue northwest on Bully Creek Reservoir Road for another 4 miles; the campground is on the left.
GPS coordinates: N44 01.455' / W117 24.071'
About the campground: This landscaped campground rests in the basin of grassy hills that contains Bully Creek Reservoir, the centerpiece for recreation. The reservoir offers boating, swimming, and catches of panfish. Shade is rare along the shore. Campsites have gravel parking; a few sites are shaded by fuller trees.

642 Cow Hollow County Park

Location: About 10 miles southwest of Nyssa, 15 miles south of Vale
Season: May–Oct
Sites: 21 hookup sites; electric hookups
Maximum length: 40 feet
Facilities: Tables, flush toilets, showers, playground, horseshoe pits, tennis court with basketball hoop, ball field; no drinking water
Fee per night: Donation for maintenance
Management: Malheur County
Contact: (541) 473-5124; www.malheurco.org/parks
Finding the campground: From US 20/26 in Nyssa (12 miles south of Ontario) drive south on OR 201 for 4.3 miles. Turn right (west) onto Grand Avenue and continue 4 miles. Turn left onto Lytle Boulevard and go 1.6 miles to its junction with Janeta Avenue. Turn right (west) onto Janeta and go 0.2 mile. Turn left, following signs for the park. The park/camp is another 0.2 mile ahead on the right. *NOTE:* RVers should take the second turn to avoid bumps.
GPS coordinates: N43 49.003' / W117 07.138'
About the campground: This rural 20-acre, lawn-and-shade-tree camp provides an oasis and base for exploring the southeast desert. Northbound, Lytle Boulevard parallels the historic Oregon Trail, with historic wagon ruts, interpretive panels, and an overlook trail at Keeney Pass. During the Depression a Civilian Conservation Corps camp operated at what is now the park to improve area irrigation. In World War II the site became an internment camp for Japanese-Americans, with workers laboring in the sugar beet industry.

643 Farewell Bend State Recreation Area

Location: On Brownlee Reservoir, about 26 miles northwest of Ontario
Season: Year-round
Sites: 101 hookup sites, 30 basic sites, hiker/biker camp, 2 cabins; water and electric hookups
Maximum length: 56 feet
Facilities: Tables, grills, flush toilets, drinking water, showers, dump station, playground, sand volleyball, horseshoe pits, fishing docks, boat launch, Oregon Trail exhibit
Fee per night: $$–$$$
Management: Oregon State Parks and Recreation Department
Contact: (541) 869-2365; (800) 452-5687 for reservations; www.oregon.gov/OPRD/PARKS/camping.shtml
Finding the campground: From I-84 (25 miles northwest of Ontario) take exit 353 and go north on US 30 Business toward Huntington. The park is on the right in 1 mile.
GPS coordinates: N44 18.314' / W117 13.596'
About the campground: Here along the Snake River, you can camp where the Oregon pioneers did more than 150 years ago. But there are a couple of notable differences: The accommodations are now first class, and the river is contained as Brownlee Reservoir. Arid canyon hills overlook this oasis of lawn and trees. The hookup sites occupy two distinct areas: One has privacy hedges,

mature shade trees, and a central lawn. The other, in the arid Snake River Canyon, has open lawn and young trees. Boating, swimming, fishing for bass and catfish, hunting (outside the park), and rockhounding in the outlying area entertain guests.

644 Lake Owyhee State Park

Location: 33 miles southwest of Nyssa
Season: Mid-Apr–Oct
Sites: 31 hookup sites, 8 basic sites, 2 tepees (at McCormack); 26 hookup sites, 9 basic sites (at Indian Creek); water and electric hookups
Maximum length: 55 feet
Facilities: Tables, grills, flush toilets, drinking water, showers, dump station, boat launch, dock, fish-cleaning station
Fee per night: $$–$$$
Management: Oregon State Parks and Recreation Department
Contact: (800) 551-6949; (800) 452-5687 for reservations (for half the electrical sites and for tepees only); www.oregon.gov/OPRD/PARKS/camping.shtml
Finding the campground: From Nyssa go south on OR 201 about 12 miles. Turn right onto Owyhee Avenue for Lake Owyhee. Follow Owyhee Avenue west and Owyhee Lake Road southwest for a total of 21 miles to the park. Road signs help point the way.
GPS coordinates: N43 37.000' / W117 15.229'
About the campground: In a stunning desert canyon in the remote southeast corner of the state, the park's V. W. McCormack and Indian Creek Campgrounds offers landscaped sites above Lake Owyhee. Lake Owyhee is an attractive, 53-mile-long, 14,000-acre reservoir open to boating, swimming, and waterskiing and known for its bass fishing. Attractive reddish cliffs, terraced walls, and unusual geological formations frame the reservoir. A nearby resort rents boats.

645 Leslie Gulch-Slocum Creek

Location: On Owyhee Reservoir, about 47 miles southwest of Adrian
Season: In dry weather, Apr–Oct
Sites: 12 basic sites; no hookups
Maximum length: 20 feet
Facilities: Tables, nonflush toilet, boat launch; no drinking water
Fee per night: None
Management: Bureau of Land Management—Vale District
Contact: (541) 473-3144; www.blm.gov/or/
Finding the campground: From OR 201, 8 miles south of Adrian, go southwest on Succor Creek Road and then west on Leslie Gulch Road (both are improved surface roads), for a combined distance of about 39 miles. The camp is on the left before the Owyhee Reservoir boat launch at road's end.
GPS coordinates: N43 19.312' / W117 19.382'

About the campground: This sun-drenched camp has limited amenities, but it enjoys a front-row seat to the reservoir and an exciting canyon location. Stargazing is unmatched. The reservoir is noted for its scenery, fishing, and boating. Washes in the Leslie Gulch area shape natural dry-weather hiking trails through the colorful volcanic ash formations: shields, beehives, hollows, and monoliths that tickle the imagination. Visitors have the opportunity to spy bighorn sheep, coyotes, bats, and golden eagles, but be alert for snakes. The camp sits at the mouth of Slocum Gulch for morning or evening strolls. Bring plenty of water, hats, sunscreen, and a freestanding shade source. A reservoir dunking is almost always in order, but water levels can fluctuate drastically, especially in drought conditions and by late summer.

646 Spring Recreation Site

Location: On Brownlee Reservoir, about 33 miles northwest of Ontario
Season: Year-round
Sites: 20 basic sites, 15 tent sites; no hookups
Maximum length: 30 feet
Facilities: Tables, grills, nonflush toilets, drinking water (seasonally), boat launch, docks, fish-cleaning station
Fee per night: $
Management: Bureau of Land Management—Vale District
Contact: (541) 473-3144; www.blm.gov/or/
Finding the campground: From I-84 (25 miles northwest of Ontario) take exit 353 and go 5 miles north on US 30 Business to Huntington. Turn right onto paved Snake River Road for a 3.4-mile winding canyon drive to the camp.
GPS coordinates: N44 22.675' / W117 14.382'
About the campground: Along Brownlee Reservoir on the Snake River, both the tent and RV camping areas rim a gravel parking lot. The tent sites are just a short walk away in an area of established shade trees. The RV spaces are typically paired with smaller trees. In this narrow, steep-sided canyon, the walls help shadow the camp. Fishing, boating, and swimming attract people to this spot.

647 Succor Creek State Park

Location: About 23 miles southwest of Adrian
Season: In dry weather, Mar–Nov
Sites: 6 primitive sites, 12 hike-in sites; no hookups
Maximum length: Small units only
Facilities: Tables, nonflush toilet; no drinking water
Fee per night: None
Management: Oregon State Parks and Recreation Department
Contact: (800) 551-6949; www.oregon.gov/OPRD/PARKS/camping.shtml
Finding the campground: From OR 201, 8 miles south of Adrian, go southwest on improved-surface Succor Creek Road. Continue 15 miles to the park.
GPS coordinates: N43 27.215' / W117 07.197'
About the campground: This isolated state park serves up a fine dose of solitude in a grand desert-canyon setting. Succor Creek, spanned by a pedestrian bridge, halves the camp; the big trees offer prized shade. There are no established trails, but jeep trails and the landmarks of the canyon suggest short cross-country outings. Photography, wildlife viewing, stargazing, and relaxing at camp entertain individuals who venture here. When scrambling among the rocks, be alert for snakes.

Burns Area

	Hookup Sites	Total Sites	Max. RV Length	Hookups	Toilets	Showers	Drinking Water	Dump Station	Recreation	Fee	Can Reserve
648 Buck Spring		7	40		NF					$	
649 Chickahominy Recreation Site		28	35		NF		X		FBL	$	
650 Chukar Park		18	28		NF		X		F	$	
651 Delintment Lake		30	30		NF		X		HFBL	$$	
652 Emigrant		6	25		NF				F	$	
653 Falls		6	22		NF		X		F	$	
654 Idlewild		22	30		NF		X		H	$$	
655 Joaquin Miller Horse Camp		18	35		NF		X		R	$	
656 Yellowjacket		20	30		NF		X		FBL	$$	

648 Buck Spring

Location: About 26 miles northwest of Riley
Season: May–mid-Oct
Sites: 7 basic sites; no hookups
Maximum length: 40 feet
Facilities: Tables, grills, nonflush toilets; no drinking water
Fee per night: $
Management: Malheur National Forest
Contact: (541) 573-4300; www.fs.usda.gov/recmain/malheur/recreation
Finding the campground: From US 20, 1 mile west of Riley, turn north onto Silver Creek Road/ CR 138. Drive 15.4 miles and turn left onto gravel FR 45. Go 7.6 mile; turn left onto FR 4540 and continue 0.9 mile to its junction with FR 4545. Turn left onto FR 4545, go 1 mile, and turn left onto FR 100. The campground straddles FR 100.
GPS coordinates: N43 47.335' / W119 42.550'
About the campground: Rimmed by buck-and-pole fence, this quiet camp in the ponderosa pines, tall grass, and goldenrod welcomes you to catch up on your reading, nap, and listen to the wind blow. Hunters favor the spot in fall. Site access is dirt or gravel; parts of camp can be muddy early in the season.

649 Chickahominy Recreation Site

Location: On Chickahominy Reservoir, 31 miles west of Burns
Season: Year-round; maintained Apr–Sept
Sites: 28 basic sites; no hookups
Maximum length: 35 feet
Facilities: Tables, fire rings, nonflush toilets, drinking water, shade shelters, fish-cleaning station, boat launch
Fee per night: $
Management: Bureau of Land Management—Burns District
Contact: (541) 573-4400; www.blm.gov/or/
Finding the campground: The campground is north off US 20, 31 miles west of Burns and 99 miles east of Bend.
GPS coordinates: N43 32.763' / W119 36.739'
About the campground: This camp rests along the open flat of Chickahominy Reservoir, which holds back the water of Chickahominy Creek. It is a sparkling, big, elongated water body in an arid basin of mixed grasses and sagebrush. Juniper-studded buttes and ridges rise in the backdrop. Birding, fishing, and boating are the pastimes. The sites have gravel pull-through parking. Bring a sturdy shade source and plenty of sunscreen lotion. Winds can be forceful, so anchor loose items. Boaters should check on water levels, as the reservoir can draw down.

650 Chukar Park

Location: 6 miles north of Juntura
Season: Year-round
Sites: 18 basic sites; no hookups
Maximum length: 28 feet
Facilities: Tables, grills, nonflush toilets, drinking water (May–Sept)
Fee per night: $
Management: Bureau of Land Management—Vale District
Contact: (541) 473-3144; www.blm.gov/or/
Finding the campground: From US 20 at Juntura, go 6 miles north on Beulah Reservoir Road to the campground.
GPS coordinates: N43 48.188' / W118 09.332'
About the campground: This campground is a pleasing oasis along the North Fork Malheur River. It sits in a rugged countryside, where the chukar—an introduced gameland partridge—is hunted in the fall. The camp unites lawn and native juniper-grassland vegetation. The 20- to 25-foot-wide North Fork Malheur races past the campground. Scenic cliffs across the river add to views. The campground is 9 miles south of Beulah Reservoir for fishing and boating.

Fishing dock on Delintment Lake, Ochoco National Forest

651 Delintment Lake

Location: On Delintment Lake, about 42 miles northwest of Burns/Hines
Season: May–mid-Oct
Sites: 25 basic sites, 5 walk-in tent; no hookups
Maximum length: 30 feet
Facilities: Tables, grills, nonflush toilets, drinking water, boat launch, all-ability-access fishing dock
Fee per night: $$
Management: Malheur National Forest
Contact: (541) 573-4300; www.fs.usda.gov/recmain/malheur/recreation
Finding the campground: From US 20 at the west end of Hines, turn north on Burns-Izee Road (CR 127) toward Yellowjacket and Delintment Lakes. Go 11.7 miles and turn left onto FR 41. Proceed 26.2 miles, keeping left to remain on FR 41. Reach the lake in another 4 miles, with the campground entrance ahead.
GPS coordinates: N43 53.508' / W119 37.898'
About the campground: This comfortable family campground occupies the ponderosa pine and willow–treed shore of Delintment Lake, a onetime beaver pond enlarged by an earthen dam to its current 57-acre size. The fishing is good, with the rainbow trout averaging between 12 and 14 inches. The lake has a 5-mile-per-hour boat speed. A footpath rings the lake and offers excellent birding, with bald and golden eagles, ospreys, ducks, coots, geese, and spotted sandpipers.

652 Emigrant

Location: About 34 miles northwest of Burns/Hines
Season: May–mid-Oct
Sites: 6 basic sites; no hookups
Maximum length: 25 feet
Facilities: Tables, grills, nonflush toilets; no drinking water
Fee per night: $
Management: Malheur National Forest
Contact: (541) 573-4300; www.fs.usda.gov/recmain/malheur/recreation
Finding the campground: From US 20 at the west end of Hines, turn north onto Burns-Izee Road (CR 127) toward Yellowjacket and Delintment Lakes. Go 23.2 miles and bear left onto FR 43. Proceed 9.9 miles; turn left onto gravel FR 4340 and follow it 0.3 mile into the campground.
GPS coordinates: N43 51.892' / W119 25.091'
About the campground: This campground is situated among the big ponderosa pines along meadow-banked Emigrant Creek. The picturesque, meandering waterway invites you to explore along its banks or go fishing. The forest has a lovely meadow and shrub understory; sites offer gravel parking. At the edges of day, deer can be spied as they drift to and from the creek.

653 Falls

Location: About 32 miles northwest of Burns/Hines
Season: May–mid-Oct
Sites: 6 basic sites; no hookups
Maximum length: 22 feet
Facilities: Tables, grills, nonflush toilets, drinking water
Fee per night: $
Management: Malheur National Forest
Contact: (541) 573-4300; www.fs.usda.gov/recmain/malheur/recreation
Finding the campground: From US 20 at the west end of Hines, turn north onto Burns-Izee Road (CR 127) toward Yellowjacket and Delintment Lakes. Go 23.2 miles and bear left onto FR 43. Proceed 8.2 miles; turn left onto gravel FR 4300.050 to reach the campsites in 0.2 mile.
GPS coordinates: N43 50.989' / W119 24.611'
About the campground: This campground occupies a ponderosa pine flat at a bend on Emigrant Creek. The beautiful, towering red-trunked pines complement the green banks and dark, meandering flow of the creek. Above the camp a few volcanic boulders stud the forest slope. The camp promises a quiet retreat, and a short, rugged trail travels the west shore downstream.

654 Idlewild

Location: 17 miles north of Burns
Season: May–mid-Oct
Sites: 22 basic sites; no hookups
Maximum length: 30 feet
Facilities: Tables, grills, nonflush toilets, drinking water, picnic shelter
Fee per night: $$
Management: Malheur National Forest
Contact: (541) 573-4300; www.fs.usda.gov/recmain/malheur/recreation
Finding the campground: The campground is east off US 395, 17 miles north of Burns and 53 miles south of John Day.
GPS coordinates: N43 48.012' / W118 59.407'
About the campground: At meadow's edge in a scenic ponderosa pine forest sits this pleasant campground, a convenient stopover for the US 395 traveler. Planted aspen and natural mountain mahogany vary the look of the forest. The campground roads and parking spaces are paved, with a few pull-through sites to accommodate longer vehicles. Two short hiking trails travel the outskirts of camp: the 1-mile Idlewild Loop and the 2-mile Devine Summit Loop.

655 Joaquin Miller Horse Camp

Location: 19 miles north of Burns
Season: May–mid-Oct
Sites: 18 basic sites; no hookups
Maximum length: 35 feet
Facilities: Tables, grills, nonflush toilets, drinking water, corrals
Fee per night: $
Management: Malheur National Forest
Contact: (541) 573-4300; www.fs.usda.gov/recmain/malheur/recreation
Finding the campground: The campground is west off US 395, 19 miles north of Burns and 51 miles south of John Day.
GPS coordinates: N43 49.607' / W118 58.403'
About the campground: At this camp you will find paved roads and parking spaces and several long pull-through sites to accommodate the horse-camping public. The corrals are located at the far west edge of the camp. The sites are partially shaded by ponderosa pines. Although there are commonly used horse routes next to the camp, there are no formal horse trails.

656 Yellowjacket

Location: On Yellowjacket Lake, about 34 miles northwest of Burns/Hines
Season: May–mid-Oct
Sites: 20 basic sites; no hookups
Maximum length: 30 feet
Facilities: Tables, grills, nonflush toilets, drinking water, primitive boat launch
Fee per night: $$
Management: Malheur National Forest
Contact: (541) 573-4300; www.fs.usda.gov/recmain/malheur/recreation
Finding the campground: From US 20 at the west end of Hines, turn north onto Burns-Izee Road (CR 127/FR 47) toward Yellowjacket and Delintment Lakes. Go 30.1 miles and turn right (east) onto FR 37. Go 2.5 miles and turn right onto gravel FR 3745. Continue 0.8 mile to the campground on the right.
GPS coordinates: N43 52.584' / W119 16.364'
About the campground: This family campground occupies a gentle, pine-clad slope above the west shore of Yellowjacket Lake. A small earthen dam creates this elongated lake at the foot of a low ridge. At the lake's north and south ends, willows and marsh claim the shallows, and coots and ducks rear their young. The deeper water toward the lake's center is suitable for fishing tubes and small boats. The camp can fill up on summer weekends and holidays.

Silver Lake Area

	Hookup Sites	Total Sites	Max. RV Length	Hookups	Toilets	Showers	Drinking Water	Dump Station	Recreation	Fee	Can Reserve
657 Antler		9	30		NF				HR	None	
658 Duncan Reservoir		4	22		NF				FBL	None	
659 East Bay		18	40		NF		X		FBL	$$	
660 Silver Creek Marsh		17	40		NF		X		HFR	$	
661 Summer Lake Wildlife Area		25–30	40		NF				HF	ODFW Parking Permit	
662 Thompson Reservoir		20	35		NF		X		FBL	$	

657 Antler

Location: About 20 miles southwest of the city of Silver Lake

Season: May–mid-Nov

Sites: 5 basic sites, 4 walk-in tent sites; no hookups

Maximum length: 30 feet

Facilities: Tables, grills, nonflush toilets, corral, hitching posts; no drinking water

Fee per night: None

Management: Fremont National Forest

Contact: (541) 576-2107; www.fs.usda.gov/recmain/fremont-winema/recreation

Finding the campground: From OR 31, 0.8 mile northwest of Silver Lake, turn south onto paved CR 4-11/FR 27 toward Silver Creek Marsh and Thompson Reservoir and go 9 miles. Turn right onto gravel FR 2804 and go 2.5 miles. Head left on FR 7645 for 5.6 miles. Turn left onto FR 036 and continue 1.5 miles. Turn right onto FR 038 and go 0.6 mile to the campground on the right. Some intersection signs will help point the way.

GPS coordinates: N42 57.692' / W121 14.308'

About the campground: On Fremont National Recreation Trail, this campground is a gateway to Yamsay Mountain Roadless Area. The sites receive partial shade in a select-cut forest of lodgepole pine and fir. The camp serves hikers and equestrians. Yamsay Mountain—an all-day ride or backpack—is an intriguing, volcanic dome with exceptional views and herds of wild elk ranging its flank. The Scenic Rock Loop Trail offers a shorter excursion, touring forest, meadow, and scenic rock near the campground.

658 Duncan Reservoir

Location: On Duncan Reservoir, about 10 miles southeast of the city of Silver Lake
Season: Year-round, dependent on weather
Sites: 4 basic sites; no hookups
Maximum length: 22 feet
Facilities: Tables, fire rings, nonflush toilets, boat launch; no drinking water
Fee per night: None
Management: Bureau of Land Management–Lakeview District, Klamath Falls Office
Contact: (541) 883-6916; www.blm.gov/or/
Finding the campground: From Silver Lake go east on OR 31 South for 5.4 miles. Turn right onto gravel CR 4-14 at the sign for Duncan Reservoir and proceed 0.9 mile. Turn right onto BLM 6197, a narrow washboard road, and continue 4.1 miles to the campground.
GPS coordinates: N43 04.259' / W120 56.665'
About the campground: This small, primitive campground occupies a juniper-sage shore of Duncan Reservoir, a moderate-size body of water cradled in an arid basin. Anglers troll the lake in hopes of catching evening supper. Stargazing is a pleasant way to cap the day.

659 East Bay

Location: On Thompson Reservoir, about 15 miles southwest of the city of Silver Lake
Season: May–mid-Nov
Sites: 18 basic sites; no hookups
Maximum length: 40 feet
Facilities: Tables, barbecues, nonflush toilets, drinking water, boat launch, dock
Fee per night: $$
Management: Fremont National Forest
Contact: (541) 576-2107; www.fs.usda.gov/recmain/fremont-winema/recreation
Finding the campground: From OR 31, 0.3 mile northwest of Silver Lake, turn south onto paved CR 4-12/FR 28 toward East Bay Campground. Go 13.2 miles and turn right onto FR 014. Go another 1.5 miles to enter the campground.
GPS coordinates: N42 56.561' / W121 03.931'
About the campground: On the east shore of 1,532-acre Thompson Reservoir, this comfortable campground borders a quiet cove, offers paved parking, and receives partial shade from its mixed-age pine forest. Thompson Reservoir harnesses Silver Creek for irrigation and is open to fishing and boating. Boat speeds are limited to 10 miles per hour. The lake has an attractive shoreline when full and serves up western views of Yamsay Mountain. The south end of the lake boasts nesting bald eagles, while the lake island is a waterfowl nesting area.

660 Silver Creek Marsh

Location: About 11 miles southwest of the city of Silver Lake
Season: May–mid-Nov
Sites: 17 basic sites; no hookups
Maximum length: 40 feet
Facilities: Tables, grills, nonflush toilets, drinking water, corrals, hitching posts
Fee per night: $
Management: Fremont National Forest
Contact: (541) 576-2107; www.fs.usda.gov/recmain/fremont-winema/recreation
Finding the campground: From OR 31, 0.8 mile northwest of Silver Lake, turn south onto paved CR 4-11/FR 27 toward Silver Creek Marsh and Thompson Reservoir. Proceed 10 miles to the campground on the left.
GPS coordinates: N43 00.390' / W121 07.982'
About the campground: This campground hugs the West Fork Silver Creek, a tiny creek with a few deep pools for fish. A semi-open pine flat with big ponderosa pines houses the camp. The sites have gravel parking, receive a mix of sun and shade, and can serve either as a stop or a base for exploring the Fremont National Recreation Trail, which traverses a corner of the camp. Thompson Reservoir, 5 miles southeast, offers more-dependable fishing and also boating (10 miles per hour).

661 Summer Lake Wildlife Area

Location: About 1 mile southeast of the community of Summer Lake
Season: Year-round
Sites: 4 camping areas for about 25 to 30 basic sites; no hookups
Maximum length: 40 feet
Facilities: Tables, nonflush toilets; no drinking water
Fee per night: None, but ODFW Wildlife Area parking permit required
Management: Oregon Department of Fish and Wildlife, Wildlife Division
Contact: (541) 943-3152; www.dfw.state.or.us/
Finding the campground: At the south end of the community of Summer Lake, turn east off OR 31 at the sign for the wildlife area. Pick up a refuge map at the office, and follow the road tour into the wildlife area to the designated camping areas at Windbreak, Ana River, Bullgate, and River Ranch. (The store in town sells ODFW parking permits.)
GPS coordinates: N42 57.013' / W120 45.960'
About the campground: The refuge offers minimalist camping on broad meadow and gravel flats; comfort is what you bring. Views are of the richly textured refuge lands: open water, channels, marsh, mudflat, and arid brush. To the west rises imposing Winter Ridge. Birding and hunting are the chief draws, with the refuge road to drive and the dikes to hike. A cacophony of sounds delights, as do the evening stars. Mosquitoes can be menacing, but remember they are part of the food chain sustaining the birds. Insect repellent, hats, binoculars, scopes, and telephoto lenses are among the preferred gear.

662 Thompson Reservoir

Location: On Thompson Reservoir, about 16 miles southwest of the city of Silver Lake
Season: May–Nov
Sites: 20 basic sites; no hookups
Maximum length: 35 feet
Facilities: Tables, grills, nonflush toilets, drinking water, primitive boat launch
Fee per night: $
Management: Fremont National Forest
Contact: (541) 576-2107; www.fs.usda.gov/recmain/fremont-winema/recreation
Finding the campground: From OR 31, 0.8 mile northwest of Silver Lake, turn south onto paved CR 4-11/FR 27 toward Silver Creek Marsh and Thompson Reservoir. Go 14 miles and turn left onto gravel FR 287 to reach the campground in another 1.1 miles.
GPS coordinates: N42 57.557' / W121 05.531'
About the campground: This campground rests on the pine-forested north basin slope of Thompson Reservoir. The large, roundish irrigation reservoir has a piney rim, treed points, and a riddling of snags. Fishing boats (10 miles per hour) ply the clear, blue water. When the reservoir is full, so is this campground. Look for mergansers, bald eagles, ospreys, and migratory shore-birds and waterfowl.

	Hookup Sites	Total Sites	Max. RV Length	Hookups	Toilets	Showers	Drinking Water	Dump Station	Recreation	Fee	Can Reserve
663 Cow Lakes Recreation Site		10	30		NF				FBL	None	
664 Fish Lake Recreation Site		23	24		NF		X		FBLR	$	
665 Jackman Park Recreation Site		6	24		NF					$	
666 Mann Lake Recreation Site		Open	35		NF				FBL	None	
667 Page Springs Recreation Site		32	24		NF		X		HF	$	
668 Rome Launch Site		5	40		NF		X		FBL	None	
669 South Steens Recreation Site		36	35		NF		X		HFR	$	
670 Willow Creek Hot Springs Recreation Site		4	Small		NF					None	

663 Cow Lakes Recreation Site

Location: About 19 miles northwest of Jordan Valley
Season: Year-round, except after heavy rains
Sites: 10 basic sites; no hookups
Maximum length: 30 feet
Facilities: Tables, fire rings, nonflush toilet, boat ramp (small boats for trolling or rowing); no drinking water
Fee per night: None
Management: Bureau of Land Management—Vale District
Contact: (541) 473-3144; www.blm.gov/or/
Finding the campground: From Jordan Valley head west on US 95 South for 5 miles. Turn right onto gravel Danner Loop Road; a sign indicates this route to Cow Lakes. Continue following the signs to Cow Lakes, heading northwest via Danner Loop and Lower Cow Creek Roads, reaching the campground in 14 miles.
GPS coordinates: N43 05.786' / W117 19.683'
About the campground: This sun-drenched campground sits between Upper and Lower Cow Lakes. The area is surrounded by sage tablelands and the Jordan Craters Lava Flow. Upper Cow Lake is a fluctuating, 1,000-acre reservoir that attracts anglers with catches of white crappie, largemouth bass, and brown bullhead. Besides fishing, guests can swim, bird-watch, or hunt. People interested in exploring the lava beds should contact the BLM for information. North of Danner, history trackers may seek out the grave of Jean Baptiste Charbonneau. He was the son of Sacagawea (formerly written Sacajawea) and Toussaint Charbonneau of the Lewis and Clark exploration party.

664 Fish Lake Recreation Site

Location: About 78 miles southeast of Burns
Season: Mid-July–Oct
Sites: 23 basic sites; no hookups
Maximum length: 24 feet
Facilities: Tables, grills, nonflush toilets, drinking water, boat ramp
Fee per night: $
Management: Bureau of Land Management—Burns District
Contact: (541) 573-4400; www.blm.gov/or/
Finding the campground: From Frenchglen (61 miles south of Burns on OR 205), head east on gravel Steens Mountain Loop Road. The campground is on the right at about 17 miles.
GPS coordinates: N42 44.314' / W118 38.605'
About the campground: This family campground occupies the shore of a mountain lake, which is large enough to support fishing and motorless boating. Willows claim the shore, and aspens dress the slope near camp, but the sites sit mostly in the open. Nearby are corrals for public use. Discovery of both Steens Mountain and Malheur National Wildlife Refuge awaits. High-clearance vehicles are necessary at Steens Mountain; four-wheel drive is recommended to complete Steens Mountain Loop.

665 Jackman Park Recreation Site

Location: About 80 miles southeast of Burns
Season: July–Oct
Sites: 6 basic sites; no hookups
Maximum length: 24 feet
Facilities: Tables, grills, nonflush toilets; no drinking water
Fee per night: $
Management: Bureau of Land Management—Burns District
Contact: (541) 573-4400; www.blm.gov/or/
Finding the campground: From Frenchglen (61 miles south of Burns on OR 205), head east on gravel Steens Mountain Loop Road for almost 20 miles; the campground is on the right.
GPS coordinates: N42 43.112' / W118 37.414'
About the campground: This small campground has a split character, with the northern half of the loop showing dry meadows and sagelands dotted with juniper and mountain mahogany and the southern half showing wet meadows and aspen groves. The camp offers a base for exploring Steens Mountain, a rugged, high-clearance-vehicle area. West of the camp are Honeymoon and Pate Lakes. Aspens put on a show in fall.

666 Mann Lake Recreation Site

Location: On Mann Lake, about 89 miles southeast of Burns
Season: Year-round, dependent on winter weather
Sites: Random camping; no hookups
Maximum length: 35 feet
Facilities: Nonflush toilets, 2 primitive boat launches; no drinking water
Fee per night: None
Management: Bureau of Land Management—Burns District
Contact: (541) 573-4400; www.blm.gov/or/
Finding the campground: From US 20/395 in Burns, go east on OR 78 for 65 miles. Turn right onto Fields-Denio Road, the gravel road signed for Andrews, Fields, and Denio, and go 23.6 miles. Turn right for Mann Lake.
GPS coordinates: N42 46.751' / W118 26.801'
About the campground: Named for an early-day rancher, Mann Lake, the centerpiece of this Oregon outback stay, is a glassy, broad natural platter at the eastern foot of Steens Mountain. This is a do-it-yourself camping area on the open plain. Bringing a shade source is desirable, along with plenty of water and sunscreen. Rainbow and the Mann Lake cutthroat trout survive in this low-oxygen water. Fishing is best early in the year before the algae build. A wildlife viewing area encompasses the lake. Alvord Hot Springs is located some 18 miles farther south; on the east side of the road, look for rising steam and a small rustic tin structure for changing your clothes.

667 Page Springs Recreation Site

Location: About 64 miles southeast of Burns
Season: Year-round
Sites: 32 basic sites; no hookups
Maximum length: 24 feet
Facilities: Tables, grills, nonflush toilets, drinking water (seasonally)
Fee per night: $
Management: Bureau of Land Management—Burns District
Contact: (541) 573-4400; www.blm.gov/or/
Finding the campground: From Frenchglen (61 miles south of Burns on OR 205), head east on gravel Steens Mountain Loop Road. Enter the camp on the right in about 3 miles.
GPS coordinates: N42 48.209' / W118 52.019'
About the campground: This arid grassland camp sits beneath a basalt rim along the Donner und Blitzen River. Both sunny and tree-shaded sites are available. The camp makes a fine base for visiting its next-door neighbor, Malheur National Wildlife Refuge, where you will find exceptional birding and natural and cultural discoveries. It is equally convenient for exploring Steens Mountain, a fascinating alpine fault-block mountain rising from the desert plain; high-clearance vehicles are needed. Steens' chiseled canyons reveal superb scenery and seclude the Kiger wild horses. Page Springs is no ugly stepsister, with the sparkling Donner und Blitzen River, prized fishing, its own birdlife, and the rugged, long-distance Desert Trail, which passes through camp.

668 Rome Launch Site

Location: Near Rome, 33 miles west of Jordan Valley
Season: Mar–Nov
Sites: 5 basic sites; no hookups
Maximum length: 40 feet
Facilities: Tables, fire rings, nonflush toilets, drinking water (seasonally), raft takeout/put-in
Fee per night: None
Management: Bureau of Land Management—Vale District
Contact: (541) 473-3144; www.blm.gov/or/
Finding the campground: The campground is south off US 95 at the eastern outskirts of Rome, 105 miles southeast of Burns and 33 miles west of Jordan Valley.
GPS coordinates: N42 50.159' / W117 37.264'
About the campground: The sites edge an open, gravel plateau above the Owyhee River. A sage-grass hillside and rocky crest overlook the camp, and planted cottonwoods provide a bit of shade. The Owyhee—one of the originally designated Wild and Scenic Rivers—flows glassy and welcoming. A rafting permit system is in effect. A nearby attraction is the Pillars of Rome. These 100-foot-tall white rock towers suggested the ruins of Rome to early travelers.

669 South Steens Recreation Site

Location: About 90 miles southeast of Burns
Season: Mid-May–mid-Nov
Sites: 21 basic sites, 15 horse sites; no hookups
Maximum length: 35 feet
Facilities: Tables, grills, nonflush toilets, drinking water, hitching posts in horse camp
Fee per night: $
Management: Bureau of Land Management—Burns District
Contact: (541) 573-4400; www.blm.gov/or/
Finding the campground: From US 20/395 in Burns, go east on OR 78 for 1.7 miles. Turn right (south) onto OR 205 and proceed another 69 miles. Turn left onto South Steens Loop Road at the sign for Upper Blitzen. Drive 18.8 miles to the horse camp or 18.9 miles to the family campground.
GPS coordinates: N42 39.386' / W118 43.599'
About the campground: These side-by-side campgrounds sit at the mouth of Big Indian Gorge and offer similar convenience and amenities. Sites are dispersed through a juniper-sage grassland and are either sunny or partially shaded. A trail explores Big Indian Gorge, following Big Indian Creek upstream from the camp. With high-clearance vehicles, visitors can drive the Steens Mountain Loop Back Country Byway for stunning vistas and scenery. Wildflowers and wildlife further recommend a visit.

670 Willow Creek Hot Springs Recreation Site

Location: About 43 miles east of Fields
Season: Dry-weather access only
Sites: 4 basic sites; no hookups
Maximum length: Small units only
Facilities: Nonflush toilet; no drinking water
Fee per night: None
Management: Bureau of Land Management—Vale District
Contact: (541) 473-3144; www.blm.gov/or/
Finding the campground: From Burns Junction (the intersection of OR 78 and US 95), 92 miles southeast of Burns and 46 miles west of Jordan Valley, go south on US 95 for 20 miles. Turn right (southwest) onto gravel Whitehorse Road and proceed 21 miles. Turn south, following a dirt dry-weather road along a fenceline for 2.3 miles. Bear right at the information board to reach the hot springs in 0.25 mile.
GPS coordinates: N42 16.490' / W118 15.864'
About the campground: This remote destination is reserved for the adventurous. The austere camp exists because of two adjoining, modestly developed hot spring pools in a natural outdoor setting of dry grass and sage. Each of the pools can accommodate several people. The hotter one is clear, has a sandy bottom, and is 3 feet deep. The milder pool is cloudy, has a muddy bottom, and is 4.5 feet deep. Biting flies can annoy, but the stars dazzle.

Paisley-Gearhart Mountain Area

	Hookup Sites	Total Sites	Max. RV Length	Hookups	Toilets	Showers	Drinking Water	Dump Station	Recreation	Fee	Can Reserve
671 Campbell Lake		18	25		NF				HFBL	None	
672 Chewaucan Crossing Trailhead and Campground		5	Small		NF				HF	None	
673 Corral Creek Forest Camp		6	30		NF				H	None	
674 Deadhorse Lake		16	16		NF				HFBL	$	
675 Happy Camp		9	25		NF				F	None	
676 Jones Crossing		8	T, small		NF				F	None	
677 Lee Thomas		8	20		NF	X			F	None	
678 Marsters Spring		10	30		NF	X			HF	$	
679 Sandhill Crossing		5	30		NF	X			F	None	

671 Campbell Lake

Location: On Campbell Lake, about 30 miles southwest of Paisley
Season: July–Oct
Sites: 18 basic sites; no hookups
Maximum length: 25 feet
Facilities: Tables, grills, nonflush toilets, boat launch and dock at day-use area; no drinking water
Fee per night: None
Management: Fremont National Forest
Contact: (541) 943-3114; www.fs.usda.gov/recmain/fremont-winema/recreation
Finding the campground: From OR 31 at Paisley, turn west onto Mill Street, which becomes FR 33 as you head left at the Y-junction. After 20 miles come to a T-junction. Turn right onto paved FR 28 and go 8.4 miles. Turn left onto FR 033 to reach this campground on the left in 1.8 miles.
GPS coordinates: N42 33.578' / W120 45.369'
About the campground: This inviting campground occupies the lodgepole pine perimeter of Campbell Lake, a pretty, circular mountain lake below Deadhorse Rim. The tight pine forest affords nearly complete shade, and the sites are well spaced for privacy. The lake is stocked with rainbow trout and open to small fishing boats (human-powered or electric motor, 5 miles per hour). Trails from the camp traverse Deadhorse Rim en route to neighboring Deadhorse Lake. The small pond near the trailhead is sometimes loud with frogs.

672 Chewaucan Crossing Trailhead and Campground

Location: About 8 miles southwest of Paisley
Season: Apr–Oct
Sites: 5 basic sites; no hookups
Maximum length: Best suited for smaller units (only 1 pull-through site)
Facilities: Tables, grills, nonflush toilets; no drinking water
Fee per night: None
Management: Fremont National Forest
Contact: (541) 943-3114; www.fs.usda.gov/recmain/fremont-winema/recreation
Finding the campground: From OR 31 at Paisley, turn west onto Mill Street, which becomes FR 33 as you head left at the Y-junction. Proceed 7.6 miles to the campground, near milepost 8.
GPS coordinates: N42 36.678' / W120 36.096'
About the campground: This campground on a pine-and-juniper flat along the Chewaucan River has gravel roads and parking pads. It is a gateway to the long-distance Fremont National Recreation Trail, which travels north to Yamsay Mountain and south to Cox Pass. A pedestrian bridge spans the river at the camp, linking the trail segments. Fishing the river, anglers can match wits with rainbow and brook trout.

673 Corral Creek Forest Camp

Location: About 30 miles northeast of Bly
Season: Mid-May–mid-Oct
Sites: 6 basic sites; no hookups
Maximum length: 30 feet
Facilities: Tables, grills, nonflush toilets; no drinking water
Fee per night: None
Management: Fremont National Forest
Contact: (541) 353-2427; www.fs.usda.gov/recmain/fremont-winema/recreation
Finding the campground: From OR 140 at Quartz Mountain (13 miles east of Bly and 30 miles west of Lakeview), turn north onto FR 3660. Go 16 miles to FR 34 and turn right. Continue 0.2 mile and turn left onto FR 012, continuing 0.3 mile on the dirt road to reach the campground on the left.
GPS coordinates: N42 27.449' / W120 46.924'
About the campground: At this relaxing getaway, the sites are nicely spaced for privacy in a setting of meadow and lodgepole pines. A rail fence isolates the camp from the picturesque meadow stream of Corral Creek. An egress in the fence allows access for fishing or admiring. At the trailhead at the end of FR 012, you will find wilderness entry and the Gearhart Mountain Trail System.

674 Deadhorse Lake

Location: 32 miles southwest of Paisley
Season: July–Oct
Sites: 16 basic sites; no hookups
Maximum length: 16 feet
Facilities: Tables, grills, nonflush toilets, boat launch, dock; no drinking water
Fee per night: $
Management: Fremont National Forest
Contact: (541) 943-3114; www.fs.usda.gov/recmain/fremont-winema/recreation
Finding the campground: From OR 31 at Paisley, turn west onto Mill Street, which becomes FR 33 as you head left at the Y-junction. After 20 miles come to a T-junction. Turn right onto paved FR 28 and go 8.4 miles. Turn left on FR 033 and continue 3.2 miles to the campground.
GPS coordinates: N42 33.517' / W120 46.528'
About the campground: This campground in the lodgepole pines sits on the shore of Deadhorse Lake. This elongated lake is one of two attractive mountain lakes below Deadhorse Rim; the other is Campbell Lake. This tranquil mountain retreat welcomes fishing, boating (5 miles per hour), and hiking. The lake is stocked with rainbow trout. Trails travel Deadhorse Rim to Campbell Lake and follow Deadcow Drainage.

675 Happy Camp

Location: About 24 miles southwest of Paisley
Season: Mid-May–Oct
Sites: 9 basic sites; no hookups
Maximum length: 25 feet
Facilities: Tables, grills, nonflush toilets, historic picnic shelters; no drinking water
Fee per night: None
Management: Fremont National Forest
Contact: (541) 943-3114; www.fs.usda.gov/recmain/fremont-winema/recreation
Finding the campground: From OR 31 at Paisley, turn west onto Mill Street, which becomes FR 33 as you head left at the Y-junction. After 20 miles come to a T-junction. Turn left onto paved FR 28 and go 2 miles. Turn right onto dirt FR 047 and proceed 2.4 miles to enter the campground on the left. FR 047 has some rough, rock-studded segments and washboard.
GPS coordinates: N42 28.596' / W120 40.981'
About the campground: This campground is loaded with rustic charm. It rests on the north shore of pretty Dairy Creek. The meadow flat of the camp is dotted with aspens and ponderosa and lodgepole pines. This is a place where you can awaken to birdsong. Fishing, reading a book, or napping are popular activities (or inactivities).

676 Jones Crossing

Location: About 9 miles southwest of Paisley
Season: Apr–Oct
Sites: 8 basic sites; no hookups
Maximum length: Best for tent and small units (abrupt lip off FR 33 into camp)
Facilities: Tables, grills, nonflush toilets; no drinking water
Fee per night: None
Management: Fremont National Forest
Contact: (541) 943-3114; www.fs.usda.gov/recmain/fremont-winema/recreation
Finding the campground: From OR 31 at Paisley, turn west onto Mill Street, which becomes FR 33 as you head left at the Y-junction. Proceed 8.4 miles to the campground on the left.
GPS coordinates: N42 36.400' / W120 35.969'
About the campground: This campground with gravel roads and parking sits on a dry sagebrush-and-grass flat above the Chewaucan River. A dotting of juniper and pine trees affords partial shade. Woodpeckers and songbirds enliven camp. Hikers find access to the Fremont Trail at Chewaucan Crossing, passed en route to camp.

677 Lee Thomas

Location: 36 miles southwest of Paisley
Season: June–Oct
Sites: 8 basic sites; no hookups
Maximum length: 20 feet
Facilities: Tables, grills, nonflush toilets, drinking water
Fee per night: None
Management: Fremont National Forest
Contact: (541) 943-3114; www.fs.usda.gov/recmain/fremont-winema/recreation
Finding the campground: From OR 31 at Paisley, turn west onto Mill Street, which becomes FR 33 as you head left at the Y-junction. After 20 miles come to a T-junction. Turn right onto paved FR 28 and go about 11 miles. Turn left onto FR 3411, heading toward Lee Thomas and Sandhill Crossing Campgrounds. Proceed 5 miles to the campground on the left.
GPS coordinates: N42 35.449' / W120 50.371'
About the campground: This campground unites a lodgepole pine stand, a marmot-inhabited rock outcrop, wildflower meadows punctuated by willow clumps, and the lovely Sprague Wild and Scenic River. A pole fence encircles camp, with an egress to the river for fishing or gazing at its sparkle. The Lee Thomas Trailhead is 1 mile east of the camp; from it, the Deadhorse Rim Trail travels 6 miles to Deadhorse Lake, with Campbell Lake a possible destination beyond that.

678 Marsters Spring

Location: 7 miles southwest of Paisley
Season: May–Oct
Sites: 10 basic sites; no hookups
Maximum length: 30 feet
Facilities: Tables, grills, nonflush toilets, drinking water
Fee per night: $
Management: Fremont National Forest
Contact: (541) 943-3114; www.fs.usda.gov/recmain/fremont-winema/recreation
Finding the campground: From OR 31 at Paisley, turn west onto Mill Street, which becomes FR 33 as you head left at the Y-junction. After 7 miles turn left to enter the campground.
GPS coordinates: N42 37.379' / W120 36.334'
About the campground: This campground fronts the picturesque Chewaucan River, currently being studied for Wild and Scenic River classification. The relaxing camp is sheltered by mixed woods of pine, juniper, cottonwood, willow, and alder. Some sites directly overlook the swift river. Chewaucan Crossing Trailhead, 1 mile upstream on FR 33, offers access to the long-distance Fremont National Recreation Trail. Fishing is popular, and this campground is a Great Basin Birding Trail site.

679 Sandhill Crossing

Location: About 38 miles southwest of Paisley
Season: June–Oct
Sites: 5 basic sites; no hookups
Maximum length: 30 feet
Facilities: Tables, grills, nonflush toilets, drinking water
Fee per night: None
Management: Fremont National Forest
Contact: (541) 943-3114; www.fs.usda.gov/recmain/fremont-winema/recreation
Finding the campground: From OR 31 at Paisley, turn west onto Mill Street, which becomes FR 33 as you head left at the Y-junction. After 20 miles come to a T-junction. Turn right onto paved FR 28 and go about 11 miles. Turn left onto FR 3411, heading toward Lee Thomas and Sandhill Crossing Campgrounds. Continue 7.3 miles to the campground on the left.
GPS coordinates: N42 35.645' / W120 52.812'
About the campground: This campground in the lodgepole pines overlooks the postcard-pretty Sprague Wild and Scenic River. Wildflower-dotted meadow banks contain the river; among nature's palette are Indian paintbrush, shooting star, and buttercup. Small gravel bars and deep pools are part of the meandering river's character, and fishing provides a challenge. Mosquitoes are the lone detractor; come prepared.

	Hookup Sites	Total Sites	Max. RV Length	Hookups	Toilets	Showers	Drinking Water	Dump Station	Recreation	Fee	Can Reserve
680 Cottonwood Complex		21	T, small		NF		X		HFBL	$	
681 Dog Lake		16	20		NF				FBL	$	
682 Drews Creek		3	25		NF		X		F	None	
683 Goose Lake State Recreation Area	47	47	50	WE	F	X	X	X	HFB	$$-$$$	
684 Hart Mountain National Antelope Refuge		30	T, small		NF				H	None	
685 Lake County Fairgrounds and RV Campground	14	14	40	WE	F	X	X	X		$$	
686 Lofton Reservoir		24	30		NF				FBL	$	
687 Mud Creek Forest Camp		7	30		NF					None	
688 Willow Creek		8	30		NF				F	None	

680 Cottonwood Complex

Location: About 30 miles northwest of Lakeview
Season: June–mid-Oct
Sites: 21 basic sites; no hookups
Maximum length: Best for tents and small units
Facilities: Tables, grills, nonflush toilets, drinking water, boat launch, horse facilities
Fee per night: $
Management: Fremont National Forest
Contact: (541) 947-3334; www.fs.usda.gov/recmain/fremont-winema/recreation
Finding the campground: From OR 140, 20 miles east of Bly and 23 miles west of Lakeview, turn north onto FR 3870 at the sign for Cottonwood Meadow Lake. Continue 6 miles to the campground.
GPS coordinates: N42 16.816' / W120 38.813'
About the campground: The sites at this pleasant campground rim Cottonwood Meadow Lake. The lake generally has good fishing and is open to rafts, canoes, and small boats (human-powered or electric motors only). The lake basin features wildflower meadows, scenic stands of ponderosa pine, groves of aspen, and views of Cougar and Grizzly Peaks. Trails explore the greater lake area and climb to the top of Cougar Peak. Cottonwood Trailhead is on the left as you arrive at camp.

Motor home in cattle drive, Oregon Outback Scenic Byway, Lake County

681 Dog Lake

Location: About 26 miles southwest of Lakeview
Season: June–mid-Oct
Sites: 16 basic sites; no hookups
Maximum length: 20 feet
Facilities: Tables, grills, nonflush toilets, boat launch, dock; no drinking water
Fee per night: $
Management: Fremont National Forest
Contact: (541) 947-3334; www.fs.usda.gov/recmain/fremont-winema/recreation
Finding the campground: From US 395 in Lakeview, go west on OR 140 for 7.3 miles. Turn left (south) onto CR 1-13 toward Dog Lake and go about 4 miles. Turn right onto CR 1-11D (Dog Lake Lane), which becomes FR 4017. Stay on it for about 15 miles to reach the campsites, which string along the lake for the next mile. A few sites still occupy the former campground area, a rise to the right.
GPS coordinates: N42 04.942' / W120 42.394'
About the campground: Dog Lake, the area's central draw, is an attractive artificial lake. It claims a pretty forested basin and displays areas of rush, cattail, and pond lily along its shallows. White pelicans, ducks, geese, killdeer, and yellow-headed and red-winged blackbirds favor this lake, as do campers, boaters (maximum speed 5 miles per hour), and anglers. Because of its popularity with recreationists, the campground has grown. Numbered sites occur in clusters accessed by dirt roads heading left off FR 4017. Bass, perch, and trout are the lake catches.

682 Drews Creek

Location: About 17 miles southwest of Lakeview
Season: June–mid-Oct
Sites: 3 basic sites; no hookups
Maximum length: 25 feet
Facilities: Tables, grills, nonflush toilets, drinking water, horseshoe pits
Fee per night: None
Management: Fremont National Forest
Contact: (541) 947-3334; www.fs.usda.gov/recmain/fremont-winema/recreation
Finding the campground: From US 395 in Lakeview, go west on OR 140 for 7.3 miles. Turn left (south) onto CR 1-13 toward Dog Lake and go about 4 miles. Turn right onto CR 1-11D (Dog Lake Lane), which becomes FR 4017. Stay on it for 6 miles to reach the campground on the left, crossing a bridge.
GPS coordinates: N42 07.168' / W120 34.827'
About the campground: Along Drews Creek, this camp sits in a ponderosa pine setting at the foot of a low hill. Besides the individual sites, the campground has a group site, with central long tables and community parking. Pole fencing isolates the camp from Drews Creek, which can flow slow and murky here. For fishing the camp is 2 miles from Drews Reservoir.

683 Goose Lake State Recreation Area

Location: About 16 miles south of Lakeview
Season: Mid-Apr–early Oct
Sites: 47 hookup sites; water and electric hookups
Maximum length: 50 feet
Facilities: Tables, grills, flush toilets, drinking water, showers, dump station, horseshoe pits (at day-use area), nearby boat launch
Fee per night: $$–$$$
Management: Oregon State Parks and Recreation Department
Contact: (541) 947-3111 or (800) 551-6949; www.oregon.gov/OPRD/PARKS/camping.shtml
Finding the campground: From the junction of US 395 and OR 140 West in Lakeview, go south on US 395 for 14.7 miles. Turn right at the sign for Goose Lake State Recreation Area, just as California welcomes you, and go 1.1 miles. Turn right for the campground (straight leads to the day-use area).
GPS coordinates: N41 59.663' / W120 19.341'
About the campground: On the Oregon-California border, Goose Lake is an enormous Great Basin lake between distant low ridges. Water levels fluctuate from year to year. The campground is slightly removed from the lake, occupying a flat of lawn and shade trees. The site parking is paved. Fields and willows, with mowed passageways through them, stretch at the outskirts of camp. Giant lupine and wild rose color these corridors where songbirds flourish. This camp is a favorite with birders. Quail roam through the camp, western tanagers decorate tree branches, and migrant and resident waterfowl visit the lake. Goose Lake welcomes fishing and boating, but the access is away from camp.

684 Hart Mountain National Antelope Refuge

Location: About 68 miles northeast of Lakeview
Season: Year-round, weather permitting (Winter snow can close the road.)
Sites: 30 basic sites; no hookups
Maximum length: Best suited for tents and small units
Facilities: Nonflush toilets, hot springs; no drinking water, but water available at refuge headquarters
Fee per night: None
Management: Hart Mountain National Antelope Refuge
Contact: (541) 947-2731
Finding the campground: From the town of Plush (40 miles northeast of Lakeview), drive 0.9 mile north. Turn east at the sign for Hart Mountain and Frenchglen. Proceed 23 miles to the refuge headquarters or 27 miles to the camp and hot springs, bearing right at the junction past the headquarters. The route is paved and gravel to the refuge. The rough road into the camp is not recommended for trailers or RVs.
GPS coordinates: N42 29.959' / W119 41.547'
About the campground: Your arrival route is part of the Lakeview to Steens National Backcountry Byway. The refuge road system then continues your discovery, serving up wildlife sightings and stunning dry landscapes. Antelope are the primary attraction. The isolated camp consists of primitive sites radiating out from the refuge hot springs—a pleasant, deep steamy pool. A refurbished enclosure houses the spring; it can accommodate six users at a time. The camp claims an aspen-shaded grassy flat between Rock and Bond Creeks. Scenic hillsides of sage, juniper, and mountain mahogany frame the setting. Near the headquarters you will find a small museum and nature garden.

685 Lake County Fairgrounds and RV Campground

Location: In Lakeview
Season: Year-round; no water Oct–Mar
Sites: 14 hookup sites, dry camping and tent camping available; water and electric hookups
Maximum length: 40 feet
Facilities: Flush toilets, drinking water, showers, dump station, food concessions (seasonal)
Fee per night: $$
Management: Lake County
Contact: (541) 947-2925
Finding the campground: The fairgrounds are north off OR 140 (North Fourth Street) at the west end of Lakeview. You will find the RV camp to the left off the West Gate entrance.
GPS coordinates: N42 11.684' / W120 21.723'
About the campground: This austere but practical RV camp primarily caters to fairgoers and participants, but it is also available to area travelers. It occupies a shadeless, gravel parking area with hookup posts. For individuals looking to dry or tent camp, ask at the office about suitable areas.

686 Lofton Reservoir

Location: About 38 miles northwest of Lakeview
Season: May–Oct
Sites: 24 basic sites; no hookups
Maximum length: 30 feet
Facilities: Tables, grills, nonflush toilets, boat launch, accessible fishing pier for individuals with disabilities; no drinking water
Fee per night: $
Management: Fremont National Forest
Contact: (541) 353-2427; www.fs.usda.gov/recmain/fremont-winema/recreation
Finding the campground: From OR 140, 13 miles east of Bly and 30 miles west of Lakeview, turn south onto paved FR 3715 toward the reservoir. Go 7.2 miles and turn left onto FR 013 to reach the camp in 1.2 miles.
GPS coordinates: N42 15.772' / W120 48.873'
About the campground: In a location that has been largely cut over, a full forest of ponderosa pine and white fir shelters this family campground along the shore of Lofton Reservoir. Developed, premium sites sit along shore. The lake was built to hold water for irrigation, but it is open to recreation. Lofton is at its prettiest when full, and the fishing is generally good. Electric motors are allowed on the lake; boating speed is limited to 5 miles per hour.

687 Mud Creek Forest Camp

Location: About 20 miles northeast of Lakeview
Season: June–mid-Oct
Sites: 7 basic sites; no hookups
Maximum length: 30 feet
Facilities: Tables, grills, nonflush toilets, drinking water
Fee per night: None
Management: Fremont National Forest
Contact: (541) 947-3334; www.fs.usda.gov/recmain/fremont-winema/recreation
Finding the campground: From Lakeview go north on US 395/OR 140 East for 4.7 miles. Turn right to remain on OR 140E and continue 8.5 miles. Turn left onto North Warren Road/FR 3615 and proceed 7 miles to campground on the right.
GPS coordinates: N42 16.924' / W120 12.321'
About the campground: At the edge of a sage prairie and along the wet meadow threaded by tiny Mud Creek, this quiet camp sits in a forest of lodgepole pine and white fir. Mud Creek is a meandering black ribbon. Across FR 3615 from the campground is Bull Prairie, a private property where the springtime camas bloom creates seas of purple. Area trails can be reached 2.2 miles south of the campground, and Drake Peak Lookout might suggest a drive. Fishing and hunting are other pursuits. Come ready for mosquitoes in early summer.

688 Willow Creek

Location: About 23 miles southeast of Lakeview
Season: June–mid-Oct
Sites: 8 basic sites; no hookups
Maximum length: 30 feet
Facilities: Tables, grills, nonflush toilets; no drinking water
Fee per night: None
Management: Fremont National Forest
Contact: (541) 947-3334; www.fs.usda.gov/recmain/fremont-winema/recreation
Finding the campground: From Lakeview go north on US 395/OR 140 East for 4.7 miles. Turn right to remain on OR 140E and continue 7.2 miles. Turn right onto South Warren Road/FR 3915 (which begins paved and becomes gravel). Go 10.2 miles to a Y-junction and bear right onto FR 4011. Go 0.7 mile and turn right onto FR 011, followed by a right onto FR 012 to enter the camp in 0.3 mile.
GPS coordinates: N42 05.575' / W120 12.122'
About the campground: A rail fence separates this campground from the meadow of Willow Creek. A mixed woods of ponderosa pine and aspen enfolds the camp, and arnica sometimes lends a cheery yellow glow to the forest floor. Signs of beaver activity are evident throughout the meadow. Fishing is the lone activity at this camp.

Campground Index

About the Authors

For decades Rhonda and George Ostertag have traveled throughout their home state of Oregon, seeking its secrets and treasures. They have documented their journey in more than a half dozen Oregon guide, travel, and photography books; hundreds of articles; and dozens of calendars. The two speak from firsthand knowledge of the campgrounds, back roads, waters, and trails.

Other Oregon titles by this duo are *Our Oregon,* a pictorial celebration of the state, and *Best Short Hikes in Northwest Oregon, 75 Hikes in Oregon's Coast Range and Siskiyous,* and *50 Hikes in Hells Canyon and Oregon's Wallowas.* Beyond Oregon's borders, their titles include *California State Parks: A Complete Recreation Guide* and *Our Washington,* as well as *Hiking Connecticut and Rhode Island* and *Hiking New York,* both FalconGuides with Globe Pequot Press.

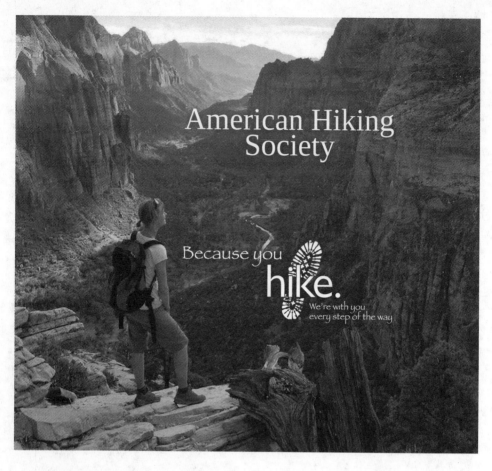

American Hiking Society

Because you hike.
We're with you every step of the way

As a national voice for hikers, **American Hiking Society** works every day:

- Building and maintaining hiking trails
- Educating and supporting hikers by providing information and resources
- Supporting hiking and trail organizations nationwide
- Speaking for hikers in the halls of Congress and with federal land managers

Whether you're a casual hiker or a seasoned backpacker, become a member of American Hiking Society and join the national hiking community! You'll enjoy great member benefits and help preserve the nation's hiking trails, so tomorrow's hike is even better than today's. We invite you to join us now!

American Hiking Society

www.AmericanHiking.org • info@AmericanHiking.org